The Future We Chose

Emerging perspectives on the centenary of the ANC

Edited by
Busani Ngcaweni

Africa Institute
of South Africa
Development Through Knowledge

The Future We Chose: Emerging Perspectives on the Centenary of the ANC

First Published in 2013 by the
Africa Institute of South Africa
PO Box 630
Pretoria 0001
South Africa

ISBN: 978-0-7983-0436-8

Opinions expressed and conclusions arrived at in this book are those of the authors and should not be attributed to the Africa Institute of South Africa or the Department of Arts and Culture.

Project manager: Nonjabulo Dladla
Copy-editor: David Merrington
Proofreader: Linda Botha Language Solutions
Layout: Dudu Coelho
Cover design: Berekile Pila
Printing:

The Africa Institute of South Africa is a think tank and research organisation, focusing on political, socio-economic, international and development issues in contemporary Africa. The Institute conducts research and publishes books, monographs, occasional papers, policy briefs and a quarterly journal – *Africa Insight*. The Institute holds regular seminars on issues of topical interest. It is also home to one of the best library and documentation centres world-wide, with materials on every African country.

For more information, contact the Africa Institute at PO Box 630, Pretoria 0001, South Africa; Email ai@ai.org.za; or visit our website at http://www.ai.org.za

Contents

Foreword

In 2012 the African National Congress (ANC) reached the significant milestone of its Centenary, and as expected, this attracted a flurry of interest from various scholars and observers alike. Being the oldest liberation movement in Africa, the ANC's survival up to a hundred years has been seen as intriguing, particularly given its inordinate share of vicissitudes and challenges over many years, which many liberation movements and parties in Africa invariably weathered with mixed fortunes. Most of these liberation movements mutated or fell by the way side, without attaining the milestone of one hundred years reached by the ANC.

More confounding to many observers is how the ANC managed its dual existence both in exile and in the country, and subsequently collapsed this impelled heritage fairly well into one collective force and entity which ushered the country to freedom and democracy in 1994. In addition, the relationship between the ANC and its political allies has been as historically puzzling and intricate as it is today.

Among the key pillars of this organisation have been its founding values of justice, freedom, democracy and equality of all the people, of all races and genders, not only in South Africa, but in Africa and the rest of the oppressed world. These values proved unassailable and timeless over all these years in the face of political oppression, a number of historical exigencies of fiercest rivalry from political organisations, political oppression and other historical exigencies. It did not succumb to organisational fluxes, nor even cave in to its pragmatism. Instead, it gained even more dynamism and vibrancy over the years in the face of the apartheid tyranny, and was enhanced strategically through a combination of decisive, pragmatic methods such as armed struggle and underground resistance activities, as well as international mobilisation of a magnitude never seen before. It is the longevity of the moral authority and universality inherent in these values which laid the basis of the trust between erstwhile adversaries and enabled negotiations to take place towards a free and a democratic South Africa.

It is now significant that this history is being visited with fresh perspectives from a wide range of dimensions. Generally, various thematic areas guide the multitude of views regarding the ANC at this important juncture. Most compelling are two aspects. Firstly, the history of the ANC including the emerging narratives, its philosophical underpinnings and how these shaped its historical trajectory, contending with the various challenges over the years, and its determined resilience enduring up to the present era. Equally enthralling is the flipside to this foregoing historical aspect, and this is the organisation today and its relevance for the future. Cutting across the said themes are the achievements of the ANC in giving form and expression to the democratic state enjoyed today in South Africa, concretized through the socio-economic transformation in the country and service delivery to the people. Also fascinating for analysts, is the kind of society shaped by this change; emerging class patterns, improving socio-economic conditions on the one hand, a humanity still grappling with overcoming the material legacy of the past and cohering as one united nation in its cultural diversity on the other. Another cross-cutting and salient characteristic throughout the ANC's existence has been its nature as an organisational entity and how this has also been personified and elevated over the years by its successive leadership.

This particular contribution is therefore most welcome. Even though it is eclectic and does not purport to be a purely historical text, it is a very important contribution to the history of this country generally, and of the ANC specifically. The book captures some of the achievements in socio-economic transformation that the country has registered so far, in education for example, and in fighting the scourges of abject poverty and unemployment. In this sense, it marks the culmination of the many principles set forth by the ANC at various historical epochs in its development, such as the Freedom Charter, which envisaged a free and equitable society. One of the most definitive influences of the ANC observed today is in the international policy locus of the government, where there is coalescence around the issues of solidarity with the African continent, the African Diaspora and the oppressed world at large, its multilateral approach to important continental and global issues, as well as a fair and equitable global order.

As this book illustrates, this is in large measure, a continuation of the values that the ANC espoused at its formation, which took shape even among certain black nationalists even prior to 1912. In all its strategic shifts and pragmatism over the years, the ANC managed to retain the confidence, support and admiration of the international community, and its broader alliance, in its unwavering commitment to realise every grain of its founding principles. Therefore the present that the country is traversing today is in many respects a vindication of the values and outlook of the ANC over the years, and indeed, in every letter, is the future we chose at that time.

After the country's transition to democracy post-1994, the ANC demonstrated its staunch resilience in the face of the challenges it navigated in establishing itself as a ruling party, championing policy changes which not only changed the legacy of apartheid, but sometimes in a true nature of democracy, stirred ructions even within its own camp. True to its mission and values, the ANC has transformed the political landscape of this country, and set it on a course towards the attainment of a better life for all people who live in South Africa. In this penultimate year towards its 20th year in government, just in the wake of the ANC centenary, and even after stoically weathering some breakaways, the attention accorded this organisation at this historical epoch cannot by any speck therefore be considered gratuitous.

The book is, in one sense, also a culmination of the various efforts which have been made over the years through other initiatives such as the South African Democracy Education Trust, contributions from academia; for instance the Southern African Historical Society[1] and various other biographical works. The candour of the book's scope and omissions points to many other intellectual spaces that still need to be addressed with regard to the centenary and beyond, and I believe that this challenge will also be seized by other scholars with a great zeal.

Lindiwe Sisulu
Minister of Public Service and Administration
Member of the National Executive Committee of the ANC
November 2013

---

[1] See the South African Historical Journal Vol. 64, No. 3, September 2012 – Special Issue on: "The ANC at 100."

Preface

The history of South Africa is characterised by colonial dominance, division and conquest, as well as unity among the dispossessed, a strong will for democracy and ultimately the triumph of the human spirit.

However, since 1994, the spirit of reconciliation and nation building, championed by Nelson Mandela as the first democratically elected president of South Africa, has laid a solid foundation and defined the future of a democratic South Africa.

Since the advent of Freedom and Democracy in 1994, working with the rest of society, we have been involved in the process of writing an inclusive South African history and narrative about our future, as outlined in the National Development Plan Vision 2030. In this we build and unite all South Africans around a common programme to achieve prosperity and equity; promote active citizenry to strengthen development, democracy and accountability; bring about faster economic growth, higher investment and greater labour absorption; focus on key capabilities of people and the state; build a capable and developmental state; and encourage strong leadership throughout society to work together to address challenges of our democracy.

In order to achieve this we have established amongst others the South African Democracy Education Trust (SADET) project with the aim of examining and analysing events leading to the negotiated settlement and democracy in South Africa. As a result of this project we are proud to have produced six volumes of work that outline our cultural heritage.

We have also erected and developed new symbols of freedom and democracy that tell a story of where we come from, including an outline of the kind of society we seek to create. We will therefore continue to support and work with all South Africans to ensure that our history is documented and preserved for generations to come.

In continuing with the work of preserving and promoting our cultural heritage, in the year 2012 we celebrated the Fortieth Anniversary of the World Heritage Convention of 1972. This we did because UNESCO was also focusing on the listing of heritage sites with outstanding universal value to humanity. We are proud that we have additional heritage sites of which, in line with the UNESCO conventions, we will ensure the preservation and as we do so we will continue to identify new sites to submit to UNESCO for consideration and listing.

In line with UNESCO's convention of celebrating living heritage, in 2012 we celebrated the centenary year of the oldest modern liberation movement in Africa, the African National Congress (ANC). The ANC has remained a popular voice fighting for human rights and in particular against apartheid in South Africa since its formation in 1912. The formation of the ANC was influenced by both domestic and international conditions; hence its character and struggle took an international outlook. This led to the ANC adopting and embracing the principle of Colonialism of a Special Type and subsequently adopting the strategic objectives of building a non-racial, non-sexist, democratic, united and prosperous society. Over time the ANC as a movement produced heroes and heroines of struggle and influenced the creation of a number of political formations.

Evidently the struggle waged by the ANC against apartheid, while it happened in many parts of the country, became stronger in the industrialised parts of South Africa. It is in this context that in the year 2012 we also celebrated the centenary of two key townships that were at the heart of the struggle against apartheid: Sophiatown and Alexandra. In essence the history and indeed the evolution of the South African struggle are included in the history of the ANC. As we continue to write and tell the story of the ANC we will also be telling the story of South Africa.

As part of promoting and preserving our history, many South Africans submitted proposals that were aimed at contributing towards the celebrations of our cultural heritage. These included the publishing of books, the production of documentaries and many other ideas in this regard.

The Africa Institute of South Africa is a natural partner in an endeavour of this nature. We are delighted that they have partnered with us in ensuring that this very important aspect of our history is captured in this publication. A word of congratulation also goes to Mr Busani Ngcaweni, the Editor and initiator of the project, for his great vision in ensuring that different perspectives of the hundred years of the ANC are represented. Most important, we are proud that we have a number of leading South African thinkers sharing their views on the history and meaning of the centenary of the ANC.

This book gives an important account of the work of the ANC since its formation in 1912. More critically, it gives an account of the future as it attempts to provide scenarios on the management of new challenges that have emerged as a result of the ANC having attained state power in 1994.

We have supported and partnered with the initiators of this book as part of our contribution towards knowledge creation, management and dissemination. I am confident that this book will add meaningful value in teaching generations to come about where we come from and where we are going as a nation.

We would like, indeed, to congratulate the initiators and all the authors who have taken time over the past two years to critically write on the work done over the past few years and in particular for their contribution to the role played by the ANC as a modern liberation movement in the fight against apartheid.

I would also like to thank Mr Siphiwo Mahala from the books and publishing unit of the Department of Arts and Culture, and my Special Advisor Mduduzi Mbada for ensuring that we partner and support this important project.

Enjoy the read!

Paul Shipokosa Mashatile
Minister of Arts and Culture
2013

Acknowledgements

This book owes its origins to the *Magubane @ 80* gala dinner hosted by the University of South Africa in August 2010. The dinner was an extension of the African Knowledge Producers conference co-organised by Unisa and the Human Sciences Research Council to celebrate the works and life of the now departed Professor Bernard Makhosezwe Magubane. Responding to the speakers celebrating his works, Professor Magubane remarked: "You know, the books that I wrote were for personal clarification and edification, to try and understand the nature of our oppression and the struggle that was being waged… that explains my writing… trying to explain what the ANC was about, trying to tackle the issues of race, class, nationalism and so forth."

These words, together with subsequent discussions with Dr Olive Shisana of the HSRC and a few sessions with Professor Magubane at his Johannesburg home, inspired me to conceive a project whose strategic intent would be to try to explain what the ANC was about, alongside the history of colonialism and racism that Professor Magubane spent his life documenting. And so, in part, this book is a tribute to this unparalleled doyen of South African history and lifetime ANC activist.

Ours is a contested history, as flowery and diverse as the nation itself. This complicates the task of writing about the whole or aspects of South African history, especially in the post-apartheid milieu where ideological considerations have been muted by the meta-narrative of inclusivity and nation building. Even the ANC itself is conscious of not repainting our historiography in its colours, recognising the diversity of contributions in the making of the nation-state.

Necessarily, we undertook this project fully aware of its weight and limitations since the story of the evolution of the ANC over one hundred years can't be told in a single volume, circumscribed by time and resources. Although we remain impenitent about the rigour and vigour of knowledge offered by this volume, chapters in this edition claim no authority over the history of the ANC. Their concern is to broaden the frontiers of academic and public discourse on the history of the African National Congress, which celebrated its first centenary on 8 January 2012. Importantly, this book further acknowledges other initiatives such as *The Road to Democracy in South Africa* series whose volumes already provide extensive scholarship on the contribution of the ANC in the making of South African history.

A question often arose in the past two years: how did you secure the commitment and confidence of such eminent scholars? My answer was simple: that each of the authors responded positively to my invitation to contribute chapters for this book speaks volumes of their commitment to the project of recording national heritage, reflecting on the future we chose and contemplating the future we choose. As editor, I am eternally grateful to all contributing authors for subjecting themselves to a tedious process, led by an unknown novice. It is an honour to have accomplished intellectuals, senior bureaucrats and renowned leaders take time off their busy schedules to write for an academic publication of this nature – especially when academic credits and material gain are not their primary objects for participating. Once again, your contributions are appreciated. Without your insights and commitment, there would be no such a book.

The most exciting moment creating this edition was dealing with the peer review report. The peer review process was as rigorous and iterative as it could be, with some of the contributors disagreeing completely with the feedback while others embraced it. Yet it was a necessity and therefore had to be taken into consideration. Authors owned the process and produced the excellent chapters that we proudly give to the reading public. To the peer reviewer: thanks for your critical comments.

Credit also goes to Professor Christopher Landsberg of the University of Johannesburg, who offered time and insight as a critical reader. He made sure that inconsistencies were addressed and restored the main narrative.

To the Department of Arts and Culture, especially Mduduzi Mbada and Siphiwo Mahala, thank you for believing and investing in this humble contribution to our liberation heritage. Your support lends credence to the department's commitment to celebrating and nurturing African scholarship and creating space for new voices to enter the publishing space. Minister Paul Mashatile's endorsement of this project and the preface he has contributed cannot go unnoticed.

Words of appreciation to my publisher – Africa Institute of South Africa – especially Solani Ngobeni, for rescuing the project and ensuring that it passes through the eye of the needle of scholarly publications. As a premier publishing house in Africa, we know we have a trusted partner in you. With the lessons learnt from the current project, the second edition of this book should be much easier to coordinate.

It would be remiss of me not to thank my employer, The Presidency of the Republic of South Africa, for both inspiration and encouragement. The book would have remained a pipe dream had it not been for the open-mindedness of the political and administrative leadership organisation that allows space for juggling punishing work schedules with intellectual engagements. The Centenary speeches he gave had a major impact on this book's narrative of shared history and inclusivity. Significantly, I wish to thank my boss, Deputy President Kgalema Motlanthe, for all his political education and lessons in humility, discipline and integrity. To my colleagues in the bureaucracy, especially Bongiwe and Nolubabalo in my office, I recognise you for ensuring that weekend and holiday schedules were cleared for this project.

Finally, my heartfelt tribute goes to my mother Nonhlanhla, retired history teacher and school principal. Thank you for introducing me to the academic discourse of history, and for echoing my grandmother's insistence that black people should go to school and rub shoulders with knowledgeable people like the ones contributing chapters to this edition. To my boys Mhlengi and Khulubuse, I hope your reading of this book will compensate for my demanding solitude whilst you wanted attention. To my partner, thank you Reabetswe for all your encouragement.

About the contributors

Alan Hirsch was born in Cape Town and educated in South Africa and the United States (US), with degrees in Economics, Economic History and History at the Universities of Cape Town (UCT), Witwatersrand (Wits) and Columbia. He also trained at Georgetown University, and was a visiting scholar at the Harvard Business School. He worked as an economics lecturer and economic policy research director at UCT from 1984 to 1986 and from 1989 to 1995. He joined the Department of Trade and Industry in 1995, and occupied several senior positions in industry and technology policy until joining the Policy Unit in the Presidency in 2002, as Chief Economist. He led the negotiations team for South Africa for its first World Bank loan in 1998, and led the first negotiations with the EU for a trade and development agreement, starting in 1994.

Most recently at the Presidency, he monitored and evaluated economic policy implementation, represented the Presidency at the G20, and was co-chair at the G20 Development Working Group from 2010 to 2012. Hirsch recently helped to found the Graduate School of Development Policy and Practice at UCT, where he is a professor and the director. He is a regular visiting professor at the Graduate School of Governance at Maastricht University and is a country director with the International Growth Centre, a think-tank based at the London School of Economics and Oxford University.

He is a member of several boards, including the Business Trust and, until recently, the Denel group board, and was chair of Denel Aviation. He is on the board of Trade and Industrial Policy Strategies, a think-tank. Hirsch has published widely on trade and industrial policy issues, including a book: *Season of Hope – Economic Reform under Mandela and Mbeki.*

Anver Saloojee is a professor in the Department of Politics and Public Administration at Ryerson University. He is a former special advisor in the Presidency of South Africa. He is also the former president of the Laidlaw Foundation and the Community Social Planning Council of Toronto. Until April 2013 he was vice-president of the Canadian Association of University Teachers. Currently, he is president of the Ryerson Faculty Association. He authored several books and articles and most recently co-authored a chapter with former Minister Essop Pahad on the Developmental State in South Africa. Professor Saloojee works closely with colleagues at the School of Public Management and Administration at the University of Pretoria.

Bengt Säve-Söderbergh is a former Ambassador and Deputy Minister of Foreign Affairs of Sweden. His long career in international relations and development cooperation inside and outside of the Ministry has had a special focus on Africa. He was the first Secretary-General of the International Centre of the Swedish Labour Movement, later renamed the Olof Palme International Centre. He was the founder and first Secretary-General of IDEA (the International Institute for Democracy and Electoral Assistance), of which South Africa was also one of the founders. He has been awarded the Order of Companions of Oliver Tambo by the Government of South Africa. He has received similar awards from Mozambique and Poland. He is the President of the Swedish Jazz Federation. He expects to publish a book about Sweden and the liberation struggle in southern Africa in 2014.

Busani Ngcaweni is Deputy Director-General (DDG) in the Presidency, responsible for heading the Office of the Deputy President. Before taking this DDG position, he worked as Head of Strategy and Special Projects in the same office. Prior to joining the Office of the Deputy President, Ngcaweni worked as Senior Policy Analyst in the Social Sector of the Policy Co-ordination and Advisory Services (PCAS) and was also responsible for establishing and heading the Youth Desk, during which time he contributed to policy formulation, analysis, monitoring and advisory. He led the development of the current National Youth Policy and facilitated the merger of Umsobomvu Youth Fund and the National Youth Commission in 2008. Before joining the Presidency, Ngcaweni was Director at Umsobomvu Youth Fund. He has contributed book chapters and regularly writes for journals and newspapers on the political economy of post-apartheid South Africa.

Ngcaweni holds degrees in education from the then Durban-Westville University and an MSc in Urban and Regional Planning from the School of Development Studies at Natal University. He has attended economic development and economic history courses offered by the London School of Economics and Graduate School of the Chinese Academy of Social Sciences. He is a Fellow of the Duke and Cape Town Universities Emerging Leaders Programme.

Chris Landsberg is South African National NRF Chair: African Diplomacy and Foreign Policy in the Faculty of Humanities, and Senior Associate: School of Leadership at the University of Johannesburg (UJ). He is a former head of Politics at UJ. Professor Landsberg was a former Rhodes Scholar at Oxford, where he obtained his M Phil and D Phil International degrees, alongside a MA International Studies from Rhodes. A former director of the Centre for Policy Studies in Johannesburg (2002–2007) and former co-director of the Centre for Africa's International Relations (CAIR) at Wits, he has published widely on South African foreign policy and African diplomacy. His latest single-authored title is *The Diplomacy of Transformation: South African Foreign Policy and Statecraft*, Macmillan, 2010.

Dan Motaung graduated from Wits University with an Honours Degree in Applied Linguistics and also holds Bachelor of Arts (Education) degree. Motaung was initiated into politics by his involvement in the youth, civic and student struggles against apartheid. He grew up in Tembisa where, apart from politics, he was initiated into jazz, a musical genre he ferociously collects and reads about. Motaung is interested in history, egyptology, philosophy, political economy and political studies. He is currently working for the Presidency of the Republic of South Africa as a speech writer.

David Maimela holds a degree in Political Science majoring in International Relations, an honours degree in the same field and is currently pursuing a Masters programme in International Relations focusing on South Africa's Foreign Policy. In April 2013, he was enrolled for the Seminar on Economic & Social Development, Academy for International Business Officials (AIBO), China, Beijing. He is former president of SASCO (December 2006 to June 2008). Among other honours, he holds the Mandela Rhodes Scholarship from the Mandela Rhodes Foundation for the class of 2007 and in 2010, he was chosen as one of the Mail and Guardian 200 Emerging Young Leaders in South Africa. Maimela has also worked in the erstwhile Gauteng Youth Commission and the Gauteng Office of the Premier in the Policy and Governance Branch. In his period in the Office of the Premier, he acquired considerable experience in policy making processes in government. David is currently Researcher at the Mapungubwe Institute for Strategic Reflections (MISTRA) in the Political Economy Faculty.

Eddy Maloka is Advisor to the Minister of International Relations and Cooperation. He previously worked for the Africa Institute of South Africa as Executive Director and for Mpumalanga and Gauteng Provinces as Adviser to the Premiers. Between 1992 and 1995 he served as Mellon Research Fellow at Cape Town University. Dr Maloka's research interests are on political and developmental issues in Africa. He writes extensively on the history of the liberation struggle in South Africa. His recent book is *The South African Communist Party: Exile and After Apartheid*, Jacana Media, 2013.

Essop Pahad has been involved in the struggle against racism and apartheid for more than 50 years. Currently, Dr Pahad is the Director of Vusizwe Media and the editor of *The Thinker*, a monthly quality journal covering broad socio-economic, socio-political issues in South Africa and the African continent.

Dr Pahad has held numerous political offices, as a member of the National Assembly from 1994 to 2008, Parliamentary Counselor to the Deputy President of the Republic of South Africa (1994 to 1996), and Deputy Minister in the Office of the former Executive Deputy President, Thabo Mbeki (1996 to 1999). Dr Pahad was appointed Minister in 1999 with specific responsibility for the Office on the Rights of the Child, Office on the Status of Women and Office on the Status of Disabled People in The Presidency as well as the National Youth Commission and the Government Communication and Information System. He was a member of the National Executive Committee (NEC) of the African National Congress (ANC), Chairperson of the Board of Trustees of the South African Democracy Education Trust and Member of the Board and Executive Committee of the International Marketing Council. Dr Pahad was a Minister in the Presidency until 2008.

He has published numerous articles in journals and is co-editor of *Africa, The Time has Come* and *Africa, Define Yourself*, a collection of speeches of former President of South Africa, Thabo Mbeki. He holds a BA degree in Political Science from Wits University, a Masters in African Politics and a PhD in History from Sussex University.

Helmi El Sharawy is currently the vice-president at the Arab and African Research Center in Cairo, Egypt and its director from 1987 to 2010. From 1960 to 1975, he was the coordinator for African Liberation Movements offices at the African Association Zamalek under the auspice of the President's Office of African Affairs. He then became a consultant to the Ministry of Sudan under the Egyptian Integration Program between 1975 and 1980. He has also taught African Political Thought at Juba University in Sudan. Then he was selected as expert for Afro-Arab Cultural Relations at Arab League ALECSO in Tunisia until 1986. He has served as a member of the executive committee of the Council for the Development of Social Science Research in Africa (CODESRIA). He has published thirteen books in Arabic and four in English.

Joel Netshitenzhe is the Executive Director and Board Vice-Chairperson of the Mapungubwe Institute for Strategic Reflection (MISTRA), a research institute dealing with strategic issues facing South Africa. He has a Master of Science (MSc) degree in Financial Economics and a post-graduate diploma in Economic Principles from the University of London (SOAS), and a diploma in Political Science from the Institute of Social Sciences in Moscow. Netshitenzhe is a member of the National Planning Commission and the ANC National Executive Committee. Before joining the Government Communication and Information System (GCIS) as CEO in 1998, Mr Netshitenzhe was Head of Communication in President Nelson Mandela's office. In addition to being the CEO of GCIS, he was appointed Head of the Policy Co-ordination and Advisory Services (PCAS) in the Presidency, in 2001. He headed the PCAS on a full-time basis from 2006 until his retirement in 2009.

John Pampallis is Special Advisor to the Minister of Higher Education and Training. He was previously the Director of the Centre for Education Policy Development (1996 to 2009) and, before that, worked at the Education Policy Unit at the former University of Natal (1991 to 1996). From 2004 to mid-2009 he was a member of the Council for Quality Assurance in General and Further Education and Training (Umalusi) and for two years served as its chairperson.

Professor Pampallis is a teacher by profession and has taught in South Africa, Botswana, Canada and Tanzania. During the 1980s he taught History and English and was Deputy Vice Principal at the Solomon Mahlangu Freedom College (SOMAFCO), a school established by the African National Congress for young exiles in Morogoro, Tanzania. Since the late 1980s he has worked extensively in the area of education and training policy and has published articles and co-edited three books on various education policy issues. He has written a book on South African history, *Foundations of the New South Africa,* Zed Press, 1991. He has also edited a series of fifteen short biographies of Southern African political leaders of the twentieth century (Series Title: *They Fought for Freedom.* Cape Town: Maskew Miller Longman).

Kgalema P. Motlanthe is the Deputy President of the Republic of South Africa. In the 1970s, while working for the Johannesburg City Council, he was recruited into Umkhonto we Sizwe (MK), the then armed wing of the ANC. He was part of a unit tasked with recruiting members for military training inside and outside the country.

In 1976 Motlanthe was arrested for furthering the aims of the ANC and was kept in detention for 11 months at John Vorster Square. In 1977 he was found guilty on three charges under the Terrorism Act and sentenced to an effective 10 years imprisonment on Robben Island, where he served alongside Nelson Mandela, Harry Gwala and Walter Sisulu. After his release from prison in 1987, Mr Motlanthe was tasked with strengthening the trade union movement in the country. To this end, he worked for the National Union of Mineworkers (NUM) as a national office bearer responsible for education. Among other things, he was involved in training workers to form shop steward committees. In 1992 he was elected Secretary-General of NUM. After serving the labour movement, Motlanthe was elected and served two five-year terms as General Secretary of the ANC from December 1997 to December 2007. This was followed by a five-year term as Deputy President of the same organisation until December 2012. In 2008 he joined government as Minister in the Presidency until 25 September of the same year, when he was elected President of the Republic of South Africa after the resignation of former President Thabo Mbeki.

As current Deputy President of the Republic of South Africa since May 2009, Motlanthe's responsibilities include serving as Leader of Government Business and chair of multi-stakeholder structures such as the South African National Aids Council, the Human Resource Development Council, in addition to coordinating the government's anti-poverty programme.

Mathethe Jeffrey Sehume holds a BA in Social Sciences and MA in Media Studies from the University of the Witwatersrand. He taught, amongst others, at Rhodes University (Grahamstown campus), AFDA College (Johannesburg) and Fort Hare University in the fields of Media, Communication and Social Sciences. He was a postgraduate student at the Centre for Cultural and Media Studies (CCMS) at the then University of Natal. From 2007 to 2010, he worked in The Presidency as a researcher and speechwriter. He joined the Mapungubwe Institute (MISTRA) as a researcher in the Humanity Faculty in 2010. He has been book review editor of the *Critical Arts* since 2000. He is co-writer of the book, *The Concept and Application of Transdisciplinarity in Intellectual Discourse and Research*.

Ntongela Masilela is Professor Emeritus of English and World Literature and also Professor Emeritus of Creative Studies at Pitzer College in Claremont, California. From 1995 to 2008 he was Adjunct Professor of African American Studies and Comparative Literature at the University of California in Irvine (UCI). While he was at Pitzer College he founded the H. I. E. Dhlomo Center of African Intellectual History which resulted in the creation of the New African Movement website and the book *The Cultural Modernity of H. I. E. Dhlomo* (2007). He has taught at the University of Nairobi in Kenya, University of Lodz in Poland, Summer Academy of Dance in Arezzo (Italy), University of California in Los Angeles (UCLA), and University of Landau/Koblenz in Germany. Presently he has just published two books: *An Outline of the New African Movement in South Africa* (2013) and *The Historical Figures of the New African Movement Volume One* (2013). Two subsequent volumes will follow. He recently relocated to Bangkok, Thailand as an independent South African intellectual and scholar.

Pali Lehohla is the Statistician-General of South Africa, a position he has held since November of 2000. He is the Chair of Africa Symposium for Statistical Development (ASSD), a country-led initiative established in 2006 the aim of which is to put statistical evidence at the centre of policy in Africa. From 2005 to 2010 he served in a variety of portfolios. He was Chair of the United Nations Statistics Commission, Chair of Statistics Commission Africa and also Chair of PARIS21, a global partnership for statistical development in the twenty-first century. He has served as an advisor to in-conflict, post-conflict and fragile political environments. In this regard he was Chief Advisor to the Monitoring and Evaluation Committee (MOC) of the 2008 Population and Housing Census of Sudan, which was part of the Comprehensive Peace Agreement signed in 2005. He served as UN envoy to the Census of Cambodia in 1998. He undertook a Population Census readiness mission in Afghanistan in 2008 and another in Iraq in 2009. He is Vice Chair of the International Statistics Institute (ISI) and led the hosting of the fifty-seventh Session of the ISI held in Durban, South Africa in 2009. Under his leadership partnerships have been established with universities in South Africa in advancing tuition of statistical training, research and applications in state planning. Of note is the establishment of the Centre for Regional and Urban Innovation and Statistical Exploration (CRUISE) at the University of Stellenbosch. Under the auspices of the Africa Census Analysis Project (ACAP), he initiated a series of publications on the Demography of South Africa as primary tuition material for higher learning and advancing Pan-African scholarship. The first book in the South African series was published in 2005.

He obtained his degree from the National University of Lesotho (NUL) with a double major in Statistics and Economics, undertook post-graduate studies in demography at the United Nations Regional Institute for Population Studies (UNRIPS) at the University of Ghana and completed a Senior Executive Programme jointly awarded by Wits and Harvard Universities.

Pekka Peltola is a retired Counsellor at the Ministry of Labour. His first profession was as a journalist at the Finnish Broadcasting Corporation covering the Biafra war. Later he joined the book publishing company Tammi in Finland and then moved to trade unions and worked for the Finnish Confederation of Trade Unions (SAK), leading a programme for training Swapo exiles in Kwanza Sul, Angola, during the 1980s. He obtained his MA and PhD in social sciences from the University of Helsinki. He has also published books in which Africa is discussed, the latest one in 2011 called *In Africa*, in Finnish, and in English, with Iina Soiri, a history of Finnish involvement in the liberation of Southern Africa, published by the Nordic Africa Institute in 1999.

Thabo Mbeki is a thought leader who remains close to visible leadership. His profile as an intellectual, policy shaper and mediator has been built over a lifetime. He is an avid reader who dabbles in poetry, his speech 'I am an African' being one example of his use of poetry to deliver a very strong message. He spent his early years in exile studying in Britain where he obtained a Master of Economics degree from Sussex University. Former president Mbeki has received honorary degrees from South African and foreign universities, awards from various organisations, orders and decorations from local public and private institutions alike. The University of South Africa (Unisa) awarded him an honorary doctorate in 1996.

Mr Mbeki has served the ANC in various capacities. He joined the ANCYL in 1956 and was elected Secretary of the African Students Association in 1961. He headed the London ANC Youth Section and mobilised the international student community against apartheid. In the 1980s he led ANC delegations to meet with Afrikaner leaders in the United Kingdom, leading to secret talks from 1988 which culminated in the negotiations for a democratic South Africa that took place under the auspices of the Convention for a Democratic South Africa – CODESA. He served as the second president of post-apartheid South Africa from 14 June 1999 to 24 September 2008.

While in government, Mr Mbeki made serious strides in ensuring that women's empowerment and gender equality took centre stage in democratic South Africa. He also helped steer the longest economic growth period in the history of South Africa since the Second World War. Amongst other initiatives, he actively participated in the transformation of the Organisation of African Unity (OAU) to the African Union (AU) and conceptualizing the New Partnership for Africa's Development (NEPAD), a vision and strategic framework for Africa's renewal.

Mr Mbeki is Patron of the Thabo Mbeki African Leadership Institute (TMALI), a partnership between the Thabo Mbeki Foundation and Unisa.

Sabelo J. Ndlovu-Gatsheni is a Professor and Head of the Archie Mafeje Research Institute (AMRI) for Applied Social Policy based at the University of South Africa (Unisa). He is also the founder and coordinator of the Africa Decolonial Research Network (ADERN) based in the College of Human Sciences at Unisa. He is a decolonial theorist who has published extensively on African history, African politics, and development.

Sifiso Mxolisi Ndlovu is Executive Director at the South African Democracy Education Trust (SADET). He has a Masters degree from the University of Natal (Pietermaritzburg campus) and a PhD from the University of the Witwatersrand. He has published extensively in all six volumes of *The Road to Democracy in South Africa* history series funded by SADET. He is the author of *The Soweto Uprisings: Counter-memories of 16 June 1976*. His other research interests include the pre-colonial history of South Africa and also the history of football in South Africa and has published articles in these fields. He is a member of UNESCO's Scientific Committee responsible for revising the *General History of Africa* series.

Siphamandla Zondi is the Director of the Institute for Global Dialogue (IGD) and an honorary professor of politics and development studies at the University of South Africa. He received his BA and BA Hons degrees from the former University of Durban-Westville (UDW), an MPhil and DPhil from the University of Cambridge. He lectured for short stints at UDW and the former Rand Afrikaans University before he coordinated the SADC integration programme at the Africa Institute of South Africa. He was then appointed director of Africa and Southern Africa at the IGD. In that position, he led the Institute's two-track diplomacy transition projects on the Burundi,

Côte d'Ivoire, Chad, Sudan and Zimbabwe before being appointed director of the IGD in January 2010. Dr Zondi has published widely on issues of regional integration, South Africa's international relations and foreign policy, governance in Africa, social policy, public health, the migration-development nexus and soft power politics.

Vusi Gumede is professor and head of the Thabo Mbeki African Leadership Institute at the University of South Africa. He previously was an associate professor at the University of Johannesburg. He also lectures public policy, since 2009, at the Graduate School of Public and Development Management of the University of the Witwatersrand in South Africa. He is also chairman of Southern Africa Trust, Editor for the International Journal of African Renaissance Studies and Editor for the Journal of African Studies and Development.

He worked for the South African government, in various capacities, for about 12 years – he was Chief Policy Analyst, among other things, in the Presidency. He was also with the Institute for African Development, at Cornell University, as Distinguished Africanist Scholar and he was also with Yale University as Yale World Fellow. He spent research fellowships with universities and institutions in Brazil, Europe and the United States, and also the University of Botswana. He holds postgraduate qualifications in economics and policy studies, including a PhD in economics (2003).

Acronyms

AAPC	All African People's Conference
ACAP	African Census Analysis Project
AfDB	African Development Bank
AME	African Methodist Episcopal
ANC	African National Congress
ANC HQ	African National Congress Headquarters
ANCYL	African National Congress Youth League
APLA	Azanian People's Liberation Army
APRM	African Peer Review Mechanism
ASA	African Student Association
ASGISA	Accelerated and Shared Growth Initiative for South Africa
ASUSA	African Student's Union of South Africa
AUC	African Union Commission
AWEPAA	Association of West European Parliamentarians for Action Against Apartheid
AZAPO	Azanian People's Organisation
AZASO	Azanian Student Organisation
BAA	Bureau of African Affairs
BAPS	Busan Plan of Action for Statistics
BBBEE	Broad-Based Black Economic Empowerment
BC	Black Consciousness
BCM	Black Consciousness Movement
BMR	Bureau of Market Research
BNDES	*Banco Nacional de Desenvolvimento Económico e Social* (Brazilian Development Bank)
BPC	Black People's Convention
BRICS	Brazil Russia India China South Africa
CI	Communist International
CIAS	Conference of Independent African States
CODESA	Convention for a Democratic South Africa
COPE	Congress of the People
COSAS	Congress of South African Students
COSATU	Congress of South African Trade Unions
CPC	Coloured People's Congress
CPSA	Communist Party of South Africa

CSS	Central Statistics Services
CST	Colonialism of a Special Type
DA	Democratic Alliance
DBE	Department of Basic Education
DBSA	Development Bank of Southern Africa
DDS	Democratic Developmental State
DHET	Department of Higher Education and Training
DNA	Deoxyribonucleic Acid
DRC	Democratic Republic of Congo
ECA	Economic Commission for Africa
ECC	End Conscription Campaign
EELAK	Isolate South Africa Campaign
ESOPs	Employee Stock Ownership Plans
EU	European Union
FET	Further Education and Training
FOSATU	Federation of South African Trade Unions
FRELIMO	*Frente de Libertação de Moçambique*
	The Mozambique Liberation Front
GDDS	General Data Dissemination Standard
GDP	Gross Domestic Product
GEAR	Growth, Employment and Redistribution Strategy
GIVAS	Global Impact and Vulnerability Alert System
GRAE	*Governo Revolucionário de Angola no Exílio*
	Revolutionary Government of Angola in Exile
GSS	Ghana Statistics Service
HDI	Human Development Index
HIV and Aids	Human Immunodeficiency Virus and Acquired Immunodeficiency Syndrome
HPI	Human Poverty Index
HSRC	Human Sciences Research Council
IBSA	India Brazil South Africa
ICP	International Comparisons Programme
ICU	Industrial Commercial Union
IFP	Inkatha Freedom Party
ILO	International Labour Organisation
IMF	International Monetary Fund
JIPSA	Joint Initiative on Priority Skills Acquisition
KANU	Kenya African National Union
KZN	KwaZulu-Natal

LMC	Labour Market Commission
MAPS	Marrakesh Plan of Action for Statistics
MDGs	Millennium Development Goals
MDM	Mass Democratic Movement
MEC	Mineral Energy Complex
MIP	Minimum Integration Programme
MK	Mkhonto Wesizwe
MPLA	*Movimento Popular de Libertação de Angola*
	The People's Movement for the Liberation of Angola
NAFCOC	National African Federated Chamber of Commerce
NAM	Non-Aligned Movement
NATO	North Atlantic Treaty Organisation
NDP	National Development Plan
NDR	National Democratic Revolution
NDS	National Democratic Society
NEC	National Executive Committee
NECC	National Education Crisis Committee
NEDLAC	National Economic Development and Labour Council
NEPAD	New Partnership for Africa's Development
NEPI	National Education Policy Initiative
NGO	Non-Governmental Organisation
NGP	New Growth Path
NIDS	National Income Dynamic Study
NP	National Party
NPC	National Planning Commission
NQF	National Qualification Framework
NSF	National Skills Fund
NSFAS	National Student Financial Aid Scheme
NSS	National Statistics System
NUNW	Nduuvu Nangolo Trade Union Centre
NUSAS	National Union of South African Students
OAU	Organisation of African Unity
ODETT	Organisational Development Task Team
OECD	Organisation for Economic Co-operation and Development
OHS	October Household Survey
OOs	Operation Objectives
OPA	African People's Organisation
PAC	Pan African Congress
PAFMECSA	Pan-African Freedom Movement of East, Central and Southern Africa

PAIGC	*Partido Africano para a Independência da Guiné e Cabo Verde*
	African Party for the Independence of Guinea-Bissau and Cape Verde
PARIS21	Partnership in Statistical Development in the 21st Century
PICC	Presidential Infrastructure Coordinating Commission
PLO	Palestine Liberation Organisation
PRSP	Poverty Reduction Strategy Papers
PTSAs	Parent-Teacher-Student Associations
R2G	Ready to Govern
RDP	Reconstruction and Development Programme
RMCs	Release Nelson Mandela Committees
RRSF	The African Regional Reference Strategic Framework
SA	South Africa
SACP	South African Communist Party
SACTU	South African Congress of Trade Unions
SADC	Southern African Development Community
SADCC	Southern African Development Coordination Conference
SADET	South African Democratic Education Trust
SAIC	South African Indian Congress
SALDRU	South African Labour and Development Research Unit
SANC	South African Native Congress
SANNC	South African Native National Congress
SANSCO	South African National Students Congress
SASCO	South African Student Congress
SASK	Trade Union Solidarity Centre (Finland)
SASM	South African Student Movement
SASO	South African Student Organisation
SAUF	South African United Front
SAYCO	South African Youth Congress
SDDS	Special Data Dissemination Standard
SETAs	Sector Education Training Authorities
SHaSA	Strategy for the Harmonisation of Statistics in Africa
SRC	Student Representative Council
SSRC	Soweto Student Representative Council
StatCan	Statistics Canada
StatCom	Statistical Commission
Stats SA	Statistics South Africa
SWANU	South West African National Union
SWAPO	South West African People's Organisation

TANU	Tanzania African National Union
TBVC	Transkei, Bophuthatswana, Venda and Ciskei
TSL	Workers Educational Society (Finland)
TV	Television
UCM	University Christian Movement
UDF	United Democratic Front
UF	United Front
UK	United Kingdom
UN	United Nations
UNC	Uganda National Congress
UNECA	United Nations Economic Commission for Africa
Unisa	University of South Africa
UNITA	*União Nacional para a Independência Total de Angola*
	National Union for the Total Independence of Angola
UNSC	United Nations Statistical Commission
UPC	Union des Populations du Cameroun
	Union of the Population of Cameroon
US	United States
USA	United States of America
WCRW	Why Civil Resistance Works
ZANU	Zimbabwe African National Union
ZAPU	Zimbabwe African People's Union

PART 1

The Future We Chose

CHAPTER 1

Locating the ANC centenary in the South African historiography: a prelude

Busani Ngcaweni

South African history – from Vasco da Gama's landing at the Cape in 1498 to its libera-tion in 1994 – frames all modern social struggles, and certainly black struggles. – Ngugi wa Thiong'o

From 1898 onwards, aspiration, opportunity and action converged to make possible the first concrete steps of a national movement in South Africa. – Andre Odendaal

The ANC centenary is a time to reflect on its multiple legacies. How can the bold vision-ary element, the willingness to venture beyond what was possible at the time, be taken forward? – Raymond Suttner

Introduction

The African National Congress (ANC) celebrated its centenary on 8 January 2012. Given that colonial and post-colonial history is not favoured with chronicles of political organisations that survive and capture the national and international imagination for such sustained periods, it was fitting for South Africans and inter-national observers to reflect on this milestone. True to the tradition of the ANC, throughout 2012, rallies, prayer meetings, cultural events and lectures were or-ganised countrywide, largely to remind South Africans of the role it played in the liberation struggle.

For the main commemoration, the organisation returned to its founding site in Bloemfontein[1] – now renamed Mangaung – where rallies, prayer meetings and com-munity engagements were conducted by the leadership. The Dutch Reformed Church in Waaihoek, where the founding meeting was held in 1912, was consecrated and declared a national monument.

Elsewhere, 'friends of South Africa' – predominantly former members of the international solidarity movement – gathered not only to discuss their historic roles in fighting apartheid but also to reflect on the road travelled by South Africa since the demise of apartheid.

Reasons for celebrating the centenary

It has been stated many times that the ANC is the oldest political organisation on the continent of Africa. Not only does this make its founders and various generations of leadership special, but also South Africa, yet again, assumes the limelight and international acclaim for its 'exceptionalism'.[2] That the ANC survived 82 years of state suppression, imprisonment, banishment, torture, murder and propaganda makes the organisation special and worthy of reflection. That two of its former presidents, Nelson Mandela and Thabo Mbeki, are not in jail, court or exile in a continent in which former liberation movements turn on their former leaders makes the ANC exceptional.

That it remains relatively intact, in spite of well-publicised growing internal contradictions and excesses occasioned by exposure to state power and resources, tells a story of the DNA that has sustained the organisation over one hundred years. After all, 'lapses are inevitable in society. The past never completely prepares one for the present'.[3]

That the ANC retains just under a two-thirds majority in parliament – notwithstanding overwhelming evidence of service delivery shortfalls, corruption, poverty, unemployment and inequality – probably suggests that the majority of the electorate retain confidence in the organisation and its political vision. Remarkable also is the ANC's sustained belief in electoral democracy rooted in a liberal constitution – although seen by some to be stifling transformation because it protects property rights and has safeguards such as judicial review which sometimes reverses decisions of the executive.

Necessarily, history compels us to pause and reflect on the phenomenology of a self-styled, left-leaning political organisation surviving internal and external contradictions, colonialism and apartheid and, more importantly, withstanding the post Cold War liberal offensive which has to a large degree annihilated progressive movements in Africa, Asia, Latin America and even Europe.

In *From Revolutionary Movements to Political Parties,* Deonandan et al.[4] chronicle the transitional schizophrenia experienced by dominant African and Latin American liberation movements from the trenches, exile and prison to political office, trading camouflage for designer suites. Besides exogenous pressures such as the changing global balance of forces after the fall of the Soviet Union, Deonandan et al. highlight intra-party contradictions and country-specific realities that weakened the hegemony of these *new* political parties and saw leaders assassinated, gaoled or exiled. From this book we derive an important yet widely documented inference that the legacy of colonialism weighed heavily on these former revolutionary parties, whether in handling devastating poverty and deprivation, ethnicity, violence, governance and leadership, or managing internal democracy within revolutionary parties themselves.

Flowing from the latter, history records elsewhere that leaders like Thomas Sankara of Burkina Faso, Kwame Nkrumah of Ghana and Patrice Lumumba of the Zaire count among the post-liberation era leaders who later become victims of either their former comrades, political rivals, tribal secessionists or foreign interests. Whether advanced by power-hungry former revolutionaries or puppets of Western powers, like in the case of Zaire (Democratic Republic of Congo), historical cleavages have reared their ugly heads in many *free* African states. Ethnic difference, for instance, became a pretext for power struggles and thus a usual suspect in the post-colonial narrative.

We single out ethnicity in this ANC narrative because, as eminent scholars Basil Davidson,[5] Mahmood Mamdani,[6] Cheikh Anta Diop[7] and Albert Adu Boahen[8] have extensively documented, pre-colonial, colonial and post-colonial Africa has had to deal with the difficult subject of nation state formation to the extent that language and ethnic differences make way for a 'new nation', united in its diversity, much like the way Shaka ka Senzangakhona tried with the formation of the Zulu nation and Julius Nyerere with the formation of modern Tanzania.

As if foretelling what would happen to post-independence Africa when compatriots would turn against each other on ethnic grounds, thus precipitating the devastating conflict seen in Nigeria and many parts of central and west Africa, Pixley ka Isaka Seme, the young ANC leader who in 1911 made the call for all provincial natives congresses to meet and form the Natives Union, instructed:

> The greatest success shall come when man shall have learned to cooperate, not only with his own kith and kin but with all peoples and with all life… The demon of racialism, the aberrations of the Xosa-Fingo feud, the animosity that exists between the Zulus and the Tongaas, between the Basutos and every other Native must be buried and forgotten; it has shed among us sufficient blood! We are one people. These divisions, these jealousies, are the cause of all our woes and of all our backwardness and ignorance to-day.[9]

Anton Lembede and successive generations of *young lions* who founded and led the ANC Youth League in 1944 sounded Seme's drum by calling for the unity of oppressed black Africans working hand-in-hand with all other oppressed groups, such as the Asians and the coloureds. This unity narrative would go on to influence the Black Consciousness Movement, which gained prominence in the 1970s – calling for the unity of blacks as the culturally, politically and economically oppressed group (although in many of his speeches and articles published in *Freedom in Our Lifetime*, Lembede was somewhat suspicious of the real commitment of Coloureds and Indians the course of African liberation – a view that resonated with many Africanists who would later break away from the ANC.)

There is arguably a view that part of what distinguishes the ANC from other revolutionary movements in the continent is that from the turn of the twentieth century its founders prioritised national unity across tribal, ethnic, linguistic, religious, gender and racial identities. This ideal of national unity informed their responses to the formation of the Union of South Africa in 1910 and the declaration of the South African Republic in 1961. In principle, the leadership was opposed not to these manifestations of concrete nation state formation but to the practice of excluding[10] the majority of South African citizens according to racial markers.

It is important to note that neither the founding leaders of the ANC nor Chief Albert Luthuli, who presided over the organisation when the Republic was declared, called for the reversal of processes to create a sovereign South African territory. This was made crystal clear in various deputations and representations to the British parliament which created the racist Union of South Africa which was inaugurated on 31 May 1910, and to Afrikaner authorities responsible for administering the Union and the Republic of the white minority.

In response, the founding leaders thought, if Africans were to be excluded from the political and economic mainstream of the 'new' South African territory, a union for all the natives of South Africa, the South African Native National Congress (later renamed African National Congress) was to be created as the alternative representative parliament of the people.

Jack and Ray Simons, in *Class and Colour in South Africa,* concluded:

> The African elite included men and women who would have risen to eminence in any open society; yet all were relegated by reason of race to a civic status lower than that of the meanest white... All Africans endured the humiliation and restrictive effects of pass laws, racial classification, residential segregation, and discrimination in public life. None could escape the state's coercive sanctions. The African National Congress spoke for the *entire African population* when it presented a claim to full citizenship.[11]

Writing in the *Business Day,* Pallo Jordan summarised the unity imperative as follows: 'The objective of the founders was to yoke the efforts of the traditional and modern African elites to defend and extend the rights of Africans within the parameters of the colonial state.'[12]

Part of the test, therefore, in the present through to the future, is whether the organisation will sustain its civilising mission of inclusivity, non-tribalism and non-racialism, the values embedded in its inherited DNA. Can it do so even at times when internal and external contradictions might tempt a reawakening of ethnic and racial demons in an attempt to give oxygen to a suffocating creature?

Commenting on how ethnic identities defined colonial and post-colonial nation state formation, Mahmood Mamdani argued:

> In the colonial period, ethnic identity and separation were politically enforced. Although forged through colonial experience, this form of the state survived alien domination. Reformed after independence, purged of its racial underpinnings, it emerged as a specifically African form of the state.[13]

Why recount known history?

We can deduce from Karl Marx's assertion that in every society and at various epochs, luminaries [like Seme, Dube, Maxeke, Thomas Mapikela, Solomon Plaatje, Lillian Ngoyi and Moses Kotane, in the South African context] would make their own history, not as they pleased or under self-selected circumstances, but under pre-existing circumstances, given and transmitted from the past. As Marx believed:

> The tradition of all dead generations weighs like a nightmare on the brains of the living. And just as they seem to be occupied with revolutionizing themselves and things, creating something that did not exist before, precisely in such epochs of revolutionary crisis they anxiously conjure up the spirits of the past to their service, borrowing from them names, battle slogans, and costumes in order to present this new scene in world history in time-honoured disguise and borrowed language.[14]

In 2012, the country observed the centenary and recounted stories of colonialism and apartheid, not so much to build a buffer between current realities and the challenges of governing faced by the ANC but rather to cast a glance over the road travelled, to look forward to the future we had chosen as part of humanity and to affirm our commitment to the 'worldwide struggles between capital and labour and between the coloniser and the colonised'.[15]

We therefore reflect on history in an attempt to repudiate the colonial image of the 'African as an object without agency, always acted upon'; to replay the drama of heroes and heroines of struggle that was 'enacted in the open theatre of organised politics [by the people] whose lives and actions and thoughts have made South Africa an integral part of the black self-imagination'.[16]

Answering the now fashionable question – has the ANC served its purpose and met its mission? – requires circumspection. A multi-pronged analytical framework should be applied when attempting a balanced response. *Inter alia*, it should include a rigorous assessment of the legacy of the political economy of colonial and apartheid South Africa and the extent to which such legacies impose their weight on the present. Second, the analysis requires conscientious interpretation of pre-1994 historic documents such as the *Africans' Claims* (1943), the *Freedom Charter* (1955), the *Strategy and Tactics* documents of Morogoro (1969), the *Ready to Govern* guidelines (1992) and the Reconstruction and Development Programme. In this regard, some would suggest that the triple challenge of poverty, unemployment and inequality ought to be the *zeitgeist* of the second centenary, in addition to transforming the state, fully democratising society and fulfilling the dream of presenting a *more human face* to the world.

Admittedly, even as mounting evidence points to serious weaknesses in the ANC of today and the government it leads, some of which are discussed in various chapters of this book, and in other scholarly works by academics like Ben Turok, Susan Booysen, Hein Marais and Sampie Terreblanche,[17] so an analytical framework that projects current challenges as the sum total of the glorious history of the ANC is methodologically flawed. Significantly, such would be ahistorical since it overlooks established historiography of the legacies of pre-colonial, colonial, apartheid and post-colonial South Africa. Furthermore, such reductionist thinking delegitimises the historicity of the centenary and national liberation struggles broadly. As a contribution to the historicity of the centenary, this book puts forward these inevitable questions as a point of departure:

- What traits in the ANC's *genetic code* have kept it alive for such a long period?
- Is it on course to meeting its *historical mission* of building an equitable, non-racial, non-sexist and socially democratic society as articulated in the Africans' Claims, the Freedom Charter and the Strategy and Tactics documents?
- Would it continue to *retain relevance* for a bicentenary?

Closing the yawning gap in our understanding of the objective and subjective conditions of survival of political organisations inspired this book, which – while also hoping to give a perspective on internal and external contradictions that shaped the ANC – also proposes a new hypothetical architecture to be employed by those studying the rise and fall of political organisations.

Surviving for a century: how?

To further illuminate this fresh approach of assessing the ANC from within in order to appreciate the present and approximate prospects for the future, let us abridge what we believe are carefully managed internal contradictions that have sustained the ANC for such a long period, but which, dialectically also constitute an axis for the anatomy of decline. We subdivide them into three: philosophical base, tactical orientation and the character of leadership.

Philosophical base

The ANC was founded on the values of representativity, inclusivity and national unity. Representativity refers to issues of mobilising society on the grounds of mass participation in determining the cause and direction of their circumstances and future.

Representativity: The leaders of the ANC understood that their mandate was to create the necessary space in which the people could raise their concerns and suggest solutions to their problems. The ANC went through a period of organisational decline in the 1930s following the deposition of Josiah Gumede. In a word, the disconnection of the conservatives – who had replaced and purged the so-called radicals - from the core constituency can be said to have occasioned this decline. Fortunately, in succeeding decades the organisation engendered mechanisms for self-correcting its internal contradictions by creating extended platforms for national unity and by forging practical alliances with other liberation movements, such as the Communist Party of South African (CPSA) and the Indian and Coloured People's Congresses. In the process, this managed to lend credence and organisational character to the ANC's policy of creating alliances across racial and ideological boundaries, a philosophical underpinning that would also inform the process and lead to the drafting of the Freedom Charter in 1955, whereby it was stated in the Preamble that: 'South Africa belongs to all who live in it'.

Inclusivity: The core values informing the ANC included the implicit promotion and explicit practice of furthering the principles of non-racialism, non-sexism and non-tribalism, all with the goal of overcoming dichotomies of material conditions between rural and urban populations, rich and poor, educated and illiterate. Also, Andre Odendaal[18] elaborates on the principle of non-sectarianism informing the early roots of the ANC in the late nineteenth and early twentieth centuries. The majority of the people who founded the ANC were Christian converts yet they did not proselytise the organisation into a narrow religious one.

The other dominant group who founded the ANC had strong royal leanings and associations and yet they did not turn the movement into a constricted traditionalist entity. These coalescences affirmed the notion and practice of the ANC as the 'parliament of the people'.

National unity: The principal objective of aligning these broad interest groups was the promotion of the grand ideal of burying the demons of tribalism and racism, as Seme had proclaimed. Subsequent generations of leaders furthered this ideal as Mandela opined that the struggle was not against whites but the oppression of the majority. Presenting his defence during the Rivonia Trial which began in July 1963 after the raid at Liliesleaf Farm where the Umkhonto we Sizwe High Command was operating from (Mandela himself was arrested in Howick in the then Natal), Mandela declared:

> We are not anti-white, we are against white supremacy... we have condemned racialism no matter by whom it is professed... During my lifetime I have dedicated myself to this struggle of the African people. I have fought against white domination, and I have fought against black domination. I have cherished the ideal of a democratic and free society in which all persons live together in harmony and with equal opportunities.

This statement is pertinent since it defines both Mandela's character[19] and the multigenerational heritage of non-racialism. They have global agency today as they did half a century ago.

Another value informing the pursuit of national unity was the creation of a sovereign state serving all citizens and ultimately aimed at severing ties with the *metropolises*. As mentioned above, the organisation did not oppose manifestations of nation-state formation, like the existence of the Union of South African. It was the exclusion and race-based policies of the 'new' South African polity that the ANC was vehemently opposed to. Precisely because of the perpetuity of racial exclusion, the declaration of the Republic in 1961 was opposed by the ANC which collaborated with other formations to organise stay-at-home strikes. After all, the nation-state formation project would be impossible in the context of systematic exclusion of the black majority from their main body politicTaking into account the manifestations of apartheid as colonialism of a special type, wherein all racial groups were classified as first (white), second (Indian), third (coloured), and fourth (African) citizens, the movement consistently declared that

> The African, although subjected to the most intense racial oppression and exploitation, is not the only oppressed national group in South Africa... A unity in action between all the oppressed groups is fundamental to the advance of our liberation struggle.[20]

From Morogoro to Mangaung, the strategy and tactics of the ANC maintain that the struggle is about liberating Africans in particular and blacks in general.

Internal democracy: The enduring belief in internal democracy has arguably helped the ANC reinvent itself. Unlike many liberation movements in Africa, Latin America and Asia, the ANC, from inception, had regular periodic elections of leadership across its structures. Its constitution safeguards this democratic principle. This is important to the extent that political scientists predict that political parties' orientation towards rules-based and democratic governance is likely to manifest itself in the handling of national affairs. We see this ethos sustaining itself even during the exile years. Because the party was banned and therefore could not organise elections with proper representation of branches, Oliver Tambo considered himself acting president after the death of Chief Albert Luthuli. Soon after the unbanning, a conference was held in 1991 to elect a leadership in accordance with the wishes of the branches.

We emphasise this point because many liberation movements have been annihilated by internal squabbles emanating from the lack of internal democracy or resulting in its demise.

Tactical orientation

Recognising the complexity of advancing national liberation under conditions of brutal oppression of political expression, the ANC had to adapt, develop and implement the four pillars of the struggle. This was to ensure that it responded to the changing political and material circumstances internal and external to the organisation, the country and the world. To remain rooted amongst the people it adopted mass mobilisation as a first pillar of struggle, followed by underground resistance, international solidarity and armed struggle. Of course, all four pillars played varying but equally significant roles in undermining apartheid.

Underground resistance: It is to be understood that all oppressive legislation that banned liberation movements unwittingly forced the ANC, amongst others, to operate underground, using subterfuge and distribution of political material, building political cells and networks aimed at conscientising the masses about the ongoing struggle against national oppression. In essence, underground resistance was responsible for mass mobilisation and a necessary vehicle for armed struggled which relied on underground cells and networks to succeed internally.

Mass mobilisation: This was premised on the consideration of the organisation remaining relevant to wider constituencies, and on keeping regular contact with all sectors of society in a consultative, participatory and relevant manner, thus building a broad front against colonialism and apartheid. For mass mobilisation to succeed, the first pillar of the struggle, underground resistance, had to be effective in order to retain the ANC in the popular imagination of the oppressed.

Armed struggle: This pillar was adopted as a culmination of a period in which all forms of civil disobedience (peaceful protests, sending deputations for negotiations) had been exhausted by the liberation movement. As Mandela expressed at the Rivonia Trial:

> We are undertaking this armed struggle to show that black South Africans will not any longer live on their knees. There comes a time in the life of any people when there are but two choices: to submit or to stand and fight. The decision is to stand and fight.

The armed struggle was no longer an option, it was a necessity.

At this point let us note that the formation of Umkhonto Wesizwe in 1961 did not represent the first turn towards armed resistance in South Africa, but rather it was a consolidation of people's wars against national oppression and dispossession. In the *Road to Democracy in South Africa* series, compiled by the South Africa Democracy Education Trust, this pillar of the struggle has been well documented. The sequel to this book will however dedicate space for critiquing the evolution of armed struggle in the making of the centenary of the ANC to close the gap that exists in the current edition.

International solidarity: arguably, this pillar predates the first two in that international anti-colonial networks began as early as the last decade of the nineteenth century, when the founders of the ANC like Seme, Dube, Plaatje and Maxeke developed alliances in Britain and the United States. Here they studied and were influenced by activists like Marcus Garvey, W.E.B. Du Bois and Booker T. Washington. This expression of diasporic connections was made against the background of the abolition of slavery and struggles against racism. It was also a period in which colonialism and imperialism were consolidating, and therefore we do well to remember Seme's 1906 magnum opus which called for the unity and the *Regeneration of Africa*. This inspired post-independence African leaders like Kwame Nkrumah of Ghana, who opined that Africa cannot be free until all colonial outposts like South Africa became free.

Necessarily, when the apartheid regime outlawed all form of legitimate protests after the 1960 Sharpeville Massacre, the liberation movement saw fit to intensify the mobilisation of the international community against a regime declared by the United Nations as perpetuating crimes against humanity.

Character of leadership

Perhaps one of the most distinguishing features of the 101-year-old organisation, for all that is said above, was the individual strength and collective character of the leadership. With few exceptions, most ANC leaders were people who had distinguished themselves as leaders in other spheres of life. Here we speak of doctors (AB Xuma and JB Moroka), academics (ZK Matthews), preachers (ZR Mahabane), lawyers (Tambo), publishers (Plaatje), autodidacts (Moses Kotane), and social workers (Maxeke).

Therefore, it can reasonably be asserted that, given all the internal and external contradictions including the ever-changing global situation, it was quality of leadership that kept the organisation alive and determined the course and pace of struggle.

The raging battle of ideas throughout the history of the organisation comes to mind at this stage. We recall the ones between the constitutionalists and the traditionalists, the conservatives and the radicals, the nationalist and communists. More specifically, we remember how leadership handled difficult discourses sparked by the Black Republic Thesis, the Freedom Charter and the race debate before and after the 1969 Morogoro Conference. Some have suggested that the handling of Wankie-Sipolilo campaigns shook the foundations of leadership in exile to the extent that the organisation, especially Umkhonto Wesizwe, might have collapsed had it not been for the character of leadership.

In recent times the leadership showed character when it handled the negotiations which paved the way for the first inclusive democratic elections in 1994; notwithstanding a political compromise seen by some as favouring the oppressor who gained legal and political protection from retribution and wealth sharing. Linked to the delicate management of the transition was the handling of political violence which spilled over to democratic South Africa.

It could therefore be argued that generations of leaders were visionary in outlook, humble and selfless in demeanour, always aiming at maintaining the broad church, inclusive and participatory in approach by working within constituencies, and unifiers in practice. Their world outlook was internationalist. Building an equitable, non-racial, non-sexist, democratic and prosperous South Africa was their course.

The book's meta-narrative

This book contends that whilst the struggle became organised on four pillars, following the banning of political activity after the Sharpeville massacre, the Treason Trial and imprisonment of political leaders, manifestations (in varying degrees) of these pillars actually predate the formation of the ANC in 1912. As demonstrated in different chapters, armed resistance is as old as colonialism itself, and international solidarity emerged towards the end of the nineteenth century, mainly through black South Africans who were studying abroad. The fact that slaves and immigrants had to be brought to South Africa to work in the plantations and the mines boosted the argument that passive resistance and open defiance, as a form of struggle by Africans, predates African liberation movements in South Africa.

Significantly, this book seeks to build an argument that each of the four pillars of struggle – in addition to what we have constructed as philosophical orientation and character of leadership – remain relevant today, with all the different lessons and meanings they represent. In so doing it addresses a number of key questions:

- Can the ANC employ the core principles of mass mobilisation to define a democratic state where, as President Jacob Zuma has been emphasising, government knows where the people are, appreciates their conditions and is responsive?
- Can the Andries Tatane, Marikana and Mido Macia tragedies reinvigorate the strategic posture of the armed struggle, i.e., to protect civilians from perceived or lived experiences of state brutality and to build a caring civilian police service?
- Will the ANC sustain its internationalist character and side with the worldwide oppressed peoples, even when national interest might seem to be threatened? and
- To what extent will underground struggle tactics of *secrecy* influence the management of public affairs in a progressive democratic state characterised by transparency and openness?

How is this book arranged?

Flowing from this meta-narrative and the sub-narratives of what has kept the ANC together for over a century, we have arranged this book in four parts.

Before we introduce each part let us cite this edition's limitations. Absent from it are specific chapters discussing the roles of women, organised labour, the religious community, the Communist Party, the coloured and Indian people's congresses and the United Democratic Front as protagonists of anti-colonial struggles. Thematic confines of the current project limited the scope and chapter selection.

As the title suggests, this book contributes to *emerging perspectives* on the centenary of the ANC. Therefore, a sequel to this and other projects should dedicate specific chapters to protagonists, events and ideas that were under contention during the period under review.

Also, we disclaim that this is a history textbook with precise dates, names and events. Chapters employ diverse methods of historiography. Some use oral and storytelling tradition, e.g., Chapter 9. Others employ theory to build their arguments, e.g., Chapters 4, 11 and 12. Some rely on popular literature, e.g., Chapters 14, 18 and 18, while Chapters 2, 3, 5, 7, 13 and 15 combine a variety of methods of documenting African history, including examination of language and statements, observations, officials and analyses of news reports.

Also important to note is that, in terms of stylistics, each section and chapter of the book varies in tenor and length. Some chapters are personal accounts whereas others are theoretical.

Part 1 provides the background to both this book and the origins of the ANC. This sets the scene for the entire edition. It contains three chapters: the prologue by Ngcaweni, followed by Masilela's tribute to Pixley ka Isaka Seme – the key historical figure driving the idea of a national union of the natives, the ANC. The third chapter by Ndlovu builds a foundation for what follows in Parts 2 and 3 by discussing the inclusivity, nationalist and internationalist outlook of the ANC from its founding. As suggested by its title, **the Future we Chose**, Part 1 is a retrospective of what was *chosen* by the organisation's leadership over the century.

Part 2 progresses from a critique of decisions made by the founders and their successors. Since we argue that it was primarily the adoption, implementation and careful management of three of the four **pillars of the struggle** that sustained the ANC, chapters in this section discuss these three pillars, i.e., mass mobilisation (Chapter 4 by Motaung and Sehume), underground resistance (Chapter 7 by Zondi) and international solidarity (Chapter 8 by Pahad *et al*).

Given the centrality of education as a site of mass mobilisation and a liberatory instrument, we complement Chapter 4 with Chapters 5 by Pampallis and 6 by Maimela which, respectively, discuss the centrality of education throughout the history of the ANC as well as the role of students in the struggle for democracy.

We were fortunate to have friends of South Africa from Sweden, Finland and Egypt agreeing to contribute to this book by penning their firsthand experiences of international solidarity in Scandinavia (Chapter 19 by Säve-Söderbergh and Peltola) and in Egypt (Chapter 10 by Sharawy).

The narrative in this second part of the book is retrospective, although Chapters 5, 7 and 8 combine both retrospective and prospective methodologies.

Given the centrality of the **battle of ideas** throughout the history of the movement, **Part 3** delves into that space by discussing issues that remain points of contention to this day. Arguable, the ANC was and remains a populist organisation. Chapter 11 by Saloojee explores this view drawing heavily from both theory and praxis. Chapter 12 by Ndlovu-Gatsheni puts forward an argument that apart from removal of legal and administrative apartheid, the ANC has a duty to dismantle all manifestations of colonialism and apartheid, especially economic exclusion and intellectual dislocation suffered by black people.

Whilst it might appear as a settled debate, the discourse on the ANC's Pan-Africanist inclinations remain. Chapter 13 by Mbeki, a modified lecture by a former president, contributes to that debate. Continuing the long tradition of debating class dynamics and the national question in the apartheid and post-apartheid era, chapter 14 by Netshitenzhe closes Part 3 by drawing on history to discuss what has come to be known as *the sins of incumbency*.

With prospective lenses, **Part 4** explores the present and the **future we choose**, which is invariably connected to the continuing *battle of ideas*, and the struggle to transform the ANC from a liberation movement (reliant on its *four pillars of the struggle*) into a modern political party based on the vision of the founders who *chose the* *future* of a South Africa characterised by non-racialism, non-sexism, democracy and prosperity for all.

Flowing from this understanding, Chapter 15 by Motlanthe offers a perspective on organisational renewal in what has been described as *the decade of the cadre*, with heavy emphasis on political education. Recognising challenges facing the century-old organisation, especially those emanating from proximity to state power and the people's unmet expectations, this chapter reinforces the idea that the ANC needs to constantly renew itself in order to meet ever-changing local dynamics and the global balance of forces.

Recognising the significance of evidence-based planning, and drawing from the regional experiences of former liberation movements' posture towards official statistics, Lehohla's Chapter 16 shares the ANC government's attitude in this regard.

Noting that state power is the principal propeller of the *great leap forward*, Gumede in Chapter 17 make a rapid assessment of socio-economic transformation and what needs to be done to accelerate transformation.

Respectively, Chapters 18 by Hirsch and 19 by Ngcaweni sum up the book by offering insights into the prospects of and practical steps required to achieve the developmental state, which has become the preoccupation of the ANC. In these chapters it is suggested that the task of building state capacity should be prioritised and accompanied by firm leadership, innovation and accountability. After all, an inefficient and untransformed public service cannot be a catalyst for transformation as envisaged in the recently adopted National Development Plan.

While they might appear as such, views contained in this book are not political statements but a contribution to a political discourse of the history of the ANC, the future chosen by the leadership from its foundation through to the centenary, and the future that the current leadership chooses in this second centenary.

Conclusion

Measured against historiography presented in this edition, it can be asserted that the history of the twentieth century and this twenty-first century tells a beautiful yet difficult story of the evolution of the African National Congress. Dialectically, it also tells the story of the uncomfortable journey towards the 'third' new South Africa founded in 1994 (some scholars have suggested that the 1910 Union was the first 'new' South Africa and the 1961 declaration of the Republic the second 'new' South Africa). After all, without colonialism and apartheid, the ANC, at least as we know it, might not have existed.

Consequently, men and women of South Africa, through the ANC and the broader liberation movement, have made their own history, not as they pleased but under circumstances pre-existing, given and transmitted from the past. Theirs was the negation of the history of oppression and the affirmation of a new modernity.

The story of South Africa is like the story of the Nile. Like the great river, South Africa and the ANC, in the context of the present project, are made up of countless springs, waterfalls and tributaries. From it, multitudes of livelihoods depend on millions of litres that flow. It is a story spanning centuries of contestation and decades of reconstruction.

The jury is out on the utility and sustenance of symbiosis between the ANC and South Africa. Read in conjunction with the ever-dynamic internal party-political contradictions occasioned by recent phenomena such as the *sins of incumbency*, history might not be kind to the ANC in the twenty-first century.

There is a Buddhist saying that if you want to know your past look into your present conditions; if you want to know your future, look into your present actions. Unless history is recalled for reflection, for assessment, for renewal, for inspiration, for planning the future, it is possible that the story of the ANC might become an urban legend, surviving, like a great dinosaur, in the museums of history. Much as the story of the Nile continues without the great civilisations that once thrived alongside it, much as the story of the animal kingdom continues to be told with dinosaurs confined to museums. So, will the struggle for justice and economic freedom continue in South Africa without the ANC – a reminder that it is solely responsible for writing itself firmly into the script of a future South Africa?

Much more has been said about the priorities of the ANC beyond its first centenary; however, it is this counsel from the organisation's moral compass, Nelson Mandela, which sets the bar for what will breathe oxygen into the ANC and thus make it germane beyond the demise of apartheid and colonialism:

> …Our single most important challenge is therefore to help establish a social order in which the freedom of the individual will truly mean the freedom of the individual. We must construct that people-centred society of freedom in such a manner that it guarantees the political liberties and the human rights of all our citizens…[21]

To paraphrase Zwelinzima Vavi of the Congress of South African Trade Unions, *democracy should not bypass the poor*. All South Africans should enjoy and participate in democracy and have their dignity restored through economic and cultural emancipation. To shoulder this weight of history, values of humility, selflessness, inclusiveness and transparency ought to be the zeitgeist. The leadership collective should win over South Africans by pursuing a realistic programme of action, win debates by advancing superior arguments, and take along all South Africans and sectors of society. Given the will, Raymond Suttner argues, the ANC and all South Africans can realise the visions of many heroes and heroines who strove to build an ever-broadening, inclusive and empowering democracy.

Endnotes

1 Details of the events leading up to this founding meeting and what happened on what has been described as a calm day in the Union of South Africa province then called Orange Free State are not recounted in this book. For some authoritative account of events leading up to 8 January 1912, readers can visit books like *The history of the ANC: South Africa belongs to us* by Francis Meli, *The Founders: The origins of the ANC and the struggle for democracy in South Africa* by Ander Odendaal, *First President: A life of John L. Dube, founding President of the ANC* by Heather Hughes and *Seme the founder of the ANC* by Richard Rive and Tim Couzens. Some of the volumes of *The road to democracy in South Africa*, published by SADET, give extensive overviews of the founding of the ANC.

2 Reference to 'expectionalism' is used advisedly here since the discourse continues on this phenomenon, especially as signs point to a post-oppression state whose path mirrors that of other post-colonial states. For example, South Africa is not the only country in Africa that made a democratic breakthrough through negotiations. Tanzania also did. Also, like many other post-colonial states, government has struggled to transform the public service to the extent that it is efficient and effective, much as other countries have.

3 Mcebisi Ndletyana, reflecting on the ANC centenary in the *Sunday Independent*, 8 January 2012.

4 Deonandan, K., Close, D. & Prevost, G., 2007. *From revolutionary movements to political parties: Cases from Latin America and Africa*. New York: Palgrave Macmillan.

5 For example see Davidson, B., 1992. *The black man's burden: Africa and the curse of the Nation-State*. Suffolk: James Currey, and Davidson, B., 1996. *Africa in history*. New York: Touchstone Books.

6 Various titles by Mahmood Mamdani (such as Mamdani, M., 1996. *Citizen and subject: Contemporary Africa and the legacy of late colonialism*. New Jersey: Princeton University Press) deal extensively with the issue of tribalism and how it has impacted on patterns of African history.

7 For example, see Diop, C.A., 1987. *Pre-colonial black Africa*. Chicago: Lawrence Hill Books.

8 Boahen, A.A., 1989. *African perspectives on colonialism*. The John Hopkins Symposia in Comparative History.

9   Statement made by Pixley ka Isaka Seme in 1911, on behalf of provincial native congresses calling for a national conference to form the Native Union of the oppressed.

10 For further reflections on the Union of South Africa, see Ngcaweni, B., 2012. *Busani Ngcaweni: Union centenary*. Avaliable at: http://www.bdlive.co.za/articles/2010/05/24/busani-ngcaweni-union-centenary; Bernard, B.M., 2012. *Bernard Magubane: Cape franchise*. Available at: http://www.bdlive.co.za/articles/2010/05/27/bernard-magubane-cape-franchise; and Magubane, B.M., 1996. *The Making of a racist State: British imperialism and the union of South Africa, 1875–1910*. New Jersey: Africa World Press.

1   See Simons, J. & Simons, R., 1983. *Class and colour in South Africa: 1850–1950*. International Defence and Aid Fund for Southern Africa.

2   See Jordan, P., 2012. Does the ANC have the courage for introspection? *Business Day*, 13 December. Jordan further writes that 'January 8 1912 was a realisation of a vision that had evolved among the educated African elite in the last 20 years of the nineteenth century... The movement was a brainchild of a generation of youth Africans educated in the US and the UK. In an age before female suffrage, it was composed exclusively of men, though Charlotte Maxeke founded an auxiliary women's league'.

3   Mamdani, 1996, op. cit. details the interplay and exploitation of ethnic and racial identities in colonial and post-colonial Africa. In essence, he argues that while some tribal and ethnic identities predate colonialism, they were shapely defined and deliberately exploited by the ruling elites in the colonial and post-colonial era.

4   Marx, K., 1852. *The eighteenth brumaire of Louis Bonaparte*.

5   Ngugi wa Thiong'o argues this in Wa Thiong'o, N., 2009. *From colour to social consciousness: South Africa in the black imagination*. See Wa Thiong'o, N., 2009. *Re-membering Africa*. Nairobi: East African Education Publishers.

6   Ibid.

7   Respectively see the following books by these authors, *From the Freedom Charter to Polokwane: The evolution of ANC Economic Policy* (2008), *The African National Congress and the regeneration of political power* (2012), *South Africa pushed to the limit: The political economy of change* (2011) and *A history of inequality in South Africa 1652–2002* (2002).

8   As a sequel to his seminal work *Vukani Bantu*, Andre Odendaal, in Odendaal, A., 2012. *The founders: The origins of the ANC and the struggle for democracy in South Africa*. Johannesburg: Jacana, mobilises evidence that elaborates the history of non-sectarianism and role of religious leaders in the formation and sustenance of the ANC.

9   See Ngcaweni, B., 2011. *Whose Mandela is it anyway?* Available at: http://kunjalo.co.za/wp-content/uploads/2011/07/Whose_Mandela_is_it_anyway.pdf in which he asks questions about value system that shaped Nelson Mandela and the leadership collective. Among others, Ngcaweni observes that history is littered with leaders who betrayed the cause of 'freedom' and Mandela is not one of them. When 'offered' a

choice by the apartheid regime to be released from jail, he refused, and for the re-lease of all political prisoners. Yet the greatest test of his character was his astute political management of the period between 1990 (when political organisations were unbanned and political prisoners released) and 1994 (when South Africa held the first all-inclusive democratic elections). In summary, he saved the country from a possible bloody civil war.

20 The African National Congress, 1969. *Strategy and Tactics document*.

21 Former Nelson Mandela making his first address to the democratic Parliament in 1994.

CHAPTER 2

Recalling the historical significance of Pixley ka Isaka Seme in the founding of the ANC

Ntongela Masilela

The death of Dr P. ka I. Seme has removed from among us one man whose stature will grow tremendously as the years go by and whom future historians of our race will regard as the greatest African of the first fifty years of the twentieth century – if not of the century as a whole. For it is to the vision of Dr Seme that we are indebted for the unity of the African people. – JORDAN KUSH NGUBANE, 'Dr P. ka I. Seme: A Tribute', *Inkundla ya Bantu*, 30 June, 1951.

That Pixley ka I. Seme was a man of action and a patriot no sane man can deny. But his weakness, and that perhaps is the weakness of every brilliant man, was that he believed in his mind only, and therefore could not listen to the advice of other men. Had he understood the value of compromise and cooperation he would have achieved greater things for the African race. But his plans were 'wrecked', to use Lord Rosebery's phrase, 'by the extravagance of his own genius'. – R. V. SELOPE THEMA, 'How Congress Began', *Drum*, July 1953.

Introduction

On this momentous occasion of reflecting on the hundredth anniversary of the founding of the African National Congress (ANC) there are perhaps four or five force fields in which Pixley ka Isaka Seme – the key figure in its founding – made seminal contributions to South African political, cultural and intellectual history in the twentieth century. His great essay of 1906, *The Regeneration of Africa*, called on Africans to initiate the decolonisation process and facilitate the construction of modernity as a historical imperative of that contemporaneous moment. He gave coherence and amplitude to the idea of the New African Movement which began a decade or two before his written reflections,[1] disseminated in many New African newspapers, thereby becoming the founder of the South African Native National Congress (from 1923 known as the South African National Congress).[2]

In the 1900s he was among the earliest, if not the first, to write portraits of the emergent New Africans (intellectuals, religious leaders, literary scholars or literary anthologists), an undertaking to be articulated in depth and systematised by Selope Thema and Henry Selby Msimang in the pages of *Umteteleli wa Bantu* (The Mouthpiece of the People) in the 1920s. Seme fostered among African people a cultural ethos of intellectual activity,[3] writing extensively from July 1932 to October 1937, also in *Umteteleli wa Bantu* – a period that largely coincided with his presidency of the ANC, calling for the creation of 'One African Nation' guided by particular political principles and ideological perspectives.

Seme was one of the principle architects of the ideology of African Nationalism,[4] through influence on his protégé Anton Lembede, who for all intents and purposes was the founder of the African National Congress Youth League (ANCYL), as well as being its ideologue and first president. He has been designated the godfather of this radical and youthful nationalist organisation by Jordan Kush Ngubane, himself a founding member, then editor of the *Inkundla ya Bantu* (Bantu Forum) newspaper, as well as being one of the preeminent intellectuals of the New African Movement.[5]

In founding the newspaper *Abantu/Batho* (The People) in 1912, which in effect was the intellectual organ of the ANC, Seme, like other New African intellectuals such as Solomon T. Plaatje, R.V. Selope Thema, John Langalibalele Dube and Mohandas Gandhi, played a critical role in modernising the historical and political imagination of the dispossessed people of South Africa in the first half of the twentieth century.

Given this colossal achievement of Pixley ka Isaka Seme, it is not surprising that within a matter of days of his death Jordan Kush Ngubane wrote the laudatory appraisal of him that is partly quoted in the epigraph. Likewise, and not surprisingly, given their deeply adversarial relationship during the turbulent 1930s, it took Selope Thema just over two years to reflect on the historical legacy that Seme had bestowed on the African people. This antagonism, though based on mutual respect, was paradoxical in that both were conservative modernisers within the New African Movement, distinct from fellow New Africans who were either progressive modernisers or revolutionary modernisers.

As the epigraph indicates, despite the originality of his political imagination, Seme was autocratic, disregarding a democratically forged consensus, in the estimation and evaluation of Thema, and thereby was more a *political visionary* than a *practical implementer* of a democratic consensus. Ngubane in his tribute sought to indicate that by means of the ideology of African Nationalism Seme had been able to construct notions or concepts such as 'New Africa', 'United Africa', 'African People' and 'Free Africa', actualised by intellectual and political practices of New African intellectuals through their political organisations, associations, societies and cooperatives to effect 'Justice', 'Liberty' and 'Truth' for the dispossessed people of South Africa or the 'New African Masses'.

Noting that Seme 'realised that the knowledge that he acquired was not only for his self-aggrandisement and enrichment, but also for the upliftment and the emancipation of his down-trodden people', Thema argues that Seme, like other New African intellectuals, struggled to reconcile his aspiration for modernity (including Christianity) with African traditional beliefs and ethos. These are exemplified in his particular instance by the great king Shaka and the Zulu Nation he founded, as well as by the great Zulu imbongi (praise poets) of the nineteenth century, Magolwana ka Makhathini and Mshongweni. This dialectical contradiction or historical tension was particularly acute amongst those New Africans who had studied abroad up to the first two decades of the twentieth century, lawyers like Seme himself, Alfred Mangena, George D. Montsioa and Richard W. Msimang.

Seme and scholarship

Seme was among the distinctively few New African intellectuals who studied both in the United States and in Great Britain, thereby experiencing their singular brands of modernity at a moment when the former was beginning to supersede the latter as an imperial hegemon.

American modernity was a much greater determinant on the political conscious-ness and historical outlook of Seme than English modernity, if nothing else because he arrived in the United States during his impressionable and formative years in 1898 at the age of 18 to study at Northfield Mount Hermon [high] School in Massachusetts. He entered Columbia University in 1902 to commence his Liberal Arts education, and received his Bachelor of Arts degree in April 1906 at the age of 26. It was at the graduation ceremony that he read his celebrated *The Regeneration of Africa* address. Five months later, in September 1906, he left New York for Jesus College at Oxford University where he obtained a degree of Bachelor of Civil Law in June 1909.

Seme returned to South Africa in 1910, just after the formation of the Union of South Africa which dispossessed Africans and other oppressed nations of their politi-cal rights. Nearly two decades after his graduation, Columbia University bestowed on him an honorary degree of Doctor of Law in 1928 for his intellectual and political work in leading the African people in the struggle against white political domination and racial oppression.

Perhaps the fundamental reason why American modernity had a profound effect on Pixley ka Isaka Seme was that, at the time of his residence in the country, the New Negro Movement was at its height in mobilising the intellectual, political and religious forces of the New Negroes in the struggle against racial oppression and 'Jim Crow' laws in the United States.

Besides Seme, others studying there at this critical moment of American history were John Langalibalele Dube, Charlotte Manye Maxeke, Charles Dube, and Alfred B. Xuma, all profoundly imprinted by a traumatising American *racial politics* of this time that stemmed from the defeat or failure of Reconstruction, as the result of the Federal Government in 1877 abandoning the recently emancipated slaves (in January 1863) to the fate of the embittered white Confederacy which had been defeated in the American Civil War.

W.E.B. Du Bois devoted one of his great historical works, *Black Reconstruction* (1935), to this enormous tragedy of black people in America. In their landmark anthology, *The Norton Anthology of African American Literature* (1997), Henry Louis Gates and Nellie Y. McKay periodised this moment as that of the 'New Negro Renaissance', beginning in 1865, the end of the American Civil War, ending in 1919 and forming a precursor to the culturally renowned 'Harlem Renaissance'.

The Jim Crow era in American history was politically characterised by several fundamental processes: the development of white supremacist ideology, and white violence against black people, which in its worst manifestation took the form of lynching, disempowerment and disenfranchising of black people on a massive scale. It could be argued that within New Negro politics at this time, the year 1895 was the most critical: Frederick Douglass died; Booker T. Washington delivered the 'Atlanta Compromise' speech; and W.E.B. Du Bois received a doctoral degree for his dissertation *The Suppression of the African Slave Trade*, which was published the following year as a book.

Seme's great manifesto of the New African Movement, *The Regeneration of Africa*, was profoundly permeated by the penetrative understanding of the philosophy of American racial politics from the perspective of the New Negro Movement, understandable given that it was the amalgamation and synthesis of particular classic documents and philosophies of African American intellectual culture. These were Frederick Douglass's essay 'The Claims of the Negro Ethnologically Considered' (1854), which Henry Louis Gates retroactively designates as having been the founding document of Black Studies that emerged in the1960s; the three essays of Alexander Crummell, 'The English Language in Liberia' (1860), 'The Regeneration of Africa' (1865), and 'The Need of New Ideas and New Aims for a New Era' (1885); and Booker T. Washington's philosophy of black self-empowerment and upliftment that made him give primacy to the construction of social institutions rather than theoretical systems.

The real genius of Seme in this essay of not more than four pages was in having transposed, transfigured and transformed American racial politics stemming from enslavement into African racial politics singular to the colonial experience. The subsequent acclamation given to it was perhaps for this unique achievement: be it its inclusion in an African American anthology of 1910 dedicated to the memory of the African American poet Paul Laurence Dunbar, adjacent to the contributions of W.E.B. Du Bois and Bishop Henry M. Turner, among others;[6] or Kwame Nkrumah, the first President of Ghana, reading Seme's whole essay in his Opening Address to the proceedings of the First International Congress of Africanists in Accra in 1963.[7]

It is plausible to postulate that it was because of his knowledge of racial politics acquired in the United States, similar to the racial politics that were at the centre of the formation of the Union of South Africa in 1910, that Seme, in preference over his three senior aforementioned colleagues who were also lawyers but had only studied in Great Britain, was given the monumental task by members of the South African Native Congress and some prominent chiefs of organising the gathering that would lead to the founding of the ANC over a century ago.

Locating Seme within the Pan-African movement

The acquisition of this knowledge of racial politics by Seme was in the context of his interacting with eminent African American intellectuals: Alain Locke, W.E.B. Du Bois, Booker T. Washington and others. It may have been due to his observations of the intellectual and political practices of the New Negro intellectuals of the New Negro Movement while he was a student at Columbia University that he came to acquire an appreciation of the concept of the intellectual, as evident in his writing the intellectual portraits of Alfred Mangena, while he was still studying at Oxford University in 1908, that of Walter Benson Rubusana immediately after his return to South Africa in 1910, and that of Alfred Mangena as an obituary notice in 1924.

In the intellectual portrait of 1908 ('Alfred Mangena of Lincolns Inn: Esquire and Barrister-at-Law', *Ilanga lase Natal*, 24 August), Seme views Alfred Mangena as one of the most outstanding first generation of New African intellectuals to have constructed the historical horizon and intellectual content of the New African Movement. In this construction he shows himself to be one of South Africa's outstanding modernists. Seme argues that Mangena acquired this modernist sensibility and outlook from the superlative education he had received in England as well as from the political praxis he was implementing in the country upon his return from overseas. He stresses the fundamental role of education Mangena had received in England in the form of both matriculation and the law degree acquired at Lincoln's Inn in London.

Seme postulated that in all probability it was the Bhambatha Rebellion of 1906 (which occurred in Natal while Mangena was completing his final degree) that made him resolute in his hostility to European oppression and exploitation of African people. As evidence of this political resolution, Seme elaborated on the two petitions that Mangena submitted to the British government on behalf of Bhambatha's men who were facing court martial in Natal. Even more impressive to Seme, Mangena initiated a political and court case in London against the Governor of Natal for having proclaimed martial law in the province, which Mangena considered illegal and unconstitutional.

When he was attacked by a representative of the Natal government in London, Mangena vindicated himself by suing for libel. To Seme, by these political and juridical actions, Alfred Mangena showed himself attuned to the legal knowledge that was necessary in order to participate fully in the new historical experience of modernity. It may have been this intellectual and political praxis by the uncompromising New African political leader and intellectual in defending the political and legal rights of New African masses that made such a lasting and profound impression on Pixley ka Isaka Seme, who was a fellow student at this time at Lincoln's Inn.

In the aforementioned obituary notice,[8] written 16 years later, Seme praised Alfred Mangena with astonishing words which were perhaps an index of the nature of the political and intellectual imprint on his consciousness that his senior colleague had on his awakening to the complex nature of modernity.

What is so revealing about this intellectual, biographical and intellectual portrait of Mangena, written four years before the formation of the ANC, is the prescient nature of Seme's political imagination. In it he alludes to certain intractable issues or problems that informed or were at the centre of South African political history in the twentieth century, perhaps even in our twenty-first century.

What is so compelling about this biographical sketch of 1908 is that Pixley ka Isaka Seme was beginning to theorise the historical context of the interaction of the New African intellectuals and political leaders within the New African Movement in the making of New African modernity in which new perspectives, new praxes and new sensibilities would be necessary in the liberation of New African masses.

In many ways this homage by a *protégé* to the *master* initiated three fundamental issues that were central in the relationship between the ANC and the New African Movement: the *political practice* of the New African Movement, and the *cultural* or *intellectual expression* of the ANC:

i) What should be the configuration of the relationship between *ethnic Nationalism* and *African Nationalism* in the structuring of the political ideology and historical consciousness of the ANC?

ii) Should the challenge to the oppressive political order of European modernity and its possible transfiguration into New African modernity be through *constitutional-ism* or *revolutionary* practice?

iii) Should it be the conservative modernisers, the progressive modernisers or the revolutionary modernisers who should be the driving force in the making of a New South Africa?

Given the complacency of the present, these issues seem to have been 'automatically' resolved with the defeat of the apartheid regime. One of the greatest African poets of the twentieth century, Mazisi Kunene, who paradoxically gave the appearance of being a conservative moderniser during his lifetime but who to posterity might turn out to have been the most incomparable revolutionary moderniser, thought otherwise since the dialectic between *language* and *history* has not as yet been resolved in South African history.

What is truly astonishing for our purposes here is that the young Pixley ka Isaka Seme already had a profound premonition of the central importance of these issues at the very moment of the inauguration of his intellectual and political practice. What should be mentioned here, without going into detail because of limited space, is that while possessing a prescient political vision, Seme had questionable, in fact horren-dous, leadership qualities. In many ways, he was an enigma.

From the perspective of the laudatory nature of the obituary notice[9] that Pixley ka Isaka Seme wrote 16 years after the earlier intellectual and political portrait, Alfred Mangena fulfilled his social and political responsibilities to the emergent New Africa. Though written in absolute sadness, Seme seems to be jubilant that the exemplary form of Mangena's political and intellectual practice will everlastingly influence and inform the wisdom of future generations of New African intellectuals and political leaders who are intent on bringing into being a 'Free Africa'. With this new construct or concept of a 'Free Africa', which should be viewed in relation to his earlier formula-tion of the notion of the 'Regeneration of Africa', Seme seems to be alluding to the inseparability of African Nationalism and Pan-Africanism.

Though it does not directly concern us here, during the deepest crisis of the African National Congress in the 1930s, due to his authoritarian and dictatorial leadership, a crisis that is comparable to the other which deeply engulfed the organisation in the 1960s during the exile period or interregnum, Seme undertook a truly remarkable project of formulating the ideology of African Nationalism in a series of extraordinary articles in the pages of *Umteteli wa Bantu* over a five-year period, as if to say that although he possessed incompetent political leadership skill his formidable mind was incomparable. This was truly the paradoxical nature of Seme, which is characterised as his 'genius' in the epigraph cited earlier from R.V. Selope Thema.

But returning to the obituary notice: in this short four-paragraph notation Seme made the following observations: the early death of Mangena at the age of 45 surprised the cultural and intellectual leadership of the New African Movement and the political ideologues of the ANC; however short his life, he certainly delivered to South Africa a high and new message of modernity, thereby inspiring New Africans and Old Africans ('Natives') to new awakenings, achievements and attainments; in his determination that Africans should strive for the best that was attainable at that particular moment, he not only made certain that they would no longer be subservient to the colonial project of domination, but he also inspired them in the direction of political resistance.

Last, his inborn political skill of leadership came directly from his fearlessness, determination and patriotism. In this absolute fortitude, Mangena exemplified a new national principle 'that no sacrifice would ever be too great' in creating and forging a new nation. The third paragraph in this appraisal deserves being quoted verbatim here for its insightfulness:

> Alfred Mangena lived under the shadow of the beautiful vision of a *free Africa*, in which he and all his countrymen would be free; free from this demon of discriminating injustice and prejudice, free from the base and contemptible political jugglery and cupidity of this day - tergiversation in word and deed... In a word he dared and dreamed of the day when Ethiopia shall lift up her hands unto God and when princes shall come out of Egypt.

With these words Seme sought not only to pay homage to the prescient nature of Mangena's political practice and intellectual vision but also to establish that the real encompassing understanding of the New African Movement went beyond creating a New South Africa towards making possible a Free Africa. This combined a realisation that African Nationalism and Pan-Africanism would be made possible by synchronising the *past* ('Egypt') with the *present* ('Ethiopia').

In this obituary piece of about a hundred words, Pixley ka Isaka Seme summarised this Pan-African vision of Alfred Mangena as his everlasting legacy.

Seme's reflections on Rubusana[10] were written in the same year as the publication of the Xhosa intellectual's second edition of the great anthology of Xhosa writings *Zemk' Inkomo Magwalandini* which had originally appeared in 1906.

Disagreeing with the translated title of the book, *Away Go the Cattle, You Cowards*, Benedict Wallet Vilakazi, the outstanding Zulu intellectual, in his doctoral dissertation of 1946, *The Oral and Written Literature in Nguni*, thought that a better title translation of this Xhosa reader was *Preserve Your Culture*. Astonishingly, Vilakazi argued in this doctoral work that the first half of the twentieth century, a period coterminous with the trajectory of the New African Movement, should be designated as the 'Age of Walter Rubusana'.

In other words, Pixley ka Isaka Seme's intellectual portrait of Rubusana was anticipatory of the high regard given to Rubusana by later generations of Zulu intellectuals, which included among others H.I.E. Dhlomo and Jordan Kush Ngubane. This anticipatory nature of Seme was one of the defining features of his greatness.

Concerning Rubusana as a historical figure – engaged with profound changes initiated and imposed by the violent entrance of European modernity into African history – Seme made pertinent observations which can be summarised as follows regarding the emergent New Age: with the publication of the book Rubusana was taking cognisance that modernity had not only changed the life experience of African people from the Old to the New but had also transformed it into a better experience.

Paradoxically this contact between Africans and Europeans had the former attain 'a higher standard of life' despite the oppression and domination exacted on them; Rubusana represented and exemplified the double-edged nature of modernity on African people – enlightenment effected through subjugation and genocidal occupation.

The efforts and achievements of Rubusana were attained despite the limitations and hindrances exacted by colonial modernity, making him the paragon of what African people should emulate, despite the exactions of this domination. Rubusana sought the making of a humane society for all South Africans and Seme was awed by the role of Christianity in making Rubusana a man of tempered measures as well as preoccupied with the role of ethical principles in life.

Seeking to understand the particular explanations and reasons for the singularity of Rubusana's high achievements, Seme reconstructed the historical lineages and his particular cultural subjectivity which were determinant of his political and social practices ranging from Ntsikana, the first Xhosa to convert to Christianity, to the quality of education he obtained from the missionaries. One major characteristic of his youth was the quality of sobriety which later in life marked the nobleness of his political maturity as well as imparting in him a deep sense of responsibility in his political undertakings.

His appreciation of nature gave him an absolute sense of determination in his beliefs. Although his family were among the early converts to Christianity, he commenced his missionary education at the late age of 16, and despite this lateness, or because of it, he never wavered in recognition of the importance of education. His early Christian teachers instilled in him an unyielding belief in Christianity and education which converged with the pastoral practice of the church. Later in life they informed his political integrity.

On commencing his education at Lovedale in 1876, he excelled in Latin, Greek, Hebrew, logic, Church history and philosophy. His ordination into the ministry of the church in 1884 marked in Rubusana a complete separation from the Old Ways of tradition to the New Ways of modernity. His preaching of the gospel made him popular within certain segments of the Xhosa Nation, and his combination of religion and politics, which he acquired from the Lovedale Literary Society and the Native Educational Society, characterised his determination in questing for the 'Truth'.

He believed that the Truth would someday free African People from sinfulness and oppression, a fundamental ambition made possible by the combination of the Way of the Church, the Life of Politics and the Truth of Knowledge in the search for freedom and liberation.

Finally, for Seme, the historical figure of Walter Benson Rubusana constituted a move beyond the politics of the church and the politics of knowledge towards the politics of an emergent African nationalism.

These two intellectual-cum-political portraits of Alfred Mangena and Walter Benson Rubusana make unmistakably clear that these two New African leaders, as well as such prominent figures as John Langalibalele Dube and Sefako Mapogo Makgatho, were fundamentally influential in Pixley ka Isaka Seme's own intellectual and political formation.

African intellectual portraits

It needs to be emphasised that Seme was not the first New African to start writing New African intellectual portraits. While he was in high school in the United States, before enrolling at Columbia University, F.Z.S. Peregrino, the Ghanaian intellectual who arrived in Cape Town in 1900 from Rochester in the United States at the age of 49 years and lived there until his death in 1919, began this political trend of portraying black intellectuals in modernity in his newspaper *South African Spectator* which he launched immediately on his arrival.

For instance, he wrote a remarkable portrait of Mongane Maake Mokone, the founder of the Ethiopian Movement,[11] as well as of Levi J. Coppins,[12] perhaps the first New Negro minister to proselytise extensively in South Africa on behalf of the African Methodist Episcopal Church, which was based and still exists in the United States.

There are two other fundamental contributions of Peregrino to the New African Movement in its early years: he brought the ideology of Pan-Africanism, the quintessential black philosophy of modernity, to South Africa immediately following the First Pan-African Congress of 1900 in London, in which he was a participant. He wrote the first truly serious historical journalistic document about the founding of the ANC just two months after the event, astonishingly labelling it the emergence of a new *movement* (see the *South African Native National Congress: What it is*).[13]

Finally, Peregrino wrote three important pamphlets on political aspects and historical conditions of New African modernity: *Life among the Native and Coloured Miners* of the Transvaal (Cape Town, 1915), *The Political Parties and the Coloured Vote* (Cape Town, 1915), and *His Majesty's Black Labourers: A Treatise on the Camp Life of the South African Native Labour Contingent* (Cape Town, 1918).

Although Solomon T. Plaatje, like Peregrino, began writing intellectual portraits of New Africans earlier than Seme, for example,[14] it is those written a decade later in his newspaper *Tsala ea Batho* (The Friend of Bechuana), at the same time as Seme, that are more germane in this context. These were written largely after the emergence of the ANC.

Similar to Peregrino, Plaatje seemed to have wanted to project the Pan-African connections or dimensions of the momentous event of 1912. Written within a year of each other on Edward Wilmont Blyden, one engaged his political and intellectual ideas[15] and the other conveyed his death.[16]

Perhaps both appraisal and reflection should be connected to the essay he wrote slightly earlier – which seemed to have been inspired by the publication of W.E.B. Du Bois' *The Souls of the Black Folk* in the previous year. In this essay Plaatjie examined the historical lineages of the concept of Negro on both sides of the Atlantic as to the kind of unity for all black people it facilitated.[17]

The transatlantic relations between Africa and the African diaspora became of paramount importance in the columns, editorials and reports of many New African newspapers at this conjuncture of South African history, the decade in which the Union of South Africa of 1910 and the Native Lands Act of 1913 were infamously effected. It was the peregrinations of New Negro political leaders in Europe that put the case of the black world to European audiences.[18]

A detailed report was made on the political issues concerning race relations in the world scheduled to be deliberated upon at the Universal Races Congress at the University of London in July, and among the speakers were to be W.E.B. Du Bois and D.D.T. Jabavu.[19] Booker T. Washington wrote directly from the Tuskegee Institute in Alabama to Solomon T. Plaatje as editor of the newspaper, advertising a conference he was planning about the situation of black people in the world:

> For some years past I have had in mind to invite here from different parts of the world from Europe, Africa, the West Indies, and North and South America – persons who are actively interested, or directly engaged as Missionaries, or otherwise, in the work that is going on in Africa and elsewhere for the education and up building of Negro peoples.[20]

Conclusion

All of these international interconnections of the black world which were in emergent form when Pixley ka Isaka Seme returned from overseas indicate that there was already a thriving New African intellectual and political culture deeply engaged with the problems and issues of modernity, although not necessarily with the concept of modernity as such. Seme's *The Regeneration of Africa* was the beginning of the engagement with the specificity of the concept in its call for the construction of a complex form of modernity and in its argumentation that Egyptian civilisation belonged to African history because it had actually been made by African people rather than by Europeans as colonialism and imperialism had imputed.

It was the New African political leaders and intellectuals and artists such as Solomon T. Plaatje, Elijah Makiwane, Sefako M. Makgatho, Richard M. Msimang, S.E.K. Mqhayi, John Langalibalele Dube and others, as well as the American Missionaries who took the young Seme to study in the United States, and who created the historical conditions that enabled him to make the aforementioned five major contributions to South African intellectual and political history in the twentieth century.

With these seminal achievements Pixley ka Isaka Seme solidified and gave coherence to the New African Movement, a movement that was tragically destroyed by the apartheid state at the Sharpeville massacre of 1960.

Yet we remain convinced that, once again, the progressive ideas of Seme, his contemporaries and future generations of intellectuals he inspired, will re-emerge in the second centenary of the ANC, thus spurring Africans into new vistas of growth, social justice and humanism.

Endnotes

1   Seme, P., 1905. The regeneration of Africa. *Journal of Royal African Society*, 5, 1905–1906. Here it is necessary to pay salutary tribute to Richard Rive and Tim Couzens for having assembled and written the following book which guided some of the reflections expressed here: Rive, R. & Couzens, T., 1991. *Seme: The founder of the ANC*. UWC Mayibuye History Series No. 2. Johannesburg: Skotaville Press.

2   Seme, P., 1911. Native union. *Ilanga lase Natal*, 20 October; and Anon. 1911. Proposed Native Congress: Caucus meeting. *Imvo Zabantsundu*, 5 December.

3   Seme, P., 1908. Alfred Mangena of Lincoln's Inn: Esquire and Barrister-at-Law. *Ilanga lase Natal*, 14 August; Seme, P., 1910. Reverend W. B. Rubusana, Ph. D., M.P.C. *Ilanga lase Natal*, 11 November; and Seme, P., 1924. The late Alfred Mangena. *Umteteleli wa*

Bantu, 6 December (published a week earlier in a slight different form: Seme, P., 1924. A tribute to the late Alfred Mangena. *Ilanga lase Natal*, 28 November).

4 Choosing at random, Seme, P., 1933. Presidential Address: 'African National Congress'. *Umteteleli wa Bantu*, 29 April.

5 Ngubane, J.K., 1951. Dr. P. ka I. Seme: A tribute. *Inkundla ya Bantu*, 30 June. Ngubane in effect partly made *Inkundla ya Bantu* become the intellectual and ideological forum of the African National Congress Youth League.

6 Webb, J.M. (ed.), n.d. *The black man, the father of civilisation in proven by Biblical history*.

7 See 1963. *Présence Africaine*, 17(5).

8 Seme, P., 1924. The late Alfred Mangena. *Umteteleli wa Bantu*, 6 December.

9 Ibid.

10 Seme, P., 1911. Biographical sketch: Rev. W.B. Rubusana, Ph.D., M.P.C. *Imvo Zabantsundu*, 24 January.

11 See Peregrino, F.Z.S., 1901. *The father of the Church: A popular native Minister*, 7 September.

12 See Peregrino, F.Z.S., 1901. *Right Reverend Levi Jenkins Coppins, D.D.: A prince of the Church*, 23 February.

13 This statement was cited in *Ilanga lase Natal* of 22 March 1912.

14 Plaatje, S.T., 1904. Mr Alfred S. Moletsane. *Koranta ea Becoana*, 13 April.

15 See Peregrino, F.Z.S., 1911. Dr Edward Blyden, Sierra Leone. *Tsala ea Becoana*, 1 April.

16 Plaatje, S.T., 1912. A great negro savant: Death of Dr. Edward Wilmont Blyden. *Tsala ea Becoana*, 9 March.

17 See Plaatje, S.T., 1904. The negro question. *Koranta ea Becoana*, 7 Loete [September].

18 Anon. 1914. Booker T. Washington: To present the case of the blackman to Britons. *Tsala ea Batho*, 31 October.

19 Ibid.

20 See Washington, B.T., 1911. International conference on the negro. *Tsala ea Becoana*, 15 July.

CHAPTER 3

The African agenda and the origins of internationalism within the ANC: 1912–1960

Sifiso Mxolisi Ndlovu

Introduction

The three racially inspired conventions that took place within four years during the early twentieth century were crucial in the making of the democratic South African state. The 1908, 1909 and 1912 conventions marked the beginning of internationalism within the African National Congress (ANC) as the organisation consciously linked the national question in South Africa with the broader anti-colonial struggles that took place throughout the world.

When the racist South Africa Act was first published in 1909, the founders of the ANC, then affiliated to provincial congresses, realised the international significance of such a profound and racially tinged political move. African resistance to white rule had begun when the first white travellers and settlers set their sights on these parts of the world. In the Eastern Cape, Africans opposed to John Tengo Jabavu's preoccupation with white politics founded the South African Native Congress (SANC), the inaugural conference of which was held on 31 December 1891 in the district of King William's Town. Thomas John Mqanda was elected as president, with Nana Ganya as treasurer and Jonathan Tunyiswa and Tiyo Soga as general secretaries.

This tradition was continued when in July 1900 the provincially based Natal Native Congress was established. Its first chairperson was Martin Luthuli, iNkosi Albert Luthuli's uncle, and its first secretary was H.C. Matiwane. In May 1903, SANC members, including J.Z. Tantsi and H.R. Ngcayiya, both members of the African Methodist Episcopal (AME) separatist church, were responsible for the formation of the Transvaal Native Congress. In 1904, the Orange River Colony Native Vigilance Association (which later became the Orange River Native Congress) was formed under the leadership of Joseph Twayi, Jan Mocher, Peter Phatlane, Jacob Lavers and Benjamin Khumalo, also of the AME church.[1]

The leaders of the provincially based native congresses convened the South African Native Convention from 24 to 26 March 1909 in order to consolidate the anti-colonial struggle. This was after white South Africans had held their own whites-only convention in 1908, which eventually led to the publication of the draft South Africa Act. The 1908 convention congregated in Durban and was essentially about reconciliation between Boer and Briton after the divisive South African war.

The counter-national convention of 1909, organised by the native congresses, met in the Waaihoek Township in Bloemfontein and emphatically rejected clauses 25, 33 and 44 of the inhuman 1909 South African Act, which proposed the promulgation of a racist colour bar that promised discrimination and oppression of the majority. The conveners also hoped to extend the African vote (applicable in the Cape) to the other provinces. They were against the incorporation of the High Commission Territories, namely Bechuanaland (Botswana), Basutoland (Lesotho) and Swaziland, into the Union of South Africa. The resolutions adopted proposed a racially inclusive negotiated solution to the national question, to be achieved through diplomatic endeavours.[2]

Subsequently, a deputation was sent to Britain in 1909, comprising Dr Walter Benson Rubusana, Thomas M. Mapikela, John Langalibalele Dube,[3] Daniel Dwanya, John Tengo Jabavu, Alfred Mangena, J. Gerrans and Sebele Sechele. This 'multiracial' deputation also included William Philip Schreiner and Dr Abdullah Abdurahman, Matt J. Fredericks and D.J. Lenders. They made contact with Mahatma Gandhi, who undertook a separate journey to London for the same purpose but on behalf of Indian people in South Africa, though with limited success. The High Commission Territories were not to be incorporated into the Union but they failed to get the colour bar clauses removed from the 1910 Union constitution.[4]

The formation of the all-white Union of South Africa in 1910 led to the unification of various native congresses that had been operating in various parts of the country. A clarion call to fight racism and narrow ethnic nationalism and promote African unity was issued by Dr Pixley Isaka ka Seme:

> There is today among all races and men a general desire for progress, and for co-operation, because co-operation will facilitate and secure that progress. This spirit is due to the great triumph of Christianity which teaches men everywhere that in this world they have a common duty to perform both towards God and one another. It is natural therefore, that there should arise even within and among us this striving for Union… I repeat, cooperation is the key and the watchword which opens the door, the everlasting door which leads into progress and all national success…[5]

The subjugated African majority responded positively to Seme's visionary call for the formation of a democratic and unified South Africa. The various political formations that had come into being in the Cape, Natal, Transvaal and Orange Free State provinces, including the educated elite, kings and chiefs, formed the South African National Native Congress (later the ANC) on 8 January 1912, with the mission to address the national question. When the ANC was formed it was an organisation of indigenous peoples only.

Defending and promoting the rights of Africans, it fought against the colour bar in the 1910 constitution, land dispossession and the pass laws – in other words, it continued the anti-colonial struggles waged by its forebears that had culminated in the 1906 Bhambatha Rebellion. The founding convention was thus one of the most notable occasions in the struggle against colonialism, racism and white supremacist rule in the history of our continent. It also signifies that the national question was now synonymous with the anti-colonial struggle.

Notwithstanding that the 1909 deputation ended in abject failure, the ANC did not desist from seeking diplomatic solutions to the national question in South Africa. As a result, in 1914 another diplomatic mission set out for London, the second trip in five years. This democratically elected ANC deputation consisted of John Langalibalele Dube, the first president of the ANC, Walter Rubusana, Solomon Thekiso Plaatje, Saul Msane and Mapikela. It was also unsuccessful. The third diplomatic venture to Britain was in 1919, again sent by the ANC, to appeal to the British government for a negotiated, peaceful settlement of the national question. The delegates were Henry Reed Ngcayiya, Selope Thema, Levi Thomas Mvabaza, Josiah Tshangana Gumede and Plaatje.[6]

The birth of the Union of South Africa in 1910 impacted on the British High Commission Territories and protectorates such as Basutoland (Lesotho), Bechuanaland (Botswana) and Swaziland. Hence, in May 1908, as soon as reports surfaced of the Union and planned incorporation of the protectorates, King Letsie II of Basutoland convened a *Lekhotla la Mahosana* (Court of Princes), to decide on a course of action.[7] Out of the deliberations, King Letsie II penned a letter to the British resident commissioner seeking clarification of the whole issue of the Union, how it was going to be implemented and the position of Basutoland in the greater scheme of things.[8] He later proposed to lead a delegation to Britain, for he was against incorporation. Its mandate was to find a diplomatic solution to the problem.

Manifestations of Pan-Africanism and inclusivity

Although the delegation was given assurances that their fears were groundless and that their interests would be safeguarded by the British government, the Basotho monarchy was not satisfied because it was unable to extract an assurance that Basutoland would continue as a separate entity. They decided to join forces with Africans

living in the Union of South Africa and in the Swaziland and Bechuanaland protectorates to oppose this Union, once the new South African constitution was sanctioned by
the imperial government in Britain.

As a result, the Basotho monarchy cooperated enthusiastically with fellow Africans in the founding of the South African Native National Congress (SANNC) in
Bloemfontein on 8 January 1912, at which Dube was elected as president. Also to
consolidate the ANC's Pan-Africanist bias and solidarity with other Africans in different parts of the continent, in 1918 a special ANC conference of *amakhosi* (monarchs)
sent a memorandum to the British king stating emphatically that white governments
of South Africa, Germany and Belgium should keep their hands off South West Africa
(Namibia), East Africa (Tanzania) and the Congo, respectively, until the wishes of
indigenous Africans were met.

The SANNC's leadership used various strategies to showcase its affinity with Pan-
Africanism – the influential political ideology during the early twentieth century. The
SANNC's official slogan *Mayibuye Africa*, coined in 1912/1913 during the more militant early days of the SANNC and popularised by its newspaper, *Abantu-Batho,* was
decidedly and unashamedly Pan-Africanist. The slogan translates as 'Let the continent
of Africa return to its rightful owners' or, more specifically, 'let the land of Africa
return to its rightful owners'.

That the SANNC was an inclusive organisation which subscribed to Pan-Africanism
as an ideology was also confirmed by its two national anthems, the first of which was
Silusapho lwase Africa, meaning, 'We are the children of Africa'. It was composed by
Reuben Caluza and became the SANNC's first anthem in 1913. It was later replaced
by *Nkosi Sikelela iAfrica* (God Bless the African continent), an anthem composed by
Samuel Mqhayi in 1927.

These anthems are not narrowly about the Union because if this were the case they
would respectively be titled *Silusapho lwase Union of South Africa* and *Nkosi Sikelela
iUnion of South Africa*. To confirm their non-racial character, they did not specifically
confine themselves to the plight of indigenous African people, hence Nkosi Sikelela
did not say *Nkosi Sikelela Abantu Abamnyama base Africa* but *Sikelela iAfrica*, meaning
the continent as a whole and the people who live in it. In a calculative move which
highlighted the political consciousness of the ANC's leadership, the organisation
changed its name from the South African Native National Congress (SANNC) to the
African National Congress (ANC) in 1923. The leadership took such a path-breathing
step in order to confirm the Pan-Africanist credentials of the organisation.

Abantu-Batho, a newspaper founded in 1912 by Pixley Isaka ka Seme, played
a prominent role in popularising the meaning of both the Afro-centric slogans and
national anthems. The ANC-supporting readers of this newspaper were inspired and
as a result submitted poems and opinion letters that focused on the meaning of Pan-

Africanism in its broadest sense. For example, the following poem titled 'We dare say' was published by the newspaper in a February 1920 edition:

> Africa is the Mother of Countless Nations
> Africa is the centre of the world
> Africa is the Richest Continent
> Africans are the most law abiding people of the world
> Africa is calling in this hour of need
> She calls her sons and daughters in all (corners of) the world to
> Save her and her children from domination
> And oppression by outsiders[9]

The early twentieth-century writings of both Richard Msimang and Pixley ka Isaka Seme were characterised by the view that a united and strong ANC was necessary for the success of the African continent. In his introductory notes to the ANC's 1919 constitution, Msimang emphasised that:

> The (ANC) constitution is now ready for operation pending final adoption by the National Congress. The only criticism that has been made against this constitution is that it is lengthy. But it is impossible to provide a couple of sheets of regulations by which to control the affairs of a big National Organisation (such as the ANC) whose scope and activities will cover a great portion of the African Continent… I crave indulgence to place on record the invaluable assistance rendered to me by Mr E. Tshongwane of the Transkei and Mr B. Nxumalo of Swaziland… (for providing help in terms of compiling this constitution).[10]

The 1919 constitution also referred to one 'Pan-African' association which included territories and protectorates. By promoting Pan-Africanism and African solidarity throughout the continent, the ANC was operating outside the limits posed by narrow nationalism. This point becomes clearer when we peruse Chapter 6, Sections 82 to 85 of the 1919 constitution:

- Ordinary membership will be opened to all men belonging to the aboriginal race of Africa and who have attained the age of 18 years.
- Auxiliary membership will be opened to all women of the aboriginal races of Africa over the age of 18 years who shall be members of Bantu Women's National League of South Africa [later to be known as the ANC's Women's League].[11]

Note that the constitution reads 'men and women of the aboriginal race of Africa', not 'men and women of the aboriginal race of the Union of South Africa'. Why was the ANC's membership predicated on Pan-Africanism and wilfully opened to indigenous

Africans from the whole continent? Why was it that its national executive included monarchies from other parts in Southern Africa, including Bechuanaland, Lesotho, Swaziland and the Barotse, a Sesotho-speaking group that had migrated and settled in the present-day Zambia?

The discovery of diamond and gold in South Africa during the late nineteenth century consolidated the early nineteenth-century human movements from the south to the north led by, among others, Zwangendaba ka Mthethwa (ended up in Malawi), Mzilikazi ka Khumalo (went to Zimbabwe), Soshangane ka Nxumalo (ended up controlling the area referred to as Gaza province in Mozambique) as well as Nqaba kaMbekana Vundla (who went as far as the areas around the borders of Zambia and Tanzania). To this day, these communities constitute significant parts of these countries.

They developed migration routes which later guided African migrant labourers to move in the opposite direction, from the north to the south. The Witwatersrand Native Labour Association, a South African recruiting agency for mining companies, offered contracts to workers from Tanganyika (Tanzania), Nyasaland (Malawi), and Southern and Northern Rhodesia (Zimbabwe and Zambia). We can argue that the early nineteenth century human movements in southern Africa, which were a result of trade and competition for scarce resources with colonial powers such as the British, the Dutch and the Portuguese, marked the initial idea about the possible formation of the Southern African Development Community (SADC).

Some of the migrant labourers travelled to South Africa on foot and joined the ANC as soon as they settled in the Union of South Africa, as its constitution was open to 'men and women of the aboriginal race of Africa'. They were also founder members of various trade union movements, and the industrious Clemens Kadalie, the founder and leader of the Industrial Commercial Union (ICU), was from Nyasaland (Malawi).

In 1923, disgusted by the repressive policies of Jan Smuts in South West Africa and the Bulhoek Massacre in the Eastern Cape, the ANC national conference opened a debate in favour of the establishment of a Republic of South Africa, but this heated debate divided the ANC membership, with Mweli Skota enmeshed in it. Confusing to some members was that the movement simultaneously advised its Cape-based members, who had the privilege to vote, to cast their vote for the whites-only pact government.

During the late 1920s, ANC President Josiah Gumede advocated a people's 'native republic', influenced by the Communist International based in the Soviet Union, which Gumede had visited in 1927. On his return he issued a hyperbolic statement that he had seen a 'New Jerusalem', to the consternation of the ANC leadership.

Notwithstanding the apparent unresolved challenges posed by the problems of race and class, in 1923 the ANC became the first organisation in South Africa to propose the enactment of a Bill of Rights, predicated on the question of land dispossession. Ironically, white liberals now claim easy victories related to the democratic dispensation in South Africa, with a Bill of Rights legally instituted in the 1996 Constitution, failing to acknowledge that the move to establish a republic with a bill of rights had been spearheaded under the presidency of Sefako Makgatho, connected to the national question in South Africa. Written in the language of the time, the proposed 1923 Bill of Rights read as follows:

> (1) That the Bantu inhabitants of the Union have, as human beings, the indisputable right to a place of abode in this land of their fathers.
> (2) That all Africans have, as the sons of the soil, the God-given right to unrestricted ownership of land**....** their land**.**
> (3) That the Bantu, as well as their brethren, have, as British subjects, the inalienable right to the enjoyment of those British principles of the 'liberty of the subject, justice and equality of all classes in the eye of the law' that have made Great Britain one of the greatest world Powers.[12]

Makgatho's presidency of the ANC also internationalised the national question in South Africa, as became apparent after the First World War. When American president Woodrow Wilson published his 14 points (see Annexure A) and made a call for self-determination for small nations, hopes for Africans in South Africa were raised. Paradoxically, white Afrikaners were also inspired by President Wilson's 14 points, particularly when the British government endorsed Wilson's call, but for different reasons.

In 1919 they sent a delegation to Switzerland to demand a restitution of the republican status of the Transvaal and Orange Free State, as it had been before the formation of the Union of South Africa. Lloyd George, the British Prime Minister, who received their petition, refused, pointing out to the Afrikaner delegation the advantages of the dominion status which the Union of South Africa enjoyed, and which gave white South Africans as citizens full control of their destiny, while allowing their representatives to take part in international affairs on a basis of complete equality with Britain and other nations.

Africans also understood the political possibilities underlining the meaning of Wilson's 14 points. They now asked for a hearing about their nationhood, the removal of the colour bar and an end to racial discrimination in the Union of South Africa. African students such as Z.K. Matthews recalled such gross injustice and wrote:

> When President Wilson published his 14 Points, the phrase, 'self-determination for small nations' caught the ears of Africans. Did the 'nations' to which he referred

include us? Did they mean us, the black peoples of Africa, too? At Fort Hare we talked of little else. The consensus was that the makers of the world did not count us as a nation or as part of any nation... We lived in South Africa, but we were not regarded as part of the South African nation. Indeed when white leaders spoke of the 'nation' of South Africa, they meant only the white nation. When they gave population figures of the nation, they only gave the number of Europeans.[13]

It is important to note that heated discussions about the African diaspora, solidarity, race and racism were the order of the day within the ANC structures. In solidarity with African Americans these discussions certainly focused their attention on Garveyism and the 'Return to Africa' movement, including Ethiopianism. Most of these vigorous and engaging debates also took place at the African Club, located at No 34 Anderson Street in Johannesburg and founded in 1915 as a 'lively centre for political and social meeting'. It was apparently under the control of the ANC and the inspiration was probably Seme, who had enjoyed club life while a student at Oxford.

The debates about race, racism and solidarity across the colour line also featured prominently in the pages of *Abantu-Batho* and an example is offered by an article published in June 1923. It was a story about white settlers in Kenya opposed to the enfranchisement of Indian settlers. The argument was that this would endanger the supremacy of the white race, which included white settlers from the Union of South Africa. The following salient points, elaborated in the newspaper article, were similar to those enunciated by ANC leaders and supporters:

The struggle in Kenya is the struggle of two ideals – white domination of the world or equality of the race of mankind. The problem of Kenya is the problem of the colour line. It is not the question of European versus Indian but of white versus black. This is our view of the whole affair. The Indian settlers are asserting a right which broadly speaking is the right of all coloured races within a British Commonwealth of Nations... We are fully convinced that the cause of Indian settlers is the cause for humanity...we are more than pleased to learn that chiefs in Kenya have disassociated themselves with some white men who wanted to exploit the interests of the African in order to attain their own ends. The time of bluffing Africans is gone.[14]

International solidarity as pursued by the ANC was about pursuing a cause for humanity, liberty and equality and a quest for freedom from colonial rule. Extensive visits to several European countries in 1927 and 1928 by Josiah Gumede, the fourth president of the ANC, highlighted the importance of international solidarity and networks fostered by the ANC in other regions of the world. He attended two conferences held in Brussels by the League Against Imperialism and Colonial Oppression. The first, in February 1927, was notable for its inclusion of the 'Negro Question' as part of its deliberations,[15] corresponding to the 'Native Question' in South Africa which had been part of the political agenda since white settlers set up base here. The 'Native Question' was a subtext which informed the South Africa Act and the formation of the Union of South Africa. During the fifth session of this conference Gumede was requested to report on the economic and political situation of the oppressed in South Africa. He emphasised the following points in his presentation:

> I have to relate to you a very sad story of what is happening to the proletariat of South Africa, white and black. I will [use] the trade unions of Europeans in South Africa (as an example). They do not work together with us. Race prejudice in Africa is even more violent than in America. There is a fear in South Africa … if the Africans increase (in numbers and if population control measures are not instituted).[16]

In October 1927, Gumede accepted an invitation from the 'Society for the promotion of cultural relations between Russia and foreign countries' to attend its World Congress to be held in Moscow from 10 to 12 November 1927. This congress of the 'Friends of the Soviet Union' formed an integral part of the 10th anniversary of the Bolshevik revolution. Gumede was part of the celebrations together with 917 official delegates from more than 40 countries who attended the three-day sessions. At the beginning of December 1927, Gumede left Moscow en route to Brussels to attend the second Congress of the League Against Imperialism.[17] In 1930 he lost the battle for the ANC's presidency and was replaced by Seme.

A decade later, A.B. Xuma, as the sixth President of the ANC during the 1940s, willingly took the baton from the founders of the ANC and uncompromisingly supported the anti-colonial struggle by using internationalism as a core strategy. This becomes obvious when one critically reviews the document about 'Africans' Claims in South Africa' formulated by the ANC in 1943. This is a remarkable document on international solidarity and human rights, drafted by the ANC in order to respond to the relatively abstract principles defining the Atlantic Charter formulated by Western superpowers during the Second World War and signed under the leadership of Franklin Roosevelt and Winston Churchill. Meant to define a post-war world that would be characterised by lasting peace, equality, justice and respect for human and social rights throughout the world,[18] it was officially adopted by the annual ANC conference on 16 December 1945.

In reviewing the eight principles of the Atlantic Charter (see Annexure B), president Xuma and the drafters were able to identify basic conditions relevant to an African continent that would be free from the yoke of colonialism and imperialism. They argued that the same rights that were accorded to Western nations by the Atlantic Charter should be extended to the African continent and to other oppressed peoples of the world. These included: peace, equality, freedom, justice, and basic human and social rights. As an example, Clause 3 demanded, 'the right of all peoples to choose the form of government under which they may wish to live… sovereign rights and self-government restored to those who have been forcibly deprived of them'.

However, Xuma and his colleagues noted that the imperial powers reserved this clause to 'occupied territories in Europe' and not to colonies owned by imperial powers throughout the world. Thus, this injustice, as was the case with the young Matthews and colleagues at Fort Hare after the First World War, raised a question as to whether the meaning of 'nations', 'states' and 'peoples' included colonial subjects. As a result, Xuma remarked, 'The Africans in Southern Africa should draw up their Atlantic Charter'. In terms of African solidarity, the 'African Claims' demanded the safeguard of the status, independence and right to sovereignty of Abyssinia (now Ethiopia), which was being attacked by Italy, and went on to demand, 'the former Italian colonies in Africa should be granted independence and their security provided under the future system of World Security'. [19] Also, the document, taking a cue from the decision of the ANC conference held in 1923, adopted a full and detailed Bill of Rights which led to common understanding for humanity and the human condition.

In 1946, three years after penning the African Claims document, Xuma took the South West Africa (Namibia) issue to the newly founded United Nations. He became the public face for the political independence of Namibia. Opposing the Union of South Africa's bid to incorporate South West Africa as a fifth province of the Union, the ANC's president forwarded a telegram in January 1946 to the chairperson of the UN General Assembly. Such a spirited display of protest moved Moses Kotane, a member of the national executive of the Communist Party of South Africa (CPSA), so much that he congratulated Xuma regarding his position on the anti-colonial struggle in South West Africa/Namibia. On 30 January 1946, Kotane wrote a note to Xuma in which he asserted:

> My quarrel with you and Congress has been over the fact that you and Congress leadership generally let things go by default, that you do not speak up when you should and when it is necessary that you should. However, well done this time, sir. The Government will gnash its teeth but the Africans will appreciate you deeply.[20]

Xuma's readiness to form alliances across racial lines was a sign of confidence and self-assurance, which became apparent when he was part of a delegation that went to the UN in 1946 and where he personally presented a memorandum to the UN authorities. Perusing the content of this memorandum, Xuma, as the president of the ANC, highlighted the point that the white minority government did not have the right to speak on behalf of African people both in the Union of South Africa and in South West Africa. Xuma also submitted to the UN a sizeable number of written testimonies collected by the ANC from the oppressed people of Namibia. An example is provided by an archival document compiled on 24 August 1946 and addressed to Dr Xuma. It reflects the following viewpoints:

Dr. A. B. Xuma,   Keetmanshoop ... S.W.A
Johannesburg
24th Aug., 1946

Dear Dr. Xuma,

Permit us to be among the first to congratulate, and to thank you for the militant part you are playing in connection with the incorporation of South West Africa as a fifth province of the Union of South Africa.

We the Non-European inhabitants of South West Africa, oppose the incorporation for the following reasons:

We are voteless.

Our movements are restricted (Pass Laws).

We are barred from privileges.

Our schools are not worth to be called as such.

Native Hospitals and Reserves are worst than prisons.

Life in this Territory is not worth living as long as one is not white.

We have no right to buy land.

Reserves are too small.

We may bring it to your notice that Africans in urban areas were not consulted, and that only those in the Reserves were asked to air their views. We are also glad to inform you that 'Bushmen' in Kalahari are also against the incorporation. Besides the above the country belongs to us, and we want it to be placed under the Trusteeship of the U.N. Organisation. The above points are some of our reasons, although not all, and we hope that same will serve the purpose.[21]

The period after World War II

To keep the Pan-Africanist flag flying, in October 1945, shortly after the end of the Second World War, and also in 1947, ANC delegates attended the fifth and sixth Pan African Congresses, in Manchester and in Dakar respectively. This was not surprising, because Xuma had established a warm, firm and lasting friendship with Kwame Nkrumah whom he met during his days in America as a university student. There exists a story that Xuma may have gone secretly, without it appearing on his passport, to West Africa during the late 1940s or early 1950s. In February 1951 he wrote a letter addressed to Nkrumah, who had recently been released from jail and was now the leader of the Gold Coast (later renamed as Ghana) wherein he sincerely expressed the following views on freedom and African solidarity:

> I hope you received my cablegram of congratulation on your release from political imprisonment and your sweeping victory at the election. In our political prison here in South Africa we feel elated when our brothers in Africa advance politically. It makes us rejoice as we believe that the freedom of any African state from political serfdom implies eventual freedom of others if the gains made are held and consolidated. Gains are made and lost unless jealously guarded.[22]

More than a year later, on 26 July 1952, Xuma, replying to Nkrumah's previous letter which 'he appreciated very much' and was 'sorry for not (having) replied to it earlier', briefly offered his opinion on Nkrumah's proposal to convene a Pan-African Conference. Xuma explained to his friend that in his previous correspondence he had not meant that he, Nkrumah, must delay his 'idea of a Pan-African Conference' but felt that 'you (Nkrumah) must consolidate African control of affairs in the Gold Coast, a Herculean task itself, before you saddle yourself with a Pan-African Conference which will be no less arduous'.[23] Nkrumah was elected as the first president of an independent Ghana in 1957 and convened Pan-African Conferences thereafter.

The first was the Conference of Independent African States (CIAS), held in Accra, attended by the then eight independent African countries on the continent in April 1958 and organised by the Bureau of African Affairs (BAA), headed by George Padmore.[24] The Union of South Africa was excluded from this conference. However, there were meetings held at the UN prior to the conference and these were between Ghana's Minister of Foreign Affairs, Ako Adjei and his South African counterpart, Eric Louw.

In 1959, Oliver Tambo visited Ghana and met Tennyson Makiwane, an ANC representative who was already in Accra and had assisted with the organisation of conferences. During his brief stay in Ghana, he was warmly received by Kwame Nkrumah, who conveyed his concern about the split in the liberation movement and said that he believed 'there was no room for opposition among patriots'.[25] Tambo was strongly encouraged by Nkrumah to initiate discussion with the Pan African Congress (PAC) representatives in exile and to work towards forming a united front. Subsequently, alliance politics were consolidated in 1960 as liberation movements from

South Africa and South West Africa, together with the South African Indian Congress, formed the United Front (UF). This umbrella organisation was established in exile in the aftermath of the Sharpeville and Langa massacres. It had become crucial that the exiled liberation movements speak with one voice.

The UF was formally launched in London in May 1960. Tambo and Dadoo represented the ANC and the SAIC respectively, while Nana Mahomo and Peter Molotsi represented the PAC. Jarientundu Kozonguizi represented the South West African National Union (SWANU). The South West African People's Organisation (SWAPO) was admitted later. A popular view claims that the UF came into being because of intense pressure exerted on both the PAC and ANC by the African states, but this is not necessarily true because most African states were both anti-Indian and anti-communist and would not have insisted on the participation of Dadoo in the UF. However, some countries from the Pan-African Freedom Movement of East, Central and Southern Africa PAFMECSA region commended the idea of such a structure.[26]

The UF had been formed, firstly, to provide a voluntary structure within which the potentially destructive political rivalry between the ANC and PAC could be healed. The existing rivalry undermined the effective functioning of both organisations in the international arena. Secondly, since both organisations together with SWANU and SWAPO lacked adequate financial and human resources in exile, the UF would allow them to combine and raise funds jointly. Thirdly, the UF intended to isolate South Africa politically, economically and culturally from the international community.

The UF soon established offices in Accra, Cairo, London and New York to disseminate information about conditions in South Africa and to mobilise international public opinion against the apartheid regime. Members strove to secure UN support for economic sanctions against South Africa, and exerted pressure on the UN to wrest control of South West Africa from the white minority regime. About the international nature of the national liberation struggle in South Africa, including the importance of the international solidarity movement in the African continent and other parts of the world, OR Tambo was to note:

> When the people decide to fight for their rights as blacks, as most deprived, people are reacting to a situation created for them. But they are not going to stay in that situation all the time, because they are fighting for human rights basically. They are not fighting white people as white people. They are fighting a white system, but not because it is white, although it is presented in that form. But basically the struggle is for justice, for human rights.[27]

Another important figure to play a salient role in addressing the national question in South Africa was iNkosi Albert Luthuli. This becomes apparent because members and leaders of the ANC in particular and the Congress Alliance[28] in general chose to entrust Luthuli with the responsibility of guiding the liberation movement through a crucial transition from politics of deputations and petitions to mass-based politics, as exemplified by the defiance campaign and subsequent militant campaigns of the 1950s, including the formation of *Umkhonto we Sizwe*. Though Luthuli was a devoted Christian whose vision was influenced by the concept of non-violence, he supported the armed, military struggle in order to attain freedom in the African continent.

Due to the inhuman atrocities committed by the German National Socialists (Nazis) during the war, the World Council of Churches was to pay specific attention to problems besetting apartheid South Africa and supported the national struggle for the liberation of the oppressed majority in South Africa. That Luthuli was comfortable with the turn to the armed struggle by the ANC in order to address the national question in South Africa is reflected in his Noble Peace Prize speech, delivered on 11 December 1961 in Stockholm:

> Our goal is a united Africa... pursued by millions of our people with revolutionary zeal by means of books, representations, demonstrations, and in some places armed force provoked by the adamancy of white rule carries the only real promise for peace in Africa... Even here (in South Africa) where white rule seems determined not to change its mind for better, the spirit of Africa's militant struggle for liberty, equality and independence asserts itself...[29]

The tendency amongst authors has been to pay too much attention to Luthuli's life after his election to the national presidency of the ANC from 1952 through to 1967, to the point of almost neglecting his life before he took over the reins in the South African liberation movement. Today our country leads the African renewal programme, better known as the 'African Renaissance', but what is almost forgotten is that we are fulfilling the mission that was pioneered by, amongst others, Chief Albert Luthuli, and Pixley ka Seme, who had called for African renewal at his famous speech at the University of Columbia in the late nineteenth century.

For his part in waging the cultural struggle against colonialism, Luthuli played a leading role in the founding of the Zulu Language and Cultural Society that was founded in 1935 as an auxiliary of the Natal African Teachers' Association. Luthuli singlehandedly led the initiative for the founding of this Zulu Society while president of the Association between 1933 and 1935.[30] The aim of the society was to preserve and promote the culture and customs of the Zulu nation, and aimed to collect for publication manuscripts and information on folklore, tradition and history.[31]

Again, Luthuli's colleagues elected him the first president of the Zulu Society at its first inaugural meeting on 24 January 1935. Other members of the executive committee were M.D. Mkhize, the first vice-president; Charles Mpanza, secretary and Dr A.W. Dlamini, assistant secretary; Dr John L. Dube, its advisor; and Fike kaSiteku, S.D.B. Ngcobo and Sibusisiwe Makhanya as its additional members. Luthuli stepped down from the presidency when elected a chief of the *amakholwa* in 1936.

Though Luthuli was conscious of the scourge of poverty, disease and under-development in the African continent, like Seme, the founder and fourth president of the ANC, Luthuli's beliefs in the African Renaissance knew no bounds. He remained an optimist committed to the successful future of the African continent, which he expected to play an important mediating role for peace during the age of the Cold War. This was highlighted in his Nobel Peace Prize speech:

> In bringing my address to the close, let me invite Africa to cast her eyes beyond the past and to some extent the present with their woes and tribulations, trials, and failures, and some successes, and see herself an emerging continent, bursting to freedom through the shell of centuries of serfdom. This is Africa's age – the dawn of her fulfilment, yes, the moment she grapples with destiny to reach the summit of sublimity saying: 'Ours was an (anti-colonial) fight for noble values and worthy ends, and not for lands and enslavement of man… In a strife-torn world tottering on the brink of complete destruction by man-made nuclear weapons, a free and independent Africa is in the making….[32]

Conclusion

The dynamic human movements and migrations of the nineteenth century, the (inclusive) first constitution of the ANC and the organisation's policy document on African Claims provided the Pan Africanist ideals which inspired the formation of the Organisation of African Unity in 1963. Later, the human migrations triggered attention to the socio-economic and development needs of southern Africa as a region. The fact that the ANC used these routes when its cadres went into exile during the early 1960s highlights the depth of political linkages within the region. Hence, it was not surprising that the Southern African Development Coordination Conference (SADCC) was officially launched on 1 April 1980 in Lusaka. It was subsequently restructured to become the Southern African Development Community (SADC). Remarkably, four months after the 1994 democratic elections in South Africa, the country became a member of the SADC. This was just a matter of formality as the roots of South Africa's membership were planted during the nineteenth century by the likes of Zwangendaba, Mzilikazi and also the Barotse of Zambia.

What is also of importance to us is that the Pan-Africanist views and policy statements propagated by the founders of the ANC during the early twentieth century and those expressed in the African Claims policy document in 1943 defined the ANC's first ever foreign policy formulated in 1993. It was soon adopted as the country's foreign policy when the ANC officially took political power in 1994. The clauses on the African continent elaborate the following:

- The right of all the peoples of Africa to independence and self-government shall be recognised, and shall be the basis of close cooperation.
- A democratic South Africa will actively promote the objectives of democracy, peace, stability, development, and mutually beneficial relations among the people of Africa as a whole, as well as a Pan-African solidarity. Grateful for the international solidarity which supported the anti-apartheid cause, a democratic South Africa will be in solidarity with all those whose struggles continue. South Africa's foreign relations will reflect our domestic character – a constitutional state bound by the rule of law.
- A belief that our foreign policy should reflect the interests of the continent of Africa.
- A belief that South Africa's economic development depends on growing regional and international economic cooperation in an interdependent world.
- A democratic South Africa's future is inextricably intertwined with that of Africa. As the new and latest member of the Organisation of African Unity, South Africa will have the opportunity to contribute towards the issues which affect the African continent.
- Therefore, our links with this continent are of particular importance but we recognise that this alone will not help arrest the declining international interest in the continent. Accordingly, we dedicate our foreign policy to helping to ensure that Africa's people are not forgotten or ignored by humankind.
- In charting this future, we will strive to contribute towards improving the basic human condition of all Africa's people. Only this will ensure that the continent's people are able to participate in the democratic processes of their respective countries. Democracy will assist necessary economic growth.[33]

On a different note, Luthuli's views are still relevant in the present century, with the economic decline of the Western superpowers and the rise of China. Africa, richly endowed with mineral resources, is caught up in a new cold war of the twenty-first century which is mainly defined by currency wars. A free and independent African continent can play a role in brokering and mediating peace between the warring factions, hence a free and independent South Africa, as a member of the BRICS countries, has a role to play in this evolving international conflict.

These currency wars and clamours for Africa's resources are leading to what Luthuli described as 'unthinkable war, destruction and desolation' of the African continent which further promotes woes, trials and tribulations, trials, failures, hunger and illiteracy. The ANC's anti-colonial struggle of the twentieth century was against this unbearable situation and it utilised international solidarity as a major weapon of this struggle. This struggle should continue and the ANC should still pursue the African agenda during the twenty-first century, as was elucidated by the delegates who attended the international solidarity conference organised by the movement during October 2012.

Endnotes

1   Odendaal, A., 2012. *The founders: The origins of the ANC and the struggle for democracy in South Africa*. Johannesburg: Jacana, p.142, 211 and 280; and Meli, F., 1988. *South Africa belongs to us: A history of the ANC*. Harare: Zimbabwe Publishing House, p.22.

2   Odendaal, 2012, op. cit., chapter 37; and Meli, 1988, op. cit., pp.26-27.

3   He was in London for 'fund raising purposes' and played a behind-the-scenes role.

4   Meli, 988, op. cit., pp.26-27; Odendaal, 2012, op. cit., chapter 46.

5   Seme, P., 1911. Native union. *Imvo Zabantsundu*, 24 October. In Karis, T. & Carter G.M. (eds), 1972. *From protest to challenge: A documentary history of African politics in South Africa, 1882–1964, Volume 1: Protest and hope, 1882–1934*. Stanford: Stanford University, Hoover Press, p.71.

6   Meli, 1988, op. cit., p.54.

7   Machobane, L.B.B.J., 1990. *Government and change in Lesotho, 1800–1966: A study of political institutions*. London: Macmillan, p.114.

8   This section on Lesotho as a case study is based on Mothibe, T. & Mushonga, M., n.d. Lesotho and the struggle for liberation. In South African Democracy Education Trust, n.d. *Road to democracy in South Africa, Volume 5, Part 1, African solidarity*. Pretoria: Unisa Press; Public Record Office, London (hereafter PRO); Colonial Office (hereafter CO) 879/97; African (South), No. 897; Confidential, South Africa, Further Correspondence (1908) relating to affairs in South Africa: Paramount Chief Letsie L. Moshesh – Resident Commissioner, Basutoland, 12 May 1908 (Enclosure 1 in No. 100), 187.

9   See Limb, P. (ed.), 2012. *The people's paper: A centenary history and anthology of Abantu Batho*. Johannesburg: Wits University Press.

10 Peter Limb forwarded to me the original copy of the 1918/19 constitution and Msimang's note. See also Karis & Carter, 1972, op. cit.

11 Thanks to Peter Limb for the copy of this invaluable document. Some extracts of the 1919 constitution are published in Karis & Carter, 1972, op. cit., pp.76-82.

12 The 1923 resolutions of the ANC's national conference are published in Karis & Carter,

1972, op. cit., p.297. See also Jordan, P., 2002. Liberalism didn't bring liberation. *The Star,* 13 June.

13 Matthews, Z.K., 1983. *Freedom for my people: The autobiography of ZK Matthews, 1901–1968.* Cape Town: David Phillip, p.62.

14 1923. White Africa. *Abantu-Batho,* 14 June. In Limb, 2012, op. cit., p.457.

15 Van Diemel, R., 2013. *In search of freedom, liberty, justice and fair play: Josiah Tshangana Gumede, 1867–1946.* Glenvista: House of Memory, p.130.

16 1927. *Iprecorr,* 25 February. In Van Diemel, 2013, op. cit., p.128.

17 Ibid, pp.142-146.

18 Section on African Claims relies on Asmal, K., Chidester, D. & Lubisi, C., 2005. *Legacy of freedom: The ANC's human rights tradition.* Jeppestown: Jonathan Ball; and Meli, 1988, op. cit., pp.94-96. The African Claims document is also published on the ANC's official website.

19 Meli, 1988, op. cit., p.95.

20 Ibid, p.263.

21 I hereby thank Peter Limb for forwarding to me some of the letters.

22 Limb, P. (ed.), n.d. *A.B. Xuma: Autobiography and selected works,* p.113.

23 Many thanks to Peter Limb who forward to me an electronic version copy of this letter.

24 These independent countries were: Ghana, Liberia, Egypt, Tunisia, Libya, Sudan, Morocco and Ethiopia. See Thompson, V.B., 1969. *Africa and unity: The evolution of Pan Africanism.* London: Longman, pp.127-135; and Legum, C., 1965. *Pan Africanism: A short political guide.* London: Pall Mall Press, pp.41-42.

25 Callinicos, L., 2004. *Oliver Tambo: Beyond the Engeli Mountains.* Cape Town: New Africa Books, p.264.

26 This section on the United Front is based on Ndlovu, S.M., 2010. The ANC in exile, 1960–1970. In the South African Democracy Education Trust (SADET), 2010. *The road to democracy in South Africa, Volume 1 (1960–1970).* Pretoria: Unisa Press.

27 Tambo, O.R., 1977. *Sechaba,* 4, fourth quarter.

28 The Congress Alliance was an alliance that was formed during the 1950s. It was made up of organisations such as the ANC, South African Indian Congress, South African Coloured People's Congress, Congress of Democrats and the South African Congress of Trade Unions. It was led by the ANC.

29 Cited in Ndlovu, S.M., 2012. On iNkosi Albert Luthuli Nobel Peace Prize speech. *Presence Africaine,* 185/186, First and Second semester, pp.121-120. Luthuli's Nobel Peace Prize speech is also posted on the ANC's website.

30 Lutuli, A., 1962. *Let my people go: The autobiography of the great South African leader.* Glasglow: Harper Collins, pp.34-35; and Pietermaritzburg Archives Repository (hereafter PAR), A 1381: *Zulu Society Papers,* Vol. 1/1 and 1/2, 24 January 1935. Wesley says the Zulu Society was formed on 24 January 1936. See Wesley, M.A., 1994. The

Zulu society: The last bastion of elite politics in Natal. Unpublished Honours essay, University of Witwatersrand, p.1. This is not possible because the Zulu Society held its second annual conference on 29 January 1936. PAR, A1381, Vol. 1/3/1, 29 January 1936. See also notes on Luthuli compiled by Jabulani Sithole and Bernard Magubane in my possession.

31 See Lambert, J., 1936. Two-page typescript, introduction into the inventory. *Zulu Society Papers* at PAR, A1381, and Ibid. Vol. 1/3/1 Minutes of the Second Annual Conference of the Zulu Society, 19 January. Also see 1950. 'Busy-Bee': Letter to Chief A.J. Luthuli. *Ilanga lase Natal*, 1 April; and Couzens, T., 1985. *The new African: A study of the life and work of H.I.E. Dhlomo*. Johannesburg: Ravan, p.293. See also notes on Luthuli compiled by Jabulani Sithole and Bernard Magubane in my possession.

32 Cited in Ndlovu, 2012, op. cit., p.129.

33 African National Congress, 1993. Foreign Policy in a new democratic South Africa: A discussion paper.

PART 2

Pillars of the Struggle

CHAPTER 4

The evolution of internal mass mobilisation as an instrument against colonialism: from pre-1912 to 1994

Mathethe Jeffrey Sehume and Dan Motaung

History is philosophy teaching by examples. – Thucydides[1]

Lex iniusta non est lex *(An unjust law is no law at all).* – Saint Augustine of Hippo

Introduction

South Africa has entered its third decade of constitutional democracy with much having been achieved in engendering a society in which collective human rights precede state authority and racial dominance. While significant structural problems remain, the country has registered notable progress in the improvement of people's civil liberties and elemental material conditions. In the popular parlance, the transition from apartheid hegemony to democracy is regarded as a 'miracle' since it disproved the predicted racial war that was anticipated, notwithstanding the party political conflict in Gauteng and KwaZulu-Natal, where over twenty thousand people lost their lives. It is a phenomenon in the sense that the presence of the 'fathers of the nation', Nelson Mandela and Desmond Tutu, during this transition was seen as a 'godsend'.

However, human agency and the congealment of internal and external factors were responsible for bringing about the 'negotiated revolution' which led to the organisation of the first non-racial elections in 27 April 1994. Mass mobilisation was largely responsible for the relatively peaceful collective decision-making process which produced the 1996 Constitution, the Bill of Rights and the 1997 National Plan of Action for Human Rights. As Mary Robinson reminded us in her 2012 Nelson Mandela Annual Lecture, 'Democracy is irreconcilable with racial inequality and social injustice. Democracy is strengthened and entrenched when society is fully aware of its fundamental human rights and freedoms and lays claim to these'.

From the outset, the period when the process was initiated towards facilitating a democratic dispensation is not coincidental. The Rubicon-crossing speech of former President F.W. De Klerk in February 1990 was arguably not the result of a lone brave politician. Nor can the eventual liberation of the country be said to be an outcome of one protagonist against another. The 1980s are a historical period of epochal proportions, remarkable for coalescing social movements around the world bent on overturning authoritarian regimes. It was a decade during which a revolutionary wave swept across the world, propelled by inspired idealism for a better human condition. For instance, one recalls the dock protests in Poland which established Lech Walesa's trade union federation Solidarność (Solidarity).

The subsequent 'velvet revolutions' would not be similar in content or ultimate results to the open violent revolutions of France in 1789, Russia in 1917 or China in 1949. The latter group of revolutions were, as George Lawson says, 'volcanic ruptures' accompanied by 'sharp breaks with the past from which societies could not turn back.'[2] Rather, it is a period in human history when the epochal ideological war of communism and capitalism came to its zenith, inopportunely spurred on by triumphalist declarations like those of Francis Fukuyama ('end of history') and Samuel Huntington ('clash of civilisations').

This chapter examines the evolution of the internal mass mobilisation in South Africa and the two historical periods which impacted on its direction. It will proceed by defining mass mobilisation and how its configuration in South Africa centred on the four pillars of the liberation struggle, namely mass mobilisation, the armed struggle, international solidarity and underground activities. Secondly, it will interrogate the products of the mass mobilisation in democratic South Africa, especially against the background of the 2011 'Arab Spring' and 'Occupy Movement', due in part to the 2008 global economic downturn.

Setting of mass mobilisation

In South Africa, as in the United States of America, race colours the policies of racial discrimination and the equivalent struggle for freedom. As the former international statesman General Jan Smuts would posit in the 1929 Rhodes Memorial Lectures delivered at Oxford University, the black social group 'has largely remained a child type with a child psychology and outlook'.[3] Such an outlook has a foundation in the writings of Enlightenment thinkers such as David Hume, Immanuel Kant and Friedrich Hegel. In the South African milieu, it would find practical expression in the colonial enterprise unleashed by the arrival of the Dutch sailor Jan van Riebeeck in 1652. Even more, it would find overwhelming manifestation in the early twentieth century with the 1910 formation of the Union of South Africa.[4] It was precisely the racial policies of socio-political segregation and economic marginalisation of the majority of the population which would, in return, lead to the establishment of the South African Native National Congress (SANNC) in 1912.

From the outset, the SANNC saw itself as 'a parliament of the people' and a movement with a historical role of uniting all Africans under the rubric of African Nationalism. As 'parliament of the people', the SANNC was formed to provide organised articulation for the needs of the large population disenfranchised from political decision-making processes. As Sol Plaatje would state in his landmark opus, *Native Life in South Africa*, directed at the 1913 Natives' Land Act – the pivotal legislation carving up territory according to racial profile – 'Awakening on Friday morning, June 20, 1913, the South African native found himself, not actually a slave, but a pariah in the land of his birth.'[5]

The SANNC would inject organisational strategy premised on uniting resistance fronts under one banner, consolidating leadership founded on the will and direction of people from diverse quarters. (Parenthetically, at this point in history non-racialism within its ranks would not be a reality until the formation of the Communist Party of South Africa more than a decade later.)

At the same time, the struggle for social justice predates by centuries the formation of the SANNC. From 1488, when the Portuguese explorers encountered the herding Khoisan people, to the battles of resistance waged by the Khoisan and the frontier wars of the nineteenth century, indigenous peoples have systematically engaged in struggles for freedom. The famed Bhambatha Rebellion in 1906 was the last vestige of resistance to colonial conquest. When this rebellion was finally broken, an old chapter was closed to open a new leg of organised resistance in the twentieth century. Debatably, unique to the twentieth-century forms of the South African national liberation struggle was not only its duration but also its evolving and changing contour and the size of organisations involved, culminating in civil society bodies, notably local community 'civics', that mobilised what the late Jakes Gerwel once called 'enormous social energy', harnessed in 'the cause of a democratic society'.[6] The seminal question is what is meant by mass mobilisation. How really different is it from passive resistance, non-violent protests, civil resistance and violent revolutions?

Mass mobilisation defined

South Africa gained its democratic dispensation long after the wave of postcolonial movements of the 1950s and 60s. It therefore managed to benefit from the lessons learnt elsewhere about functional strategies for manageable independence. In the twentieth century, mass mobilisation has resonance in the activist philosophies of Mahatma Gandhi, Martin Luther King, Aung San Suu Kyi, Desmond Tutu and Nelson Mandela. These philosophies are sometimes defined as a 'third way', meaning neither passive acceptance of oppression nor violent opposition to it, but an active commitment to nonviolent means (e.g., direct action, civil disobedience, boycotts, strikes, protests and education) to resist evil and to seek justice for those who are oppressed.[7]

What is more, mass mobilisation differs from open warfare in that the central aim and end is not to overtly inflict physical violence on the opponent or oppressor. As Gandhi would argue, it is a 'doctrine of rejecting violence in favour of peaceful tactics as a means of gaining political or social objectives.'[8]

The most prolific profiler of the theory of 'nonviolent action', Gene Sharp,[9] divides its methods according to:

i)   protest and persuasion (speeches, letters of opposition, signed public statements, group or mass petitions, slogans, leaflets and banners, deputations, picketing, prayer and worship, vigils, mock and demonstrative funerals);

ii) economic boycotts (rent withholding, lockout, refusal to pay fees and debts, revenue refusal, domestic embargo, blacklisting of traders, international trade and buyers' embargo, economic shutdown); and

iii) political non-cooperation (withdrawal of allegiance, literature advocating resistance, boycott of elections, popular and disguised non-obedience, general administrative non-cooperation, severance of diplomatic recognition, refusal of membership in international bodies).

As such, mass mobilisation has assorted methods which are considered by its protagonists, depending on the pertaining objective circumstances. In the history of nonviolent resistance, either in Africa, Chile or the former Soviet Republics, one cannot isolate one method as definitive in the overthrow of authoritarian regimes.

The effectiveness of mass mobilisation is measured by the selection of a group of methods or sub-methods at given points in a country's historical trajectory. Factors responsible for this relate to the equally changing responses and initiatives by the ruling governments of the time to counter and quell mass mobilisation. At various times, the authoritarian regime may shift between using force to gain public authority and material rewards to seek legitimacy in the suppressed social groups.[10] For a time this was the policy embarked upon for the population reserves brought about by the 1913 Land Act. What is not contestable, though, is that force and violence are certainly not sustainable in the medium to long term. As Niccolò Machiavelli pronounced: the prince '...who has the public as a whole for his enemy can never make himself secure; and the greater his cruelty, the weaker does his regime become'.[11]

Historical overview

Two identifiable ethical strains behind mass mobilisation that congealed in the SANNC and later the African National Congress (ANC) came from the Free Ethiopian Church of Southern Africa and Mahatma Gandhi's *Satyagraha*. Long before the principles and values of black consciousness entered the public discourse in the 1940s – through the first president of the ANC Youth League (ANCYL), Anton Lembede, and Steve Biko in the 1960s to 70s – the seeds of self-awareness had already been promoted by the Ethiopian Church. One of its founding members, Mangena Maake Mokone, would instil a Pan-African and diasporic flavour in its teachings by calling for 'Africa for the Africans'.

As Mandela would acknowledge in his 1992 *Speech to the Free Ethiopian Church of Southern Africa*, such a political stance was important, as colonialism was viewed as 'a one-teated cow that only feeds the whites'. What was required therefore was an ethical creed that would empower the wretched of the earth with a belief that would gain them a superior moral claim.

Similarly, *Satyagraha* would lay a basis for the organisational orientation of future mass struggles whereby a synthesis of liberation and theology would impel cause-driven social action. Defined as 'truth-oriented' or 'holding on to truth', *Satyagraha* was different from *duragraha* or 'power-oriented' action.[12] As Sharp would argue in his 1973 classic, *The Politics of Nonviolent Action*, *Satyagraha* as a form of nonviolent action is 'adopted by those who seek to achieve their objects without the infliction, or threat of infliction, of physical injury on opponents.'[13]

In essence, its variant in South Africa drew upon the truism that ultimately power is ceded by people to ruling authorities and it is possible for them either to challenge its imposition or recoup it through means of mass mobilisation.[14] As an early pamphlet of the South African Communist Party (SACP) would urge, '(t)he real advantage of the liberation forces over all the planes, armoured cars and other superior equipment of the enemy is the support of the masses. This is our decisive weapon, without which we cannot win'.[15] Furthermore, the argument holds that while the state may have recourse to instruments of force and infliction of violence, civic engagement can be effective in challenging the effectiveness of violence.

Specifically, mass mobilisation made its pronounced impact on the local landscape in two historical periods. The first was the period following the formation of the ANCYL in 1944. A second period roughly emerged before and in the aftermath of the 1976 student uprisings. The cumulative bearing of these two periods crowned the mass mobilisation campaigns of the 1980s. The following questions are often asked about the underlying purpose of the relatively peaceful mass mobilisation beginning from the 1940s until the banning of the ANC in 1960: What were the intended outcomes of mass mobilisation at this stage in history? Did the ANC intend to overthrow the regime by this form of mass engagement? Alternatively, was the peaceful mobilisation aimed at seeking accommodation with the status quo ante, and if so, under what terms?

For the co-drafter of the 1955 Freedom Charter, Ben Turok, the intended outcome of mass mobilisation informs the instruments adopted for its realisation. He distinguishes between two useful concepts to throw light on the nature and goal of mass mobilisation. 'On the one hand there has been what I shall call Conventional Democracy, which is based on a belief in the need to extend the existing parliamentary structure to embrace the black people. On the other hand there is a conception of Revolutionary Democracy, which envisages a seizure of power by the oppressed and the creation of a new state structure with a wholly new popular power-base which will give expression to the democratic will of the people as a whole and particularly its black majority.'[16]

Beginning with the creation of the 1910 Union and the 1913 Land Act, the choice for the SANNC was reducible to the fight for conventional democracy, hence the reliance on Sharp's protest and persuasive methods, by for example sending delegations to the former colonial power, Great Britain, to register grievances against unjust laws of exclusion. This initial preferred method was supplemented by campaigns against pass laws and supporting the mineworkers' strikes of 1946, when more than 70 000 mineworkers downed their tools.

From conventional democracy to revolutionary democracy

This movement consisted of a select group of representatives from the provinces. As regards active engagement, to quote one of the first African communists, Thabo Mofutsanyane, from a largely conciliatory outlook, '...will be seen that from its inception, Congress thus was wedded to a timid and reformist conception of the status of the African people. Lacking any clearly formulated long-term policy, Congress limited itself to immediate partial struggles against one or other aspect of discrimination.'[17]

Early African nationalism accepted the emerging society that resulted from colonial conquest as a starting point from which to build the struggle for emancipation. However, a qualitative difference between pre- and post-1944 years, when the ANCYL was formed, does not imply that the movement thereby adopted revolutionary democracy as a leitmotif of the struggle.

Admittedly, the Youth League did inject radicalisation in rhetoric and limited militant African nationalism. Nonetheless, this does not automatically translate to a violent revolutionary position. Even then, there was no conscious decision to dismantle the state. In response to the 1948 electoral victory of the National Party (NP), the ANCYL introduced what they called the 'Programme of Action' intended to directly confront the regime through strikes, boycotts and defiance of the unjust laws. In particular, it agitated for: 'Appointment of a council of action… to implement our resolve to work for: (a) the abolition of all differential political institutions… (b) …preparations and making plans for a national stoppage of work for one day as a mark of protest against the reactionary policy of government.'[18]

Instead, what separated the ANCYL from its mother body was its advocacy approach for demographic recognition of the social structure of the country, in that it (the ANCYL) "…accepted the goal of eradicating racial discrimination as the means to untrammelled African progress, but [also] went on to declare the African political intention and urgent need as being the assertion of this numerical majority".[19]

It recalled Gandhi's *Satyagraha*, as highlighted by the 1906 revolt against the imposition of immigration restrictions on people of Indian descent in the Transvaal that also engendered permissive conditions for the subsequent germination of peaceful intents like the 1952 Defiance Campaign.

Perhaps the conceptual and organisational bedrock to this non-violent mass mobilisation was the non-racial character of the Alliance movement led by the ANC. Introduced into the ideological bloodstream of the ANC by the then Communist Party of South Africa, non-racialism became the fulcrum of cooperation between Africans represented by the ANC, Coloureds represented by the African People's Organisation (OPA), the SACP, the Natal and the Transvaal Indian Congresses, and the Congress of Democrats, comprising white democrats.

Dubbed the Congress Alliance, these formations constituted the core of the resistance movement whose wide spectrum of South African society not only lent legitimacy to the struggle but also posited the possibility of alternative ontological relations in South Africa. Still, one of the most celebrated moments in the struggle was the process leading up to the Congress of the People, meant to draw up the Freedom Charter in Kliptown, Soweto, on 26 June 1955.

The Charter provided a platform for the expression of popular yearning for a united, democratic, non-racial, non-sexist and just society envisioned in the iconic preamble that '…South Africa belongs to all who live in it, black and white, and that no government can justly claim authority unless it is based on the will of all the people'. This wider political conjuncture comprised a virulent form of Afrikaner nationalism that saw the NP ascend to power in 1948, counterweighted by a stirring yet somewhat catholic African nationalism championed by the Youth League, against the background of receding historical underpinnings of Christian idealism that had shaped the ANC founding fathers' political conception; that is, conventional democracy.

Following the successive events that influenced the body politic of the country between the formation of the Youth League and the social engineering project of the NP from 1948 onwards, right up to the epochal events of Sharpeville in 1960, South Africa entered a storm of uncertainty, unlike at any other time in history. The banning of the SACP in 1950, followed by the banning of the liberation movements, the ANC and the Pan African Congress (PAC), in 1960, compounded by the imprisonment of key leaders such as Nelson Mandela, became triggers that dictated a turning point in the political outlook of the ANC. The closing down of democratic space for expression of popular discontent with the status quo, accompanied by insufferable political oppression manifested by arrests, detentions and banning – acts that amounted to state terror – effectively opened up the possibility for alternative means of resistance, namely the war for revolutionary democracy.

The Sharpeville 1960 events decidedly marked an end to civil disobedience[20] as a means of seeking accommodation with the regime. In other words, this marked the end to passive resistance that had been the hallmark of the ANC from inception, culminating in the resurgence of militant albeit non-violent resistance spurred on by the youthful energies of the Youth League. As Turok points out, 'to the leaders of the liberation movement it was now obvious that the state had been geared to maximum repression and that white public opinion supported it fully in this role. The foundation for transfer from non-violence to armed struggle was being laid.'[21]

Accordingly, it held out the antithetical alternative of establishing the ANC's revolutionary wing, *Umkhonto we Sizwe* (MK), and the PAC's Azanian People's Liberation Army (APLA).

June 1976 represented yet another epochal point in the historical trajectory of revolutionary democracy. It was the attempt to introduce Afrikaans as a medium of school instruction which catapulted the revolutionary struggle onto a completely new trajectory following the relative silence, at least on the surface, since Sharpeville. One of the first priorities of the NP upon assuming power in 1948 was the elevation of Afrikaans as the language of government. This was partly driven by the Anglicisation foisted on South Africa since the days of Lord Milner. Now, in an ironic twist of history, the Afrikaner government was to repeat the mistake of their erstwhile enemies by seeking to impose Afrikaans on black people.

For black people Afrikaans was thus perceived as the cultural manifestation of racial domination at all levels of society. Unleashing the full savagery of the apartheid police on unarmed students who were protesting at the imposition of Afrikaans in African education occasioned both international and national opprobrium, though on the national front such moral recoil tended to be limited to liberal quarters of society.

In consequence, the status of the apartheid government as a polecat of the world was confirmed. Consequently, the United Nations (UN) Security Council passed

Resolution 392 condemning government's handling of the student protests and the apartheid regime at large. Those liberal and Afrikaner sections whose conscience was pricked nailed their colours to the mast. In the event, 300 white students from the University of the Witwatersrand marched through Johannesburg as a protest against the deaths of the schoolchildren.[22] Perversely for the government, the school uprisings strengthened the hand of the anti-apartheid movement.

The formation of the United Democracy Front (UDF) in 1983 manifested traces of the Congress Alliance, such as the Freedom Charter and its non-racial outlook. Underlying the intensifying mass action against apartheid were the increasingly insufferable socio-economic conditions bedevilling the lives of black people in general and Africans in particular. These chronic conditions themselves spurred the rise of community-based organisations partly targeting an improvement in the basic lives of people in addition to explicit political goals. As Mark Swilling argues:

> with the exception of the crucially important election boycotts of 1984, the driving force of black resistance that has effectively immobilised the coercive and reformist actions of the state has emanated from below as communities responded to their abysmal urban living conditions. The result was the development and expansion of local struggles and organisations throughout the country. The UDF played a critical role in articulating common national demands for the dismantling of the apartheid state. In so doing, the black communities have been drawn into a movement predicated on the notion that the transfer of political power to the representatives of the majority is a precondition for the realisation of basic economic demands such as decent shelter, cheap transport, proper health care, adequate education, the right to occupy land and the right to a decent and steady income.[23]

The sheer size and ambitions of the UDF do not escape notice. It was made up of more than 400 organisations and had about three million members. It represented a plethora of organisations, including students, trade unions, religious bodies as well as black and white youth formations, among others. Undoubtedly, the UDF era transformed mass mobilisation to unprecedented levels. Raymond Suttner contends that the '1980s introduced modes of practising politics that previously had never been seen in South Africa, and that continue to condition many people's expectations today'.[24] Notions of 'popular democracy', 'people's power', 'self-empowerment', 'the masses driving the process', 'democracy from below', and 'creativity of the masses' were all introduced as new ideas and practices into South African politics.

It should, however, be noted that the ANC did not form the UDF, even though individuals with ANC ties may have been part or members of its affiliates. The UDF's time as a political formation had come, in keeping with the historical moment, driven by the need for such an entity to come about. Most significantly, in 1989 the UDF and the Congress of South Africa Trade Unions (COSATU) cooperated under the banner of a Mass Democratic Movement (MDM), each bringing its immeasurable numerical strength to the partnership, which would further sound the death-knell of apartheid. In this period, mass mobilisation, conceptualised as 'ways of bringing people together whether by spontaneous acts or by organised and planned methods of mass action', came full circle.[25] The uniting mantra of the 1980s became 'Organising for People's Power', which encapsulated the four pillars of the struggle. People's power would merge directly with focused agitation for political change.

Effectiveness of mass mobilisation

It could be said that the mixture of violent and non-violent resistance was adopted as a last resort, given the equally violent and terror-inflicting response of the state. This is borne out by the community for which racial privilege was enforced by the state, the white community, shifting loyalty as young white men began to resist the annual draft to the army. In the process, the ranks of the enlightened began to swell in liberal white parties from the *herstigte* (reconstituted) conservative political parties, and the End Conscription Campaign gained political currency in its opposition to the draft. In such circumstances one could argue that the South African resistance was assuming the character of a normative revolution that was a 'swift, basic and comprehensive transformation of socioeconomic and political institutions (often accompanied by and effected through class upheavals from below, as Lenin reminded us).'[26]

In a study examining violent and non-violent revolutions of the twentieth century, from 1900 to 2006, the authors of *Why Civil Resistance Works* (hereafter, WCRW) argue in short that: '[o]ur findings show that major non-violent campaigns have achieved success 53 percent of the time, compared with 26 percent for violent resistance campaigns'. One of the main reasons for the viability of civil resistance or mass mobilisation was that these 'campaigns appear to be more open to negotiation and bargaining because they do not threaten the lives or well-being of members of the target regime'.[27] Based on the evidence of the 1989 'velvet revolution' and the 2010 'Arab Spring', there is space for arguing for the usefulness of passive resistance by non-state actors complemented by mass mobilisation.

On the other hand, for Mao Zedong a gentle revolution was inconceivable because to him a revolution was an 'uprising', 'an act of violence' that required 'exceeding proper limits.'[28] To him, 'power is never given, it is always taken'. However, such a conceptualisation does not adequately reckon with the long-term effects of the violent overthrow of unpopular governments.

Another argument from those who prize non-violent struggle is that it is advantageous because such forms of resistance are able to mobilise across various sectors of the population, such as was the case with the Congress of the People. It may have been foreseen by the ANC that the armed struggle should be a supplementary wing of their struggle for freedom and not their main leitmotif.

As stated above, one of the main reasons they argue for the viability of civil resistance or mass mobilisation is that these 'campaigns appear to be more open to negotiation and bargaining because they do not threaten the lives or well-being of members of the target regime'.[29] Moreover, it can reasonably be argued that the accumulated catalogue of largely non-violent resistance to an oppressive system in South Africa proved effective. The collective action of the broad coalition of resistance strategies did bring the system to heel and contributed to a climate in which a negotiated settlement was thought ideal by both non-state and state actors.

Gene Sharp argues that nonviolent struggle:

…produces change, when it succeeds, by four possible mechanisms. 1. *Conversion*: This occurs when members of the opponent group are emotionally or rationally convinced that the resister's cause is just. Sometimes this happens, but it is rare. 2. *Accommodation*: When the issues are not fundamental, the settlement may be produced by compromise. Striking workers may settle for half of their demanded wage increase, for example. 3. *Nonviolent coercion*: Mass non-cooperation and defiance can so change power relationships, that the opponents' ability to control the economic, social, and political processes of government and the society is taken away. The military forces may no longer obey orders to repress resisters, for example. 4. *Disintegration*: Due to the mass non-cooperation and defiance, the regime loses its ability to act and its own structures of power disintegrate.[30]

Conclusion

To some extent, in the negotiated settlement which delivered a democratic dispensation in the local environment, all four mechanisms can be said to have been at play. Social organisations like the Black Sash, white student groups like NUSAS and the End Conscription Campaign (ECC) saw the moral repugnance of apartheid. The CODESA talks produced a broadly accepted transition path towards the 1994 electoral process. Given that more than half the members of state security structures came from the ranks of the oppressed it is not difficult to take note of the political quandary in which they found themselves.

In this way, South African internal mass mobilisation cannot be likened to, for instance, the 2011 UK riots, which for someone like Slavoj Žižek fit into the 'Hegelian notion of the rabble', more like "irrational' outbursts of destructive violence – what Hegel called 'abstract negativity"; while the collective action of the South Africans had a clear political programme from which stemmed strategic actions of civil resistance. Moreover, the local resistance cannot be likened to the Occupy Wall Street operation, which did not follow a sustainable pragmatic model but rather came across as a utopian project which was making a 'subjective statement'.[31]

The mobilisation of society against political injustice, in the context of both conventional democracy and revolutionary democracy, happened at the time it did owing to contingency, if not conjuncture. While conventional democracy resulted in revolutionary democracy under the doctrine of historical necessity, the latter played a preponderantly weighty role in arousing international consciousness about the racist policies of the apartheid state.

From the historical turning point following the Sharpeville massacre to the Soweto student uprisings of June 1976 and the resurgence of popular uprising in the 80s leading up to the 90s, revolutionary mass mobilisation had become a political culture across large swathes of oppressed South Africa. While the apartheid state did not hesitate to unleash its deathly force on unarmed protesters, the all-too-real prospect of certain death did not dispirit the oppressed masses from taking on the racial behemoth of apartheid force. On the other hand the continued social instability not only ruined the economy but increased the international isolation of the country. The impending defeat of the apartheid state was preceded by the characterisation of apartheid as 'a crime against humanity' by the United Nations.

Ultimately though, the objective and dream for which the struggle was waged can be summarised in the words of the first president of democratic South Africa, Mandela, at his inauguration on 10 May 1994: 'We enter into a covenant that we shall build a society in which all South Africans, both black and white, will be able to walk tall, without any fear in their hearts, assured of their inalienable right to human dignity'.[32]

Endnotes

1   Thucydides, n.d. The History of the Peloponnesian War.
2   Lawson, G., 2005. Negotiated revolutions: The Czech Republic, South Africa and Chile. Aldershot: Ashgate.
3   Smuts, J., 1930. Africa and some world problems, including the Rhodes Memorial lectures delivered in Michaelmas Term, 1929. Oxford: Clarendon Press. Smuts is defined by his biographer, Antony Lentin, as 'a universal man such as might have stepped from the pages of Plutarch. I have touched life at so many points, he wrote – as warrior and

commander in three wars, as scholar, jurist, philosopher (he read Spinoza at the Peace Conference)' (Lentin, A., 2010. General Smuts, South Africa: Makers of the modern world. London: Haus Publishing, p.x).

4   A Union covered eloquently by Magubane, B., 1996. The making of a racist State: British imperialism and the union of South Africa 1875–1910. Eritrea: Africa World Press.

5   See Plaatje, S., 1916. Native Life in South Africa where he further laments: 'Similarly, if you see your countrymen and countrywomen driven from home, their homes broken up, with no hopes of redress, on the mandate of a government to which they had loyally paid taxation without representation – driven from their homes, because they do not want to become servants; and when you know that half of these homeless ones have perforce submitted to the conditions and accepted service on terms that are unprofitable to themselves…you would, I think, likewise find it very difficult to maintain a level head or wield a temperate pen'.

6   See IDASA Annual Report, n.d. The state of civil society in South Africa, 2000.

7   Semester at sea: Course syllabus – Philosophy of nonviolence. N.d. Available at: http://www.ise.virginia.edu/syllabi/S11/COPENHAVER_RELG_3559_NonViolence.pdf.

8   General notions of nonviolence. N.d. Available at: http://mkgandhi.org/africaneeds-gandhi/general_notions_of_nonviolence.htm.

9   See Sharp, G., 2010. From dictatorship to democracy: A conceptual framework for liberation. East Boston: The Albert Einstein Institution, pp.80-86.

10 'Authority denotes the capacity to command obedience to orders, or the acceptance of one's judgment, not because of the threat of sanctions but because of position or status…Government authority depends critically on the strength of its claims to legitimacy in the eyes of the population, and its assumed tight to command obedience within the limits of a given constitutional or traditional framework' (Randle 1993: p.4).

11 Cited in Sharp, 2010, op. cit.

12 Ostergaard, G., 1974. Gandhian nonviolence and passive resistance. Available at: http://civilresistance.info/ostergaard.

13 Ibid. A further motivation for adopting a physically non-confrontation stance is that 'what is morally right cannot be pragmatically wrong or politically wrong or invalidated on grounds of apparent futility'.

14 As Hannah Arendt would say in her seminal work On violence… 'power I rooted in voluntary cooperation'. It refers, she says, 'to the human ability not just to act but to act in concert. Power, is never the property of an individual; it belongs to a group and remains in existence only so long as the group keeps it together' (Randle 1993: p. 2)

15 Problems and perspectives – Discussion statement, n.d. Available at: http://www.historicalpapers.wits.ac.za/inventories/inv_pdft/AD1897/AD1897-A8-2l-01-jpeg.pdf.

16 See Turok, B., 2011. The ANC and the turn to the armed struggle: Understanding the ANC today. Johannesburg: Jacana.

17 Ibid.

18 The African National Congress, 1949. Programme of action: Statement of policy adopted at the ANC National Conference, 17 December.

19 See Turok, 2011, op. cit.

20 Which John Rawls understands as a "public, nonviolent, conscientious, yet political act contrary to law usually done with the aim of bringing about a change in the law with policies of government", and it is to remembered that 'People practicing Civil Disobedience break a law because they consider the law unjust and want to call attention to its injustices, hoping to bring about its repeal or amendment. The people are also willing to accept any penalty such as imprisonment for breaking the law. It means the refusal to obey laws using nonviolent means to force concessions from government. It is mostly taken by large number of people against government principle', op. cit.

21 Turok, 2011, op. cit., p.80.

22 Mills, W.G., n.d. Origins and development of African Nationalism. Available at: http://husky1.stmarys.ca/~wmills/course322/17African_natm.html.

23 See Swilling, M., n.d. The united democratic front and township revolt. Wits History Workshop. Available at: http://wiredspace.wits.ac.za/bitstream/handle/10539/8147/HWS-405.pdf.

24 Suttner, R., n.d. Legacies and meanings of the UDF period, September 2003. Unpublished paper.

25 From a study by the UNICEF-commissioned study led by Southern African Development, Education and Policy Research Unit (SADEP) 1997, University of the Western Cape, quoted from Mkhabela, I., 2011. Community mobilisation: Constraints and opportunities for change and development done by the people, not to people. Leadership Forum. 9–10 February. Spier Estate Conference Centre, p.1.

26 Coetzee, J.K. & Wood, G., 2006. Review essay: Negotiated revolutions or evolutionary regime transitions? The Czech Republic, South Africa and Chile. African Sociological Review, 1(10), p.238.

27 Stephan, M.J. & Chenoweth, E., n.d. Why civil resistance works: The strategic logic of nonviolent conflict. International Security, 33(1), pp.8-13.

28 Lawson, 2005. p.51.

29 Stephan, M.J. & Chenoweth, E., n.d. Why civil resistance works: The strategic logic of nonviolent conflict.

30 See Sharp, op. cit.

31 Žižek, S., 2011. Shoplifters of the world unite. London Review of Books, 19 August, pp.1-3.

32 After all: 'Nonviolent action has several advantages when compared to violent struggle, including: It does not accept that the outcome will be decided by the means of fighting chosen by the opponents, it is difficult for the regime to combat, it can uniquely aggra-

vate weaknesses of a dictatorship and can sever its sources of power, it can in action be widely dispersed but can also be concentrated on a limited objective, it can effectively use the population as a whole and the society's groups and institutions in the struggle to end the domination by a few, it helps to spread the distribution of effective power in the society, making the establishment and maintenance of a democratic society possible' (Sharp, op. cit., pp.20-21). Also see Nelson Mandela at his inauguration as RSA President, 10 May 1994. (Sisulu, W.M., 1957. South Africa`s struggle for democracy. Available at: http://www.anc.org.za/show.php.)

CHAPTER 5

The doors of education and culture shall be open: the centrality of education in the history of the ANC

John Pampallis

Introduction

From its inception, the African National Congress (ANC) was focused primarily on the expansion of the political rights of African people. From its earliest days it sought to gain for Africans equal rights with whites. In the latter half of the twentieth century this goal became more explicitly associated with the overthrow of the apartheid state and its replacement by a democratically elected government. From 1994, having been elected as the government of a democratic South Africa, the ANC turned its attention to consolidating its power and ensuring that Africans overcame their inferior societal position resulting from the centuries of colonialism and apartheid while maintaining its decades-old commitment to a non-racial democracy.

These were the overarching aims of the ANC – rather simplistically stated here for the sake of brevity – with which virtually all members would have agreed. Of course there have been disagreements among the membership over various areas of strategy and tactics in both the pre- and post-democratic periods, but never about these broad strategic goals.

As regards education, there has always been general agreement that the ANC stood (and stands) for more and better-quality education for more people. In particular, it has stood for those whose education has been neglected or worse by the various white-supremacist governments which started with colonial occupation. This is the context within which the ANC has made policy and against which its practice must be evaluated.

The early years

Until the early twentieth century, virtually all formal schooling for blacks was in mission schools, although a few government schools were also established for Africans, particularly in the Natal Colony. Mission schools catered for only a small proportion of black South African children, with the overwhelming number of pupils being in the early years of primary school. The colonial states provided some subsidies to mission schools, which provided the state a degree of control over them. At the time of the establishment of the Union of South Africa in 1910 there were approximately 110 000 African pupils receiving state aid across the country, approximately 70 per cent of whom were in the Cape Colony.[1] For the far smaller white population – 1.27 million compared to 4 million Africans[2] – countrywide enrolment (in better equipped schools) was approximately 160 000.

From the earliest years of the twentieth century, Africans – including those who established the ANC in 1912 – made known their opposition to government education policies, expressing their views with differing and increasing levels of intensity over time. In the period before and immediately after the establishment of the Union of South Africa, African leaders complained about both the quantity and quality of education available to black South Africans and about the unequal state funding to black and white pupils and the poor salaries of teachers.[3]

Many of these leaders were missionary-educated professionals, and included a number of teachers such as the ANC's first President, John L. Dube, who established the Ohlange Institute which provided both academic and vocational education for Africans. They saw education as a key instrument for African political and economic advancement. They called for the state to make schooling more widely available, and on occasion called for compulsory education. They also called for the curriculum to be made more relevant and intellectually stimulating, often calling for more and better-quality vocational training which would allow Africans to become skilled workers or independent craftsmen.[4]

In its seminal document, *Africans' Claims in South Africa*, adopted in 1943, the ANC called for 'the state to provide full facilities for all types of education for African children,' including for 'secondary, professional, technical and university education'. Similar demands were reiterated in the ANC's 1949 Programme of Action, which also called for 'the provision of large-scale scholarships tenable in various overseas countries'.[5]

Responses to Bantu Education

After the National Party (NP), with its policy of apartheid, came to power in the 1948 elections, the use of education as an instrument of white domination became increasingly overt. The Bantu Education Act of 1953 provided for a separate education system for Africans, under the national government's Department of Native Affairs. All unauthorised schooling for blacks was banned. Government subsidies for mission schools were reduced, thus forcing most of them to close or join the state system. The aim of the Bantu Education system was to provide basic knowledge for unskilled manual workers, to convince African children to accept an inferior position in society and to promote an ethnic (as opposed to a national) consciousness in students.

As the various Bantustans were established from 1963 onwards to the early 1980s, the administration of education in these areas was transferred to the Bantustan administrations, but continued to be (poorly) funded, directly or indirectly, by the central government, and remained very much under its influence. The central government retained control of the education of Africans outside the Bantustans through the Department of Education and Training. Private schools for blacks could not be established without government permission.

The ANC – and African people in general – reacted with outrage to the introduction to Bantu Education. The ANC's December 1954 national conference called on African parents to prepare to withdraw their children from primary schools from April 1955. This call, however, was not met with general support by parents who faced a dilemma in that the alternative would probably be no education at all for their children. The ANC's National Executive then called off the school boycott, but agreed it could go ahead in places where it had popular support. Sustained boycotts did take place in the East Rand, Bethlehem in the Orange Free State and Port Elizabeth, but state repression – in the form of expulsions and the firing of problematic teachers – ensured that the campaign ultimately failed. In areas in which there was a boycott, local leaders and community leaders set up alternative schools, called 'cultural clubs', in an effort to get around the restriction on unauthorised schools. However, a shortage of resources and teachers as well as police raids ensured that the schools did not last long.

The Extension of University Education Act of 1959 then closed 'white' universities to black students, unless they had special government permission. The University of Fort Hare was to be restricted to Xhosa students and new segregated universities were to be opened for other African ethnic groups as well as for coloureds and Indians. The ANC as well as other African organisations and the English language universities protested strongly, but to no avail. Most African lecturers at Fort Hare, including the Vice-Principal, a prominent ANC leader, ZK Matthews, resigned in protest.

After the banning of the ANC its most prominent leaders were imprisoned or left the country to carry out the struggle in exile, or were forced to operate clandestinely in the underground. The heavy repression by the regime in the post-banning period led to a period in which the movement was less visible in public life. In these circumstances black political opposition to apartheid surfaced most prominently through the black consciousness movement, which had its roots in the 1960s in the black student organisation, the South African Student Organisation (SASO). SASO's membership was largely active on the segregated black campuses and it united African, coloured and Indian student leaders and activists in opposition to white domination.

Born partly in opposition to the white liberal leadership of the multi-racial National Union of South African students (NUSAS), which was experienced by black students as paternalistic and domineering, SASO and other black consciousness organisations such as the Black People's Convention (BPC) excluded whites of whatever political persuasion. This break with the non-racial tradition of the Congress movement represented an obvious difference in outlook from that of the ANC. Nonetheless, the ANC welcomed the emergence of the black consciousness as a reflection of the African people's opposition to oppression and, though communication was difficult, it worked to influence the students and others in the black consciousness movement.[6]

Meanwhile, black opposition to apartheid was growing in the schools as well as the universities. The introduction of Bantu Education coincided with a period of rapid economic growth and industrialisation – particularly in the 1960s. The schooling system expanded rapidly to cope with the demand for more educated workers – first mainly at primary school level and later spreading to the secondary schools. Total enrolment at Bantu Education schools grew from 882 000 in 1953 to 2 737 900 in 1970.[7] This resulted in large numbers of young people gathered together in schools and unhappy with the education they were receiving. The regime had unintentionally created propitious conditions for a mass uprising.

Open revolt broke out against Bantu Education with the uprising of school students that began in Soweto on 16 June 1976 and spread to many other parts of the country. The Soweto Uprising, as it came to be known, began as a protest against a new language policy introduced into secondary schools in the South Transvaal region of which Soweto was a part. It required black schools to use Afrikaans as a language of instruction for half of the subjects and English (previously the only language used) for the rest. Student protests quickly turned into pitched battles between students and police after the latter fired on unarmed students, killing several.

While the uprising began as a protest against the use of Afrikaans as a medium of instruction in schools, it quickly became a movement against the system of Bantu Education and against the apartheid system in general. In the year-and-a-half that followed the uprising, over a thousand lives were lost across the country – most being the result of police action. Thousands of others were arrested, many were tortured in prison and others fled into exile.

The Soweto Uprising was a watershed event in South African history, marking a qualitatively new, more openly confrontational stage in the opposition to apartheid. Educational institutions became important sites of struggle against the apartheid system for almost two decades, with more or less continual confrontation between students and authorities at the school level and between democratic organisations (including student and political organisations) and government at the national political level.

For the ANC, the education arena became a priority area of the struggle against apartheid and it made a concerted effort to increase its influence over the student movement. In 1979, students established the Congress of South African Students (COSAS) and the Azanian Students Organisation (AZASO), both of which were initially oriented towards a 'Black Consciousness'. Through the efforts of the ANC, and particularly of older cadres, both organisations changed their thinking and declared their support for the Freedom Charter, and thus implicitly for the ANC. Cooperation grew between student organisations and community and trade union structures so that student activists increasingly saw themselves as part of the wider struggle against apartheid.

In the wake of the Soweto Uprising, thousands of young people left South Africa and joined the ANC structures in exile, with a smaller number enlisting with the PAC or other organisations. Most of the young ANC exiles joined the ranks of *Umkhonto we Sizwe*, while those who wished to continue their schooling were placed in schools in various countries in African countries, Cuba and elsewhere.

By 1979, the ANC decided to bring them together in one place and to begin to develop an alternative form of education. It established the Solomon Mahlangu Freedom College in Morogoro, Tanzania, which was initially a secondary school for young exiles but later grew to include a primary school and a day care centre. A vocational training centre was later established about 50 kilometres away in Dakawa. Most students who completed their secondary schooling were found scholarships to study at universities and colleges in various countries.

One of the main tactics of the student movement – at schools, colleges and universities – was the class boycott. A breakdown in discipline among both students and teachers in many black schools led to a disintegration of the 'culture of learning and teaching' (as it later became known). Concerned that many children were not getting any education at all, community leaders associated with the ANC-aligned United Democratic Front (UDF) established the National Education Crisis Committee (NECC) in 1986. It called for an end to school boycotts and for students and teachers to unite to create an alternative system of 'People's Education'.

This meant, *inter alia*, the establishment of Parent-Teacher-Student Associations (PTSAs) at schools and commencement of work on the development of new curricula.[8] Despite the intentions and best efforts of the NECC, these attempts were not very successful, particularly given the continuing repression of activists by the state.

Education after apartheid

Even before the ANC was unbanned, the NECC began to make arrangements for the development of an education policy for a democratic South Africa. In 1989 it established Education Policy Units at the Universities of the Witwatersrand and Natal in cooperation with the respective universities. The National Education Policy Initiative (NEPI) produced a thirteen-volume report on policy options on various aspects of education policy, followed by the establishment of the Centre for Education Policy Development, which coordinated a wide array of researchers, activists and even some members of the government's educational bureaucracy to produce the Policy Framework for Education and Training (popularly known as the 'Yellow Book'), which outlined the policy with which the ANC entered the April 1994 general election.

There is no space to elaborate on the details of these policies here, or the nuances of the discussion they embodied, save to say that their stated aim was an equitable education system which would redress past injustices and which consciously sought to promote non-racism, non-sexism and democratic participation by the people in the governance of the education system.

These pre-election policy intentions influenced, although not determined, the post-1994 policies of, first, the ANC-led Government of National Unity and then the government of the ANC. Major structural changes followed the 1994 election. Linda Chisholm summarised the main ones a decade later:

> Since 1994, there has been a significant refashioning of the education and training landscape in South Africa. Eighteen racially-divided departments have been restructured into nine. Education budgets are designed in principle to achieve equitable outcomes and overcome the racial disparities that marked apartheid budgeting allocations. Education control has been decentralised, and schools, colleges, technikons and universities have been opened to all races. Curricula, their review and design, have been revamped, and management and administration reorganised. Novel forms of assessment, qualification and certification have been introduced through an entirely new body (sic), the National Qualifications Framework (NQF). Teacher education is now provided under the auspices of the higher education sector. Higher Education itself has been reorganised. A new multilingual policy has been

articulated for schools. Skills levies and Sector Education and Training Authorities (SETAs) have been brought into being to provide training for workers. Substantially altered educational philosophies now suffuse policy documents.[9]

In addition, compulsory schooling legislation was introduced and enrolments expanded at both school and post-school levels. By 2010, 98.7% of children between the ages of seven and fifteen were attending an educational institution,[10] with almost exactly equal numbers of boys and girls. The difference in enrolments by race was small, with the highest enrolment among Indians (99.8%) and among Africans (98.6%). University enrolments increased over 80% from 495356 in 1994 to 899120 in 2011.

Formerly white schools took in rapidly expanding numbers of black students and the same happened in former white universities. In 1994, 55% of students at all public universities were black (African, coloured and Indian), 43% were African and 55% were male. By 2010 these figures were 80% black, 67% African and 43% male.

Measures such as the school nutrition programme were introduced and supplemented the expansion of social grants to alleviate poverty, particularly in underdeveloped rural and peri-urban areas. The National Student Financial Aid Scheme (NSFAS) was established in 1996 to provide funding for poor students. It grew from R441 million in 1996 to R2.375 billion in 2008. By 2011, the funds made available through NSFAS had grown to R6 billion and were expected to continue rising. This rapidly growing allocation of funds is a reflection of strong demand for free education from youth and parents. In 2007, a resolution of the ANC Conference, partly the result of student pressures, called for the progressive introduction of free education up to undergraduate level for poor students. From 2011, fees for further education and training (FET) colleges were abolished for poor students, i.e., those from families with a family income of R122 000 per annum or less.

At school level, the 1996 SA Schools Act allowed schools to charge fees if the parents voted to do so. In practice this resulted in virtually all schools, even in the poorest communities, charging school fees, with parents often acquiescing to pressure from principals who felt the strain of trying to manage schools with insufficient state funding. The distress caused to poor communities by this policy resulted in the introduction of no-fee schools, initially in the poorest 20 per cent of schools but gradually rising to the poorest 60 per cent.

These are all significant accomplishments. However, overall there was an inability to fundamentally transform the South African education system. Former whites-only educational institutions, now racially integrated, continued to have relatively good facilities, better qualified teachers and a better quality of education. Former blacks-only institutions, while seeing some improvements to their physical infrastructure and teacher qualifications, remained unable to provide anything near the quality of education in the former white, suburban public schools. It is clear that most of the educational opportunities created for blacks were enjoyed by an emergent middle class and in turn contributed towards the development of that class.

Poor communities may have seen some (though still insufficient) improvements in the infrastructure of their schools, and teachers in these schools may have seen improvements in remuneration. However, very few of these schools have turned into institutions from which children (and their parents) can expect to get the type of education that would act as a basis for social mobility. Historically black universities and colleges similarly lag behind their previously whites-only counterparts.

A number of reasons for this lack of progress in overcoming past legacies have been given in public debates and academic writing. Some of the main ones with regard to the schooling system include: bureaucratic incompetence leading to inefficiency and ineffectiveness, particularly in some of the provincial departments of education; the weak capacity of many of the teachers in schools serving poor, largely black, communities, and particularly their low levels of subject knowledge; ill-discipline, including frequent absenteeism, on the part of teachers who are allegedly more concerned with their salaries than with the education of students in poorer schools; high levels of poverty in communities, many of which suffer high levels of unemployment and lack basic amenities at home; low levels of parental education, which make it difficult for parents to assist their children with schoolwork; inadequate pre-school provision; and most children not learning in their first language, especially at primary school.

Probably the most persistent criticism of the schooling reforms in both the popular media (and to a lesser extent in academic writing) was aimed until recently at out-comes-based education (OBE). This was said, especially after its introduction, to have been complex and difficult for most teachers and even education department officials to understand. This perceived complexity was largely attributable to the new and unfamiliar (and often impenetrable) vocabulary in which it was presented. Professors Ken Harley and Volker Wedekind have argued convincingly that the outcomes-based curriculum was not very different from what had been the practice in former white schools and was easily adopted by them, while the former black schools had great difficulties adapting to its expectations. The new curriculum, like the new governance and funding arrangements, benefited the (racially integrating) middle class. In November, as a result of mounting public criticism and on the basis of a curriculum review, Minister of Basic Education, Angie Motshekga, declared OBE to be dead.

In the post-school system, also, a number of reasons have been put forward for the lack of transformation, or rather for the type of transformation which has largely benefited only the middle class. These include the poor state of readiness of students entering higher education because of the poor foundations provided by the schooling system; the difficulty that young black students have in adapting to an alien university culture, especially in the former white universities; the persistence of racism in former white institutions and of sexism and other forms of discrimination in all institutions; the lack of a concerted intervention by the state to strengthen the historically black universities, especially those in the former Bantustans; the relative neglect of vocational education (especially in FET Colleges) and adult education by the state; the failure of the Department of Education (DoE) to develop strong, mutually supportive links between the universities and the FET Colleges, including a lack of clear pathways for FET students who wish to further their studies at higher education level; and the disconnect between the funding mechanism established for workplace-based training under the Department of Labour, i.e., the Sector Education and Training Authorities (SETAs) and the National Skills Fund (NSF), and the educational institutions which fall under the DoE.

Although many of these problems are expected to be addressed by the relevant government departments, the ANC has been involved in finding solutions at a strategic level, through the decisions of national and provincial conferences as well as of its elected committees and officials. After the 2007 election, President Zuma announced a reorganisation of cabinet posts which included a fundamental restructuring of the administration of education and training. This resulted in the division of the DoE in order to create departments which are more focused in their scope. The Department of Basic Education (DBE) was established to focus its efforts almost exclusively on schooling. The Department of Higher Education and Training (DHET) took over responsibility for higher education, further education colleges and adult education. In addition, the DHET took over responsibility for the skills development branch of the Department of Labour (including the SETAs, NSF and the trade testing centres).

The DBE, responding to a widespread view that schools had not been producing youth, especially black youth, with the educational basics to prepare them adequately for either the labour market of for further or higher education, turned its focus to achieving what it considered the fundamentals of a decent education. Specifically it aims to ensure that all learners attend school regularly and punctually, understand the importance of doing their schoolwork and are adequately fed (with those in poor communities getting a good meal at school each day); to have well-qualified teachers who are dedicated to providing a good education to their learners; to have principals who focus on ensuring learning in their schools and ensuring a well-functioning school; and to have adequate teaching and learning materials, including books and computers, in every school and adequate school infrastructure.

A major intervention by the DBE has been the introduction of the Annual National Assessments in Grades 3, 6 and 9 to monitor learner performance across the system in language and mathematics.

The DHET, which brought together functions which were not previously in the same department or (in the case of universities, colleges and adult education institutions) were hardly coordinated, took a different tack and undertook a major policy initiative. A study released a short while before the department was established[11] found that in 2007, of 3 million young people between the ages of 18 and 24, the overwhelming majority were black, and not in employment, education or training. The department estimated a similar number in the same predicament between the ages of 24 and 35. This has impelled the department to plan for a major expansion of study opportunities for young people over the period to 2030. Its Green Paper released in 2011 proposes to expand university enrolments from nearly 900 000 in 2010 to 1.5 million in 2030, and to expand enrolment in colleges and other post-school institutions (currently smaller than the universities) to 4 million.

The DHET has developed a concept of post-school education and training in which universities, colleges, other post-school institutions and the SETAs and NSF cooperate to strengthen one another and collaborate to expand study opportunities in 'a single, coherent, differentiated and highly articulated post-school education and training system'.[12]

The major departures from the previous system included the priority placed on expanding and strengthening the quality of FET colleges and improving articulation between them and universities; the direction given to SETAs to shift their funding from short courses offered by private providers to training for full occupational and professional qualifications offered in public colleges and universities; and the effort to revive artisan and other mid-level skills training in the form of apprenticeships and learnerships to greatly expand the capacity of the labour force.

In the university system, while continuing efforts to improve the quantity and quality of research outputs remain, there is a new emphasis on improving the infrastructure and quality of education in previously disadvantaged universities to ensure that they can provide decent education to their students, especially at undergraduate level. At the time of writing, plans were being put in place for a large expansion of post-graduate training opportunities, using universities in both South Africa and abroad. There is also an emphasis on increasing 'scarce and critical skills' in science, engineering and technology while not losing sight of the importance of the humanities and social sciences.

Conclusion

These priorities to a large extent reflect the overall development policy trajectory of government, which from 2009 embraced the concept of a developmental state. The decision to create a department bringing together higher education and training allows greater coordination of the production of skills for the labour market and thus an attempt to overcome the skills shortage which has been one of the chief constraints on economic growth.

The ANC government's main economic policy interventions include measures to support and strengthen infrastructure and manufacturing and to ensure job creation, as demonstrated in the National Development Plan, the New Growth Path, the second Industrial Policy Action Plan and the large infrastructure development programme outlined by President Zuma in early 2012. The DHET's skills development focus fits directly into this programme and a cabinet decision to use all large infrastructure projects as sites for practical training of engineers, artisans and other professionals should ensure that economic growth and education are mutually reinforcing.

The approaches of both the DBE and DHE offer hope for turning the education system into a more effective instrument for national development for the nation and for the personal development of individuals. Many obstacles remain to be overcome before the ANC meets its goal of a decent and equitable education for all – in particular growing the capacity to implement government's intentions, especially in some provincial departments of education and some of the weaker colleges and universities. Nevertheless, the ANC and its government have gained valuable experience and learned important lessons over the period since 1994. They have sharpened their priorities, based on past achievements and challenges, and linked their educational aims to the overall developmental policy of the government. The current direction of development for both the DBE and the DHET, I believe, offers grounds for cautious optimism that the legacy of poor education left by colonialism and apartheid can steadily be overcome.

Endnotes

1   Hartshorne, K., 1992. *Crisis and challenge: Black education 1910–1990*. New York: Oxford University Press.

2   Larson, E., n.d. Formation of the Union of South Africa. In Gorman, R.F., 2007. *Great events from history: The 20th century, 1901–1940*. Available at: http://salempress.com/store/samples/great_events_from_history_20th_1901/great_events_from_history_20th_1901_south_africa.htm.

3   Karis, T. & Carter, G., 1972. *From protest to challenge: Documents of African politics in South Africa, Volume 1*. Stanford: Hoover Institution Press. Also see 1973 and 1977 Volumes 2 and 3.

4   Ibid.

5   African National Congress (ANC), 1943. African claims in South Africa. In Karis, T. &

Carter, G., 1973. *From protest to challenge: Documents of African politics in South Africa, Volume 2.* Stanford: Hoover Institution Press.

6   Francis Meli (1988:182) quotes documents of the 1985 ANC Conference which reported that by 1976 Steve Biko had accepted that the ANC was the leader of the South African revolution, that the Black People's Convention (BPC) should focus on mass mobilisation within the broad strategy of the liberation movement (i.e. the ANC) and that a meeting between the leadership of the BPC and the ANC was necessary. Meli, who was the editor of the ANC's official journal, *Sechaba*, states that arrangements for exiled ANC leaders to meet Biko were made in 1976 and 1977 but both meetings failed because it was impossible to get Biko out of the country.

7   Unterhalter, E., 1992. Changing aspects of reformism in Bantu Education, 1953–89. In Unterhalter, E., Wolpe, H., Botha, T., Badat, S., Dlamini, T. & Khotseng, B., 1991. *Apartheid education and popular struggles.* Johannesburg: Raven Press.

8   Gardiner, M., 1990. Efforts at creating alternative curricula: Conceptual and practical considerations. In Nkomo, M (ed.), 1990. *Pedagogy of domination: Towards a democratic education in South Africa.* New Jersey: Africa World Press. Also see Pampallis, J., 1991. *Foundations of the new South Africa.* London: Zed Books and Cape Town: Maskew Miller Longman.

9   Chisholm, L., 2004. *Changing class: Education and social change in post apartheid South Africa.* Cape Town: HSRC Press.

10 Although this certainly represents an increase in enrolments, accurate figures are only available from 2002.

11 Cloete, N. (ed.), 2009. *Responding to the educational needs of post school youth.* Cape Town: CHET.

12 Department of Higher Education and Training. 2011. *Green Paper for post-school education and training.* Pretoria: DHET.

CHAPTER 6

Revisiting the role of the student movement in the making of democratic South Africa

David Maimela

Introduction

The nature of the liberation struggle in South Africa, like most anti-colonial struggles elsewhere in the world, has involved a wide variety of social forces, one of which was the student movement that in the past 60 years has played an important political role in the evolution of the national liberation struggle and the evolution of the ANC itself.

The student movement is a universal phenomenon and has taken different forms in different social contexts, across times and geography. It has been argued that: "whereas the origins, evolution and proliferation of the student movement can be traced far back in history, the modern student movement is traceable from the beginning of the twentieth century and grew more pronounced and dominant as a phenomenon in the mid to latter half of the century".[1] We can refer to the 1817 German experience, the Chinese experience of 4 May 1919 or the Young Hegelians of the early 1800s, when philosophers (professors) and students shared one space, or even as far back as the eighth century BC, when students were mere protégés. The modern student movement has a distinct character, developed and sustained over time: mass composition, radicalisation, mobilising and organising on constantly changing technological platforms, and locating struggles within broader local and international contexts.

The focus of this chapter is on the South African black student movement that sprang out of the political conditions of the 1960s. The socio-political context was radically different from the present day, a period in which national oppression and class exploitation were consolidating, yet at the same time the liberation forces had just retreated, after several years of remarkable radicalisation and visible campaigns against the apartheid state. The social and political milieu shaped the form and content of the struggles and in return the student leadership shaped them within that historical period.

While acknowledging the formation of the National Union of South African Students (NUSAS) in 1924, it recognised that the black student movement was novel in that it mounted a decisive fight against the apartheid state and apartheid education, and played a prominent role in the life of the ANC and the ultimate triumph of the struggle for freedom. Objectively, for a black student, national oppression often meant that surviving through education and life was subject to a simple choice: submit or fight. Material conditions could either demobilise one to submission or drive one to fight for a better education and for freedom.

The aim of the chapter is to show how the student movement helped to shape national liberation struggles and, in particular, how this was done using the various ideological platforms and strands that not only informed the liberation movement but also in turn shaped the very character of the student movement. The emphasis will be on the connection the student movement made with the foremost political formation: the ANC and its alliance partners. At a secondary level, the aim is to identify the key ideas that informed the consciousness of the student movement and how these informed the activism of students in community and national struggles. Ultimately, based on the lessons arising out of the history of the student movement, the chapter will propose some ideas on the current and future role of the student movement under democratic conditions.

Foundations of the student movement

Wherever they appeared, the radical and progressive student movements of the world have sought to add impetus to social agency. Selassie suggests that:

> …it seems to us that the essential characteristic of all student movements is, first and foremost, to be the reflection of the many historical, political, economic and cultural contradictions of the societies and countries where they manifest themselves by revealing the problems set, with varying acuteness, by the relevant place and time.[2]

The South African Student Organisation (SASO), as modern, radical and progressive, aptly fitted this description.

Long before its formation in 1968, a forerunner to the South African Students' Congress (SASCO), there had been black student resistance and mobilisation in one form or another in institutions such as Fort Hare University, Lovedale College and others. Duma Nokwe argues that even the formation, ideology and posture of the Congress Youth League (youth wing of the ANC) were influenced by the student movement. He cites the "growing militancy of the students which was demonstrated by student strikes at Fort Hare and Lovedale"[3]. However, more than any other organisation, SASO pioneered the enduring tradition of radical and progressive student politics which has now spanned almost seven decades.

The term 'student movement' can refer to "the sum total of action and intentions of students individually, collectively and organisationally that are directed for change in the students' own circumstances and for educational and wider social change."[4] There are other definitions but for the purposes of this chapter this will suffice.

Saleem Badat, in setting the scene for the rise of radical black students in the 1960s, writes that:

> ...during the early twentieth century, the twin concerns of the South African state were guaranteeing capital accumulation on the basis of cheap unskilled black labour and consolidating the structures of white political domination and privilege.[5]

Apartheid and apartheid education were introduced to consolidate this political economy structure, as the capitalist state devised a grand social engineering strategy with education as one of its pillars. Its goal was to consolidate white power and privilege, and white minority dominance.

This had been preceded by defiance campaigns in the mid 1950s, which saw the ANC and particularly its youth taking a new radical and actively confrontational tactical posture in fighting the apartheid system. This period presented a crisis simultaneously to both the apartheid machinery and the liberation forces. Apartheid was facing increasing protest and rebellion from the oppressed masses and the liberation forces had to endure a period of suppression and persecution.

The 1960s then saw prominent national leaders facing either arrest or imprisonment, banning orders and exile, as the struggle went underground. The student movement gave the liberation struggle new impetus, with the primary organ and voice being SASO, to be joined by, amongst others, the University Christian Movement (UCM) and the South African Student Movement (SASM). After the ANC and PAC were banned in 1960, their work was taken up briefly by the African Students' Association (ASA) and African Students' Union of South Africa (ASUSA). The Non-European Unity Movement attracted student support in the Cape and Natal.[6]

Out of necessity, the student movement was essentially *political*. From its inception it had to make sense of reality within the prevailing social context so that it could exist for both its constituency and the broader community. When SASO was formed in 1968 it had at least three identifiable tasks:

1) To close the gap opened by the crushing of a liberation movement by the apartheid security establishment;
2) To define students and their place and role in society, in education and in the black community; and
3) To respond to the unfavourable conditions of students in black higher education.

With these in mind, it became apparent that if the student movement was to be effective it had to locate itself in society, understand national oppression and devise strategies to fight its manifestations in education and keep in contact with the broader community. It introduced a particular consciousness and theoretical construct; that is, the idea of students being members of the community before they are members of institutions of learning. It was this consciousness that kept the student movement organic and embedded in community struggles and, by extension, national struggles.

The interconnectivity of student, youth and community struggles

The student movement, both in universities and high schools, engaged in various creative ways to form an interface with local and youth struggles. There were a number of community projects and networks that gave practical meaning to the idea of being members of the community before they were students. These went beyond projects in tackling social ills such as crime or gang violence in the community. For instance, Mamphele Ramphele, a Black Consciousness Movement and SASO activist, later to become vice-chancellor of the University of Cape Town, recalls how, around 1973: "…student activists from Fort Hare and the Federal Theological Seminary in nearby Alice called regularly to enquire about new developments or to participate in community development projects."[7] These included literacy projects and medical assistance, while churches and seminaries in the early 1970s funded Zanempilo clinic, run by Mamphele near King William's Town,[8] and to be operated by students.

Already, as Glaser notes, "from around 1971, it (SASO) recognised the need to reach beyond the isolated campuses, to forge links with a wider black community."[9]

The South African Student Movement (SASM), having originated in Soweto in 1968,[10] had several community engagements as part of the work to get the out-of-school youth to believe in and support their causes, as well as the migrant workers in the hostels and parents at large.

However, soon after the 1976/7 Soweto school uprisings, the incidence of gangs and criminality increased and discipline declined. Inadvertently the scholars had created a vacuum to be filled by tsotsis,[11] with growing acrimony and non-cooperation between the student activists and other youths. Glaser has traced the ebb and flow in the relationship:

> ...on one occasion, after receiving complaints that train passengers were being molested by criminal youths, two hundred students patrolled a Soweto station to protect commuters... The drop in gang crime was primarily a result of student crackdowns.[12]

Although there were tensions and fights, stay-away blockades and protest marches, the students understood that the out-of-school youths who engaged in criminal activities and gangsterism were victims of a political and social order that rejected them. Such was the level of consciousness within the politicised student movement that many attempts were made to reach out to the youths, but often with little success. The situation only improved when SASM became affiliated to the National Youth Organisation, and then in the 1980s when the local youth congresses were launched – in the case of Soweto, the Soweto Youth Congress (SOYCO) in 1983.

SASM, using networks such as the Transvaal Youth Organisation (regional structure of the National Youth Organisation) and black community projects, reached out to the local youth, and meetings were convened at which the goals were explained and discussed.[13] At community level, beyond the winter and summer schools, SASM and the Soweto Student Representative Council (SSRC) campaigned successfully against rent increases and the Urban Bantu Council system.[14] Also, interaction between students and migrant workers in particular increased, as the students mobilised the support of workers to sabotage white shops in towns and generally undermine the apartheid regime.

The understanding of community did not end with South Africa but spread across borders through the influence of the underground movement. Printed materials and exile added to the consciousness of the students. Pro-Frelimo rallies helped to sharpen the consciousness of students, enabling them to locate local struggles for social justice within the wider international context.

For the purposes of this chapter, what is more important is not how much community work was done by students but whether they saw themselves as members of the community first in their social agency or whether this was practised in reality, not as an add-on but as a way of living life and conducting the struggle itself. In the author's opinion, the students did live up to the idea and expectation of being members of the community before they were students, and in some respects they still do today.

In the following years, the dialectic of the tensions and cooperation between the students and youth affected most townships across the country, parallel to the evolution, intensity and success of the youth and student struggles of the two crucial decades of South Africa's history, the 1970s and 1980s.

Students and national struggle for freedom: ideas and strategy

National oppression and apartheid meant the oppression and exclusion of the black majority from the national life of South Africa. In other words, blacks did not enjoy full citizenship or political and human rights. Harsher forms of repression resulted in political organisations and leaders being targeted and banned, in response to the momentum of active resistance. Black higher education was sub-standard, with bad living conditions, control and authoritarianism combining to produce a resistant radical black student movement. Frustrations of blacks in general, and black students in particular, led to the origination of the 'Black Consciousness' concept as a theoretical tool to interpret national reality at the time. It was later used to politicise, mobilise, organise and conceive programmes and activities – in short, it evolved into a movement.

The concept of Black Consciousness in simple terms was defined as a state of mind and way of life, propagating the idea of self-reliance, self-discovery and self-sufficiency of the black community, and the ability to live independently of the white oppressors, their structures and their cultures. Although the white person was seen as the enemy, the real enemy was the white system of supremacy and domination, encapsulated in the apartheid system.

As stated elsewhere, whereas the BC concept was "inspired by thinkers and leaders such as Pixley ka Isaka Seme, Charlotte Maxeke, W.E.B. du Bois, Thomas Sankara, Haile Selassie, Marcus Garvey, Frantz Fanon, Kwame Nkrumah, Mwalimu Nyerere and other figures who espoused a pan-African philosophy,"[15] the 1960s generation was also buoyed by the recently triumphant anti-colonial and national liberation struggles elsewhere on the continent. These developments gave hope to the struggle in South African that freedom was indeed attainable.

In the struggles of the early period of the formation of a black student voice and platform, white liberal students in NUSAS accused SASO of promoting black racism and reversing the gains of a national multiracial student union. NUSAS argued that it was relevant and legitimate as a representative of all South African students. Steve Biko, first President of SASO, argued fiercely and yet eloquently that white liberals could not claim to be opposed to white minority rule and yet continue to enjoy the privileges associated with whiteness.

Biko went on to explain the need for a black student organisation, and black solidarity and unity:

The fact that we have differences in approach should not cloud the issue [SASO not being anti-white]. We have a responsibility not only to ourselves but also to the society from which we spring. No one else will ever take the challenge up until we, of our own accord, accept the inevitable fact that ultimately the leadership of non-white people in this country rests with us.[16]

The student movement also had the ambition of shaping black political thinking in South Africa, which illustrated that it was organic and understood its role in shaping ideas in society. In addition, the student struggles were intricately linked to the broader national struggle for liberation, making it possible to either lose or win the struggle.

Another important question of consciousness and identity was a shift from the 'non-white' concept to strictly referring to blacks as 'blacks'. This was a victory for self-articulation and assertiveness. It was felt that the oppressed could not be defined as 'the *other*' and certainly not in relation to whites as 'the *non-white other*'. It was asserted that black people existed, just as much as whites existed, and that blacks were also human beings, not non-beings. Black people and black lives were of equal worth to white people and deserved equal citizenship status.

As time went on, and as the student movement increased its contact with the ANC and the SACP underground, Black Consciousness came under serious criticism from within SASO itself. It was now seen by some as merely an idealism of values and standards. While for some these were important traits, for others their exponents failed to fully understand and confront the reality of the situation.

On the other hand, most of the cadres who kept close contact with the student movement did so either as underground operatives or under code names. Several current leading figures of the ANC and government, such as Joe Phaahla, former President Thabo Mbeki (ASA), and Barney Pityana, either cut their political teeth in the student movement or had irregular contact with ANC underground operatives.

It is prudent to make two points at this stage. Firstly, Black Consciousness as a body of ideas was essentially built on Pan-Africanism and both have roots in the student movement, the liberation movement and more particularly the ANC, as well as the global Pan-Africanist Movement of the late nineteenth century. For example, it was Seme who spoke in 1906 of the 'Regeneration of Africa' and 'I'm an African', while Maxeke, in her student and youth days, was close to Du Bois and the Pan-African Movement in America, having an immense role in the formation of these Pan-African ideas, in and outside South Africa. Although they were generations apart, Seme/Maxeke's Pan-Africanism and Biko/Pityana's Black Consciousness were essentially one movement, albeit with ebbs and flows at different historical times.

Secondly, Black Consciousness must be credited as a helpful body of ideas, making an important and valuable contribution to liberatory politics in South Africa. The contestation of ideas within the student movement, especially the influence that the ANC and the Congress Alliance sought, was not a zero-sum game, but rather it was a triumph of hegemony by the ANC when it won over the student movement to a class–race approach. For the student movement, meanwhile, it was a triumph when it influenced and sold the idea of black consciousness to the ANC.

The ideological orientation of SASO became the subject of fierce debate within the student movement, culminating in changes of ideological character: from Black Consciousness to a class–race approach to analysis. In large measure, this change was influenced by the Congress Alliance and its blueprint Freedom Charter of 1955, as well as the Colonialism of a Special Type (CST) thesis by the Communist Party. These debates took place in the Azanian Student Organisation (AZASO), essentially a re-emergence of the student movement on the political scene which coincided with the revival of mass movements aligned with the Congress Alliance tradition. By adopting the Freedom Charter, AZASO was further demonstrating the extent of interaction and influence by the ANC on the student movement.

Again, as argued in the Inaugural SASCO-Nelson Mandela Lecture, the interaction and influence partly explains why the "race–class and gender analytical approach… *became* a worldview and platform that was to inform its ideology, organisation, mobilisation and activities".[17] The transformation was not straightforward but characterised by political contest between the national liberation movements, in particular AZAPO and other Black Consciousness formations and the ANC, who wanted to reproduce their ideas within the student population.

In addition to these influences, the student movement in South Africa, as in many other parts of the world, gradually gravitated towards using Marxist-Leninist tools of analysis. More frequently, Marxist literature became increasingly popular with radical students in institutions of higher learning. The debate about the ideological character of the student movement is not frozen in history, but is forever present in the ranks of the student movement. Even at the time of activism of the author, the debate was alive, given permanency due to the very composition and character of students, who tend to come from different socio-economic backgrounds and after graduation assume different positions in society.

Re-emergence of mass mobilisation

The period between 1976 and 1991 saw South Africa undergoing serious crises again, with political changes and drastic changes in political student struggles. During this period, the liberation movement was revived and had a presence in various ways, through progressive mass movements at community and shop floor level. The ideals contained in the Freedom Charter increasingly appealed to the toiling masses, and at this stage it was clear domestically and internationally that the ANC, more than any other political formation, enjoyed widespread support from the South African people.

The student uprisings of 16 June 1976, led by high school students, became one of the key political moments in the history of South Africa's struggle for freedom. When the students fled from apartheid security agencies in the aftermath of these uprisings, some were welcomed by the ANC and its *Mkhonto weSizwe* military wing outside the country, and others sought exile and/or joined underground liberation movements. Later, in 1979, on the formation of the Congress of South African Students (COSAS, the successor of SASM), the direct hand of the ANC and its partners the SACP was quite apparent. Its first president, the late Ephraim Mogale, was an underground operative of the Communist Party, as were many others who helped form COSAS.

When the United Democratic Front (UDF) was founded in 1983, the student movement became an affiliate. A wide coalition of mass democratic formations, it also adopted the Freedom Charter and ran campaigns such as Release Mandela and held Anti-Republic Day demonstrations alongside the student movement. COSAS and AZASO, and later SANSCO, also organised solidarity campaigns under their worker federation, such as forerunner FOSATU and later COSATU. For instance, in 1981 COSAS and most of the mass movements were mobilised in a solidarity campaign to support struggles of workers in factories such as Fattis and Monis and Wilson Rowntree, where workers faced dismissals and bad working conditions.

Again, it was COSAS and AZASO that played a key role in the formation of the South African Youth Congress (SAYCO), a process that took five years to complete between 1982 and 1987. When the ANC Youth League (ANCYL) was re-launched in 1990, the student movement played a role in different ways.

In the course of engaging in broader questions of struggle, the student movement never lost sight of the conditions of the students on campuses or stopped tackling inappropriate sectoral policies in the education system. There are many progressive campaigns and policy propositions that have over the years originated in the ranks of students, and some of these find expression in official government policy today. For instance, the legalisation of student representative councils was a victory for democratising institutional governance, and the campaigns for greater institutional autonomy could mean that academic freedom was enhanced and a backward narrow managerialism challenged. COSAS campaigned for many years against the brutality of corporal punishment, now mercifully abolished. Campaigns around access, more funding and more support material for learning have yielded positive results and helped transform education sector policies.

Locating the student movement in the liberation struggle is a matter requiring careful treatment and consideration by historians.

The above historical account simply affirms that the student movement is a product of history as well as an initiative on the part of the oppressed. Even more profoundly, it gives practical testimony to the theory of the founding generation of SASO which concluded, quite correctly, that students are members of the community before they are members of institutions of learning.

A few basic lessons and observations can be made at this point:

- One can conclude that, throughout the evolution of the student movement, theory was met with practice by and large. It was the students who formed alliances with workers and youth. It was the students who connected with communities through the concepts of self-reliance and self-sufficiency, and later community service.

- Not only did the student movement influence the ANC and other liberation movements, these also had an impact on the orientation, policies and programmes of the student movement.

- The student movement itself was also a theatre for the battle of ideas. Among those were the contests among the well-known liberation movements which sought to influence the student movement in one way or another.

- The students have always sought to theorise, debate and think about the best ways to understand society, and have devised strategies to change it. They tend to have an appetite for abstract thinking as well as application. At times they illustrate in practical terms that theory can follow practice.

- It is apparent that the mainstream student movement that sought to challenge the system of apartheid and apartheid education gradually adopted and identified with the Charterists or the Congress tradition.

- The student movement has made a significant contribution to the broader struggle for freedom, as well as to changing higher education and improving the conditions of the students on campus.

- The student movement has had the ability to adapt and change over time and in different contexts, so that it remains relevant and discharges its responsibilities.

- The dynamism of the student movement is derived in part from its penchant for ideas and critical thinking. Not just any ideas, but progressive mobilising and transformational ideas that seek to understand changing reality. Although located in traditionally elitist institutions, the majority of students globally have identified themselves with popular struggles. This could be a function of heightened consciousness.

Contemporary student movement and the future

We have already stated that *wherever they appeared, the radical and progressive student movements of the world have sought to add impetus to social agency*. Accordingly, history places a heavy burden upon successive generations of students to continue in this tradition, especially when – as is the case in South Africa – it is one of heroic and triumphant feats.

Today the student movement evolves in a different socio-political milieu characterised by freedom and democracy as opposed to oppression and autocracy. The tasks and challenges, both subjective and objective, are vastly different from those preceding the two decades of universal suffrage and freedom.

At a subjective level, the contemporary student movement faces a serious challenge of decline, in terms of both the quality and quantity of members. The problem of decline is not a new problem *per se* and, I believe, is certainly not the greatest concern. The greatest concern is whether the progressive student movement can adapt and survive for another 60 years and so to its centenary and beyond.

Today, the political traditions of SASO are carried through the progressive student movement in the form of SASCO (a 1991 merger between a white liberal NUSAS and a black radical SANSCO) as well as COSAS. There are indeed other formations of students locally placed and some with a national footprint; however, these two organisations remain most visible of all. Of course, the youth movement as a whole can now be found in universities. Here one can cite the existence on campuses of the ANCYL, the Young Communist League and others. Could it be that adaptation means a return to the past, a period in 1948 when the ANCYL launched in Fort Hare University?

In the twenty-first century, society has changed dramatically. The role of science and technology has revolutionised the way human beings interact among themselves and with their environment. The technology is not the same as that of the 1960s, when there were no cell phones, no television and no internet. What was convenient then in terms of mobilisation, organisation and building an organisation may not be convenient today.

Equally, the nature and intensity of the battle of ideas has changed and so should those who mobilise to improve the human condition. In other words, the world has become more complex and yet full of opportunities to advance the struggle for a better society. The ANC has also changed tremendously and, at one hundred and one years, will surely continue to metamorphose in ways that greatly impact on the student and youth movement as a whole.

It is within this context that the student movement of today should strive to renew itself. The constant is change, and the student movement must find ways, as it did before, to grapple with a rapidly changing, increasingly unpredictable and complex inter-dependent world.

It is possible that the rapid modern technological platform of transmitting demo-bilising ideas affects the mobilisation capacity of the student movement, such that a hostile outcome is produced against its revolutionary and progressive ideas.

One contends that, for the reasons stated above, every society needs a student movement that will operate within the broad context of a progressive movement yet remain independent and never collapse formally into structured party political affili-ation. It must maintain this posture so that it continues to be a critical voice in the youth and liberation movement. For this reason, there is a role and a future for the student movement in South Africa.

The other pressing challenge is the dearth of a historiography of the student move-ment in South Africa. Arguably, its impact, place and contribution to the liberation history are under-researched and poorly documented. The danger about this limita-tion is that an important story about the evolution of the country and the struggle for freedom will be forgotten, or at worst lost completely. This problem partly arises from the fact that the student movement itself is usually underfunded and unable to archive properly and conduct proper handover processes. It could also be due to lack of funding in the research community or lack of innovation in terms of research areas. This is a challenge laid on the doorstep of the student movement, and perhaps it must rethink its structures, sources of funding and mobilisation strategies.

Conclusion

If the story of the student movement must be told, clearly and properly, then students must tell their own. This is a rich history which must partially define who we are, where we come from and where we ought to go.

As Mbeki put it:

> ...the fierce struggle we had to wage to win the right to determine our future was also a struggle to achieve the possibility to discover our past. Its victory gave us the possibility to assert the truth that our erstwhile overlord was as much a product of history as we were, and that we both were, in our different ways, makers of that history.[18]

This shows the importance of writing our own histories.

To put it another way, there is a need to rethink, more broadly, the role of history:

...a present-minded generation, interested mostly in the market and its utilitarian values, demonstrates an impatience with history. As a result, history is often peripheral...
The overall development since 1994 has been characterised by a growing 'non-use'
of history as well as by the declining prestige of the discipline... to what extent was
South African historical writing actually liberated with the fall of Apartheid?[19]

The above question and concern about history will require a separate treatment in
future. In the experience of the author of this chapter, an interesting phenomenon is
emerging in the South African public and the youth: there is an increasing demand
for the blind spots of history to be cleared. The curse and blessing of being the last
country to be freed is now experiencing its historical awakening. Hopefully the momentum will be sustained.

So indeed, in the 101 years of the ANC's existence, in a century of struggle for
national liberation, the student movement has been a reliable ally and source of
inspiration.

Endnotes

1 Maimela, D., 2011. The student movement and society. *Umrabulo*, (36), Q2 June.
2 Selassie quoted in Maimela, 2011, op. cit.
3 Nokwe, D., 1956. Problems of the Youth Movement. *Liberation*, (19), June.
4 Jacks quoted in Badat, S., 1999. *Black student politics, higher education and apartheid: From SASCO to SANSCO 1968–1990*. Pretoria: HSRC Press.
5 Badat, 1999, op. cit.
6 Ibid.
7 Ramphele, M., 1995. A life as cited. In Denis, P., 2010. Seminary networks and black consciousness in South Africa in the 1970s. *South African Historical Journal*, 62(1), p.172.
8 Denis, 2010, op. cit., p.172.
9 Glaser, C., 1998. 'We must infiltrate the tsotsis': School politics and youth gangs in Soweto, 1968–1976. *Journal of Southern African Studies*, 24(2), pp.301-323.
10 Note that SASM was founded in 1968 as African Student Movement and later changed to SASM. The chapter does not discuss the reasons for the change of name.
11 Cillie Report as cited in Glaser, 1998, op. cit.
12 Ibid.
13 Diseko, N.J., 1992. The origins and development of the South African Student's Move-ment (SASM): 1968–1976. *Journal of Southern African Studies*, 18(1), Special Issue: Social history of resistance in South Africa (March), p.59.

14 Ibid.

15 Maimela, D., 2012. Inaugural Nelson Mandela Lectured delivered at University of Johannesburg for SASCO Johannesburg Region.

16 Steve Biko made a Presidential Address in 1969 at the 1st National Formation School of SASO. In this chapter in *I write what I like*, it has a title: 'SASO – its role, its significance and its future' (Stubbs, A. (ed.), 2000. *I write what I like: Selected writings: Steve Biko*. Chicago: University Of Chicago Press, pp.3-8.)

17 Ibid, p.3.

18 Mbeki, T., 2004. Foreword to *The road to democracy in South Africa*. Volume 1 (1960–1970), pp. ix–xiii.

19 Stolten is quoted in Stolten, H.E. (ed.), 2007. *History in the new South Africa: An introduction*. pp.5-50.

CHAPTER 7

Through the shadow of death: the ANC's underground struggle

Siphamandla Zondi

The ANC at that time was in a very big lull. It was all quiet... We operated a cell of three people and I was the only female. It was the most dangerous work of the ANC underground. – Dillies Maboshane Mahlatsi, SADET Oral History Project.[1]

You know by 1963/1964 the entire leadership of the Transvaal Indian Congress and the Transvaal Indian Youth Congress were either arrested, banned or in exile. Others were not, but were too scared to come out into the open... In some ways, it was safer to work underground than to work in an open organisation ... there was no formal structure. As progressives, we kept in touch as a family, visited each other, talked to each other, kept contact with the outside world, visited people on Robben Island, tried to organise funding... – Prema Naidoo, SADET Oral History Project.[2]

Our problem was not whether to fight, but was how to continue the fight. – Nelson Mandela, Testimony to the Treason Trial, 1956–1960.

Introduction

The banning of the African National Congress (ANC) on 7 April 1960, the incarceration of its top leaders, the banishment of its activists and the closure of its offices seriously disrupted the political programme and the very presence of the ANC on the ground. For a time, especially in the immediate aftermath of these measures and because of sustained surveillance and clampdown by the security forces of the apartheid government, the basic structures through which the ANC mobilised were either destroyed or weakened, sometimes severely.

This is what Dillies Mahlatsi means by the situation on the ground being 'all quiet'. As Naidoo's testimony above indicates, many ANC supporters and activists who were not banned, killed or arrested were simply paralysed by fear. This was fear of being banned, killed or arrested. It was fear of being spied upon or being 'sold out' to the notorious security police by their acquaintances. Some even feared leaving their houses for work during the day or sleeping at night as rumours of police brutality spread, including the fear of being buried alive.[3]

However, the lull was not as significant as it is sometimes thought in that success in clamping down upon known structures and leaders of the ANC only helped accelerate the growth of the underground structures and leadership. In fact, from interviews conducted it emerges that many activists and leaders simply went into hiding and concealed their activism, even as they increased the intensity of the mobilisation of disobedience, canvassing for ANC support and recruiting activists.

The impression that active resistance lost momentum from 1960 until the sudden explosion of the Soweto uprising in 1976 is an exaggeration, for it is clear from oral evidence that activism had become so mass-based by 1960 that it continued and later went underground, while facing the many new obstacles presented by the brutal regime. It is evident that the spirit of resistance found other avenues to express itself, including cultural activities, infiltration of South Africa from neighbouring countries and the creation of new student and youth formations, including the South African Students Organisation (SASO) in the 1960s.[4] Many of these activities were not really led by the ANC, but it is the organisation that supported and provided further leadership once volunteers had started them.

This chapter posits that the ability of the apartheid regime to annihilate the structures of resistance was limited by its ability to deal only with leaders it knew, while the mass of activists, often working under their own volition, with some guidance by loose networks of leaders at local community levels, were hard to detect or pin down for any violation of draconian laws.

In this sense, the Soweto uprisings were a culmination of a decade-long process of conscientisation and rebuilding mass structures of resistance by the ANC, other organisations and volunteers, leading to the buildup of resistance against Afrikaans in 1971/1972.[5] They were thus not a sudden explosion of resistance but rather were connected with the evolution of the ANC underground and other forms of mass resistance after 1960, including the Black Consciousness Movement and SASO. State repression and the 1960s state of the emergency had a significant impact on ANC structures, particularly leadership and aboveground structures. They caused citizens to fill the void through voluntary political activism, preventing elitism and a lull in political resistance.

The argument of this chapter is inspired by theoretical work on hidden transcripts of resistance. James Scott's *Domination and Arts of Resistance: Hidden Transcripts*[6] aptly describes how the relationship between the dominant and the dominated is mediated by both public roles and hidden discourses (he calls them 'transcripts'), that seek to secretly undermine the dominating power. He analyses what seemed to be a successful clampdown on a theoretical proposition that was unable to openly resist the ruthless power of the authorities.

The dominated feigned deference, they created secret discourse to critique power behind the dominators' backs, and they invented anonymous gossip, folktales, songs, jokes and theatre, using ambiguity to resist domination. This book also analyses the hidden transcripts of the dominant or powerful force, which included ostentatious display of power in parades and ceremonies and crude deployment of force to ensure subordination.

This recognition of voices and actions of the dominated as agency from below underlies my analysis of the underground experience, hence the reliance on oral history, mainly from the ground-breaking subaltern project by the South African Democracy Education Trust. A careful analysis of the insights from participants, many of whom were ordinary activists, suggests that the reduction in overt political activities led to growth in covert underground political work, drawing in younger people, women and rural folk in larger numbers than before.

This means the blow to the ANC's aboveground struggle enabled activists and ordinary citizens to help shift the struggle during the 1960s and 1970s to an organised underground terrain. The liberation movements, including the ANC, were forced to support this or risk becoming irrelevant. Through this support that they were quick to provide, the underground struggle grew in the 1980s to become a significant factor alongside the armed struggle, exile politics and internationalism.

Escalation in state repression and resistance

The period between 1948 and 1960 saw an increase in mass resistance to oppression with what were called 'convulsive campaigns' in the form of bus boycotts, anti-pass protests, women's protests, worker strikes, peasant revolts and mass demonstrations.[7] Active participants in the resistance movements generally regard this as a heroic period, with major advances and growth in the size, number and intensity of open and organised resistance.

The political situation had changed with the electoral victory of the Nationalist Party in 1948 and the formal introduction of the ideology of apartheid as a total programme of societal change designed to make white interests paramount and dominant. A brand of nationalism, born out of exclusion of poor Afrikaners from the British colonial political economy, was based on a belief that the only way for Afrikaners to prosper and dominate was if they gained state power and used it to privilege themselves and dominate blacks.

'Apartheid, therefore, is more than mere racial discrimination or casual exploitation of one group by another,' contends Magubane. 'It is a strict ideology of white supremacy, racial oppression, and exploitation, whose logical extremity – genocide – is tempered by the need for African labour.'[8] For this reason, Afrikaner nationalists tried to make apartheid pervasive by imposing it on urban planning and human settlement, education, health, social welfare, travel and transport, leisure activities, birth and death.[9]

A scholarly perspective that gives space to the hidden transcripts of the struggle, the efforts of the subalterns, generally, must resist the temptation to view events on the basis of the propaganda of the dominant. This is because Eurocentricism is not something that is generally declared, but it lives on invisibly through assumptions of rationality and common sense among mainstream scholars.

This leads to either scepticism or neglect of the power and effect of the agency of the dominated in response to the visibly strong power of the dominant force in society. This is apparent in mainstream scholarship on the struggle, in which are prevalent dichotomies between the uncelebrated underground resistance and celebrated above-ground political activism. I suggest that, fundamentally, the problem is that the former is associated with uncivilised, unlawful and shadowy politics of norm-breaking, while the latter is assumed to be civilised norm-creation.

Notwithstanding the rise of 'histories from below' involving social historians such as Peter Delius and Philip Bonner, SADET, UNISA's Hidden Histories and others, pro-normality perspectives – both Africanist and Eurocentricist – continue disproportionately to influence scholarship on resistance to apartheid. This conservative slant in South African scholarship continues to limit the spread of alternative perspectives, such as Marxist theories, subaltern studies, decolonial thought, post-colonial studies, radical feminist perspectives and other epistemologies.

Thanks to efforts to unearth the buried voices of history, especially about the struggle, there is a basis for giving expression to subaltern interpretations of historical complexity. The studies mentioned above, and T. Karis and G. Carter's publication series entitled *From Protest to Challenge*, provide rare written records on the struggle. Another initiative called the Wits History Workshop has, through its interviews initiative, collected 'voices from below', but it is the *South African Democracy Education Trust*, with over six thick volumes of analysis, that has cemented the importance of oral evidence in analysing a period marked by secrecy and propaganda.

The underground struggle involved the trespassing onto structured space in the form of protests and transgression of legitimate normative order in the form of subversive activities. On coming to power, the Nationalists immediately outlawed the Communist Party of South Africa, a key ally of the ANC, through the Suppression of Communism Act of 1949. Thus began a clampdown on institutions and leaders of the anti-apartheid resistance movement.

In doing so, the Nationalist Party had decided to act against the winds of political change that were beginning to sweep through colonial territories, leading to independence. This forced the resistance movement to increase its resistance, and in 1949 the ANC adopted a programme of action which entailed militant activities on a larger scale and in greater frequency than seen before.

These activities culminated in the Defiance Campaign launched in 1951 by which the ANC and its allies set about defying 'unjust laws' in civil disobedience campaigns. This escalated resistance to levels not seen before and in turn the apartheid regime upscaled suppression of dissent and general oppression. The activities spilled over to matters of capital–labour relations with a number of militant strikes.

Parts of the countryside, such as Pondoland, Zeerust and Ga-Matlala, also saw radicalisation of resistance in militant peasant revolts that surprised the apartheid regime. Now it was urban blacks who were brewing trouble for them. In the same decade, women made a bold march on the Union Buildings to demand their rights and defy pass laws.

In the state clampdown that began in 1949, many activists and leaders were harassed, gaoled, or killed. In 1957 alone, 14 500 000 people were committed for trial, of whom 1 448 582 were convicted for political crimes. This meant an average of 4 200 were being arrested and tried daily.[10]

Oliver Tambo, a key ANC leader, saw this growth in mass struggle and resistance to the apartheid regime as fraught with challenges relating to the difficulty of giving guidance and leadership in the form of an intelligent paradigm and strategy for the many activities and tactics undertaken.[11] He argued that the ANC leaders should think ahead in order to give effective leadership to the next phases of the struggle.

In 1955, he was already worried that the masses might, on their own, shift one gear up in terms of modes of resistance and he probably feared a spontaneous shift towards armed resistance. 'The situation in South Africa today,' he argued, 'is such that alternative modes of struggle have been reduced to the barest minimum, and we shall not wait long for the day when only one method will be left to the oppressed people of this country.'[12]

It was on this basis that forward thinking about armed struggle and the underground began, at least at the highest level of ANC leadership. The split within the ANC that gave birth to the Pan Africanist Congress must have also been read as an indication that there were some within the ANC who were impatient for some form of radicalisation of the struggle or elements of it.[13]

Indeed, with many top ANC leaders and its great minds facing the Treason Trial in 1959, the leadership baton passed to the hands of those who could take the lead. 'In town and countryside, events were unfolding that necessitated the ANC to tail-end community confrontations, rather than guide them.'[14]

This was of great concern to Tambo and other leaders, but what worried them more was that many community structures or branches of the ANC were battling because of a need for national guidance and support. Based on recent history that suggested no single blow would cause the apartheid regime to acquiesce, the ANC under the leadership of Tambo and Duma Nokwe argued for a multi-pronged struggle strategy that would allow ANC structures on the ground to engage in a variety of struggles and to focus more on quietly recruiting activists.

The decision of the ANC national leadership to make sure that its leaders were the most visible in the community would explain the ease with which the apartheid security forces were able to severely weaken the aboveground struggle. That they had also decided to build branches and recruit large numbers of sympathisers, however, meant that with the leaders gone there were activists and branches that would become the backbone of the underground struggle.

Before turning to analyse in some detail this mode of struggle I make the point that part of the challenge is that the aboveground struggle had been the focus of both the ANC and the regime, creating a sense that it was the most significant, and therefore its destruction led to a collapse in resistance. The story of the underground struggle on the basis of active participants illuminates what researches like Vinthagen saw as historical battles between social forces which decide who and what belongs to the 'underground' or the 'normality' – the affirmation of one terrain of struggle and minimisation of another.

In the case of South Africa, this comes together with the dominance of Eurocentric ideas about what is a normal and civilised form of politics, and to treat all resistance to a minority white rule of apartheid with some caution, giving the political underground the least credit in the greater scheme. In this sense, the hidden transcripts of the dominant voices in the history of the struggle, in the disciplines of both politics and history, are a form of a subtle assertion of the mastery of the powerful over the powerless.[15]

Some ANC activists in exile and in armed struggle had such an exaggerated sense of the importance of the aboveground terrain that the underground became obscured and somewhat forgettable. 'We always make a terrible mistake of thinking that the ANC is those who were visible in exile,' writes Joe Mathews, 'But we left hundreds of thousands of people, the ANC members, here in South Africa ... And we forget that all the activists of the movement were basically in the country.'[16]

One key reason the bans would not eliminate political activism associated with the ANC was that, in the 1950s, various loose associations and forums engaged in local struggles, especially around state services in townships. There was also an impact of the Bantu Authorities Act on livestock farming in the countryside, with uprisings in Pondoland and Thembuland in the modern-day Eastern Cape, Zeerust and Phokeng in the North West, Vhembe in Venda and Ga-Matlala near present-day Polokwane.[17]

Through these localised and widespread struggles the ANC (and to some extent, the PAC and other liberation movements later) existed both in formal structures and non-formally in associated structures that were formed as part of local communities' own activism.[18]

In parallel to these rural struggles was a rise in worker-based urban and peri-urban resistance, organised around issues of working conditions, the quality of employment, living conditions and apartheid policies. They too created many auxiliary structures, including committees and forums that sustained the political momentum.[19] These galvanised urban communities to such an extent that the banning of the ANC had little if any material effect on popular mobilisation.

The implication of this is that the arrest of elected leaders and the banning of the formal organisation simply forced the ANC-aligned political activism to exist only through these non-formal structures. This is what Dennis Goldberg meant by the 'ripeness' of the countryside in the late 1950s for a variety of rural struggles. The aboveground resistance generated such political consciousness that underground activists would find in rural communities many villagers who were ready to participate in the underground political activities, including the transmission of goods, as well as those across the borders ready to join the ANC and PAC in exile.[20] Even the ANC leadership found itself overwhelmed by 'hunger for action' in resistance to encroaching apartheid in the rural areas, as people continued to demand arms and space to resist well into the late 1960s.[21]

Astute and streetwise operatives like Pharaphare Mothupi exploited this 'ANC spirit' in communities to recruit trainee soldiers for Umkhonto Wesizwe (MK), the armed wing of the ANC. The likes of Nelson Diale were actually trained for sabotage in the villages of Ga-Sekhukhune in Limpopo in the mid 1960s. A network of cell groups connected many of these activists who worked mostly as individuals or small groups taking advantage of the 'ripeness' of the countryside and townships to keep the ANC struggle alive. They found it provided links between the ANC activism of the pre-1960 period, when youth-led political activism culminated in the 1976 student revolts.

Samson Ratshivhanda Ndou, for instance, paints a picture of a hive of activities managed by elaborate networks through which he and his comrades were able to shuffle between what are now known as Limpopo, Gauteng, North West and the Eastern Cape provinces, addressing meetings and giving leadership to political programmes. This story is corroborated by the likes of Lawrence and Rita Nzanga.[22] The continued existence of ANC-led activism in non-formal structures and forms deceived the apartheid regime for a short while, before another state clampdown in 1969.

The underground prior to 1976

There is growing evidence that there was a strategic decision taken at the highest leadership level of the ANC to keep the movement alive by immediately and deliberately moving underground. As OR Tambo's statements quoted above show, the ANC responded to community and individual initiatives against growing oppression, and filled the void left by the arrest of ANC leaders. Had the ANC not responded positively and harnessed this energy it would have been unable to control the underground struggle the way it eventually did.

Describing its strategic response to the proclamation of a state of emergency and the declaration of the ANC as unlawful, which happened after the Sharpeville massacre in 1960, Nelson Mandela explained during the Rivonia Trial four years later that:

> My colleagues and I, after careful consideration, decided that we would not obey this decree. The African people were not part of government and did not make the laws by which they were governed. We believed in the words of the Universal Declaration of Human Rights that 'the will of the people shall be the basis of authority of the Government,' and for us to accept the banning was equivalent to accepting the silencing of the Africans for all time. The ANC refused to dissolve, but instead went underground. We believed it was out of duty to preserve this organisation, which had been built up with almost fifty years of unremitting toil.[23]

Thus, its leaders gave a new strategic orientation to the ANC and the struggles of communities and individuals. It did this for its own survival as the leader of the struggle for freedom in South Africa. In the same testimony, Mandela went on to say: 'What were we, the leaders of our people, to do? Were we to give in to the show of force and the implied threat against future action, or were we to fight it and, if so, how?'[24]

They, of course, refused to surrender after 50 years of 'unremitting toil' for freedom and democracy. 'Our problem,' he explained, 'was not whether to fight, but was how to continue the fight.'[25]

The armed struggle was chosen because violence had become institutionalised by the regime in response to mass mobilisation. The exile front was forced on leaders who escaped mass arrests and the underground was partly forced by the illegality of the movement and partly occasioned by a strategic choice to remain rooted in the masses of the people. It was decided that the ANC would have neglected its historic responsibilities were it to leave it to the people to organise, mobilise and put up the fight on their own, and at a time when the apartheid regime was becoming increasingly ruthless in its suppression of the struggle.

Actually, in the Treason Trial testimony, Mandela saw the armed struggle and the underground resistance as different parts of the same strategy. Both were a response to a realisation that the time comes in the life of the oppressed when there remain only two choices – to submit or fight. As their strategy document drawn up after consultations in May and June of 1960s declares, 'We shall not submit and we have no choice but to hit back by all means in our power in defence of our people, our future, and our freedom.'[26] Mandela was on the side of those who argued that it was also time for an armed struggle. In this sense, 'all means' included armed and unarmed, open and secret activities, activities inside and outside the country. That was what the ANC as a mass political organisation could realistically do at the time.

The plan was also that the banning would not drastically change the nature of the ANC or its political ideology. The underground work would not be allowed to deviate from the organisation's political ideology of finding peaceful or negotiated ways of helping to bring about popular democracy. Thus, the ANC needed to move swiftly to remain the leader of the resistance. The type of armed struggle decided upon was sabotage, not only because it ensured that civilians would not be targeted deliberately, but also because it would become a source of inspiration for the oppressed to ensure that they could still be mobilised for political activism.

It is on this basis that the ANC president, OR Tambo, was able to declare before African presidents in 1975 that while international isolation and armed struggle would help bring about change in Africa, the real hope was that, 'the revolutionary mood of the oppressed of our country is surging forward.'[27]

This was the ubiquitous mood of resistance that enabled the ANC, when it took advantage of it, to make a comeback from the state clampdown of 1960.

As Mandela insisted during the Treason Trial, 'the ANC remained a mass political body of Africans only carrying on the type of political work they had conducted prior to 1961.'[28]

A secret meeting of ANC leaders had failed to agree to make the armed struggle a policy (a decision that could be made by conference, and with the organisation banned, such a conference could not be convened).[29]

The ANC's *Strategy and Tactics* document of 1969 underlined the point that Mandela made in the dock, that the political struggles conducted through fraternal organisations and any structure that could be found useful at community level were considered critical to keeping the banned ANC alive. It also directed ANC members and activists who worked underground to keep masses galvanised to continuously resist the authorities. In the following years these activists would work through the Black Consciousness Movement to keep masses mobilised around their duty, to further the struggle started by banned organisations. This is why the communities were ready to respond positively to the outbreak of student uprisings in 1976, a 'heightened political ferment' that was also the basis for the ANC's belief that the masses were 'the Main Force of Liberation.'[30]

The primary task of ANC leaders assigned to work on the underground was to keep the body alive and connected to the soul of the struggle, namely the battlefields in townships and villages. The likes of Lawrence Nzanga and Samson Nzou went about addressing meetings of youth, women and traditional structures and mobilising support behind programmes mostly designed in exile. Seeing the vacuum created by the incarceration of leaders and the fact that many others had been forced into exile, experienced activists who went underground, such as John Nkadimeng, John Phala and Albertinah Sisulu established, managed and led underground networks of leaders who helped multiply the number of underground structures and activists. They formed committees, issued instructions about how the networks were going to operate, resolved disputes and conflicts, and laid out the rules of operation.

In some cases, the underground network was sufficiently sophisticated to have hubs and spokes dynamically linked to each other and capable of mobilising people in large areas without detection. The Johannesburg hub of the network, in which Nkadimeng and Sisulu were leaders, would grow into a pivot for the regional networks covering Natal, the Orange Free State and the Cape. As Nkadimeng recalls: 'We cut off this national committee thing so that the enemy is not going to pounce on us and destroy us again. Meanwhile we created this regionally linked structure ... in accordance with the M-plan.'[31]

On this basis, the entire underground network was able to communicate with relative safety and secrecy, sending messages between them and the leadership on Robben Island or in exile. The regional structures were linked to the Transvaal body, which acted as an apex of the network through chairpersons of regional bodies. Leaders from various parts would travel to Soweto for interaction and consultations and to receive new orders.[32]

Underground structures would, by the late 1960s, become useful for reintroducing ANC activists released from prison.[33] This would be a major boost for underground activism because the released prisoners were leaders with experience in popular mobilisation. They also helped replenish activist leadership depleted by mass bannings, arrests and exile. They were given a heroes' welcome back to their communities and these turned out to be rallies of sorts.[34] Those who had held significant political positions prior to their arrest would become even more useful for managing the whole underground network.

This was the case with Henry Makgothi, who was the ANC Youth League president in the 1950s and a member of the National Secretariat before the Rivonia Trial, a body created to understudy the National Executive Committee. He was arrested during a police swoop on ANC leaders in May 1963 and sentenced to 10 years. On release, he became a major catalyst for a nationwide underground network of cells of activists working closely with MK operatives engaged in campaigns of sabotage.

In some cases, on release from jail, activists would be instructed to skip the country immediately. There was, however, fear in certain instances that losing activists to the external mission would not only weaken the activities of the underground struggle but also demoralise the large numbers of volunteers recruited to underground activism.[35]

James April remembers an experienced ANC activist and a lawyer for many detainees, Albie Sachs, complaining about the decision by activists to leave for exile quickly after release from prison, saying, 'It will be alright to go out and save your skins and all that. But what effect will it have on the morale of the people here? We must think of that because a lot of our leaders have left. And that is already demoralising.' These underground leaders could understand cases in which cadres were earmarked by the leadership in exile for training in order to be used for specific purposes or for deployment in exile duties. Their concern was that many were skipping borders out of curiosity or personal circumstances rather than as part of a political plan. 'If you run away,' cautioned Sachs, 'although you can still work here – it will have a very bad effect on morale.'[36]

James April, a member of the Coloured People's Congress (CPC), remembers the vibrancy of the ANC's underground structures in Cape Town as the result of the dedicated work of the likes of Barney Desai, Reggie September, Elijah Loza and Archie Sibeko. He recalls that as the main leaders were discovered by the Special Branch and arrested, the baton for leadership passed to the inner circle of members, which was always being replenished by new members. Thus, sometimes frequently and sometimes not, members moved from the outer circle into the inner circle. The CPC became a useful platform for underground work because it had not been banned, thus allowing underground activists to use its offices to communicate, print leaflets and hide from spies.

The links between the internal underground networks and the international campaign had also been strong from the outset. For instance, Joe Mathews recounts the many occasions when he and others, like Johnny Makhathini and Robert Resha, moved around the continent and the world making sense of major developments and discussions, including those of the international communist movement, and reporting back to internal structures in underground meetings.

The idea was that, although it was underground, the internal leadership should not be cut off from the thinking, developments and decisions of the ANC in exile, or the rest of the progressive movements in the world. Underground leaders like Samson Ndou and Theophilus Cholo, Henry Makgothi, John Nkadimeng, Joe Gqabi, Indres Naidoo and Griffits Mxenge communicated with Thabo Mbeki and Jacob Zuma in

Swaziland and Mozambique and other senior ANC leaders in Zambia and Tanzania, thus bringing the underground struggle into the centre of high-level political discussions and strategising.[37]

The underground structures were crucial for managing the very tricky and risky business of infiltrating operatives of the MK and ANC activists and for sending cadres out of the country. Lawyers who worked with detainees, defending them for political crimes, were themselves part of the underground structures, men like Advocate Albie Sachs, Dullar Omar and Babla Cachalia; shop owners like Abbas Gadief and other professionals like Dr Jassat, Mosie Moola and Molvi Cachalia. They were instrumental in the movement of underground activists who the security police were already looking for.[38]

Conclusion

The underground struggle required a good understanding of the cause of struggle, superior skills in popular mobilisation, the ability to disguise and the agility of top leadership in the face of ever-changing political fortunes. It became a strategic site not just for keeping the struggle alive but also for improving the mass-based resistance. Replenished by the release of gaoled leaders, the underground network of cells would benefit immensely from their political knowledge and connections with the ANC in exile.

As Mandela's court testimony paraphrased above put it, the ANC refused to acquiesce to the state's intention to kill activism through arrests and bans by shifting the struggle to the underground. By so doing it opened a new and powerful terrain of the struggle, one that involved widespread and mass-based conscientisation, recruitment, training, couriering and reconnaissance on behalf of MK, linking exile and domestic politics and volunteer work. In this sense, it may be that the ANC was more effective in prosecuting the struggle and the mobilisation of masses underground than it had been when it was engaged in activism in the open.

While this was largely spontaneous underground work driven by activists who were less prominent than those arrested and banned in 1960, the ANC was wise enough to seize the opportunity to lead and give direction to this mass struggle, thus helping to formalise and extend it. Many of these activists were ANC-aligned, supporters and even members. In this sense, the ANC could claim responsibility for part of this voluntarism.

Endnotes

1   SADET, 2008. Dillies Maboshane Mahlatsi. In South African Democracy Trust (eds), 2008. *The road to democracy: South Africans telling their stories*. Vol. 1. Cape Town: Zebra Press, pp.175-8.

2   SADET, 2008. Prema Naidoo. In South African Democracy Trust, 2008, op. cit., pp.351-5.

3   Interview with Nelson Diale, 8 July 2001, Ga-Masemola, Limpopo, SADET Oral History Project.

4   George Nene recalls a hive of activities by young people, from study groups using Eastern European material and Marxist literature in Soweto and later at the University of Zululand where he studied with the likes of Siphiwe Nyanda and Welile Nhlapho to cultural groups that disguised political mobilization in the late 1960s. SASO increasingly came to take centre stage in this below-ground political resistance. Interview with Ambassador George Nene, 18 February 2013, Pretoria, IGD's diplomatic memoirs project.

5   See George Nene, op. cit.

6   Scott, J., 1990. *Domination and arts of resistance: Hidden transcripts*. New York: Yale University Press.

7   Quoted in Callinicos, L., 2004. *Oliver Tambo: Beyond the Engeli Mountains*. Cape Town: David Philip, p.244.

8   Magubane, B.M., 1979. *The political economy of race and class in South Africa*. New York: Monthly Review Press, p. 250.

9   Ibid.

10 Figures quoted from Magubane, B.M., n.d. The report of the South African Commissioner of Police. *Political Economy*, p.307.

11 Callinicos, 2004, op. cit., p. 224.

12 Callinicos, 2004, op. cit., p. 225.

13 Callinicos, 2004, op. cit., p. 248.

14 Ibid.

15 The idea of hidden transcripts of the powerful is borrowed from Scott, 1992, op. cit.

16 Interview with Joe Mathews by Bernard Magubane and Gregory Houston, 9 March 2004, Pretoria, SADET Oral History Project.

17 For fuller discussion of these struggles on the basis of interviews with surviving participants of these struggles, see Zondi, S., 2004. Peasant struggles of the 1950s: GaMatlala and Zeerust; and Ntsebenza, S. & Ntsebenza, L., n.d. Rural resistance in Mpondoland and Thembuland, 1960–1963. Both chapters in South African Democracy Trust (eds), 2008. *The road to democracy in South Africa*, pp.147-76 and 177-208.

18 See, for instance, the interview with Thomas Nkobi, conducted by Philip Bonner, Shell

House, Johannesburg, 24 November 1993; interview with Govan Mbeki, conducted by Sifiso Ndlovu and Greg Houston, Port Elizabeth, 18 November 2000, SADET Oral Project; and interview with John Nkadimeng, conducted by Sifiso Ndlovu, 13, 18 and 27 March 2001, Johannesburg, SADET Oral History Project.

19 Interview with Mathews Oliphant, conducted by Jabulani Sithole, 3 February 2005, SADET Oral History Project.

20 Interview with Dennis Goldberg, conducted by Peter Delius, London, 24 August 1994, Wits History Workshop. Interview with Samson Ratshivhanda Ndou, conducted by Siphamandla Zondi and Norman Mulaudzi, 21 May 2001, Thohoyandou, SADET Oral History Project.

21 Magubane, B., Bonner, P., Sithole, J., Delius, P., Cherry, J., Gibbs, P. & April, T., n.d. The turn to armed struggle. In South African Democracy Trust (eds), 2008. *The road to democracy*, pp.53-145.

22 See interviews with them at SADET Oral History Project.

23 *Nelson Mandela's Testimony to the Treason Trial, 1956–1960*. Available at http://www. anc.org.za/show.php?id=3743 [Accessed 12 July 2012].

24 Ibid.

25 Ibid.

26 Ibid.

27 *Speech by OR Tambo at the ninth ordinary session of the Council of Ministers of the Organisation of African Unity, 7–10 April 1975, Dar es Salaam*. Available at: http:// www.anc.org.za/show.php?id=4326 [Accessed 2 August 2011].

28 *Nelson Mandela's Testimony to the Treason Trial, 1956–1960*. Available at http://www. anc.org.za/show.php?id=3743 [Accessed 12 July 2012].

29 Interview with John Nkadimeng.

30 ANC, n.d. *Strategy and Tactics of the ANC*. Available at www.marxists.org/subject/africa/anc/strategy-tactics.htm [Accessed 2 August 2012].

31 Interview with John Nkadimeng.

32 Ibid.

33 Interview with Samson Ratshivhanda Ndou.

34 See Houston, G., 2004. The post-Rivonia ANC and SACP underground. In South African Democracy Trust (eds), 2008. *The road to democracy*, pp.643-59.

35 See the biography of James April, in South African Democracy Trust (eds), 2008. *The road to democracy*, pp.52-7.

36 Ibid.

37 Interview with John Nkadimeng. Interview with Bambela Manci, conducted by Sifiso Ndlovu, 8 March and 14 June 2001, Roodepoort, SADET Oral History Project

38 Houston, 2004, op. cit., p.649.

CHAPTER 8

The fourth pillar: a century of solidarity in ANC politics

Essop Pahad, Chris Landsberg and Eddy Maloka

Introduction

South Africa's democratic breakthrough in 1994 did not fall from the sky; it came about through long and hard struggle, including the most unprecedented international solidarity movement in world affairs, and it should be remembered that international solidarity represented the fourth pillar of the African National Congress's struggle. The international solidarity movement against white minority domination is almost as old as the ANC as various pockets of the international community, spread across continents and countries, pushed for, and ultimately succeeded in prompting political changes in South Africa long before the start of the democratisation process in 1994. Sanctions, isolation, sports, cultural and academic boycotts, and arms and oil embargoes were critical tools of international solidarity.

International solidarity against apartheid marked the fourth pillar of struggle,[1] a key feature of which was the economic front, and on this score we witnessed numerous conferences dealing with implementation of sanctions; the role of trans-national corporations; seminars on loans to and disinvestments from; and determining the socio-economic implications of apartheid. Later on, by the 1970s onwards, conferences against nuclear collaboration became a central focus.

The international anti-apartheid crusade focused on a vast array of topics, such as discrimination and colonialism; support for the victims of apartheid; trade union actions against apartheid; conditions of prisons and human rights violations of prisoners; NGO conferences for action against apartheid; international youth and student solidarity with the oppressed people of South Africa; the exploitation and oppression of children under apartheid; strategies for resistance against apartheid; the role and position of women under apartheid; culture against apartheid; education against apartheid; campaigns against apartheid sports; and the mass media and apartheid.

In the fourth pillar, internationalism, international solidarity and pan-African unity and cohesion occupied a central place in the strategy, tactics and principles of the national liberation and working-class movements in South Africa. Anti-colonial, anti-imperialist interaction between political organisations in South Africa with those in India and Africa can be traced to the 1880s. At the time of Mahatma Ghandi's political activities in South Africa, relations were developed between the Indian National Congress of India and the Indian Congress in South Africa.

A struggle anchored at home

The party-to-party relationship between the congress movements in South Africa with that of the Indian National Congress of India is one of the most enduring and oldest party-to-party relationships in the world. At the ANC's inaugural conference, in 1912, representatives from neighbouring countries were present.

The Communist Party of South Africa (CPSA) (1921) and its successor the South African Communist Party (SACP) played an exceptionally prominent role in promoting, defending and enhancing the theory and practice of proletarian internationalism. Critical to this approach was solidarity with the Soviet Union and the international working class movement, as well as anti-colonial and anti-imperialist struggles worldwide. Throughout its history the Communist Party was greatly influenced by the Second Comintern Congress of July 1920.

It is worth recalling some parts of the thesis on the national question adopted at that congress. That thesis had a profound impact on the thinking and activities of communists in South Africa and the world. As Brian Bunting points out in his biography of Moses Kotane:

> Point 4 of the thesis on the national question set out the perspectives of the movement as follows: 'The policy of the Communist International on the National and Colonial questions must be chiefly to bring about a union of the proletarian and working masses of all nations and countries for a joint revolutionary struggle leading to the overthrow of capitalism, without which national inequality and oppression cannot be abolished.[2]

The thesis distinguished sharply between proletarian internationalism and petty-bourgeois nationalism. Point 10 of the thesis declares:

> Petty-bourgeois nationalism proclaims as internationalism the mere recognition of the equality of nations, and nothing more. Quite apart from the fact that this recog-

nition is purely verbal, petty-bourgeois nationalism preserves national self-interest intact, whereas proletarian internationalism demands, first, that the interests of the proletarian struggle in any one country should be subordinated to the interests of that struggle on a worldwide scale...[3]

Point 11 places upon the Communist Parties of all countries the responsibility of assisting the bourgeois-democratic liberation movement in the more backward countries, and of establishing the closest possible alliance between the Communist Parties of the metropolitan countries and the revolutionary peasant movements in the colonies and backward countries.

The CPSA and later the SACP never flinched (even under conditions of illegality) from defending the Soviet Union and other socialist countries in Europe, Cuba, China and Vietnam. Unremitting, unqualified and uncritical support and solidarity with the Soviet Union was the foundation on which the South African Communists developed their internationalist consciousness.

In turn, the Soviet Union offered the struggle in South Africa unstinting, unqualified and immense political material and international solidarity. With historical hindsight one could be critical of such a relationship.

The banning of the ANC in 1960 and the formation of *Umkhonto we Sizwe*, in 1961, made urgent the need to strengthen international solidarity with the South African struggle exponentially and qualitatively. MK cadres needed to be trained in the science of military warfare and guerrilla war. Some of the countries that heeded this call were Algeria, Egypt, Sudan, Morocco, People's Republic of China, the Soviet Union and other socialist countries. Without this support in the early 1960s it would have been exceedingly difficult to build the people's army as a selfless, courageous and cohesive fighting force.

In exile, the ANC, SACP and SACTU embarked on a concerted, concentrated campaign for the international isolation of racist apartheid South Africa. These efforts were met with hostility from the major Western powers. It is worth pondering that at the time when these major Western powers were ready to abuse the UN Security Council by imposing sanctions on countries such as Gaddafi's Libya, Iran, Syria and Northern Sudan, and bring about regime change, they refused to take any action against an oppressive racist order.

In those extremely difficult days in exile the ANC was superbly led by OR Tambo.[4] He gave his energy, drive, strength, intellectual capacity and unmatched leadership to build the ANC underground and MK, as well as to develop one of the most powerful and influential international solidarity movements, the anti-apartheid movement, the world has seen.[5]

To win support for the ANC from some African countries was a serious challenge.

These countries were more favourably disposed to the PAC due to their anti-communist posture and erroneous belief that the PAC was more committed to pan-African unity.[6] There were also very strenuous efforts made to impose a false unity on the ANC and PAC. They conveniently ignored the earlier attempts that were made by the formation of the South African United Front after the Sharpeville massacre. The SAUF comprised the ANC, PAC, South African Indian Congress and the South-West African National Union. That front was dissolved due to the behaviour and the role of the PAC. Behind the back of the United Front, the PAC representatives worked for privileged contacts with governments and public organisations abroad.

The ANC gradually won over the majority of African countries due to the escalation of the struggle at home, actions of MK, the support of Sweden, the Soviet Union and other progressive forces, international organisations such as the World Peace Council, Afro-Asian People's Solidarity Organisation, World Federation of Democratic Youth, World Federation of Trade Unions, International Union of Students and the international Union of Socialist Youth and above all the unrelenting work of the ANC led by OR Tambo. The work of the ANC was greatly facilitated by the hard-won independence of Guinea-Bissau and Cape Verde, Angola, Mozambique, Zimbabwe and Namibia.

The sports, cultural and academic boycott of apartheid as well as the boycott of South African products grew in scope and impact due to the work of the ANC, African countries and the worldwide anti-apartheid movement.

The ANC and its allies also offered solidarity and support to anti-fascist struggles in Spain and Greece, the heroic and courageous Cubans and Vietnamese, the embattled Palestinians, and to movements for a nuclear-free world, world peace and an end to imperialist, neo-colonialist intervention and diktat.

The fourth pillar and the international anti-apartheid offensive

Apartheid easily qualified as the world's foremost *racistocracy*. That racial engineering project was ethno-chauvinism par excellence and a crime against humanity. The UN was founded on the principle of equality for all human beings, and its *Universal Declaration of Human Rights*, which was adopted by the General Assembly on 10 December 1948, was at the very least politically binding on states; some say that it was in fact legally binding on states.

Relations between states, said the UN, should be 'based on respect for the principle of equal rights and self-determination of peoples'. Even before the adoption of the UN Universal Declaration of Human Rights in 1948, the UN Charter boldly identified 'equal rights' as a UN principle.[7] In Chapter I of the Charter, the UN committed itself to 'promoting and encouraging respect for human rights and for fundamental freedoms for all without distinction as to race, sex, language, or religion.'[8]

In the preamble itself, the UN reaffirmed: '…faith in fundamental human rights, in the dignity and worth of the human person, in the equal rights of men and women, and of nations larger and small.'[9] The UN explicitly called on member states to practice 'tolerance'.

Thus, from its very inception, the UN has been acutely conscious of its obligation to promote the elimination of all forms of racial discrimination. On 12 July 1948, India cautioned the United Nations that, 'if the belief that there is to be one standard of treatment for the white races and another for the non-white continues to gain strength among the latter, the future for solidarity among the members of the United Nations and, consequently, for world peace, will indeed be dark.'[10] These were prophetic words indeed.

Yet those words fell on the proverbial deaf ears in Pretoria. Throughout the post-Nazi Germany era, apartheid South Africa acted in ways as if such norms did not exist. It believed it could simply do as it pleased without showing any regard for the consequences of its actions. South African officials often hid under the non-interference doctrine of the UN.

In the end, apartheid South Africa came to pay a dear price for its actions and crude defiance of international norms. Third World states were in the vanguard of efforts firstly to isolate the white-ruled state and secondly to democratise the *pariah* state; they largely succeeded in this quest.[11] South Africa's fourth pillar of ostracism was therefore a crucial aspect of democratisation. It covered four areas of isolation, namely the diplomatic, economic, military and socio-cultural.[12] The white-ruled Republic developed a *pariah* image.

Because apartheid was contrary to this global spirit of self-determination and equality of peoples, an international anti-apartheid struggle became globalised.[13] Calls for boycotts, sanctions, pickets and the like transcended state boundaries. The establishment of anti-apartheid bodies abroad in the 1960s coincided with the anti-colonial revolution and the liberation of many 'Third World' states; a clash between the immorality of apartheid and the morality of democracy was inevitable. The subjected people of Africa, Asia, the Caribbean and the Pacific region, who struggled for their own independence, quickly took up the anti-apartheid struggle.

The United Nations became an important platform and agent for the waging of the international anti-apartheid offensive. In 1948, the UN debated the issue of apartheid in South Africa on India's request.[14] Following this debate the system of white minority domination and apartheid gradually grew into an issue of major importance that confronted the international community. In 1950, the General Assembly for the first time stated that apartheid was decidedly anti-democratic as it was necessarily based on 'doctrines of racial' discrimination that were contrary to the UN Charter.[15]

By the 1950s and early 1960s, apartheid stood out uniquely in the world with the effect that it began to unite the United Nations, pro-democratic states and international civic movements, in ways that few issues could. As former Swedish Prime Minister Olof Palme once remarked, the 'struggle against apartheid' was a 'universal cause'.[16] Kadar Asmal opined in similar fashion that 'opposition to racism and apartheid' established 'the only universal consensus the world has seen since the Second World War'.[17]

From early on, the Afro-Asia-Caribbean members requested that 'the question of race conflict in South Africa resulting from the policies of apartheid of the government of the Union of South Africa should be urgently considered by the United Nations'.[18]

In 1960, domestic opposition to apartheid culminated in an event which quickly drew the inequity of that system onto the centre stage at the UN. This event was the Sharpeville massacre on 21 March, followed by the subsequent bans on the African National Congress and Pan-Africanist Congress. Following the Sharpeville massacre in which 69 people were gunned down by apartheid's security forces, the UN Security Council began to debate South Africa's apartheid policies, and began to threaten it with deeply punitive measures.[19]

Representatives of 29 African and Asian members requested an urgent meeting of the Security Council to consider 'the situation arising out of the large-scale killings of unarmed and peaceful demonstrators against racial segregation in the Union of South Africa'.[20]

In January 1961, UN Secretary-General Dag Hammarskjöld visited South Africa and declared that it was impossible to find 'mutual understanding' with the Pretoria regime on its country's race policies. That year South Africa was compelled to withdraw from the Commonwealth. The racist Prime Minister H.F. Verwoerd had to save face with his white electorate and provided the rider that South Africa would withdraw in the interests of its 'honour and dignity'.[21] In private, however, Verwoerd conceded that the 'pressure was on' and South Africa declared itself a Republic on 31 May 1961.

After 1962, the world witnessed attempts by international actors to institutionalise many anti-apartheid institutions as mobilising agents against apartheid South Africa. In that year, for example, the *United Nations Special Committee against Apartheid* was established. With this action the UN moved towards a heightened form of international democratisation by effectively institutionalising punitive measures against the white-dominated Republic.[22]

In October 1963, prominent leaders of the ANC and allied organisations were charged with 'treason' in the Rivonia trial, which ended in Mandela, Mbeki, Sisulu,

Goldberg, Kathrada, Mhlaba, Mlangeni and Motsoaledi being sentenced to life imprisonment. The UN requested the South African government to grant 'unconditional release to all political prisoners and to all persons imprisoned'.

After Pretoria's defiance of this call, the Security Council agreed to a voluntary arms embargo against South Africa by member states. Also in that year, the UN adopted the all-important *Declaration on the Elimination of all forms of Racial Discrimination*, which expressed alarm at 'the manifestations of racial discrimination' in South Africa. It considered apartheid to be 'scientifically false, morally condemnable, socially unjust and dangerous'.[23] In the mid 1960s, the apartheid issue became gradually internationalised with this type of action.

The Organisation of African Unity, the highest institutional expression of Pan-Africanism, had long been at the forefront of international entities and initiatives to intervene against apartheid. The OAU campaigned for sanctions, ostracism, international propaganda and armed struggle against apartheid. The objectives of this campaign were very clear in their intent: bring about democracy in South Africa through '…an end to the illegal government of settler minority'.[24] Not only did the OAU set out to discredit and de-legitimise the white minority regime, it also sought to legitimise in its place the national liberation movements. The ANC and other liberation movements were baptised as 'the sole and authentic representatives of the peoples of South Africa'.[25]

The OAU played an extraordinary role in support of the resistance movements. It called into existence a Liberation Committee in the 'Service of the Liberation of Africa'. In line with this move, the OAU established a 'Special Fund for the Liberation of African Territories still under Colonial and Racist Rule'.[26] It was the duty of the Liberation Committee to strengthen its support to the liberation movements in order for them to 'intensify the struggle and carry it to its logical conclusion, namely independence based on the principle of one man, one vote'.[27] The OAU appealed for Afro-Arab solidarity and co-operation to ensure the strictest implementation of the oil embargo. The OAU specifically targeted the following list of countries: Ecuador, Indonesia, Iraq, Malaysia, Kuwait, Qatar, Saudi Arabia, the United Arab Emirates and Venezuela. As oil-producing countries, these states were all expected by the OAU to lead the charge of imposing an oil embargo against the Republic.[28]

The six African states of Angola, Botswana, Mozambique, Tanzania, Zambia and Zimbabwe regarded themselves as being in the 'frontline' of 'the struggle against the racist Pretoria regime'.[29] They sought to maintain a solid front that was able to wear down the regime to the point that it yielded on the major demand of black majority rule.[30]

By the early 1970s, the UN began to expose the anti-democratic nature of apartheid by passing resolutions condemning the practice as 'a crime against the consciousness of mankind' and 'a threat to international peace and security'.[31] In 1971, the UN General Assembly rejected grand apartheid in the form of the establishment of Bantustan Homelands and the forced removals of African people.[32]

The 'Third World' states of Africa, Asia, the Caribbean and Latin America were in the forefront of attempts to isolate the apartheid regime. Many of these states sought to use the UN as a mechanism through which intra-state relations became a fundamental principle of inter-state relations.[33]

Increasingly, a majority of states in the international system repudiated in different ways and to different degrees South Africa's racially based domestic order. In a dramatic move in 1974, the UN General Assembly deprived South Africa of its rights to participate in UN activities following the rejection of the credentials of the South African delegation. The then president of the General Assembly, Abdelaziz Bouteflika of Algeria, announced that the UN 'refused to accept the credentials of the South African delegation'.[34]

The high-water mark of this new wave of intervention against South Africa occurred in 1977. The Security Council, in response to the anti-apartheid revolt that started in Soweto in 1976 and the murder in custody of Black Consciousness leader Bantu Steven Biko, voted in favour of a mandatory arms embargo against South Africa. This was the first time that the Security Council had adopted such drastic actions against any member state. After the passing of the mandatory arms embargo, symbolic opposition to apartheid was turned into widespread demands for the total isolation of South Africa and the application of hard-hitting sanctions against its government.

It was in the aftermath of these events that the former president of the ANC, Oliver Tambo, urged the international community to pursue the comprehensive isolation of the South African regime.

Cognisant that white South Africans were fanatical sports lovers, the Commonwealth launched a sports boycott that culminated in the 1977 Gleneagles Agreement, announcing major restrictions on sporting contacts with the country. The UN General Assembly also adopted the 1976 Resolution on Apartheid in Sports.

One year later, in 1978, the UN passed the *Declaration of the World Conference to Combat Racism and Racial Discrimination*. Mainly targeting South Africa, it depicted apartheid as: 'a crime against the conscience and dignity of mankind, and [which] constitutes serious dangers which will inevitably lead to great conflict with enormous repercussions on international peace and security'.[35] No other state in the post-World War II era's domestic body politic and legal dispensation had ever been branded as such by the UN.

Another example was that, on 18 July 1978, there was a worldwide observance of the sixtieth birthday of Nelson Mandela, a move initiated by the ANC and the UN *Special Committee Against Apartheid*. The motivation was to show international solidarity with the struggle against apartheid and publicise the cause of political prisoners. While languishing in apartheid's gaols, Nelson Mandela soon graduated from ordinary political prisoner to one of the world's most authentic leaders. He certainly became the world's most famous political prisoner.

Rhodesia became liberated in 1980 and in March of that year the independent Republic of Zimbabwe came into existence. From then on, black-led regional states were even more militant in their anti-apartheid opposition. South Africa's project of creating a buffer zone of friendly states in southern Africa was dealt a severe blow. On 1 April 1980, less than one month after the election in Zimbabwe, a summit meeting of nine southern African countries in Lusaka decided to form the Southern African Development Co-ordination Conference (SADCC).[36]

Far from acting as a shield for apartheid, the SADCC sought to expose and isolate apartheid South Africa. It quickly articulated three avowed objectives: one, to promote regional development; two, to decrease dependence on South Africa; and three, to challenge Pretoria's aggressive destabilisation campaign in the region. Several progressive international states, notably the Nordic countries, decided to strengthen and widen their co-operation with SADCC countries. Co-operation took the forms of trade promotion, investments, technology transfers, cultural exchanges and communications, and building up the developmental capacities of such states.

The camaraderie that developed during World War II prompted many in the West to emphasise South Africa's status as an ally rather than focus on the morality of apartheid. Even during the 1960s and 1970s, Western powers dealt with South Africa based on the erroneous strategic premise that it was a 'bulwark against the red communist menace'.

This dominant ethos of engagement with South Africa was particularly rife in the US. For example, US policy towards Pretoria could still best be explained by Washington's preoccupation with containing Moscow's thrust into regional vacuums and trouble spots. The anti-apartheid crusade was confined chiefly to the Civil Rights Movement, academics, students, church activists, the Congressional Black Caucus and a handful of black officials who had become targets of recruitment for the US federal government and foreign service, particularly in the Kennedy and Johnson administrations.

It was not only in the USA that anti-apartheid lobbies had significant impact on governments' policy directions vis-à-vis South Africa. In Western Europe too, anti-apartheid movements campaigned on the basis that 'apartheid was an evil to be combated by every means within their power'.[37] Demands for sanctions and isolation were the chief arsenals in these movements' strategies. These movements worked in creative ways with multi-lateral organisations such as the UN, the Commonwealth, the Non-Aligned Movement (NAM) and the OAU to increase the pressure against

South Africa. More importantly, they forged close working relations with the ANC, as well as the United Democratic Movement (UDF) and the Mass Democratic Movement (MDM) inside the country. The anti-apartheid movements took the art of lobbying to new heights. As Kadar Asmal observed, the anti-apartheid movements showed a 'combination of tenacity and clarity of purpose with vision and imagination as to how to win support for [their] aims'.[38]

By the mid-1980s, the efforts of non-governmental anti-apartheid lobbies became important pressure points that worked on the political psyche of the Afrikaner governing elite. The message from such movements was a clear one: apartheid will have to go. The role of the fourth pillar of international solidarity in forcing De Klerk to the negotiating table in 1990, which resulted in a major opening for the negotiated settlement, should not be underestimated.[39]

Post-Apartheid South Africa

The ushering in of post-apartheid South Africa in 1994 was a culmination of decades of struggle on all fronts, including international solidarity. However, the end of apartheid did not mean an end to international solidarity for the ANC. Instead, the ANC, now as a ruling party in post-apartheid South Africa, re-oriented its international solidarity work using both its party structures and the state machinery. Its foreign policy perspective and values were to be informed by the vision of 'Peace and Friendship' as articulated in the Freedom Charter and what OR Tambo had said during struggle days, that: 'We will have a South Africa which will live in peace with its neighbours and with the rest of the world. It will base its foreign relations on mutually advantageous assistance among the peoples of the world'.

The focus of the ANC's international relations is in six areas, namely building a better world and Africa; international and continental solidarity work; strengthening party-to-party relations; transformation of global governance; policy development issues; and campaigns on specific international issues.

Through the party-to-party relations the ANC has established active bilateral relations with a host of parties around the world. However, in establishing such relations, the ANC makes a distinction between like-minded and non-like-minded partners. Besides bilateral relations, the ANC continues to interact with former liberation movements through their coordinating forum, and is also a member of the Socialist International.

The ANC guides government on policy issues through decisions and resolutions of its policy organs such as the National Conference, the National Policy Conference and the National Executive Committee.

As the international solidarity posture of post-apartheid South Africa evolved under the leadership of the ANC, four main themes emerged. First is the strategic focus of the ANC-led government on Africa and the many challenges that prevent this continent from realising its full potential. Beginning with the presidency of Nelson Mandela and up to the present, Africa became the centrepiece of the foreign policy of the new South Africa. Mandela's successor, Thabo Mbeki, became a leading champion of what became known as the 'African Renaissance' – a movement that cuts across governments, regional and inter-governmental organisations, and civil society, with the objective of taking responsibility and full charge of the destiny of the African continent.[40] This movement transformed the OAU, established primarily for decolonisation, into a new continental body, the African Union, which was launched in South Africa in 2002 with the purpose of driving the development agenda of the continent and eradicating poverty and wars.

The formation of the AU was accompanied by the establishment of the New Partnership for Africa's Development (NEPAD), a continental initiative whose purpose was to galvanise Africa's collective energy around the continent's development challenges.[41] Through the NEPAD, the African Peer Review Mechanism (APRM) was born as a mechanism through which African leaders subjected themselves to periodic reviews by other Africans on their leadership and its impact on their people for a better life.[42]

The Mbeki-led government was at the centre of all these three initiatives to the point that the secretariats of both NEPAD and the APRM were given to South Africa to host.

The philosophy behind the ANC's emphasis on Africa in the foreign policy of the post-apartheid government is grounded in the tradition of international solidarity. The ANC does not see South Africa, with its comparatively more developed economy in Africa, in isolation from the rest of the continent. To the ANC, South Africa's present situation and its future are inseparably linked to those of the African continent.

There is also a historical consideration at play here. The ANC was formed as a Pan-African movement and defined itself as such. It has always considered its struggle in South Africa as part of the decolonisation wave on the African continent. Its cadres fought side by side with other liberation movements in different parts of Africa. In exile, the ANC benefited from the selfless generosity of African sister countries, some of which were subjected to destabilisation by the apartheid regime because of their association with the ANC. Therefore, it would have been difficult for the post-apartheid ANC to define its international relations outside its Pan-African heritage.

The second theme that has emerged since 1994 in the international solidarity posture of the ANC pertains to the international system that remains undemocratic and biased towards the interests of countries of the developed North.[43] Not only do these countries control institutions of global governance such as the United Nations and the Bretton Woods bodies but they also use this dominance to perpetuate the second-class position of the countries of the developing South. Through the Non-Aligned Movement (NAM) and the G77 plus China, among others, the countries of the South have constituted themselves into a force contesting the hegemony of the North in the international system and working for the transformation of its supporting institutions. The NAM and the G77 plus China were strong supporters of the ANC during the struggle against apartheid. After 1994, it therefore became natural that the ANC would continue its association with these two bodies.

In addition, the ANC established bilateral relations with like-minded parties (at party-to-party level) and governments (at inter-state level) with certain countries of the South with the view to strengthening the voice of this constituency in the international system. In making a determination of countries with which to establish strategic relations, the ANC has been guided by its experience of international solidarity during the struggle years. It is in this context that the IBSA and BRICS groups emerged with South Africa as a member.

The third is about how the ANC, through government and the party, has continued international solidarity in a traditional sense, providing support to, among others, Palestinians, and the peoples of the Western Sahara and South Sudan in their quest for self-determination, as well as Cuba in its struggle to determine its own socio-economic system without interference from Western powers. At the level of the party, the ANC is engaged in a series of campaigns through its structures and partners such as its Alliance to mobilise South Africans. The ANC provides political, moral and material support to leading organs in the aforementioned countries. At the level of government, the ANC uses its membership of a number of international organisations to support measures that promote the plight of its solidarity allies. The government also provides material support, knowing how this helped the ANC when it was an exiled movement.

The fourth theme revolves around the complex challenge of building a global progressive movement. It was in this context that the ANC organised its 3rd International Solidarity Conference in Tshwane from 25 to 28 October 2012. The conference was a follow-up to the 1st and 2nd Solidarity Conferences that the ANC had organised in 1987 in Tanzania and 1993 in Johannesburg, respectively. The conference was the implementation of a resolution taken by the 52nd National Conference of 2007 which called upon the ANC to organise a gathering of this nature for the mobilisation of international progressive forces. The conference took place in the context of the ANC's Centenary Celebrations in the month dedicated to the celebration of OR Tambo.

Whereas the 1st and 2nd Solidarity Conferences were organised, respectively, at the height of the struggle and during the negotiations, the 3rd conference was an opportunity for the ANC to reconnect with its international friends from the days of the anti-apartheid movement. Accordingly, it aimed at recognising the contribution of the international community to South Africa's liberation, re-establishing historic links with progressive forces, restoring the hegemonic voice of progressive forces in global political and economic relations, and celebrating the life and memory of OR Tambo.

The conference was attended by more than 800 participants, about 170 of whom were from outside South Africa from over 50 countries. International participants included fraternal parties, the former Anti-Apartheid Movement and other like-minded formations. Some international inter-governmental organisations were also represented. From within South Africa, the ANC and Alliance as well as MDM structures also attended. The conference mandated the ANC to steer the coordination of the global effort to convene the next conference, and to rekindle the international solidarity movements.

Conclusion

Over its hundred years of existence as a liberation movement, and today as a party at the helm of post-apartheid South Africa, the ANC was shaped and enriched by international solidarity, which by the 1960s had become the fourth pillar of its struggle for liberation and justice. From its inception in 1912, the ANC was influenced by its own experiences in South Africa, as well as by developments elsewhere in the world. Over the years, it came to define itself as part of a global progressive movement which was struggling for a world that is democratically governed and free of wars, inequality, hunger and poverty. This is the agenda of the international solidarity movement today.

In 2013 we celebrate the 58th anniversary of the adoption of the Freedom Charter at the historic Congress of the People. This remarkable and timeless document spelt out the internationalist positions of the ANC and its Congress allies. Under the clause 'There shall be Peace and Friendship' the ideals of an independent state that respects the 'rights and sovereignty of all nations' are clearly articulated. The clause commits the movement to 'strive to maintain world peace and the settlement of disputes by negotiation and not war.' Finally, at the end of November 2012, we held the Solidarity Conference as part of the centenary celebration activities. One of the main lessons from that conference, from both philosophical and ideological perspectives, is that solidarity and co-operation amongst progressive forces are as relevant today as they were a century ago.

A century after the ANC's formation in 1912, the movement would be well advised to take a leaf out of the fourth pillar of its liberation book, which emphasised internationalism, international solidarity, world peace, self-determination of peoples, pan-African unity and African solidarity. Since joining government, the ANC has adapted these steadfast principles to a set of modern, cosmopolitan principles.

All post-apartheid governments have appropriated and claimed these principles, and stated that they informed the Republic's foreign policy. It is incumbent on the ANC to live by its stated values and principles of the fourth pillar of international solidarity, and to be seen to be doing so.

Endnotes

1   Landsberg, C., 2012, 100 years of ANC foreign policy. *The Thinker*, 35, p.24.
2   See Bunting, B., 1975. *Moses Kotane: South African revolutionary*. London: Inkululeko.
3   Ibid.
4   Landsberg, 2012, op. cit., p.25.
5   Ibid.
6   For a perspective on the 'Africanist' split within the liberation movement, see Jordan, P., 2012. The evolution of ANC leadership: Lessons from history. *New Agenda*, Fourth Quarter, pp.11-12.
7   Quoted in United Nations, 1994. United Nations and apartheid 1958–1994. *United Nations Blue Book Series*, Vol. 1, p.2.
8   Ibid.
9   Ibid.
10 Ibid., pp.167-168.
11 Geldenhuys, D., 1977. *The effects of South Africa's racial policy on Anglo-South African relations, 1945–1961*. Unpublished Ph.D thesis, Cambridge University, p.334.
12 See Geldenhuys, D., 1990. *Isolated States: A comparative analysis*. Johannesburg: Jonathan Ball.
13 Geldenhuys, 1977, op. cit., p.334.
14 Reddy, E.S., n.d. *The United Nations and apartheid, a chronology*. p.2. Available at: http://www.anc.org.za/un/un-chron.html.
15 Ibid.
16 Palm, O., 1997. World Conference for Action against Apartheid. *Struggle against apartheid is a universal cause*. 22 August. Lagos, Nigeria.
17 Asmal, K., 1999. Anti-Apartheid Movement. *Address to the closing session of the symposium organised by the anti-apartheid movement archives committee to mark the 40th anniversary of the Anti-Apartheid Movement*. 26 June. Africa House, London.
18 Quoted in Geldenhuys, D. The head of government and South Africa's foreign relations, op. cit., p.255.
19 Reddy, n.d., op. cit., p.2.

20 Ibid.

21 Geldenhuys, op. cit., p.255.

22 United Nations General Assembly Resolution. 1962. *The policies of Apartheid of the Government of South Africa, A/res/1761 (xvii)*. 6 November. New York.

23 United Nations, 1994. United Nations and Apartheid 1958–1994. *United Nations Blue Book Series*, p.8.

24 Organisation of African Unity. 1967. *Assembly of Heads of State and Government, First Ordinary Session*. 17–21 July. Cairo, Egypt.

25 Organisation of African Unity. 1975. *The Council of Ministers of the OAU, Twenty-fifth Ordinary Session*. 18–25 July. Kampala, Uganda.

26 Ibid.

27 Ibid.

28 Ibid.

29 Shamuyarira, N.M., 1969. *The Lusaka Manifesto on Southern Africa*. Proceedings of the Fifth Summit Conference on East and Central African States, Commentary. Lusaka, Zambia.

30 Ibid.

31 United Nations, 1994, op. cit., p.167.

32 Ibid.

33 Reddy, n.d., op. cit., p.7.

34 Ibid.

35 United Nations, 1994, op. cit., p.155.

36 For an assessment of the SADCC, see Khadiaghala, G.M., 2007. *Allies in adversity: The frontline States in Southern African security, 1975–1993*. Lanham: University Press of America, pp.229-248.

37 Asmal, K., 1999. Anti-Apartheid Movement. *Address to the closing session of the symposium organised by the anti-apartheid movement archives committee to mark the 40th anniversary of the Anti-Apartheid Movement.*

38 Ibid.

39 Landsberg, C., n.d. Directing from the stalls? The international community and the South African negotiating forum, op. cit., p.282.

40 For a perspective on the 'African Renaissance', see Kornegay, F., Landsberg, C. & McDonald, S., 2001. Participate in the African Renaissance. *Washington Quarterly*, 24(3), pp.105-112.

41 For an analysis on NEPAD, see Rukato, H., 2012. The new partnership for Africa's development: Past, present, future. *Africa Insight*, 42(3), pp.91-103.

42 An account of the APRM is provided by Landsberg, C., 2012. The African peer review mechanism: A political retort on Africa's most innovative governance instrument. *Africa Insight*, 42(3), pp.104-118.

43 For a perspective on the nature of global governance and how it serves the interests of the industrialised powers, see Landsberg, C., 2010. South Africa's transformational approach to global governance. *Africa Insight*, 39(4), pp.23-34.

CHAPTER 9

The Scandinavian anti-apartheid movement: international solidarity in action

Bengt Säve-Söderbergh and Pekka Peltola

Introduction

In this chapter we[1] present case studies from Scandinavia which, arguably, led both Europe and North America in its solidarity work against racial oppression. Although we focus on Sweden and Finland as European epicentres of the anti-apartheid movement, our presentation also resonates for Norway, Denmark and the greater region. Bengt Säve-Söderbergh contributed the part about Sweden and Pekka Peltola wrote the second part dealing with Finland and the anti-apartheid movement.

The ANC and Sweden, a very special relationship

When the Prime Minister of Sweden, Olof Palme, was killed in Stockholm in February 1986, Oliver Tambo had been his close friend for almost 25 years. He reacted with deep sorrow and made a statement upon learning of this tragedy:

> We have received with extreme shock and heartfelt grief news of the death of our dear brother, the Prime Minister of Sweden. We had come to know him as the leader of the Swedish people, but also as one of us, a fellow combatant who made inestimable contributions to the struggle for the liberation of South Africa.[2]

Oliver Tambo attended the memorial service for Palme in Stockholm with a strong ANC delegation.

Palme and Tambo first met in the 1960s on one of Tambo's first visits to Sweden. During that visit, he also spent time with Palme's family and they soon became close personal friends. This friendship lasted for the rest of their lives and went far beyond being representatives of a liberation movement, government and social democratic party. Warmth, trust and solidarity were always there. Palme would always ask for news about Tambo and the struggle.

Olof Palme was the most important person in Sweden in mobilising support for the liberation struggle in South Africa, not only because of his being Prime Minister and party leader but very much because of his interest in international affairs, his disgust with apartheid and his continuous close monitoring of how things developed in the struggle. He refused to accept a common view in major Western countries to look upon the conflict in southern Africa as part of the cold war. Apartheid had to be seen for what it was: a gross violation of fundamental human rights, which also created extreme inequalities and injustices. Sweden is and was not part of NATO and strongly defended its own policies of non-alignment and the rights of smaller nations.

Olof Palme was definitely not alone in Sweden in supporting the struggle in South Africa. Thousands of persons and many organisations took part, with a large majority of Swedes involved one way or the other over four decades. Sweden achieved a special role in the struggle, as many South Africans have pointed out. We agree with this view.

The following sections of this chapter deal with highpoints of this solidarity action, how this special relationship developed and its significance.

The early days

South Africa and Sweden are geographically very far apart, but already in the middle of the nineteenth century some Swedish and Norwegian missionaries found their way to South Africa and opened missionary stations. Relations were established. Joseph Zulu, a cousin of King Cetshwayo, was ordained at the Uppsala Cathedral in 1901 and became the first African priest in the Church of Sweden. Dean Gunnar Helander served in South Africa between 1938 and 1956, when he was expelled from the country by the government because of his opposition to apartheid. Helander was probably the first Swede to warn against the political developments and wrote a great number of articles in the Swedish press, an activity he continued and combined with far-reaching solidarity work when back in Sweden as a priest. Later, relations between anti-apartheid churches in South Africa and different churches in Sweden developed quite remarkably and played major roles in the struggle against apartheid. A key person in South Africa in this connection was of course Beyers Naudé.

In 1949, when the new apartheid government had just been installed, the chief editor of *Expressen*, a major daily newspaper in Sweden, paid a long visit to South Africa and wrote eleven critical articles for his paper. In 1953, Herbert Tingsten, chief editor of Sweden´s largest morning paper, the liberal *Dagens Nyheter*, visited South Africa for more than a month. He interviewed a great number of persons. Tingsten was at the time one of the most influential opinion makers in Sweden. His articles, which in 1954 were published in a book, constituted a most powerful condemnation of the policies of racist South Africa. He had become convinced that this system could not survive in the long term. It would result either in a bloody and cruel civil war or in a realisation that apartheid would not be in the interest of any part of the society.

The Swedish Student Union, which comprised all students studying at universities, had started a scholarship programme for foreign students in the early 1950s as part of their membership of the International Student Association. In 1955 they were informed from South Africa that only white students in South Africa were allowed to take part in this exchange, a signal that resulted in a delegation to be sent to South Africa to find out what it was about. The report suggested that the white Student Union of South Africa was to be expelled from this programme and triggered the Swedish Student Union to focus its scholarship programme on students from Africa working for freedom from colonialism and racial segregation. Olof Palme was active in the Swedish Student Union at the time, and probably his first concrete act of international solidarity was to donate blood in order to raise funds for the scholarship programme.

The cause of Algeria and its struggle for independence created a strong voice in Sweden, not least among young persons with a new view of the world. The Swedish Social Democratic government in 1959 became the first Western government to vote in favour of a resolution in the United Nations to support the right to self-determination, a controversial issue when major Western countries still occupied colonies around the world. A growing opinion was being formed to the effect that Sweden had to be active in support of freedom in developing countries and that a public aid programme should be developed.

What these examples describe is that already, before 1960, some information had filtered through to an interested Swedish public about what was about to happen in South Africa and that a public opinion in favour of solidarity was in the making.

The turning point

Sharpeville and the ensuing banning of ANC and other anti-apartheid organisations in 1960 created anger and shock around the world, very much so in Sweden. It became a turning point, not only in the struggle in South Africa but also in the commitment to organise support for the struggle. We would do well to remember the resolutions that were blocked at the United Nations General Assembly as well as in the Security Council where major Western countries ideologically looked at the South African issue through East–West or Cold War lenses rather than seeing apartheid as a continuation of imperialism and white supremacy.

But what more tangible could be done in support of the victims and for the cause? The ANC asked for boycotts of certain South African goods. There was a need to accommodate asylum seekers and, in some cases, to provide scholarships for victims of apartheid who had to flee their own country. The first student from South Africa, who studied with a scholarship at the University of Lund in southern Sweden, was Billy Modise. Modise later became the ANC representative in Sweden and eventually became the first ambassador of democratic South Africa in Canada.

Evert Svensson, a young social-democratic parliamentarian, managed to collect a list of 33 other parliamentarians, who signed a request to the Norwegian Nobel Peace Committee to award the Peace Prize to Chief Albert Luthuli. This proposal was approved and Luthuli came to Oslo to receive the Nobel Prize, a year after he was nominated. The South African government had given him strong restrictions regarding his visit if he wanted to return to South Africa from Oslo. Part of the conditions included barring him from visiting Sweden or any other country while travelling to Oslo.

Oliver Tambo was invited to speak at the 1962 May Day demonstrations organised by the Social Democratic Party, something he did several times in the years ahead. He was received by Prime Minister Tage Erlander and other prominent politicians and opinion makers. He developed a relationship with many persons representing different political parties, trade unions, students and media. His warmth, clarity, modesty and, of course, his cause had a strong appeal for the persons he met and he built a relationship for life with many Swedes.

In his speeches and contacts, Tambo made pleas for the boycott of South African commodities such as wine, oranges and marmalade. He called for support in the UN and asked for sanctions and an arms embargo. The National Council of Swedish Youth, an umbrella organisation embracing many kinds of youth organisations, including the youth wings of all major political parties, launched a national campaign in 1963. So did the student movement.

The ANC's Secretary-General, Duma Nokwe, took part in the launch. Consequently, every young person who was a member of any youth or student organisation learnt about South Africa and took a position. The trade union and the cooperatives movement launched boycott campaigns as well. A number of articles about South Africa were printed in Swedish media in those years. This movement became a broad learning experience which prepared the ground for more active involvement of other sectors of society. The first voices of opinion in the previous decade were primarily addressed to elites. At this time, opinion voices had become broad-based, thus popularising the anti-apartheid sentiment across Sweden.

In subsequent years, mobilisation initiatives resulted in a number of political demands made to the Swedish government, including economic sanctions and the closing of the Swedish Embassy in Pretoria. In those days, Sweden had a long tradition of non-alignment and a low-key voice in international matters, a policy that had kept it out of two world wars. The appeal of countries fighting for independence and against poverty had strong support, however, particularly among the younger generations. The new demands of solidarity with South Africa created a new perspective on foreign policy to which the immediate reaction was slow in government circles. Together with the other Nordic countries, a resolution was introduced to the UN, condemning apartheid but avoiding calling for economic sanctions. But many Swedes wanted more action from their government. A new era in Swedish foreign policy was taking shape.

A new government institution for international development cooperation to assist developing countries came into being in the early 1960s. Could this government institution do something for the victims of apartheid?

A special budget post was created for refugee assistance and a number of persons from South Africa, Namibia, Zimbabwe and the Portuguese colonies were assisted with scholarships. More personal relations were created and demands for more political action came from party activists, student organisations and other opinion makers. The South Africa committees were established in different parts of the country, and across the region, albeit at difference times and with different configurations.

In 1969, the most important agreement came into being in Parliament between the Social Democratic government, the Liberal Party and the Left Party. This pact committed the government of Sweden to provide direct support to liberation movements in southern Africa. The Moderates (Conservatives) were hesitant, to put it diplomatically, but all other parliamentary parties came along, including the Centre Party. The new aid agency, Sida, was to implement these new policies, which had the label of *humanitarian assistance* and excluded military involvement. The assignment was to provide support directly to liberation movements as well as to international organisations and NGOs directly involved. Much of the assistance had to be delivered secretly. A special committee of parliamentarians and other concerned individuals was formed to oversee and give advice to Sida.

By 1969 the ANC as an organisation was in trouble. The core of the leadership, excluding Oliver Tambo, was jailed on Robben Island and the apartheid government had devoted enormous resources to try and crush the ANC and other organisations fighting apartheid. At the same time, the struggle against Portuguese colonialism had increased with the PAIGC (party for the liberation of Guinea and Cape Verde), Frelimo (of Mozambique) and the MPLA (of Angola) leading in the advance of that cause. The Portuguese empire was slowly collapsing. Liberation movements in Namibia and Zimbabwe were also making progress. Given these events, it was no coincidence that the initial focus of Swedish support to liberation movements went to these organisations and only later to the ANC, which was experiencing problems due to the banishment and imprisonment of its leaders. Oliver Tambo would later tell friends that this was regrettable but unavoidable given the difficulties under which the ANC was operating.

The first formal meeting between the ANC and the Swedish government through Sida resulted in an agreement that saw it deliver basic commodities such as food and other necessities to the ANC members in exile. There was also an agreement that regular consultations should be a defining feature of this formal cooperation, which also made provision for accountability and prudent resource management.

More importantly, this period saw the evolution of cooperation between the ANC and the Swedish government beyond a humanitarian mission. The main question became: how to assist the ANC to become a 'government in waiting'? This meant that the organisation had to be supported to create different departments and missions in different countries. Sweden, mostly through Sida, assisted in this regard. As these engagements progressed, high levels of trust and confidence developed. The ANC was represented by more or less the same persons year after year. Oliver Tambo, Thomas Nkobi, Alfred Nzo, Thabo Mbeki and others were involved. Oliver Tambo ensured that the ANC was open to the Swedes, even on very delicate matters, except the armed struggle, to which Sweden was not a partner.

Signs of a very special relationship were there for all to see, both inside Sweden and in other Scandinavian countries. The relationship was to continue for about 20 years until democracy was achieved in South Africa in 1994. At this time there was no other government, certainly not in the West, that worked with the ANC in such regulated forms and with a recurrent annual planning cycle as did Sweden. Sweden had no other agenda in the cooperation with the liberation movement except to assist with whatever would be useful in the struggle against apartheid and for democracy. Acknowledging this, Lindiwe Mabuza, for many years the active and respected ANC representative in Sweden, would later say in an interview:

> The cooperation started with a limited view of what we were doing and that was reflected in the amounts and in the negotiations. But our perspective of what ought to be accommodated grew as we had more people coming out of South Africa. We were forming departments as we were having increased assistance. The Nordic countries were actually helping us to form the nucleus of the future ministries.[3]

From humble beginnings, the anti-apartheid movement and formal cooperation between the ANC and the government of Sweden grew from strength to strength, covering a wide range of areas. For instance, with the large exodus of refugees after the 1976 Soweto Uprising, the issue of the right to education become a priority. As the government of Tanzania made land available for the ANC in exile to educate its cadres, governments of Sweden and Finland gave support which resulted in the creation of the Solomon Mahlangu Freedom College. Meanwhile, cooperation in the sphere of arts and culture also grew as evidenced by the exploits of the Amandla Ensemble, Miriam Makeba and many South African artists and cultural groups who either performed or took refuge in Sweden. The people of Sweden were now learning about the conditions of Africans in southern Africa and were inspired to help. To this day, arts and culture bind our people.

For the first time since 1932, the Swedish Social Democrats lost power in the 1976 Parliamentary Elections. The new government, consisting of the Liberals, the Centre Party and the Moderates (Conservatives), initially created uncertainty within a solidarity movement and the ANC, but the Centre Party and the Liberals decided early on that the Conservatives should not have any serious influence on foreign policy, especially on the solidarity work with the liberation movements of southern Africa. As a result, the cooperation with the ANC and other parties was sustained.

The role of the trade unions was elevated in the 1970s, thanks to local and international pressure on the apartheid state, which had to allow labour organisations. This allowed solidarity work between Swedish unions and organised labour in South Africa to increase. For example, Cyril Ramaphosa, who became involved with the Mine Workers Union from 1982, made his first visit to Sweden a year later and established working relations with the Swedish brothers. Ramaphosa was later quoted as saying he had visited almost every Swedish mining pit and learnt most of his negotiating skills from interactions with the unions of Sweden. Even in the formation of the Congress of South African Trade Unions, organised labour from Sweden had influence.

When the United Democratic Front (UDF) was formed in 1983, the International Centre of the Swedish Labour Movement (AIC and later renamed the Palme Centre) quickly initiated relations and provided funds, which increased over the years. It is estimated that more than sixty per cent of UDF funding came through this Swedish centre. The same is true of millions of South African rands which went to other civil society organisations active inside South Africa during and after apartheid.

Olof Palme returned as Prime Minister of Sweden in 1982 after a strong election victory. He continued and stepped up his commitment to the liberation struggle. His strategy changed as he intensified his effort to get more Western capitals to be on the side of the oppressed. As we demonstrate later in this chapter, the international solidarity movement consolidated in other Nordic countries, as well as in the Netherlands, yet most Western powers followed the policies formulated by Henry Kissinger who believed that the apartheid regime was there to stay and suspected the ANC of a friend of America's opposing forces in the cold war.

Swedish politicians argued that for as long as politicians from the West failed to listen to the ANC they would continue to judge it by applying narrow Cold War rhetoric. For instance, it was only in 1987 that Oliver Tambo had the opportunity to meet the Secretary of State of the USA. All the while, it was evident to everybody that Kissinger had always been wrong.

The end of apartheid

When South Africa became ungovernable around 1985, the ANC faced a new set of challenges. In addition to pressing for the final collapse of apartheid, it had to ensure that innocent lives were protected from state brutality, while at the same time preparing itself to govern. As President PW Botha's administration was showing signs of fatigue, questions arose: Is it possible to talk to the enemy and negotiate a settlement? How would the leadership of the ANC be coordinated from abroad, in prisons such as Robben Island and from the UDF and the broader mass democratic movement? If negotiations took place, how would trust be established between the ruling party and its supporters and the liberation movement? What of the new structure of democratic government? Some of these issues are dealt with in the preceding and remaining chapters of this book.

What can be added from our point of view is that the Swedish and Finnish governments were fully behind the liberation movement and readily availed material and non-material support during the negotiations process.

Unfortunately, Oliver Tambo fell sick in 1989 and needed medical care. He was taken to a hospital in Stockholm where in February 1990 he received the news of the release of Nelson Mandela and other leaders of the ANC. Soon thereafter Nelson Mandela travelled to Sweden to see Oliver Tambo, a comrade and colleague he had not seen in 28 years. His week-long stay in Sweden was greeted by just about every Swede with joy and pride.

For the first time, Nelson Mandela addressed a Parliament and attended a state banquet hosted by Prime Minister Ingvar Carlsson, who had succeeded Olof Palme in 1986, something Mandela had not done in his own motherland. Mandela addressed many gatherings in Sweden including a large rally at which Miriam Makeba was on stage.

In 1991, Sweden held elections that saw the Social Democrats lose power and be replaced by the conservative Moderate Party of Carl Bildt. Bildt initially viewed the ANC as a party in a new position, preparing for elections in competition with other parties. It would be difficult for the Swedish government to provide financial support to one of the parties in this competition, he argued. Friends in Sweden found ways to overcome this obstacle and the support for the ANC from Sida continued up to 1994.

Finally, apartheid ended in 1994 and the ANC became a government. As if arranged by the forces of nature, Sweden held elections in the same year which saw the return to power of the Social Democrats. This ushered in a new era of Sweden–South Africa cooperation, solidifying government-to-government and people-to-people relations.

Pursuing justice and equality: Finland's opposition to apartheid

As seen above, Finland was not an early bird in the fight against apartheid in Europe. After the Second World War, in which Finland had at one stage fought the Soviet Union alongside Hitler's Germany, and lost, all the energy in foreign policy was used to build a working relationship with the allied victors. The relationship with the Soviet Union was especially crucial. Presidents J.K. Paasikivi and Urho Kekkonen were successful in this endeavour and Finland built little by little an area for independent foreign policy. Its focus was on the United Nations, of which Finland became a member in 1955, eight years after its application for membership.

Finland avoided taking stands in international disputes, preferring to play the role of a 'doctor' rather than a 'judge'. The country adopted a non-aligned position and preferred cooperation in the Nordic family of nations – Sweden, Norway, Denmark and Iceland – with whom there were long historical ties and shared culture and language commonalities. This meant that the bilingual Finland took its cue from the sentiments and policies of other Scandinavian countries.

Limitations in movements in the international sphere, as well as a relatively marginal geographical position in Europe, naturally created time lags in the movement of ideas and their political expressions inside Finland. It must also be remembered that after a long and lost war Finland was very poor, with about 400 000 internal refugees from Soviet-occupied regions of the country looking for shelter. This was organised through the distribution of small pieces of rather unproductive land, but the situation became untenable in the 1960s, resulting in the expatriation of 300 000 Finns abroad, especially to the far richer Sweden, which had avoided joining the Second World War. Some seven per cent of the population of Finland thus migrated to Sweden.

At the same time, in the 1960s, the anti-apartheid movement had grown strong in Scandinavia. Led by Swedish-speaking Finnish students, information of the dire situation of blacks in South Africa was spread. Amplified by the victorious struggles of the black movement in the USA, led by Martin Luther King, the idea of equal rights regardless of the colour of the skin was also largely accepted in Finland. However, it still did not mean that the Finns should concretely do something to alleviate the situation outside their borders. Inside, there were almost no blacks or other people with a different skin colour. At this stage, for many people the struggle was abstract.

Something else was concrete, however. At the time, the Finnish industrial base consisted of wood and paper. Metal industries, including mining technology, were also growing rapidly. These branches of the economy had developed interests with related South African industries and were keen to maintain relations with the apartheid government. Their discreet influence set the tone of the foreign policy of Finland toward South Africa. It did not include any meaningful criticism of apartheid but actually tried to down-play any attempts to join the growing anti-apartheid movement around the world based on economic interests.

During the early years of the 1960s, the first articles criticising apartheid and calling for democracy appeared in the Finnish student press. The Swedish language *Studentbladet* and the influential *Ylioppilaslehti* published articles describing the appalling situation and demanding action. Pamphlets and books followed, including that of Erkki Tuomioja, presently a long-serving minister of foreign affairs of Finland. It took almost a decade, however, before the authorities began to take these demands seriously. Paper-selling politics were more important.

The first non-governmental organisation (NGO) against apartheid in Finland was called the South Africa Committee, established in 1965 and led by journalist Erkki Hatakka, with upcoming leftist politician Kati Peltola as secretary. Important support for the committee was given by the leader of the strong Seamen's Trade Union, Niilo Wälläri. One result was an effective boycott of alcohol imports from South Africa.

In the spirit of growing international support during the early 1970s, many NGOs launched projects in support of the Southern African liberation movements. These include the South Africa Association, Finnish Namibian Friendship Society, Africa Committee of Finland, Espoo Namibia Committee and the National Union of Students. Mikko Lohikoski and Börje Mattson were invited to walk through liberated areas of Angola and to write about the journey. Scholarships for exiled Southern Africans were granted and diverse contacts increased tremendously. Officers from the ANC representation in Stockholm visited Finland regularly. Two friendship associations of Finland–South Africa were founded, one for business people not so interested in the liberation struggle and the other for the remainder of Finns.

Support from the trade unions

A great change in Finnish foreign policy took place in 1973 when Finland decided to start supporting liberation struggles politically and materially. Included from Southern

Africa were the ANC and the Pan Africanist Congress, Swapo of Namibia and Frelimo of Mozambique. This opened many opportunities for the NGOs in increasing their support activities and helped to rally the public behind the demands for democracy and the end of colonialism.

Towards the end of the 1970s, trade unions joined the Finnish international solidarity movement. They supported the building of the labour camp in Kwanza Sul settlement, later named Nduuvu Nangolo Trade Union Centre (NUNW) for Swapo. Trade union support for the NUNW continued until Namibian independence and long afterwards.

After the founding of the Trade Union Solidarity Centre (SASK) in 1985, coopera-tion with the Congress of South African Trade Unions (COSATU) started immediately and has continued to this day. Trade unions benefitted from the experience of the Finnish *missionaries* in the training and a good and effective cooperation was formed between these two large organisations. Almost all Finns belong to either the Lutheran church or a trade union, or to both. Progressively, every political party in Finland announced its support for the liberation struggles against apartheid. This signalled the rapid growth of the Finnish anti-apartheid sentiment, a complete turn of events compared to the situation 35 years earlier.

From 1980 onwards, the people of Finland, like their counterparts in Sweden, Denmark and Norway, were fully behind the southern African liberation struggles. Markku Vesikko arrived in Luanda, Angola, on behalf of the Finnish Taksvärkki-cam-paign and helped to make the Luanda printing shop operative and later to build, on behalf of Finnsolidarity, the Moses Kotane Self-Reliance Centre in Vienna. He stayed a decade working with activists in Luanda. Pertti Koivusalo and many other Finns worked with him. Elsewhere, the Workers Educational Society (TSL) started to work in the Dakawa settlement in Tanzania, where Leo Söderqvist remained permanently.

In Finland, the Isolate South Africa Campaign (EELAK) was initiated by a large network of NGOs, trade unions and churches calling for the boycott of South African goods. The Transport Workers Union called a strike to stop trade with apartheid South Africa in 1985. It was a high point for the Scandinavian solidarity movement and the oppressed people of Southern Africa.

Eventually, the Finnish parliament passed a law that in practice stopped all import and export trade with the apartheid regime in 1986. In a further symbolic move, par-liamentarians from most parties founded an anti-apartheid group known as AWEPAA.

The Information Office of the ANC was opened in Finland towards the close of the decade and helped to increase popular awareness of the plight of the oppressed. Pirjo Virtaintorppa worked in that office for many years. The opening of the office was possible as the movement against apartheid had grown in popularity and stature, thus making it easy to mobilise resources (including funds from government) for running the offices. This period was momentous, given the intensity of projects benefiting Swapo and ANC.

The solidarity movement gains traction in Finland

By this time, as was the case in other Scandinavian countries, mainstream activities were supported by the public from all walks of life, as the evils of apartheid had become widely known. For example, Nelson Mandela's seventieth birthday was celebrated outside the then South African official mission in Finland. In addition, the boycott of *Royal Dutch Shell* was initiated in Finland, replicating the events in the United Kingdom and the Netherlands. This boycott was supported by both the trade union movement and the churches.

Open confrontations between the more radical activities and the police also occurred, but in a peaceful manner, as there were never any violent radical elements in the Finnish anti-apartheid movement.

Altogether, during the years from 1978 to 1993, Finnish humanitarian assistance to the ANC and other organisations in South Africa amounted to about 87 million Finnish marks, corresponding to about 23 million US dollars.

In the last decade of the twentieth century, when the transition to democracy became certain, Finnish activists dissolved the EELAK and re-established the Finland–South Africa Campaign. Nelson Mandela's visit to Finland in 1992 was a great occasion celebrated throughout the region. Finally, many people thought, good was winning over evil. Mandela was free and he personally travelled to Sweden and Finland to thank the people and government for choosing to align with and support the struggle for political freedom.

Today, as the ANC edges closer to one hundred and two years of existence and twenty years in political office, the Finns are aware of the obligations of the ANC as a political party and a governing party. They equally appreciate the ANC's geopolitical responsibilities, especially in southern Africa. They ask questions about South Africa's leading role in multilateral institutions such as the United Nations and the African Union, as well as in geopolitical blocks such as the BRICS group (Brazil, Russia, India, China and South Africa).

The people of Finland commend the programmes of the ANC government aimed at improving the living conditions of the great majority of South Africans. They follow the lively political discussion in the free media, including some of the running battles between people demanding services and the authorities. They follow developments in South Africa, hoping that the country can use its influence in neighbouring countries in order to help overcome at least the most serious problems undermining democracy and fair play, which are evident in Zimbabwe. They feel that the ANC could break the stalemate in Zimbabwe, if it wanted to.

The Finns support equal trade relationships between South Africa, Finland and the European Union as a whole. The Organisation of Economic Cooperation and Development (OECD) has set up an informal tax task force for Tax and Development with representation from member states, enterprises and civil society. South Africa is active in representing the voices of emerging economies as well as developing countries in such discussions. Finland, too, has an interest in developing an international tax system in a way that would leave more of the proceeds of mining, for instance, to the country in which the extractions take place. Currently, too much revenue goes for paying patent rights and transfer pricing to countries in which the owners of corporations reside.

Several Finnish NGOs, municipalities and governmental organisations have close ties and constant cooperation with their South African counterparts. Trade is growing and people travel between the countries. Affection that emerged from the contacts during the struggle for freedom carries these activities on its shoulders.

Conclusion

Therefore, as we observe a new milestone in the history of the ANC which has surpassed a century in existence, we take inspiration in both history and what lies ahead, believing that ours is a special relationship sustained by the common pursuit for social justice and equality. However, that should not be taken for granted by anybody, especially the century-old organisation to which we are dedicating this chapter. The relationship with Scandinavia should be treasured and respected in part as a tribute to the fallen heroes and heroines of the liberation struggle and the anti-apartheid movement. More importantly, the relationship should be nurtured further for the benefit of future generations to whom we should bestow our best traditions of solidarity, humanism, democratic expression, peace, justice and a better life for all.

It is our hope that the people of South Africa, Sweden, Finland and beyond, will continue to enhance relations stretching beyond the borders of the two regions because ours is a special relationship, forged over time and premised on the universal principles of justice, freedom and equality for all. That is the burden on the shoulders of the ANC. Lest we forget!

Endnotes

1   Bengt Säve-Söderbergh is a veteran anti-apartheid activist from Sweden who worked with leaders like Olof Palme for decades mobilising the Swedish society to reject apartheid as an inhumane system. He contributed the section of this chapter discussing the role of Sweden in the anti-apartheid struggled. Pekka Peltola is an activist and scholar from Finland who has contributed to a body of knowledge documenting the Finnish anti-apartheid movement. He has a long history of leading civil society groups in Finland that organised various sectors of society against the unjust system of apartheid. He contributed the part of this chapter discussing the Finnish anti-apartheid movement.

2   See 1986. ANC pays tribute to Olof Palme. *Sechaba*, April.

3   Lindiwe Mabuza cited in Sellström, T., 2002. *Sweden and National Liberation in Southern Africa: Solidarity and assistance 1970–1994*. Uppsala: Nordiska Afrikainstitutet.

CHAPTER 10

The presence of African liberation movements in Egypt after the Bandung Conference in 1955[1]

Helmi Sharawy

Introduction

After the Second World War, the Cold War saw countries newly independent from colonialism torn between the communist pull of the Soviet Union and China on one side, and the capitalist West on the other.

One of the greatest shocks to those global schemes was the Bandung Conference in Indonesia, April 1955, in which great leaders in the circle of the developing world met, including Nehru, Sukarno and Abdul Nasser, and with the support of the Socialist Bloc, represented by Chou En-lai. It was the real beginning of building a New World bloc with its pros and cons. About 30 Asian and African countries attended the conference, though the majority were Asian, with only six African. Not all had the same spirit of liberation, some being involved in Middle Eastern and Indochina alliances; however, the democratic experiments of liberal India, leftist China, Indonesian frontism and Egyptian nationalism remained the most significant for the new alliance on a global scale.

The leaders of the world, whether attending the Bandung Conference or not, realised that the young 33-year-old Gamal Abdul Nasser, representative of Egypt, signified the weight of African people and the leaders of liberation movements aspiring for independence. Egypt asserted this view with its valiant resistance to the tripartite aggression of France, Britain and Israel in October 1956 after the nationalisation of the Suez Canal. Nasser wanted to affirm the independence of his country after ending British occupation in a 1954 Treaty as he acquired the main source of the wealth of his country, the Suez Canal.

The academic intelligentsia stirred passions by looking at the role of the military with anticipation, waiting for the nationalist undertakings that accompany democratic achievement in such circumstances. However, the consecutive successes on both the domestic and foreign levels earned Nasser's leadership great status with the people of Egypt and beyond.

The leaders of Asia and Africa aspired to join Egypt in grand strategic plans for national liberation. Frequent visits of Nehru and Sukarno to Cairo and Nkrumah's arrival made the dreams of young people seem attainable. A conference on the Asian and African levels in Cairo, the Afro-Asian People's Solidarity Conference, in January 1958, was attended by all parties and national liberation movements from both continents. In its Cairo headquarters the conference established a Permanent Secretariat formed of the representatives of these powers, one that has continued functioning to this day.

The conference was attended by more than 100 popular and political organisations and hundreds of representatives who filled the auditoriums of Cairo University and its students' hostel. For the author of this article, then a student, it was among the best of memories, accompanying great leaders in auditoria while he was only a young activist, a member of the African Association established in Zamalek in 1956. This chapter therefore examines subsequent developments in a country subjected to the push and pull of national and international politics, particularly as they relate to the continent of Africa with its various liberation movements.

Political culture in Egypt was associated with the culture of national liberation due to Egypt's early support of the Palestinian people in the forties, a national movement in Sudan, media support of the Mau Mau Revolution in Kenya since the early 1950s and its crucial support of the Algerian Revolution in the mid-fifties in support of decolonisation from French rule around the Maghreb (Arab African North). These developments were soul-stirring for the young people of Egypt as they welcomed Oliver Tambo, Joshua Nkomo, Oging Odinga, F. Moumie, Musazi, J. Kale, and the representatives of Sam Nujoma among other African and Asian leaders in the space of the university.

Supporting African liberation movements was important for President Nasser for many reasons, almost all of which were direct. Colonial and imperialist powers surrounded the Nile Basin, with British colonies in East Africa and a US military base in Ethiopia, formerly Abyssinia. Various colonial or neo-colonial regimes persisted in Southern Africa, including Rhodesia (English), Namibia (German), Angola and Mozambique (Portuguese), and apartheid South Africa. Israel, meanwhile, was looking forward to extending its influence in the African region and the Nile Basin. There was a struggle again French colonialism in Algeria and the whole of Francophone Africa. However, there was also potential support from the Socialist Bloc in order to confront what was known as the 'Western Bloc'; that is, against the entire imperial project.

Nasser adopted the principle of accepting representation of all liberation movements that wanted to be represented in Cairo directly after the Afro-Asian People Solidarity Conference. He authorised the opening of permanent offices for them in the African Association in Zamalek, directed by the representative and acting as the movement's window to the world, the voice of its members and the link with other African liberation movements, global powers and international organisations.

When one African leader met Nasser this meant permission for official representation of the leader's movement in Cairo. The Uganda office (UNC), Kenya office (KANU), South Africa Office (ANC), Cameroon Office (UPC) and Namibia Office (SWAPO) were among the first to be opened for liberation movements in Cairo since 1958. The first Head of the National African Congress Office, Ntimi Piliso, was succeeded by Tennyson Makiwane, Alfred Nzo and (later) Joe Nhlanhla. They were to become prominent leaders in South Africa and were good friends of the author.

Besides the direct intellectual effect of ANC representatives in Cairo, there was also the academic and democratic influence of Professor Archie Mafeje. Although politically limited, as his presence was not officially recognised in Cairo and he rarely expressed his affiliation to the unity movement, as a prominent professor of anthropology Mafeje's own CV was for us a testimony of the apartheid repression against nationalist researchers. In his life in Egypt as husband of an Egyptian intellectual, and as a friend of a number of us, he was helpful to the cause of democratic issues of South Africa.

Likewise, a group of the strongest leaders were also in these offices and were keen teachers of the struggle, especially Félix-Roland Moumie of Cameroon, John Kale of Uganda, Oginga Odinga of Kenya and Mahmoud Harbi of French-Somalia, as well as Woldeab Woldemariam of Eritrea. Some of these leaders had developed previous international relations, especially in London, the US or Scandinavia. However, those relations were only in the framework of African immigrant communities or Afro-American minorities, along with some support from democratic powers in Europe. All were facing difficulties with the Western conservative stance towards the liberation of rising nations, but their support was not on a governmental or national level, as was the case with Cairo, extending to Ghana, Algeria and Tanzania and through the developments in those countries after the Congo Crisis in 1960 and the establishment of the Organisation of African Unity in 1963.

The liberation movements' offices used to find an easy way to international representation in Cairo. Among my duties was to connect their representatives to Egyptian government departments and popular spaces of support and activism. Within a few years, there were more than 20 offices for African liberation movements in Zamalek, as well as more than 25 radio programmes in African languages, such as Zulu, Matebele, Shona, Swahili, Hausa and others.

Pan-African connections

Within the framework of implementing this duty, the connection between some liberation movements and the Egyptian society became more profound, in spite of foreign
languages being an impediment to this connection due to the prevalence of Arabic
in Egypt. However, comrades Piliso and Makiwane (ANC office) were strongly connected to Egyptian leftist circles in the *Al-Ahram* newspaper, the World Peace Council
and the Secretariat of Afro-Asian People's Solidarity.

The traditional Egyptian society (Islamic and bourgeois) was sensitive towards
the coalition between the ANC and the communists in South Africa, and even to some
Jewish leftist leaders in the party. Nasser himself was reserved about Marxism and
Marxists, though he had broad coalitions with the Socialist Bloc. It was the rising
wave of national liberation that was to transcend most of these sensitivities, a wave
that was also felt at the level of the Arabic world.

This spirit of solidarity moved Egypt and Ghana to support the Congolese liberation movement, thereby further expanding the anti-colonial movement throughout
the continent. This support evolved into military support as seen in the Congo, where
the struggle was led by Patrice Lumumba.

Flowing from this anti-colonial spirit, Egypt severed its consular relations with the
South African government in 1960, a relationship that had existed between apartheid
South Africa and the monarchy that ruled Egypt before the July 1952 Revolution.

The new rulers of Egypt joined hands with 28 other countries in raising the apartheid case at the Security Council for the first time in 1962, in consultation with the
leaders of the ANC. Within the continent, the Organisation of African Unity established a presidential Committee of Coordination of Liberation of African Colonies
which took a firm stand against apartheid South Africa which was oppressing its
people and destabilising neighbouring states that were gaining independence.

The activism of liberation movements in Cairo and in a number of progressive African countries strongly affected the broadening of the national liberation circle – from
the horizons of the Communist International (CI) and its centres in Eastern Europe to
the democratic forces in the Western Bloc, to the effective circles in the third world,
especially in African capitals.

This activism was demonstrated by the Casablanca Group in 1960 (the six countries in North Africa and across the continent: Egypt, Algeria, Morocco, Ghana, Guinea
and Mali) and made them influential in national coalitions and the establishment of
the Organisation of African Unity.

It is no coincidence that this spirit of resistance would irk the racist regime in
South Africa, a regime that promptly banned and even criminalised the lawful presence of parties opposing it in 1960. Then, the trial of Nelson Mandela came after his

visits to a number of North African countries and the rest of the continent in 1963. The Sharpeville massacre had a significant impact on Egyptian youth, who linked it to Lumumba's death. This led most of them also to accept the versions of the events as narrated by the Pan-Africanist Congress (PAC), besides those of the ANC about these developments.

This power of national liberation countries pushed the resistance movement in Portuguese colonies and in North and South Rhodesia. This led to the development of the diplomacy of liberation movements themselves and doubled their importance for the powers supporting them with humanitarian aid and media support in the North, especially from Scandinavian countries.

Given the development of the diplomacy of African liberation movements, they were not bound to politics or political diplomacy only. The slogan of armed resistance since the killing of Lumumba became a lawful slogan in all circles previously influenced by Gandhism or by the practical difficulties associated with this method of struggle.

The sixties were a backdrop for several differences, and then clarity prevailed in this respect. Since the All-African People's Conference (AAPC) in Ghana in late 1958, new features began to crystallise with regard to means of struggle. The great psychological impact Frantz Fanon had, when he came to Accra from the heart of armed Algerian struggle, saw leaders of the Algerian Revolution rally around him, getting to know the leaders of national African political action. After that, the Nkrumian and Gandhian policy of non-violence was reconsidered.

After the killing of Lumumba, violent resistance broke out from east and mid-Congo, led by Muleli. The spirit of Guevara was vibrant at that time, influenced by his visit to the Congo and by Cuba's long-time support for its rebels. Then, the resolution came to establish the Liberation Committee in the Organisation of African Unity, recognising armed struggle officially, and at the level of an international organisation that could not be rejected by the frameworks of the UN.

The latter's General Assembly, as well as the OAU, was armed with the International Declaration of Decolonisation in December 1961, when global leaders such as Nehru, Nasser, Nkrumah and Khrushchev attended this meeting in New York in September 1961.

This added to our burdens in Cairo as we needed to provide support to the steps taken by the representatives of the African liberation movements in all directions, regional and international. The rivalry due to Egypt's power or distinguished position was palpable. This was normal as Algeria was a newly independent country (1962) and its new diplomatic system led by Abdelaziz Bouteflika was known to be dynamic. Thus, rivalry with Egypt was normal and even resulted in broader support for liberation movements, especially those adopting armed struggle in Portuguese colonies.

Another example was that the dream of President Kwame Nkrumah to free Africa first and achieve its independence imposed the slogans of Pan-Africanism on movements that were primarily concerned with putting themselves into order and overcoming their domestic situations. President Nyerere then came newly into the line of competition after the independence and unification of Tanzania while he was the one hosting the Liberation Committee in Dar es Salaam.

In this respect, we do not forget that there was a strong move toward reconsidering all these directions, based on what were known as reactionary countries such as Ivory Coast, Senegal, Tunisia and others. Those countries believed that solutions reached through agreement (entente) were better than the hardships of armed struggle and that negotiation was more useful and maybe faster.

However, the intransigence of racist regimes in South Africa and Rhodesia (reaching the point of Ian Smith's Unilateral Declaration of Independence in November 1965 and the continuation of the apartheid policy of Bantustan) did not give conservative countries the chance to push for their views to be considered. In fact, liberation countries even rushed to declare the severance of diplomatic relations with Britain to let it be responsible for confronting the racist policy in Southern Rhodesia, considering that it was the colonising country. More than ten African countries supported Egypt's stand in this connection.

These developments may have pushed forward the diplomacy of violence against racist systems because the Palestinian Liberation Organisation (PLO) was established in the same period (1964) and the organisation adopted the philosophy of armed struggle. These ideas flourished in the ANC with the influence of early youth organisations and the arrests of leaders, which became an inspiration. In Cairo, and outside of Cairo across the continent, we were more concerned with the situation in South Africa as it confronted settler colonialism and how it resembled and co-operated with the racist system in Israel.

There was also some impact on the activism and competition of the PAC, whose representation was acceptable for Islamic circles and countries. The Morogoro Conference was held by the ANC in Tanzania, with a great momentum of parties and struggle which we heard about in Cairo, especially as the Congress elected Alfred Nzo, the party representative in Cairo, as its Secretary-General. We considered this strong proof as to the value of the Cairo office for the ANC's politics.

The Cold War era

The Cold War was the momentum behind the 1960s, but its final years were not as glorious as its beginnings. The end of the decade saw many African *coups d'état* (for example in Ghana and Mali) and a military setback for the Nasserian regime in Egypt, with Israel's victory over Egypt. The Soviet–Chinese conflict was at its peak and it also influenced various African policies, including the African liberation movements.

In the African Association, we were suffering from the consequences of that conflict and the deterioration of the relationships between a group that called itself 'authentic' and was considered pro-Soviet. It included representatives of the ANC, SWAPO, ZAPU, MPLA, FRELIMO and PAIGC, and other pro-China groups that did not even maintain distinct 'Maoist' ideologies. It mainly included the PAC from South Africa, ZANU from Rhodesia, UNITA and GRAE from Angola, COREMU from Mozambique and SWANU from Namibia.

The difficulty was personal when it came to planning any meetings, joint statements or relations with diplomatic or administrative authorities. This also starkly impacted on working in the Afro-Asian Solidarity Secretariat as the Soviets used to facilitate services abundantly for conferences and meetings. Also, the Egyptian Nasserist atmosphere and the pro-Soviet leftist movement helped keep that conflict going. The deeper truth is that the political reality and struggle of the authentic group or the one that was pro-Soviet was clearer for African and Arabic public opinion, whereas the weakness of other organisations was also a sign of the triviality of the support they were receiving.

With the beginning of the seventies, the policies of peaceful coexistence of the Soviet Union with the West began to encourage the idea of moderation, in spite of all the victories of national liberation movements in Angola, Mozambique, Guinea-Bissau and Cape Verde. Western campaigns were intensified against the Cuban presence in Africa and critical problems began to be transferred to countries that had achieved independence through armed struggle, such as Angola, Mozambique and Guinea-Bissau. This led us, the young people of Egypt, to wonder about the outcome of armed struggle within the social and cultural transformations of those people.

Sadatism depended on this disappointment, as the new regime rushed towards more loyalty to American politics and agreements with Israel. We, the young people of Egypt, were concerned about that, which is why the Algerians gave such support for African liberation movements financially and militarily. It was satisfactory for the Egyptian left. If it were not for the conflict between Algeria and Morocco, the Arabic Maghreb would have served the African national struggle movement more. Then, the Libyan Revolution led by Muammar Gaddafi entered the arena in 1969, with the complexity of its policies in the seventies and after.

The rising Libyan leader's (1969) attempts to push Nasserism and its methods towards supporting African liberation movements financially and militarily failed because he linked this with a crude Arabist tone for a long time before he switched to Africanism. It was difficult to tolerate this in African liberation movement circles and Algeria was affected by the problems arising from its reform policies and radical Islamism. Also, Morocco started to suffer from the problem with the Western Sahara and its crisis with the Polisario being either a national liberation movement or a separatist one. This disturbed the wider African theatre, not just the Arabic North.

The scenario was not miserable all the time in the area of African-Arab activism. The Arab-African coalition was able to support the leaders of the PLO and SWAPO at the General Assembly of the United Nations in reviving the diplomacy of the third world. The eruption of the Revolution of the people of South Africa in Soweto in 1976 also revived the nationalist movements across the continent, while confrontation with the apartheid system remained at the top of African concerns.

Within these circumstances, the campaign to release President Nelson Mandela at the end of the 1980s was a great impetus in raising awareness among the people of North Africa. One cannot remember such broad popular participation as with the signatures campaign for freeing Nelson Mandela. In Egypt, we used to move from one meeting to the other among civil society organisations and the leaders of professional and trade unions to have them sign documents demanding the release.

It is no coincidence that when he was released and visited Cairo in the winter of 1991/1992, even the police could not adequately help him walk among the huge crowds thronging Zamalek, as he had to give a speech remembering his previous visit to Cairo – before his imprisonment – in late 1962 as part of his tour of North African countries to support the struggle of South African people. This is what he himself related in detail in his personal memorials.

Post-Apartheid reflections

Declaring the beginning of full democratic transformation in South Africa had a great impact on the people of northern Africa. It started as a great victory for the phase of national liberation, especially with Nelson Mandela's release from the Robben Island prison. The influence of Egyptian TV played a part in this connection. Mandela's release came at a time in which Leftists were mourning the collapse of the Soviet Union and the leading socialist experience, while Nasserists were lamenting Abdul Nasser's reign of freedom. Egyptians generally considered the release a victory for their history in supporting African liberation movements and their symbol, the hero Nelson Mandela.

Egyptian intellectuals added to the event a perspective that was even broader, as they linked the triumph over apartheid in South Africa with the suffering of the Palestinian people in their own land, in spite of wide media coverage of Palestinian uprisings. Many questions followed this as a result of the African and Arab revival following the transformation in South Africa. We could briefly mention some of those questions because it is important to follow some of them up for the coming two decades.

The major question was about the secrets behind this great transformation at that time. The importance of the question was not solely related to the relationship with South Africa but, as pointed out, it was related to different worlds. The globalising phenomena became essential, especially with the beginning of the 1990s. Many phenomena became more intertwined and this was generally the first lesson learned from the events in Africa.

Indeed, the events became related to those in Angola, and the extent to which the Cubans would be able to stay there. In the Egyptian mind remained the great attack of President Anwar Al-Sadat against Cuba and the Soviet presence throughout Africa. From another perspective, for some of us, the events were associated with the Nkomati Agreement with Mozambique to mitigate the intense unrest there and with Angola suffering from Savimbi, besides the news about negotiations for settlement with the ANC. Those were thought to be similar to the Camp David Treaty, an infamous Treaty, associated in Egypt with the policies of submission in the Arab region and Palestine and the expansion of the American and Israeli powers in the region.

Questions kept following, positively and negatively, about what was considered by Sadatists a victory of 'peace politics' and the end of the 'fad' of struggle and liberation! It was even pointed out that the Congress abandoned its belief in Marxism and socialism. We progressives used to argue strongly against this, noting the importance of the hegemony of African liberation (before socialism) on governance that was for long solely dominated by a racist colonialist regime, hoping the same development would take place in Palestine. We even pointed out the importance of the fall of the Pretoria–Tel Aviv axis, which we had talked about for long, and its nuclear arms. The news of creating the new constitution in South Africa came to send strong messages to the regime in Egypt, a regime of police and security control. This was welcomed by progressives and the supporters of human and women's rights.

Conclusion

The South African events and their developments remain a source of reflection and excitement in different ways. Mandela's refusal to run for a second term as president made a joke of Hosni Mubarak's constant need to stay in power. Then, the Durban Review Conference came to confront racism in the beginning of September 2001 and the people of South Africa started demonstrating in support of the people of Palestine, with the attendance of President Bush and the Israelis. However, their intensity was decreased by the air attacks on New York on 11 September 2001 two weeks after the

Durban Review Conference. The USA and Israel made the September 2001 events the deathbed for Palestinian and Arab rights and declared a steady fight against so-called Islamic terrorism. This introduced the Arab and Islamic region into the great debate about 'religion', 'political Islam' and 'terrorism'.

The liberal and progressive trend in the region accused American institutions – security ones as well as cultural ones – of being the force behind pushing political Islam to the surface as part of the anti-communist wave. They were accused of using members of this movement in the war against the Soviets in Afghanistan or supporting the rulers in the Gulf for a time through religiosity and Islam, until the phenomenon turned upside down with the influence of the Muslim Brotherhood in competition with Mubarak himself over power in Egypt.

The great question which remained was about the nature of the relationship between the rise of the current of political Islam opposing some powerful and pro-USA regimes with the American interests in the Middle East and the Greater Middle East project itself. The answer was clear, especially after the popular uprisings that have appeared since 2011. This could be interpreted by the 'Islamic project' being founded by a group of Islamists who form a bourgeois business-oriented class in countries with relatively complex economies (e.g. Egypt and Algeria) supported by rentier-petroleum regimes carrying the name of Islam.

This formation of commercial capitalism does not in any way contradict American globalisation, particularly on the policy of the completely free market (as Islamic laws, mainly) and adopting an Islamic Middle East project. It also could, as a globalising system, accept the view of 'Islamic internationalism' that the Muslim Brotherhood calls for.

Even as he continued to rise, Colonel Gaddafi came up with the 'Third International Theory' and did not stop at the Arab, African or Islamic circles because it was a rentier system anyway, or what was called 'rentier-capitalism' and 'global' petroleum at the same time.

This is why political culture in the Arab region in North Africa looks at the impact of globalisation with great apprehension. It was behind the fragmentation of African countries and led them to conflict even after the latest revolutions. It seems also that globalisation is behind regional groupings or empowering some of its supporting regimes that are able to take the path of global capitalism such as South Africa, Nigeria and Ethiopia, hoping Egypt, Algeria and Morocco will join. This worries many Arab countries in North Africa that there will be competition with South Africa in the world of capitalist development or stirring any Africanist inclinations against Arabism or Islam, considering how this separates them from the single globalist path. This does not negate the effect of the African national liberation movement on progressive people and the youth behind the uprising of 25 January 2011.

This relates to the attempts to push for an Egyptian role in Africa, after the Mubarak regime was accused of destroying Egypt's interests in this continent by isolating it from the events there for long. When Egyptians think of Africa after the 25 January Revolution, they quickly remember Egypt's role in national liberation in particular. It is fortunate that the South African experience of truth, reconciliation and transitional justice after its 'great transformation' came as a new model for the need of Arab 'revolutions' to follow, as the path of the revolution was threatened by the rising power of Islamists who do not have a reputation of respecting democracy in any way. The intelligentsia in North Africa feels the negative effect of the Libyan events in particular and the miserable scene of Gaddafi's end – who was loved and respected to a certain degree on the African level. This led to the revolution or the uprising not being the main cause of exchanging emotions. Scenes of violence or chaos in Libya were the sources of negative impressions about what went on in North Africa instead.

Many remain unresolved about the relationship between the global capitalist system and the regimes in Southern or Northern Africa, or the one between great American projects for the Middle East with the power of the Muslim Brotherhood in Egypt or Islamists in general in Libya, Sudan and Algeria. The question remains: do imperialist polices reassure their supporters in Africa about Islamist conduct? Or are typical African fears of Islamists in North Africa doubled? The remaining questions abound and nothing answers them but the developments witnessed by our people within the greater circles of this world.

Endnote

1 This chapter was translated from Arabic to English by Mrs Nihal Nour of Cairo University.

PART 3

The Battle of Ideas

After the centenary: reflecting on the growth and development of the ANC from a revolutionary populist movement to a governing party

Anver Saloojee

Introduction

The African National Congress (ANC) is now over one hundred years old and democratic South Africa is rapidly approaching its fourth post-apartheid elections in 2014. Over the course of the one hundred years the ANC has undergone major and significant transformative changes. Since 1994, the ANC has been victorious in the first three democratic elections in South Africa it contested, and there is every likelihood the ANC will win a fourth consecutive victory in 2014 – this despite challenges including service delivery failures, corruption, 'tenderpreneurship' and the increasing use of the state apparatuses for personal gain, and the interpenetration of political and economic elites.

The central questions that arise particularly in the light of these challenges and of the tragedy at Marikana are whether the ANC has now abandoned its ethos of revolutionary populism and whether a new leadership will be able to steer the organisation back onto the path of a pro-poor economic growth and development strategy that combats unemployment, redistributes wealth and promotes greater states of equality among all South Africans. Will a renewed debate about inclusive nation building and democratic citizenship emerge as a significant counterweight to both the disturbing shades of ethnic chauvinism that emerged in sections of the ANC in the run-up to the Polokwane leadership elections and the xenophobia and concomitant violence that gripped parts of South Africa early in 2008?

This chapter will analyse the historical evolution and development of the ANC through the theoretical prism of populism and crisis. Theoretical reflections on populism, Laclau's notion of fusion of popular democratic and working class demands and Gramsci's notions of hegemony, crises and organic intellectuals provide us with important insights and interpretations, which can also be very profitably applied to an understanding of the historical evolution and development of the ANC.

The simultaneous existence in apartheid South Africa of two very different forms of populism, one revolutionary – the ANC – and the other reactionary – the Inkhata Freedom Party (IFP) – and their different responses to the various crises of the regime suggests that any theory linking crisis and populist responses must be cognisant of the large spaces open for alternate forms of political leadership and organisation to exist. Furthermore, the alternate responses suggest that populist movements do not respond in a vacuum but are directly shaped by the context of struggle, state repression, crises in the conjuncture, and spontaneous and semi-spontaneous actions initiated by the ensemble of dominated classes.

There were a number of political moments leading up to the first democratic elections and the formal political end of apartheid when space was open for creative political leadership to emerge, for political activists to reconstitute the counter-hegemonic bloc and challenge the state, and even for the two forms of populism to come into direct conflict with each other.

Since populist movements can take on a variety of organisational forms and populist ideologies can vary widely, it is imperative to show how popular democratic 'interpellations' are articulated into the ideology of the working class in a manner antagonistic to the state and the prevailing ideology.[1] For a national liberation movement like the ANC there are a number of organisational implications which flow from this. Popular participation predicated on this antagonism towards an oppressive state requires mediation by politico-organisational structures. These structures have to mediate (i) the relationship between a charismatic leader and a heterogeneous mass base; (ii) class contradictions internal to the organisation; and (iii) ideological thrusts which stem from the internal conflicts.[2]

What distinguishes revolutionary from authoritarian populism are class interests. A revolutionary populist movement like the ANC, which under apartheid challenged the state and the dominant discourse, is one that:

• Incorporates and articulates working-class demands within its political agenda,
• Avoids racism and ethnocentrism as mobilising tools,
• Politically organises the dominated classes into a strong counter-hegemonic bloc,
• Has an organisational and membership bias in favour of the working class,
• Incorporates the organic intellectuals of the working class into its decision-making structure,
• Is politically autonomous from any sector of the ruling class, and
• Challenges the state and the prevailing ideology and provides an alternative to it.

These characteristics, it can be argued, can also be used to distinguish the ANC pre-1991 and the ANC after 19 years as the governing party in post-apartheid South Africa.

In an organisation like the ANC, the central question is, how does the working class come to assert hegemonic control over a revolutionary populist movement, which is structured on a multi-class base? It is only when this process of assertion is complete that there can be agreement with Laclau when he says:

> In socialism, therefore, coincide the highest forms of 'populism' and the resolution of the ultimate and most radical of class conflicts. The dialectic between 'the people' and classes finds here the final moment of its unity. There is no socialism without populism and the highest forms of populism can only be socialist.[3]

In South Africa, for the most part, throughout the 1900s to the present there has existed a well-organised black working class with its own organic intellectuals, which continually sought to assert its hegemony over the national liberation movement (the ANC). The process was historically uneven and the working class had to continually work at asserting its hegemony over a multiclass alliance. For example, in the 1950s the organic intellectuals of the black working class came to play a vital role in increasing working-class influences in the ANC. This was reflected in the fusion of working-class and popular democratic/community demands and the development of political unionism amongst trade unions representing the interests of black workers.

Once the ANC was banned and forced into exile, the process of fusion and the working-class bias in the ANC were rendered problematic. The extent to which the ANC could directly influence the black community in general and the black working class in particular was constrained by the reality of illegality. Thus the ANC had to find new ways of initiating popular protests and influencing the people. The history of the ANC, particularly since the mid-1940s, is the history of balancing working-class and community demands and of drawing on and being influenced by both the nationalist and socialist thrusts of resistance politics.

The ANC, populism and formative episodes

Populism has to be analysed in the context of a crisis of capitalism at the level of a social formation and this requires an understanding of the nature of the crisis (hegemonic or transformative) and its impact on classes affected by it. Theoretical reflections on populism and Gramsci's conception of 'organic intellectuals' and his notions of 'hegemony' and 'crises' provide us with important insights and interpretations and allow us to look at what we will call formative episodes in the development of the ANC.

Between 1940 and 1994 there have been at least seven such moments in the history of the ANC: the formation of the ANC Youth League (ANCYL), the Defiance Campaign, the Congress of the People and the adoption of the Freedom Charter, the decision to launch the armed struggle, the 1979 decision to refocus and intensify internal reconstruction, the call to 'ungovernability', and the decision to enter into negotiations with the apartheid regime.

At each of these moments, options had to be weighed, costs and benefits calculated and key decisions taken. With the decisions taken, the dye was cast, a political approach was articulated and internal unity within the movement was cemented around the political principles. Those who opposed the new directions (for example Africanists opposed to the multi-racial, multi-organisational Congress Alliance) ultimately had little option but to leave the organisation.

Shortly after it won the first democratic elections in South Africa, tension in the ANC surfaced around whether to accept an International Monetary Fund loan, cancel the debt of the apartheid regime, open South Africa to trade liberalisation and institute a de facto policy of structural adjustment. More recently there have been tensions within the ANC that revolve around leadership struggles – first with respect to who would replace President Nelson Mandela and then in 2007 the leadership struggle between President Mbeki and then Deputy President of the ANC Jacob Zuma. These two leadership struggles, and particularly the latter, polarised the ANC and ultimately led to President Mbeki resigning as President of South Africa in September 2008.

Theory of populism

There is much confusion surrounding the term populism. Is it a political movement, an ideology, a regime or merely a tendency that appears in diverse types of political movements? This chapter evolves from the premise that populism is both an ideology and a political movement but that it can take different political forms on the same political terrain.

For Ernesto Laclau, populism is linked to the existence of the entity 'the people' in an ideological discourse, in such a manner that the latter is transformed into a populist ideological discourse by the particular form of articulation of the popular-democratic interpellations in it. Where the ruling class is unable to neutralise popular democratic demands, space is opened for the emergence of a revolutionary populism in which the dominated classes incorporate popular democratic demands into their discourse and present their ideology and their practice as an antagonistic option to the dominant bloc.

Populism therefore has its origin in crisis. Its emergence is linked to a crisis of the dominant ideological discourse, which is symptomatic of a more generalised crisis. It can result from contradictions between fractions of the power bloc in which a new fraction seeks to assert its hegemony, thereby precipitating a hegemonic crisis, which potentially allows for the emergence of authoritarian populism.

It can result from the inability of the ruling class to meet or contain the demands of subordinate classes. In this case, the system is challenged and there develops what Gramsci calls a crisis of 'transformism'. Such a crisis threatens the political and ideological underpinnings of the system and threatens to transform it.

In such a crisis, the dominated classes weld into a 'counter-hegemonic bloc'. They unite, develop a counter-hegemony, challenge the system and pose alternatives to the existing form of the state. The specific form of populism (revolutionary, reformist or authoritarian) will depend on the nature of the crisis and on which class or fraction is able to galvanise 'the people' against the established order and ideology. For Laclau the people/class dialectic (one is simultaneously a member of the people and a member of a class) attains ultimate unity for there is 'no socialism without populism and the highest forms of populism can only be socialist'.[4]

In the case of South Africa, the ANC emerged initially as a reformist movement, which sought political accommodation with British colonialism. In the 1940s a transformation began which affected both the structure and politics of the ANC – namely the formation of the ANCYL and the black working class and its leadership who came to play a much larger role. With the consolidation of the Congress Alliance the movement adopted a 'Programme of Action' and then the Freedom Charter. With these developments began the maturation of the ANC into a revolutionary populist movement – one that challenged the system, mobilised the dominated classes, fused popular democratic and working-class demands, gave expression to this multi-class heterogeneity and posed an alternative to the apartheid state.

The value of Laclau's formulation is that it points us to the importance of the fusion of working-class and non-working-class demands, and this is precisely what was important to the development of the ANC from the 1940s onwards. Despite this, Laclau's formulation has two significant weaknesses which his preoccupation with populism as ideology obscures; these are his neglect of populism as a political movement and the class basis of the populist movement.

To fill these two gaps we turn to a reformulation of the theory of populism drawing on the work of Gramsci, who alerts us to the importance of organic intellectuals in transforming political organisations, which respond to and are shaped by political moments. Gramsci provides an analysis of populism as movement and organisation that are shaped by political moments, by internal and external crises and by political action.

In the case of the ANC, a Gramscian analysis alerts us to two important areas of enquiry – the nature of the counter-hegemonic bloc as a multi-class alliance that has a particular organisational expression (the Congress Alliance) and the role played by organic intellectuals of the black working class in reshaping the ANC into a revolutionary populist movement. Over a period of five decades from the 1940s, the ANC demonstrated a great deal of latitude for creative forms of leadership and organisation. A large share of the responsibility for this was left to political activists in the ANC and the broader Congress Alliance. They had to gauge the mood and tempo of actions initiated by the people against the power bloc. These political activists had to organise opposition on what Gramsci called the 'terrain of the conjunctural', which was also the terrain on which the ruling class in apartheid South Africa sought to hold onto to power. This was particularly true after 1960, when the state declared the ANC illegal. Forced underground and part of its leadership imprisoned or forced out of the country, the ANC decided to wage an armed struggle.

The first two formative episodes that were important in the development of the ANC into a revolutionary populist movement were the creation of the ANCYL and the Defiance Campaign. At both of these political moments the leadership was faced with significant choices. The pressure they were under and the decisions they took altered the organisation, the terrain and forms of resistance and the nature of alliances. They also precipitated organisational problems for the ANC and ideological tensions within the leadership.

The inception and growth of the ANCYL was a central ingredient in the radicalisation of the ANC. Many of the Youth Leaguers were from working-class and peasant backgrounds, while others were teachers and lawyers from the nascent black middle strata. Nelson Mandela, Walter Sisulu and Govan Mbeki would in very short order assume leadership roles in the ANC.

They became the organic intellectuals of the oppressed black people of South Africa. And in order not to be removed from their roots they had to devise ways of reaching down and establishing a rapport with their roots. This was accomplished by the ANC working much more closely with the black trade union movement (particularly after the 1946 mineworkers' strike), a close cooperation that resulted in the development of political trade unionism in South Africa.

Political trade unionism and all it entailed (stay-at-home campaigns, the £1/day campaign, the bus boycotts, the rent boycotts and eventually the Defiance Campaign) constituted the specific mechanism through which popular democratic and working-class concerns and demands were being fused. These protest mechanisms pioneered by the organic intellectuals of the ANC in the 1940s and 1950s withstood the test of time and the waves of repression by the apartheid state.

With regard to the class basis of the ANC, Dan O'Meara[5] has argued that the African mineworkers' strike of 1946 was crucial in transforming the ANC into a much more militant organisation, responsive to the demands and interests of the black working class. The petit bourgeois leadership of the ANC was groping its way to common cause with the black working class.

After the violent suppression of the strike, 53 trade union, ANC and Communist Party officials were put on trial for aiding and abetting in an illegal strike.[6] The organic intellectuals of the black working class were beginning to fuse working-class and national demands. They were simultaneously radicalising the ANC, and politicising and mobilising the people for mass action. The process of assertion of working-class dominance in the ANC was very uneven. The leadership of the ANCYL supported the 1946 Mineworkers' strike but worked against the 1950 May Day 'stay away'.

The Defiance Campaign was one of the first attempts to implement the ANC's Programme of Action. It saw 'a notable influx of working-class men and women into leadership positions' in the ANC.[7] The decision to embark on the Defiance Campaign opened two fissures in the ANC leadership. The first was between those who wanted to embark on mass action and those who did not. The second and more significant split was between those who advocated cooperation with non-Africans and those who did not. The role of leadership was again central and they made the choice to create a multi-racial front against apartheid – it was a stand from which the ANC has not backed down.

The working class had not yet achieved a hegemonic position in the ANC. Its intellectuals were laying the basis for that possibility, but first the radicalisation of the ANC had to continue, its strategy had to be altered and new tactics had to be developed. And the ANC had to increase its membership base.

The Defiance Campaign became instrumental in the radicalisation of the ANC, the heightening of national consciousness and the heightening of the people/power bloc contradictions. A broad multi-class, multi-racial, multi-organisational campaign to defy unjust racial laws was led by the ANC. It was successful and it led to the call for the convening of a Congress of the People to draw up a 'people's charter of rights'.

This was a shrewd political calculation by the organic intellectuals in the ANC to develop a charter that would reflect a fusion of working-class and popular democratic demands. Through the fusion the Freedom Charter would come to reflect the populism of the dominated classes. The two elements that are significant are first that it reflects the populism of the dominated classes and the fusion of demands and second that it posits an alternate vision which cannot be implemented without first bringing the populist movement into direct conflict with the apartheid state.

The ANC of the 1950s reflected the populism of the dominated classes. The Congress Alliance, the growth of the South African Congress of Trade Unions, the struggles of labour and of women and youth communities, the use of boycotts and the stay-at-homes had the cumulative effect of heightening the people-power bloc contradictions. This populism of the dominated classes was revolutionary precisely because of its political autonomy from any sectors of the ruling class. Internal crises (in 1926, 1935/36, 1948/49 and 1958/59) all enabled the organisation to deal with latent and manifest tensions, to jettison those opposed to its political line and to reconstitute unity. In the late 1950s and beyond such unity was reconstituted around principles articulated in the Freedom Charter.

Once it was wedded to a multi-class, multi-racial, multi-organisational form of political organisation, the ANC had to deal with a recurring series of tensions and potential splits. These can only be understood in the context of the internal development of the movement and are illuminated by a theory of populism that focuses on the role of creative leadership which is able to chart a political course such as the ANC leadership undertook in the 1940s, 1950s and beyond.

The Freedom Charter was not a socialist document – it proclaimed the will of the people and reflected the aspirations of the dominated and the oppressed, and in its calls posited a radically different vision from apartheid South Africa. It posed a radical alternative to the status quo that it could not be achieved without the suppression of the apartheid state as an antagonistic force. Its adoption was another critical step in the ongoing radicalisation of the ANC, provoking an outcry from the Africanist wing of the ANC – a number of whom were expelled from the ANC in 1958. The revolutionary populist thrust in the ANC found expression in its strict avoidance of political mobilisation on the basis of national chauvinist or racist interpellations.

The campaigns launched and the protests conducted, the alternate vision embodied in the Freedom Charter, these all challenged the apartheid state through a powerful counter-hegemonic bloc. The ANC directly confronted the state and questioned its legitimacy and its right to rule.

For its part, the state had to deal with what it perceived to be an impending crisis of transformism. The Sharpeville crisis was provoked by the politics of popular resistance and the state responded with a massacre of innocent protestors.

In the aftermath of the Sharpeville massacre the ANC was banned and a large portion of the leadership imprisoned. Forced underground and eventually into exile by state repression, the ANC was initially cut off from its mass base. In deciding to launch the armed struggle in the face of intense and mounting state repression, the ANC was forced into a strategy and a set of tactics with which it was quite unfamiliar. Sharpeville represented the inevitable moment of confrontation between the people and the state, a moment when the state felt it necessary to use excessive repression against the counter-hegemonic bloc in an attempt to crush it physically, organisationally and psychologically.

A banned organisation, further incapacitated by the banning of its leaders, is unable to sustain the same level of political confrontation. Either the organisation is destroyed entirely or the leaders of the organisation have the foresight and the courage to dispense with the known and the familiar and begin the task of restructuring the organisation. Thus some of the leaders in the ANC decided to embark on the armed struggle and *Umkhonto we Sizwe* (MK), or 'the Spear of the Nation' was formed in 1961 and a new era of struggle was born.

Cut off from South Africa, deprived of being able to mobilise the people on the legal terrain, the ANC had to find a variety of creative ways to reach them. For the first 15 years in exile this proved very challenging. In that period new organisations such as the Black Consciousness Movement (BCM) sprang up to fill the political void. The 1976 Soweto Uprisings derived a great deal of impetus from the BCM. For its part the ANC never claimed a direct role in the Soweto uprisings. What is clear from the political trials of student leaders is that the ANC did have an indirect role. By its own admission the ANC was not fully prepared for the Soweto uprisings. It was ill prepared and organisationally still weak inside the country, and it had relatively few armed units operating in South Africa.

The Soweto uprisings signalled the re-emergence of black resistance and it had a profound effect on the ANC. The ANC had to adapt as the uprisings generated a continuous flood of students willing to leave South Africa for military training abroad. By 1979 the ANC was directing its energy at internal reconstruction. In 1980 pressure on the ANC increased as nationwide boycotts began anew. Release Nelson Mandela Committees (RMCs) sprang up throughout the country and the ANC took the decision to popularise the Freedom Charter inside South Africa once again. The Release Mandela and the Freedom Charter campaigns gained momentum throughout the 1980s as student organisations such as SAYCO (The South African Youth Congress), trade unions (including the National Union of Mineworkers) and eventually COSATU (the Congress of South African Trade Unions) all adopted it.

Through these organisations the banned ANC once again had a strong 'on the ground' organisational presence. At the same time armed attacks against the apartheid state were increasing in regularity and intensity.

The campaign to adopt the Freedom Charter was successful beyond anyone's expectations. All the organisations that adopted the charter echoed sentiments reminiscent of the 1950s – unity, and the building of a multi-class, multi-racial, multi-organisational alliance linking the charter to the everyday demands of workers, students and their communities.

These two campaigns merged with other campaigns (for example the anti-Republic Day campaign, and the anti-South African Indian Council elections). Not since the 1950s were such large numbers of South Africans actively engaged in struggle. The models of political organisation and the forms of protest were patterned along the lines of those initiated by the Congress Alliance in the 1950s.

What is remarkable is the speed with which the ANC was able to regroup in the immediate post-Soweto era. The strength of the ANC was its ability to perceive developments on the ground and attempt to influence and guide them. Such influence and guidance, such insertion in the conjuncture, could not be attempted without drawing on the legacy of protest – thus the need to popularise all the iconography of the ANC, including the colours, songs, slogans, the Freedom Charter and the leadership. The ANC was at no time entirely absent from the terrain of struggle and its organising principles were not entirely forgotten by the people.

In a sense the campaigns unlocked the recesses of political consciousness in which were stored the history of past political protest. Once unlocked, the past proved invaluable in the present. Political organisations grew, mass protest spiralled and in 1982 a Johannesburg newspaper concluded that the ANC was 'the most popular movement in the country'.[8]

Faced with its own renewed popularity and seeking to draw on its increasing ties with internal organisations and self-defence units, the ANC issued a call to render South Africa 'ungovernable'. At roughly the same time the ANC leadership took the decision to engage in talks and negotiations with government. At first glance it might seem that these two formative episodes mark a difference, perhaps even a contradiction, between an attempt on the part of the ANC to 'seize' power via rendering the country ungovernable and an attempt to 'transfer' power via negotiations. However, what both formative episodes clearly demonstrate is that a legal populist movement, once banned, need not disappear from the terrain of resistance. It has to constantly adapt to the changed conditions, reorganise its structures and reconceptualise its strategy and tactics so as to mount a new offensive, challenge the state and deepen the organic crisis of the state.

By the mid-1980s the ANC was under pressure to develop a multifaceted strategy to coordinate its armed struggle with the struggle of workers, students and communities. The ANC turned to armed propaganda which placed emphasis on the political dimensions of the struggle. With the creation of the United Democratic Front (UDF) and COSATU, the revival of the South African Indian Congress, an increase in the militancy of the black working class and a huge upsurge in community resistance even prior to the formation of the UDF, the terrain of extra-parliamentary organising and mobilisation had altered.[9] The ANC now had new avenues to access in order to bring influence to bear on the black population and to challenge the state. As Davis notes, 'The shortcut through the UDF and COSATU gave the ANC access to huge numbers of blacks in townships and on shop floors …'.[10]

As a result of these cumulative developments, 'here followed an extraordinarily pervasive re-introduction of ANC history and symbols into black community life and it had a profound effect on numbers of post-Soweto youth militants'.[11]

Another reason for the gravitational pull of the ANC was its ability to up the ante on the military front and intensify the guerrilla warfare campaign. By 1985 the ANC felt sufficiently strong inside the country to issue the call to render South Africa ungovernable. The crisis of apartheid was being deepened. Through its political structures the ANC hoped to give direction to the 'organs of people's power' on the ground and through MK it hoped to protect liberated townships.

Through its deep connection to both COSATU and the UDF, the ANC was successful in reaching the people. In so doing it provided the context in which populism (the politics of popular protest) and armed struggle (military action by a trained group of political cadre) could be fused. The ANC had transformed armed propaganda into a people's war. Through the creation of a 'revolutionary people's army' the ANC was able to mobilise its constituency as it sought to heighten the people/power bloc contradiction and pave the way for the seizure of power. These were the mechanisms by which an illegal populist movement kept touch with its mass base.

People's war was the next logical extension of the fusion of popular democratic and working-class demands. It entailed mass mobilisation of the counter-hegemonic bloc and a heightening of the people/power bloc contradiction. It would pose a threat to the status quo and put the people at the centre of the struggle. In directly challenging the state and the ruling class, and making South Africa ungovernable, it posed anew the question of the seizure of power.

By 1986, the crisis in South Africa had reached the point at which the old was dying and the new was struggling to be born. The apartheid state was still able to exercise power but with diminishing capacity and significantly diminished external support. A rupture between the state and the economically dominant class was emerging, power was being centralised in the executive of the state and all the hallmarks of a Bonapartist state were becoming evident. The crisis of the apartheid state was deepening. The state continued to resort to military as well as legal repression.

The fourfold intervention strategy by the state (military pacification of the townships, township upgrading, the creation of Joint Management Committees and coercive legislation) were all designed to contain and solve the crisis of transformism which was all-encompassing as it involved an economic crisis, a military crisis, a crisis of the state of hegemony and a crisis of transformism. It was an organic crisis that limited the ability of the state to continue its course of action. The conditions for talks about talks and for negotiations were in place. Global and regional conditions were changing rapidly and both the ANC and the apartheid government realised that a negotiated settlement could be reached.

Without the decision to render South Africa ungovernable and the concomitant

ability to deepen the crisis of apartheid, the ANC would not have been able to legitimately call for negotiations with the apartheid state as there would have been no
stalemate forcing the latter to the negotiating table.

On 7 August 1990, nearly 29 years after it took the decision to wage the armed
struggle, the ANC signed the Pretoria Minute and agreed to suspend the armed
struggle.

The study of the ANC in the period of illegality to legality informs us that the
viability of a populist movement depends on the extent to which it is capable of (i)
articulating the grievances of the people; (ii) organising popular dissent and channelling it into an effective challenge to the state; (iii) deepening the generalised crisis
of the state; (iv) weathering intense state repression; and (v) being flexible enough
to revise its strategy and tactics to take account of changing political circumstances.
The ANC both responded to and deepened the crisis at various moments in South
African history. A banned populist movement is capable of asserting its primacy on
the political terrain if it draws on its legacy, its internal capacity, its large reservoir of
iconography and its ability to interface with, influence and lead legal organisations
of resistance. The history of the ANC forces the theory of populism to recognise
that a legal populist movement, once banned, need not disappear from the terrain of
resistance.

The ANC after three general elections: revolutionary populism or gradual demise?

Today, the rhetoric of the ANC is still steeped in revolutionary populism. For example,
at Mangaung, the ANC committed itself to the 'task of ensuring decisive and accelerated progress towards the eradication of the legacy of apartheid colonialism and
the construction of a National Democratic Society'.[12] And the document continues,
'Strategy and Tactics 2007 affirms the strategic goal of the NDR as the resolution
of the three basic and inter-related contradictions of Colonialism of a Special Type
in South Africa (where the colonized and the colonial metropolis lived within one
nation-state): racial oppression, class super-exploitation and patriarchal relations of
power. These antagonisms found expression in:

> ... National oppression based on race; class super-exploitation directed against
> black workers; and the triple oppression of the mass of women based on their race,
> their class and their gender. The main content of the National Democratic Revolu-
> tion (NDR) therefore remains the liberation of Africans in particular and blacks in
> general from political and socio-economic bondage. It means uplifting the quality

of life of all South Africans, especially the poor, the majority of whom are African and female.[13]

The ANC calls for popular participation of the people in the process of development, and with special focus on the poor and marginalised. The 'Strategy and Tactics' document adopted at Mangaung is replete with such rhetorical flourishes, which leads one to believe the ANC is still a revolutionary populist organisation. But the use of sexist and ethnocentric appeals in the run-up to Polokwane and in the 'two centres of power debate' post-Polokwane demonstrate how permeable is the membrane separating revolutionary rhetoric from chauvinist rhetoric. Interestingly, in a discussion document, the ANC acknowledges 'the level of trust in local government has declined sharply since 2004. Participatory government has lost its meaning and content and in its place has risen communities who feel alienated and disconnected from decision-making processes and disempowered in influencing the affairs of the municipality.'[14] By its own admission the ANC now acknowledges it has strayed from its revolutionary ethos.

For former Minister (and senior ANC leader) Ronnie Kasrils, this departure began prior to the ANC's first term in office:

From 1991 to 1996 the battle for the ANC's soul got under way, and was eventually lost to corporate power: we were entrapped by the neoliberal economy ... What I call our Faustian moment came when we took an IMF loan on the eve of our first democratic election. That loan, with strings attached that precluded a radical economic agenda, was considered a necessary evil, as were concessions to keep negotiations on track and take delivery of the promised land for our people. Doubt had come to reign supreme: we believed, wrongly, there was no other option... To lose our nerve was not necessary or inevitable.

The ANC leadership needed to remain determined, united and free of corruption – and, above all, to hold on to its revolutionary will. Instead, we chickened out. The ANC leadership needed to remain true to its commitment of serving the people. This would have given it the hegemony it required not only over the entrenched capitalist class but over emergent elitists, many of whom would seek wealth through black economic empowerment, corrupt practices and selling political influence... However, at the time, most of us never quite knew what was happening with the top-level economic discussions.

As Sampie Terreblanche has revealed in his critique, *Lost in Transformation*, by late 1993 big business strategies – hatched in 1991 at the mining mogul Harry Oppenheimer's Johannesburg residence – were crystallising in secret late-night discussions at the Development Bank of South Africa. Present were South Africa's mineral and energy leaders, the bosses of US and British companies with a presence in South Africa – and young ANC economists schooled in western economics. They were reporting to Mandela, and were either outwitted or frightened into submission by hints of the dire consequences for South Africa should an ANC government prevail with what were considered ruinous economic policies.[15]

The ANC has now governed South Africa for 19 years and poverty and unemployment are still critical issues. Kasrils continues: '… in South Africa in 2008 the poorest 50% received only 7.8% of total income. While 83% of white South Africans were among the top 20% of income receivers in 2008, only 11% of our black population were. These statistics conceal unmitigated human suffering. Little wonder that the country has seen such an enormous rise in civil protest.'[16]

Peter Alexander, the South African research chair in social change and professor of sociology in the Faculty of Humanities at the University of Johannesburg, analysing data on the number of 'crowd management incidents' for a three-year period from April 1 2009 to 2012, provided to the South African Parliament by the Minister of Police Nathi Mthethwa, notes that:

- In 2010–2011 there was a record number of crowd-management incidents (unrest and peaceful),
- The final data for 2011–2012 are likely to show an even higher figure. The number of gatherings involving unrest was higher in 2011–2012 than any previous year, and
- During the period 2009 to 2012, there was an average of 2.9 unrest incidents a day – an increase of 40% over the average of 2.1 unrest incidents a day recorded for 2004–2009.

For Alexander, these statistics point to a 'rebellion of the poor' that has intensified over the past three years:

The main conclusion to be drawn from the latest police statistics is that service-delivery protests continue unabated. Government attempts to improve service delivery have not been sufficient to assuage the frustration and anger of poor people in South Africa … it is clear that although service-delivery demands provide the principal focus for unrest incidents, many other issues are being raised, notably a lack of jobs. As many commentators and activists now accept, service-delivery protests are part of a broader 'rebellion of the poor'. This rebellion is massive. I have not yet found any other country where there is a similar level of ongoing urban unrest. South Africa can reasonably be described as the 'protest capital of the world'. It also has the highest levels of inequality and unemployment of any major country and it is not unreasonable to assume that the rebellion is, to a large degree, a consequence of these phenomena. There is no basis for assuming that the rebellion will subside unless the government is far more effective in channelling resources to the poor.[17]

Challenges around service delivery were also identified in the *African Peer Review Report* on South Africa which noted that 'While there have been successes in terms of service delivery and decision-making, there were also shortfalls due to poor co-ordination among different departments and spheres of government. A lack of capacity and of skills and resources is particularly acute at the local government level and this has had a negative impact on service delivery'.[18] The rhetorical flourishes in the ANC Strategy and Tactics document are not matched by this reality of ineffective and ineffectual state strategies to promote pro-poor ecologically sound growth and development. The tradition of revolutionary populism of the pre-1994 ANC has not carried over into the post-Polokwane ANC. Critics of the ANC, like Professor Bond, would go further and argue that since coming to power in 1994, the ANC only talks the language of revolutionary populism but does not walk the talk.[19]

Saloojee and Pahad argue that the biggest challenges facing the South African developmental state (a state whose governing arm is controlled by the ANC) include the corruption arising from the circularity and interpenetration of economic and political elites:

It can be argued that in the case of South Africa the developmental state is essential to the NDR and to protecting democracy. It is about protecting the interests of the vast majority of the oppressed people over advancing the interests of fractions of capital – Black and White. The developmental state in South Africa is suffuse with its own tensions and internal contradictions – advancing the interests of fractions of capital through Black Economic Empowerment; corruption (both grand corruption and petty corruption), wage inequalities and increasing inequality in general; inter and intra state elite competition; political elite–bureaucratic elite competition and strife; weakening social cohesion especially with increasing labour strife; integration into a global economy that brings with it the challenges of external competition for domestic capital.

The South African economy is constituted around three distinct forms of integration into the global economy – attracting foreign investment and embedding it in the local economy; second the promotion of local firms that have huge global scope; and third the creation of a macro-economic environment that allows for transformation of the South African economy and its integration and even domination of the regional African economies.[20]

More recently the South African state has shown a distinct penchant for dealing with protests by state repression. Most dramatic and tragic in this regard was the Marikana massacre, where 34 miners were killed by police in a show of force and in a radical departure from the ethos of service (embedded in the Constitution) to one of force.

Conclusion

The ANC showed that, despite fluctuations in its political fortunes, an illegal populist movement can still have an active political presence and a wide base of support. It can also act as a centrifugal force for legal organisations, and can mobilise an effective counter-hegemonic bloc. In order for this to occur a number of conditions must, however, be present. The organisation has to have a rich legacy on the terrain of resistance and political, ideological, psychological and organisational presence among the people. The organic intellectuals need to be creative and flexible. The organisation must have consistent political principles. There must exist or be created sympathetic legal organisations capable of organising the dominated classes, and the organisation waging the armed struggle must dovetail the latter with mass political action.

However, once power is transferred and the will of the people prevails, new tensions will best the populist movement. Central to those tensions will be the ongoing interpellation of working-class demands with broader demands of a non-class nature. In the case of South Africa, these tensions find expression in leadership debates, the configuration of class forces internal to the populist movement and debates about core principles, for example nationalisation, land restitution, wealth and income distribution, taxation policy and the role of the state as employer.

Populist movements like the ANC that gain power via the ballot box will invariably face the ongoing challenges associated with a structural accommodation of a market-based economy. The very heterogeneity of populist movements makes them lightening rods for criticisms from all quarters. Once in power it is almost impossible for a populist movement to satisfy all within its multi-class, multi-organisational umbrella.

Tensions around economic direction, the role of the state in the economy, the redistribution of wealth, dealing with political dissent in the party and in society, the increased militarisation of the state machinery, as evidenced by the Marikana massacre, and the way in which service delivery protests are dealt with point to a potential rupture of state–society relations. This, along with other challenges – the abject failure to deal with service delivery to the poorest, the rise of 'tenderpreneurship', corruption, the interpenetration of economic and political elites and blatant open corruption of bureaucratic and political elites by wealthy families – points to a governing party that is on a slippery slope to abandoning its claims to being a revolutionary populist movement.

The political moment is now for the ANC to undertake a thorough assessment of itself and of state–society relations. Failure to do so will only increase the distance between the ANC's rhetoric of revolutionary populism and the reality of its actions as the party in power for close to two decades.

Endnotes

1   See Laclau, E., 1977. *Politics and ideology in Marxist Theory: Capitalism, facism, populism*. London: NLB.

2   See Mouzelis, N., 1978. *Modern Greece: Facets of underdevelopment*. New York: Holmes & Meier, p.50.

3   Laclau, 1977, op. cit.

4   Ibid.

5   O'Meara, D., 1983. *Volkskapitalisme: Class, capital and ideology in the development of Afrikaner nationalism, 1934–1948*. Johannesburg: Ravan Press.

6   Francis, M., 1989. *South Africa belongs to us: A history of the ANC*. London: James Currey and Bloomington: Indiana University Press.

7   Gerhart, G., 1979. *Black power in South Africa: The evolution of an ideology*. Berkeley: University of California Press, p.109.

8   *The Star*, 9 January 1982.

9   Swilling, M., 1987. Living in the Interegnum: Crisis, reform and the socialist alternative in South Africa. *Third World Quarterly*, 9(2), April.

10 Davis, S., 1987. *Apartheid's rebels: Inside South Africa's hidden war*. New Haven, Yale University Press, p.114.

11 Johnson, S., 1988. *South Africa: No turning back*. Basingstoke: Palgrave Macmillan, p.106.

12 African National Congress, 2012. *Unity in action: Towards socio-economic freedom, strategy and tactics of the ANC*. Available at: http://www.anc.org.za/docs/pol/2013/strategyp.pdf. Also see, ANC, 2002. *Contribution to the NEC/NWC response to the Cronin interviews on the issue of neo-liberalism*. Internal ANC paper by the Political Education Unit, September.

13 Ibid.

14 Cited in Tabane, R., 2012. Addressing citizen distrust. *Mail & Guardian*, 9 March. Available at: http://mg.co.za/article/2012-03-09-addressing-citizen-distrust.

15 Kasrils, R., 2013. How the ANC's Faustian pact sold out South Africa's poorest. *The*

Guardian, 24 June. Available at: http://www.guardian.co.uk/commentisfree/2013/jun/24/anc-faustian-pact-mandela-fatal-error.

16 Ibid.

17 Alexander, P., 2012. A massive rebellion of the poor. *Mail & Guardian*, 13 April. Available at: http://mg.co.za/article/2012-04-13-a-massive-rebellion-of-the-poor.

18 African Peer Review Report on South Africa, p.80.

19 Bond, P., 2004. *Talk left walk right: South Africa's frustrated global reforms*. Scottsville: University of Kwazulu Natal Press.

20 Saloojee, A. & Pahad, E., 2011. The bureaucratic, flexible and democratic developmental state: Lessons for South Africa. In Plaatjies, D. (ed), 2011. *Future Inheritance: Building state capacity in democratic South Africa*. Johannesburg: Jacana.

CHAPTER 12

The idea of the African National Congress, democratic paradox and the stubborn spectre of coloniality

Sabelo J. Ndlovu-Gatsheni

Introduction

Many stalwarts of the South African liberation struggle, including Nelson Mandela, spent all their time fighting for liberation and freedom, but what they earned at the end of administrative apartheid was democracy and human rights. This was inevitable because coloniality, as before, continues to actively discipline liberation forces and movements into emancipatory-reformist formations. Coloniality is a global power structure and central leitmotif of modernity that works through disciplining antisystemic opposition forces as it sustains the long-standing racially hierarchised, patriarchal, Christian-centric, Western-centric, Euro-American-centric, colonial, capitalist and modern global system that began to expand into the non-Western world in 1492.[1]

This global system is resistant to change, but what is shifting is the international order, in the direction of disciplining and then accommodating antisystemic forces and movements into the lower echelons of the world system to continue serving the global imperial designs they had set out to destroy.[2] This global imperial strategy did not affect the African National Congress (ANC) alone but also all anti-colonial liberation movements. The general epistemic poverty of the decolonisation project was well expressed by Ramon Grosfoguel:

> One of the most powerful myths of the twentieth century was the notion that the elimination of colonial administrations amounted to the decolonisation of the world. This led to the myth of a 'postcolonial' world. The heterogeneous and multiple global structures put in place over a period of 450 years did not evaporate with the juridical-political decolonisation of the periphery over the past 50 years.

> We continue to live under the same 'colonial power matrix'. With juridical-political
> decolonisation we moved from a period of 'global *colonialism*' to the current period
> of 'global *coloniality*'.[3]

Taking into account Grosfoguel's trenchant critique of the trajectory of decolonisation, the next fundamental task is to interrogate whether liberation and freedom as decolonial utopic imaginaries directly translate into modernist-liberal notions of democracy and human rights. Put in other words, how can an African struggle for liberation and freedom that emerged as revolt against the inimical processes of slavery, Eurocentrism, imperialism, colonialism, apartheid, neo-colonialism, and coloniality, end up being celebrated in terms fashioned by liberalism and neo-liberalism cascading from European and American bourgeois revolutions that never questioned the edifice of Eurocentric modernity?

These are fundamental questions that cry out for reflections and responses as we celebrate the ANC's centenary and the post-apartheid government grapples with the intractable and complex question of transformation. It is a moment to reflect on the true meaning of the compromises that were made by the ANC as it sought a transition from apartheid to freedom. It is a great moment to reflect critically on the celebrated South African constitution that was adopted in 1996, with the then Deputy President gracing the occasion with the widely quoted 'I am an African' speech. Whose interests are served by this constitution? Was it wise for the African liberation movements to let those who benefitted from the racist and corrupt apartheid colonial system keep their loot in exchange for the universal franchise? Has the constitution not turned out to be an albatross on the dynamo of structural economic transformation?

This chapter, therefore, is a deep historical and political reflection by a concerned African scholar on the idea of the ANC and how it has grappled with colonialism, apartheid and coloniality as well as radical Africanism and cultural nationalism. The insights of the chapter benefit from a combination of historically informed flash-backs and political imagination that enable flash-forwards. The chapter is organised into the following sections: the first introduces the idea of the ANC and reveals some of the shifts it has made since its formation as it was disciplined from being a liberation movement into a simple administrative anti-apartheid political force. The second section fleshes out the spectre of coloniality which has haunted the African liberation movements, disciplining them into emancipatory movements. The final section is a critical reflection on the direction the ANC should take if it has to survive in the twenty-first century.

The idea of the ANC and the democratic paradox

As the ANC is the oldest modern African liberation movement in Africa that is still in existence it means that its long history, dating back to 1912, embodies and reflects a macrocosm of trials, tribulations, crises, tests, resilience and triumphs. While its resilience in the face of colonialism, apartheid and coloniality must be celebrated, at the same time we use the moment of its centenary to engage in deep and critical reflection on the broader essence of African struggles for liberation, the suitability of nationalism for the task and the meaning of the project of decolonisation.

Anthony Butler, in his booklet titled *The Idea of the ANC,* has dealt with the question of survival of the ANC from a clearly liberal perspective.[4] He argues that: 'One secret of its longevity has been its capacity to accommodate changes in its objectives, membership and modes of operation.' But from a decoloniality perspective the celebrated plasticity and flexibility of the ANC across time reveal the gradualist betrayal of the decolonial project of liberation and freedom and the increasing entry of the modernist-emancipatory liberal project. Sabelo J. Ndlovu-Gatsheni had this to say about the differences between emancipation and liberation:

> Emancipation is genealogically rooted in modernity, whereas liberation is genea-logically rooted in colonial difference, where the darker aspects of modernity such as the slave trade, imperialism, colonialism and apartheid were manifest. The teleology of emancipation is supposed to be liberal democracy and realisation of individual rights, whereas liberation is supposed to lead to decolonisation, social justice and the birth of humanity divorced from colonial modernity.[5]

The history of the ANC is indeed a history of resistance, disruption, adaptation and accommodation of doses of coloniality as a survival strategy. The ANC had also to respond to the resilient forces of radical Africanism and cultural nationalism through displacement, accommodation and suppression. The ANC emerged as 'a Native Congress' (the South African Native National Congress – SANNC) as a direct response to the white creation of a Union of South Africa that excluded those categorised as 'natives'. This is clear from Pixley Ka Isaka Seme's speech at the founding of SANNC:

> The white people of this country have formed what is known as the Union of South Africa – a union in which we have no voice in the making of laws and no part in their administration. We have called you, therefore, to this conference, so that we together devise ways and means of forming our national union for the purpose of creating national unity and defending our rights and privileges.[6]

In the ANC in particular one finds a political formation that has always been in search of identity and acceptable terms of the struggle for liberation. By 1923 the concept of 'native' was dropped as the movement became known as the African National Congress (ANC). This change took place within a context of rising pan-Africanism with Marcus Garvey's 'Africa for Africans' being embraced by many colonised peoples as a slogan of liberation. Garveyist ideas revealed themselves in the ANC Youth League's new leaders, such as Anton Lembede, Jordan Ngubane, A.P. Mda and Zeph Mothopeng, who projected what became known as 'Africanism'. Three issues troubled the history of the ANC, namely Africanism founded on racial consciousness, multiracialism predicated on anti-apartheid inclusivist thought and class consciousness informed by capitalist exploitative development.[7]

A broad critical reflection on the SANNC reveals the dropping of the name 'native' and adoption of a simple ANC nomenclature as the movement shifted ideologically into Charterist formation with its inclusivity inclination. This inclusivity practice was interpreted by some ANC members such as Robert Mangaliso Sobukwe as a complacent attitude towards racism, a betrayal of Africanism and a misunderstanding of the racial nature of apartheid colonialism that affects the black race more than anyone else. This is how Sobukwe articulated his position, which led him and others to break from the ANC to the Pan-Africanist Congress (PAC) in 1959:

> First of all we differ radically in our conception of the struggle. We firmly hold that we are oppressed as a subject nation – the African nation. To us, therefore, the struggle is a national struggle. Those of the ANC who are its active policy makers maintain, in the face of all the hard facts of the S.A. situation, that ours is a class struggle. We are, according to them, oppressed as WORKERS both white and black. But it is significant that they make no attempt whatsoever to organise white workers. Their white allies are all of them bourgeoisie?
>
> Secondly we differ in our attitude to 'co-operation' with other national groups [...]. We believe that co-operation is possible only between equals. There can be no co-operation between oppressor and oppressed, dominating and dominated. That is collaboration, not co-operation. And we cannot collaborate in our own oppression! The A.N.C. leadership, on the other hand, would seem to believe that all that is required for people to be 'equals' is that they should declare that they are equal, and lo! The trick is done!
>
> We claim Africa for Africans; the A.N.C. claims South Africa for all. To the A.N.C. leadership the nationalist government is the properly elected government of South Africa whose policies it does not approve. And the A.N.C's main struggle is to get 'Nats' out of power [...] We, however, stand for complete overthrow of white domination.[8]

This was the beginning of robust reflection on the political trajectory of the ANC. With the adoption of the Freedom Charter in 1955, the ANC shifted from being a liberation movement standing for the oppressed black people into standing for everyone who claimed to be opposed to apartheid. The ANC began to project more of a humanist proclivity ahead of decoloniality. Its alliance with the South African Communist Party (SACP) brought the notion of class into the liberation discourse, without the ANC necessarily dropping its nationalist identity. From this time onwards a difficult debate emerged, focusing on the identity of the subject for liberation. Who was the beneficiary of the liberation struggle?

It would seem the ANC adopted more of the Freireian conception, which specified that what was needed was a radical resolution of the complex 'oppressor-oppressed'/'coloniser-colonised' contradiction. The therapy took the form of liberation of both the 'oppressor/coloniser' and 'oppressed/colonised' subjectivities. This was considered to be a pragmatic solution. But most solutions to complex problems that are advertised as pragmatic often embody betrayal and constitute an easy way out of complex problems. In the same manner, the ANC ballooned into what is today termed a 'broad church', containing rival nationalisms and populisms. The fact that South Africa had to be liberated into a black African republic remained active within the ANC, taking the form of what can be termed a 'hidden script'.[9] The gospel of multiracialism assumed the form of a 'public script'.[10] This point is well articulated by Steven M. Davis:

> Africanism as an ideology would not wither with the PAC. Its popularity as an alternative to multiracialism was undiminished and was to manifest itself in later years through intermittent revivals of the PAC and through the rise of black consciousness. Black republicans were of the opinion that citizenship in post-apartheid South Africa should be rooted in African communal identities, values, and virtues. A true citizen of South Africa was an 'Azanian' fully committed to the right of the African people to self-rule and reclamation of all of their ancestral land.[11]

What has continued to haunt the ANC since its formation is a set of very clear but difficult questions which could not be dealt with from a reformist perspective. These questions were well articulated by CRD Halisi:

> Nascent questions of national identity (how the people are to be defined, who belong to the political community, and what are the criteria of inclusion and exclusion) embedded in various schools of liberation thought profoundly influence black popular attitudes towards South Africa's fledgling democracy.[12]

To merely declare that 'South Africa belongs to all who live in it, black and white', became a form of ideological surrender in the face of diversity and it is surprising that this thinking has been celebrated as revolutionary. No wonder that it has not really managed to produce a stable South African national identity. The ANC used 'rationality' rather than 'reason' on this issue. Rationality as a product of modernity is all about pragmatism and expediency (scientificity). Reason takes into account many factors of history, culture, morals, spirituality, identity and justice (head, mind and heart issues).

The European Diaspora that began to come to South Africa in 1652, the Indians who were forcibly uprooted from their continent by global imperial forces and placed in South Africa and the diverse indigenous peoples found in South Africa have not easily gelled into a singular South African national identity. This reality led Vincent Maphai to argue that:

> When convenient to them, members of both groups were quick to abandon the idea of South African identity and adopt an exclusive racial identity. The blacks argued that, while they accepted the principles of non-discrimination and merit, history and context demanded the retention of a racial criterion to prevent the perpetuation of white domination of top positions in the private sectors [...]. Likewise, the whites adopted a group identity when minority rights were at issue. They argued that without minority rights, majority rule would lead to black domination.[13]

One can say that the idea of the 'rainbow nation' which the ANC proposed in 1994 and has continued to re-propose is open to serious crises and contestations. As noted by Chantal Mouffe, the neo-liberal democratic therapy chosen by the ANC as the framework within which nation- and state-building projects have to crystallise is not easily open to tackling 'the question of citizenship [beyond] a conception of the subject which sees individuals as prior to society, bearers of natural rights, and either utility-maximising agents or rational subjects'.[14] She elaborated on this 'democratic paradox' saying:

> In all cases they are abstracted from social and power relations, language, culture and the whole set of practices that make agency possible. What is precluded in these rationalistic approaches is the very question of what are the conditions of existence of a democratic subject.[15]

Mouffe's concept of 'democratic paradox' can be extended to reflect on how the ANC approached the complex issues of identity in a complacent rationalist way that precluded deep reasoning. CRD Halisi and Mahmood Mamdani have helped us gain a deeper appreciation of the extent of the 'democratic paradox' from the perspective of ideology and identity. Halisi alerted us to this reality:

> Rival populisms, nourished by competing visions of liberation, are bound to have an impact on the evolution of South African citizenship because popular democratic traditions, of which populism is one manifestation, are among the most durable sources of inspiration for democratic thinkers. After centuries of racial domination, it would be unrealistic to expect an ethos of non-racial citizenship to prevail unchallenged by older political perceptions. Eventually, the black liberation struggle may come to be viewed by all South Africans as a national achievement and, therefore, a cornerstone of non-racial citizenship identity; but for the immediate future, successive governments will have to cope with sensibilities grounded in both non-racial and race politics.[16]

In the face of all this the ANC finds itself having to project its identity as a liberation movement as well as a champion of democracy in the face of the emergence of such political formations as the Democratic Alliance (DA) and Congress of the People (COPE) that try to claim the niche of being superior advocates of democracy and human rights. Consequently the 'democratic paradox' becomes even more complicated if one tries to make sense of how some advocates of apartheid made the 'Damascus Road' biblical transition from rabid racists to active human rights defenders.[17]

But the challenge that is facing the ANC in its implementation of the 'rainbow nation' project is that of how to turn 'settlers' and 'natives' into equal citizens. This difficulty arises partly from the compromised transitional arrangements and the current constitution which benefited and continues to benefit 'settlers' at the expense of 'natives'. Michael Neocosmos dramatised the problem of South Africa involving processes of creating 'foreign natives' (writing indigenous people out of the nation) while producing 'native foreigners' (putting the colonists into the centre of the nation).[18] The so-called 'Madiba Magic', the philosophy of ubuntu and President Thabo Mbeki's African Renaissance that defined Africanness in inclusive terms of a product of coalescence of various histories and experiences could not solve the settler–native problem in South Africa. This reality was well captured by Mamdani:

> In the context of a former settler colony, a single citizenship for settlers and natives can only be the result of an overall metamorphosis whereby erstwhile colonisers and colonised are politically reborn as equal members of a single political community. The word reconciliation cannot capture this metamorphosis [...]. This is about establishing, for the first time, a political order based on consent and not conquest. It is about establishing a political community of equal and consenting citizens.[19]

What is often ignored is that both 'native' and 'settler' identities were recent construc-tions of settler colonialism. The challenge is not how to turn a settler into a native but how to completely destroy both as colonial creations if a new identity is to emerge. The ANC is yet to succeed on this. The challenges facing the ANC are compounded by the fact that apartheid existed as both colonialism (direct administrative domination) and coloniality (visible socio-political-economic engineering of radical difference) simultaneously.

Apartheid as both colonialism and coloniality

When the British granted 'independence' to the white minority in 1910, South Africa was emerging from imperialism and colonialism into coloniality, which became popu-larly known as 'Colonialism of a Special Type (CSP)'.[20] This thinking produced the idea of South African exceptionalism. The reality was that apartheid was special only in that it embodied both colonialism and coloniality. The danger is that coloniality is invisible but it functions to hijack the African liberation project and channel it into unintended directions. Leading decolonial thinker Nelson Maldonado-Torres provided the most comprehensive definition of coloniality:

> Coloniality is different from colonialism. Colonialism denotes a political and eco-nomic relation in which the sovereignty of a nation or a people rests on the power of another nation, which makes such nation an empire. Coloniality, instead, refers to long-standing patterns of power that emerged as a result of colonialism, but that define culture, labour, inter-subjective relations, and knowledge production well beyond the strict limits of colonial administrations. Thus, coloniality survives colo-nialism. It is maintained alive in books, in the criteria for academic performance, in cultural patterns, in common sense, in the self-image of peoples, in aspirations of self, and so many other aspects of our modern experience. In a way, as modern subjects we breathe coloniality all the time and every day.[21]

When colonialism and coloniality operate simultaneously they make sure that forms of resistance are confused conceptually. Nationalism that emerged in South Africa, while having a long pedigree that pre-dates the official adoption of apartheid in 1948, continued to be haunted by conceptual problems of mimicry at one level and at another of dilution by liberalism. How was African nationalism going to differ from English (Anglicisation) and Afrikaner (Afrikanerisation) as imaginations of the nation? African nationalism also faced the challenges to navigating forces of culture, ethnicity and nativism. D. William argued that South African nationalism was watered down from different ideological springs, namely the Eastern Cape Frontier tradition of resistance, Christian liberalism, Ethiopianism, Garveyism, Zulu warrior tradition, Pan-Africanism, Gandhism, Victorian liberalism, African-American civil rights movements, ideas of Frantz Fanon, republicanism and socialism. He elaborated that:

> In the twentieth century, the Port Elizabeth-East London-Alice triangle remained [a] highly significant area for nationalist ideas and action, and this derived from the effects on the Xhosa of the Black–White confrontation which began here 150 years earlier. In the early part of the nineteenth century the fundamental competition for land and cattle led to white military and missionary actions [which, when] coupled with preaching of Christianity, promoted attitudes among Xhosa which may be seen in all subsequent African Nationalism.[22]

A comprehensive book on the foundational stages of African nationalism in South Africa is Andre Odendaal's *The Founders: The Origins of the ANC and the Struggle for Democracy in South Africa*.[23] The point that emerges poignantly, not just for the South African nationalism but African nationalism in general, is that it was compromised by a conceptual crisis, well captured by the Asian scholar Kuan-Hsing Chen:

> Shaped by the immanent logic of colonialism, Third World nationalism could not escape from reproducing racial and ethnic discrimination; a price to be paid by the coloniser as well as the colonised selves.[24]

This problem of nationalism was further well articulated by Ramon Grosfoguel:

> Nationalism provides Eurocentric solutions to a Eurocentric global problem. It reproduces an internal coloniality of power within each nation-state and reifies the nation-state as the privileged location of social change. Struggles above and below the nation-state are not considered in nationalist political strategies. Moreover, nationalist responses to global capitalism reinforce the nation-state as the political institutional form par excellence of the modern/colonial/capitalist/patriarchal world system. In this case, nationalism is complicit with Eurocentric thinking and political structures.[25]

Grosfoguel raises an important point that was highlighted by Frantz Fanon in terms of 'repetition without change' cascading from pitfalls of national consciousnesses and intellectual laziness of the bourgeois class.[26] Butler raises these questions with specific reference to the ANC, noting that the struggle against apartheid and the pre-occupation with anti-apartheid activities deflected serious introspective analysis and critical reflection on the character of ANC nationalism and the form of liberation they wanted at the end of apartheid beyond the mantra of building a multiracial democracy.[27] Across the world there is a scarcity of future-oriented discourses.

Former liberation movements are caught up in the dung-beetle syndrome of being fixated on the past while heading into the mysterious future. Those which try to focus on the future tend to embrace coloniality as they fail to originate authentic alternatives and options to Marxism which failed to come to terms with the complexities of a black people's history and liberal democracy which emphasised elitist notions of civil and political rights within contexts such as South Africa that cried out for economic and social justice. The ANC's fixation on removal of administrative apartheid made it fail to realise that apartheid was just a mutated form of colonialism that took the practice of indirect rule to extremes involving what Mahmood Mamdani described as a 'define and rule' form of governmentality.[28]

Today, it seems most of the former liberation movements are stuck in disingenuous celebrations of empty political independence while failing to deliver economic independence. The cardinal mistake that former liberation movements made was to demobilise as they celebrated the myth of decolonisation. The reality is that liberation of Africans cannot be understood only in political terms of gaining the right to vote within a context in which African leaders are still subordinates of leaders of the developed North. African leaders continue to be monitored, to take orders from Europe and America and to account more to Europe and America than to African people. This is because it is impossible for genuine decolonisation to take place as long as the world system remains resistant to decolonisation. This point is well captured by Frank Chikane who stated that 'our post-Second World War international governance system—which has not changed since it was implemented—leaves much to be desired, especially from the perspective of the victims of past imperial and colonial systems'.[29] Genuine decolonisation requires a broader and radical transformation of economic, gender, spiritual, epistemic, linguistic, sexual and racial hierarchies imposed on Africa from outside.

It would seem that the ANC is still searching for identity as it continues to carry the burden of a history of liberation while at the same time managing coloniality. When it engaged in negotiations with the apartheid regime it entered another challenging phase in which it had to demonstrate its readiness to govern a multi-racial country dominated by black expectations and white fears. The minority white constituency feared the advent of majority rule and possibilities of losing their economic status. The majority black constituencies expected radical change, particularly reversal of colonial dispossession. The ANC had to play a balancing act informed by a 'give and take' formula. Joel Netshitenzhe, a member of the ANC, argued that 'a critical element of that settlement, from the point of view of the ANC, was the logic of capturing a bridgehead: to codify basic rights and use these as a basis for thoroughgoing transformation of South African society'.[30]

The way the ANC thought it was possible to engage in 'thoroughgoing transformation' within the context of an orderly, democratic and legal framework reveals its complacent view of coloniality and neo-apartheid. It lost the decolonisation battle when it allowed whites to keep material privileges accumulated under apartheid in exchange for universal franchise. Once whites were assured of keeping their material privileges they worked actively towards the production of a neo-liberal constitution with very clear property rights clauses to protect their loot. The ANC naively believed that those who accumulated wealth under apartheid would voluntarily accept sharing it with the dispossessed Africans as part of reciprocal acknowledgement of 'the historical grievance and a commitment to contribute actively to righting the historical injustice'.[31] This was a romantic approach to questions of decolonisation that failed to take into account that those who are powerful always want to remain powerful.

Understood from a decolonial perspective, the settlement of 1994 reflected a stalemate if not outright betrayal of black people rather than triumphalism of the ANC. The ANC could not dictate anything to the apartheid regime beyond revealing the unsustainability of administrative apartheid. It had lost the communist world that armed it and the apartheid regime was totally isolated. Militarily, the apartheid regime had maintained its superiority. The ANC had demonstrated its ability to make the country ungovernable, albeit at a human cost. Under these circumstances both the ANC and the apartheid regime wanted a new lease of life for South Africa. Indeed administrative apartheid was unsustainable in a post-Cold War dispensation that privileged neo-liberal democracy as the only triumphant ideology. The ANC had to negotiate for a democracy with a 'social content'.[32] It is this democracy for which it is still fighting, 20 years after the fall of administrative apartheid.

The reality is that the negotiations enabled black 'nationalists' together with 'liberals' and 'communists' in the ANC to find each other with whites in the now defunct National Party (NP) in a context of the post-Cold War era informed by new normative values of democracy and human rights. Black nationalists, communists and liberals, and white nationalists, liberals and communists negotiated themselves into a post-Cold War neo-liberal democratic ocumene. They had to adapt to the post-Cold War concrete circumstances in which ideas of revolution were declared dead, administrative apartheid was not tolerated, and any form of radicalism that was acceptable was supposed to be in support of the neo-liberal *status quo ante*.

The ANC has been given the mandate to manage and maintain the neo-liberal democratic arrangement in accordance with the negotiated settlement of 1994. The constitution that emerged from the negotiations is placed beyond amendments, but symbolically the ANC is not just 'another party'. It is still expected to carry the burden of history. The post-apartheid nation is associated with its history of fighting for a new civilisation superior to apartheid. Its supporters are still confident that it will deliver social and economic transformation beneficial to blacks. To deliver this social and economic justice and transformation, the ANC needs to reclaim its decoloniality mission that is aimed at giving social content to democracy and human rights. This burden entails the ANC fighting a three-pronged battle: in South Africa, in Africa and at the global level to decolonise the international system, banish neo-apartheid and build pan-African unity. It must prepare itself for a more complex struggle against global colonial matrices of power that make transformation hard to achieve at home and on the continent.

Conclusion: the ANC and the future

What has not been clearly understood by liberation movements is that the modern world system that produced the slave trade, imperialism, colonialism, apartheid, neo-colonialism, neo-liberalism (structural adjustment programmes and the Washington Consensus) and globalisation is highly resistant to systemic change. What has been changing has been the world order, albeit in accordance with the logic of coloniality that works to sustain the modern world system. What has been celebrated as decolonisation was in fact a strategy of dealing with antisystemic movements and forces that threatened to affect the global system in place since 1492. Even such regional bodies as the Southern Africa Development Community (SADC) operate as acceptable parts of the international order and are not considered subversive of the world system. This is why the SADC was given space to reign in Zimbabwe's President Robert Mugabe, who fast-tracked a land reform programme that included some physical attacks on white commercial formers which were considered antisystemic. White farmers as part of the European Diaspora carry ontological density that is higher than that of Africans in the racially hierarchised world system's order of humanity.

The duality between capitalism and socialism that manifested itself as competition between the Western and Eastern Blocs led by the USA and Soviet Union respectively did not touch the core structures of the modern world order because both socialism and capitalism were modernist projects that unfolded according to modernist logic of imperiality and coloniality mediated by ideology and violence. Socialism and capitalism were fraternal twins of modernity. African liberation movements became caught up in this struggle which was termed the Cold War.

This means that the armed and unarmed liberation forces participated in a global modernist-emancipatory project that served the Euro-American project. With decolonisation, ex-colonised states were set a place at the lowest echelons of the world system to serve the same Euro-American dominated international order. This is why there is no African state that was given a permanent seat at the United Nations Security Council. The United Nations only helped the international order to shift from the exclusionary Westphalian form of sovereignty to the United Nations sovereignty system that opened space for African states to be admitted into the organisation as junior members with no veto power on anything.

As the ANC looks into the future the business of decolonising the modern world system must be intensified. African states must not seek a place within a racially hierarchised, patriarchal, Western-centric, Euro-American-centric, Christian-centric, capitalist and modern world order because there is no dignity for Africa there. This world order must be destroyed for a new humanism to emerge. This modern world order has been reproduced and re-proposed in Africa in general and South Africa in particular. This is why it is hard to liberate women and blacks of any gender from coloniality.

The next decolonial struggle must specifically focus on global power structures, on the question of being black and on epistemologies of alterity. This in simple terms means focusing the decolonial project on politics of life, production and knowledge with a view to create a pluriversal world in which many would fit.

Endnotes

1   Wallerstein, I., 1974. *The capitalist world-economy*. Cambridge: Cambridge University Press; Wallerstein, I., 1979. *The modern world-system*. New York: Academic Press; Mignolo, W.D., 1995. *The darker side of the Renaissance: Literacy, territoriality and colonization*. Ann Arbor: University of Michigan Press; Mignolo, W.D., 2000. *Local histories/global designs: Coloniality, subaltern knowledges and border thinking*. Princeton: Princeton University Press; Grosfoguel, R. & Cervantes-Rodriguez, A.M. (eds), 2002. *The modern/colonial/capitalist world-system in the twentieth century: Global processes, antisystematic movements and geopolitics of knowledge*. Westport and London: Praeger; and Mignolo, W.D., 2011. *The darker side of Western modernity: Global futures, decolonial options*. Durham and London: Duke University Press.
2   Ndlovu-Gatsheni, S.J., 2013. *Empire, global coloniality and African subjectivity*. New York and Oxford: Berghahn Books; and Hardt, M. & Negri, A., 2000. *Empire*. Harvard: Harvard University Press.
3   Grosfoguel, R., 2007. The epistemic decolonial turn: Beyond political-economy paradigms. *Cultural Studies*, 21(2-3), March/May, p.219.
4   Butler, A., 2012. *The idea of the ANC. A Jacana Pocket Book*. Johannesburg: Jacana Media.

5   Ndlovu-Gatsheni, S.J., 2012. Fiftieth anniversary of decolonization in Africa: A moment of celebration or critical reflection? *Third World Quarterly*, 33(1), p.74.

6   Thema, R.V., 1953. How Congress began. *The Drum,* July. Available at: http://www.anc.org.za.ancdocs/history/congress/began.html [Accessed 17 March 2013]. See also Ndlovu-Gatsheni, S.J., 2009. From Pixley Ka Isaka Seme to Jacob Zuma: The Long Walk to Freedom and the future of the national democratic revolution in South Africa. In Kamusella, T. & Jaskulowski, K. (eds), 2009. *Nationalism Today*. Berne and Oxford: Peter Lang AG, pp.287-314.

7   Halisi, C.R.D., 1999. *Black political thought in the making of South African democracy*. Bloomington: Indiana University Press.

8   Karis, T.G & Gerhart, G.M., 1997. *From protest to challenge: A documentary history of African politics in South Africa*. Bloomington: Indiana University Press, pp.505-506.

9   Scott, J.C., 1990, *Domination and the arts of resistance: Hidden transcripts*. New York: Yale University Press.

10 Ndlovu-Gatsheni, S.J., 2008, Black republican tradition, nativism and populist politics in South Africa. *Transformation: Critical Perspectives on Southern Africa*, 68, pp.53-86.

11 Davis, S.M., 1998. *Apartheid's rebels: Inside South Africa's hidden war*. Cape Town: AD Donker, p.13.

12 Halisi, C.R.D., 1997. From liberation to citizenship: Identity and innovation in black South African political thought. *Society for Comparative Study of Society and History*, 39(1), p.61.

13 Maphai, V., 2004. Race and the politics of transition: Confusing political imperatives with moral imperatives. In Manganyi, N.C. (ed.), 2004. *On becoming a democracy: Transition and transformation in South African society*. Pretoria: University of South Africa Press, p.12.

14 Mouffe, C., 2000. *The democratic paradox*. London and New York: Verso, pp.95-96.

15 Ibid.

16 Halisi, 1997, op. cit., p.78.

17 The idea of 'Damascus Road' syndrome is borrowed from the postcolonial theorist Achille Mbembe. It speaks to the event when Saul was hit by lightning while on his to Damascus to persecute Christians only to rise up as ardent defender of the Christian project and become a leading apostle operating under the new name Paul.

18 Neocosmos, M., 2010. *From 'foreign natives' to 'native foreigners': Explaining xenophobia in post-apartheid South Africa: Citizenship and nationalism, identity and politics*. Dakar: CODESRIA Books.

19 Mamdani, M., 1998. *When does a settler become a native? Reflections on the roots of citizenship in Equatorial and South Africa*. Text of inaugural lecture delivered as A.C. Jordan Professor of African Studies. 13 May. University of Cape Town.

20 Wolpe, H., 1975. The theory of internal colonialism: The South African case. In Oxxal,

I., Bernett, T. & Booth, D. (eds), 1975. *Beyond the sociology of development*. Boston: Kegan Paul.

21 Maldonado-Torres, N., 2007. On the coloniality of being: Contributions to the development of a concept. *Cultural Studies,* 21(2-3), March/May, p.243.

22 William, D., 1970. African nationalism in South Africa: Origins and problems. *Journal of African History*, 11(3), p.383.

23 Ondendaal, A., 2012. *The Founders: The origins of the ANC and the struggle for democracy in South Africa*. Johannesburg: Jacana Media.

24 Chen, K-C., 1998. Introduction: The decolonization question. In Chen. K.H. (ed.), *Trajectories: Inter-Asia cultural studies*. London: Routledge, p.14.

25 Grosfoguel, R., 2011. Decolonizing post-colonial studies and paradigms of political economy: Transmodernity, decolonial thinking, and global coloniality. *Transmodernity: Journal of Peripheral Cultural Production of the Luso-Hispanic World*, 1(1), p.18.

26 Fanon, F., 1968. *The wretched of the Earth*. New York: Grove Press.

27 Butler, 2012, op. cit., p.119.

28 Mamdani, M., 2013. *Define and rule: Native as political odentity*. Johannesburg: Wits University Press.

29 Chikane, F., 2013. *The things that could not be said: From A{ids} toZ{imbabwe}*. Johannesburg: Picador Africa, p.117.

30 Netshitenzhe, J., 2012. Second keynote address: A continuing search for identity: Carrying the burden of history. In Lissoni, A., Soske, J., Earlank, N., Nieftagodien, N. & Badsha, O. (eds), 2012. *One hundred years of the ANC: Debating liberation histories today*. Johannesburg: Wits University Press, p.16.

31 Ibid, p.17.

32 Ibid, p.23.

CHAPTER 13

The centenary of the ANC: prospects for the realisation of the pan-Africanist project

Thabo Mbeki

Introduction

In 2012, we all convened[1] as part of the African ceremonies to celebrate the establishment one hundred years ago of the South African 'African National Congress' on 8 January 1912. Throughout that year of 2012, even as the South Africans celebrated the historic ANC centenary, all of us knew that the achievements of this centenary do not belong exclusively to the people of South Africa.

Part of our collective heritage in this regard is that not only did the establishment of the ANC help to emphasise the point that we are, together, Africans. It also gave us the symbolic representations of this togetherness, including the national anthem, expressed in the South African languages as 'Nkosi Sikelel' iAfrica', and here as 'Mungu ibariki Afrika', and in Zambia in other words, as well as the national colours of black, green and gold, which also distinguish the national flags of South Africa and Tanzania as well as the African Diaspora flag as far afield as Jamaica, which, it is believed, the Jamaicans borrowed from this country's flag. Driven by this understanding, Tanzanians and South Africans decided that something would have to be done also to celebrate the centenary of the ANC outside the borders of South Africa as well.

This has resulted in the happy outcome that we have convened here this afternoon.

In this regard I would like to emphasise an important historical fact that a century ago the ANC was established by delegations drawn from many African countries, including those from as far afield as present-day Zambia.

It was therefore an African regional liberation and anti-colonial movement rather than a narrowly South African national movement.

This development, a century ago, was informed by the very antecedents of the ANC itself, in terms of which the emerging anti-colonial movement in our country, towards the end of the nineteenth century, asserted that the peoples of Africa could only solve their problems within the context of a Pan-African perspective.

The ANC's Pan-Africanist orientation

Accordingly, I have no hesitation in asserting that, from its very foundation, the ANC was Pan-Africanist in its outlook and its intentions.

Inspired by all this we thought it right that we should convene in Tanzania, because of and as a tribute to the immense contribution which Tanzania has made, especially under the leadership of the late Mwalimu Julius Nyerere, as well as the University of Dar es Salaam, to advance the Pan-Africanist project.

In this regard I have absolutely no hesitation in affirming that there is no better African domicile than Tanzania and the University of Dar-es-Salaam to reflect seriously on the future of the Pan-Africanist project today, taking advantage of the celebration of the centenary of the ANC, which is the subject of this lecture. The South African antecedents of the ANC were represented essentially by the first modern African intelligentsia in our country which emerged from and rebelled against the European Christian mission.

Out of this was born one of our first modern anti-colonial movements, in the form of the Ethiopian Church. As early as 115 years ago, in 1897, one of the African leaders of this Church, the Reverend J.G. Xaba, said: "The aim of the Ethiopian Church is to promote...unity in the whole Continent of Africa."

In this context we must also recognise and pay tribute to the role of other and earlier religious leaders, such as the Muslim Sheik Yusuf al-Taj al-Khalwatial-Maqasari, an aristocrat from Sulawesi in Indonesia, who was brought by the Dutch to the South African Cape in 1694 as a slave, but whose religion sustained the determination of the African enslaved to achieve their liberation. The essential point to emphasise relating to the ANC is that, even at its foundation, it inherited a Pan-Africanist liberation perspective.

One of its most outstanding founders, Pixley ka-Isaka Seme, inspired by the then-prevailing Pan-Africanist views in Africa, and the African Diaspora in the US and the Caribbean, published a famous article in 1906, six years before the ANC was established, in which he said:

> The brighter day is rising upon Africa. Already I see her chains dissolved, her desert plains red with harvest, her Abyssinia and her Zululand the seats of science and religion, reflecting the glory of the rising sun from the spires of their churches and universities. Her Congo and her Gambia whitened with commerce... and all her

sons employed in advancing the victories of peace – greater and more abiding than the spoils of war...

The regeneration of Africa means that a new and unique civilisation is soon to be added to the world... More particularly, (the new civilisation) resembles a plant; it takes root in the teeming earth, and when its seeds fall in other soils, new varieties sprout out. The most essential departure of this new civilisation is that it should be thoroughly spiritual and humanistic – indeed a regeneration moral and eternal!

Much earlier, another distinguished son of Africa, the Reverend Tiyo Soga, celebrating victory of African-Americans over the system of slavery, envisioned the unity of all Africans inside the continent and in the diaspora with free slaves "looking forward to the dawn of a better day for (the African-American) and all his sable brethren in Africa."

Let us cite comments that were made 55 years after Seme published his 1906 article, which underline the entrenched views of the peoples of Africa we dare not betray, even today.

Here is part of what the first African laureate of the Nobel Peace Prize, the eminent South African and African patriot, Chief Albert Luthuli, then president of the ANC, said in 1961 in Oslo when he accepted this prize:

In bringing my address to a close, let me invite Africa to cast her eyes beyond the past and to some extent the present with their woes and tribulations, trials and failures, and some successes, and see herself an emerging Continent, bursting to freedom through the shell of centuries of serfdom. This is Africa's age – the dawn of her fulfilment, yes, the moment when she must grapple with destiny to reach the summits of sublimity, saying – ours was a fight for noble values and worthy ends, and not for lands and the enslavement of man...

Could it not be that history has delayed her rebirth for a purpose...?

Though robbed of her lands, her independence and opportunities... should she not see her destiny as being that of making a distinctive contribution to human progress and human relationships with a peculiar new African flavour enriched by the diversity of the cultures she enjoys, thus building on the summits of present human achievement an edifice that would be one of the finest tributes to the genius of man?...

To us all, free or not free, the call of the hour is to redeem the name and honour of Mother Africa...

Acting in concert with other nations, (Africa) is...qualified to demand of the great powers to "turn the swords into plough-shares" because two-thirds of mankind is hungry and illiterate...

Africa's qualification for this noble task is incontestable, for her own fight has never been and is not now a fight for conquest of land, for accumulation of wealth or domination of peoples, but for the recognition and preservation of the rights of man and the establishment of a truly free world for a free people.

As an African these words impelled me always to act to help ensure the realisation of the vision they projected, mindful that they represented the then-unrealisable dream of a particular age, but nevertheless, and still, a dream which we must continue to share and sustain, in our own interest.

Apart from, and in addition to the passionate sentiment we all share, that we are proudly African, our practical experience of 50 years of independence, and more, must surely have convinced us that we will not achieve the Renaissance towards which we aspire if we do not act together in unity as Africans. By now we have recognised and accepted the hard reality that none of us acting alone as our different nation states can succeed to achieve our most fundamental Renaissance objectives and therefore that the objective of African unity is practically a matter of life and death for us as Africans.

In other words, as much as the *African Renaissance* is not possible without *African unity*, African unity is also not possible without the African Renaissance.

As South African activists for our own liberation, we were immensely privileged that we had the possibility of interacting with virtually the entire cohort of the most eminent African post-Second World War leaders, to be exposed to the liberation project during this period and to observe at close hand what was done to use the victory of independence to achieve the Renaissance of Africa of which Xaba, Seme and Luthuli had spoken.

It may be that because of our rare privilege in this regard, and our practical experience of the invaluable united African action to defeat the apartheid system, as members of the ANC we had no choice but to be particularly sensitive to the historic dream of the peoples of Africa for their unity and shared renaissance. In this context, let us present to you two propositions.

The first of these is that during this centenary year of the establishment of the first modern African national liberation movement, the ANC, and therefore a heritage of all Africans as a whole, regardless of our contemporary partisan political views, we have an obligation to unite around the objective of the Renaissance of Africa.

The second proposition is that the African Renaissance is not possible unless we unleash the same national and continental forces which were responsible for the formation of the ANC itself, equivalent to the masses who participated in the Maji Maji Rebellion, whose ghosts were present even as Tanganyika achieved its non-violent transition to independence in 1961.

This second proposition, practically, means that the masses of the African people have to be mobilised to achieve the objective of the African Renaissance, organised and empowered to act consciously as their own liberators.

On the Renaissance of Africa

It is important to make the honest admission that it was a privilege to have had the opportunity to interact with Mwalimu Julius Nyerere and other esteemed leaders of Tanzania in the context of the struggle for the liberation of Southern Africa, including our country, the reconstruction and development of the liberated South Africa and its role on our continent.

In this context we were most fortunate that we had the opportunity to draw on Mwalimu Julius Nyerere's views, as well as the practical experience of the African states of Tanganyika and Tanzania, to help inform us about what practically we needed to do to achieve the Renaissance of Africa, understanding that our dream had to respond to Africa's practical realities.

Reference should be made to the important speech Mwalimu Julius Nyerere delivered in 1966 during the inauguration of the University of Zambia, titled *The Dilemma of the Pan-Africanist*.

As you will recall, the burden of his argument was that in pursuing the Pan-African dream of African unity we had to take into account the fact of our existence as independent states. Thus he warned that we should not allow our individual nationalisms to supersede the larger Pan-Africanist goal.

Specifically in this regard he said:

It was as Africans that we dreamed of freedom; and we thought of it for Africa. Our real ambition was African freedom and African government. The fact that we fought area by area was merely a tactical necessity... simply because each local colonial government had to be dealt with separately.

The question we now have to answer is whether Africa shall maintain this internal separation as we defeat colonialism, or whether our earlier proud boast – 'I am an African' – shall become a reality. It is not a reality now. For the truth is that there are now 36 different nationalities in free Africa, one for each of the 36 independent states – to say nothing of those still under colonial or alien domination. Each state is separate from the others: each is a sovereign entity. And this means that each state has a government which is responsible to the people of its own area – and to them only; it must work for their particular well-being or invite chaos within its territory.

Can the vision of Pan-Africanism survive these realities?

I do not believe the answer is easy. Indeed I believe that a real dilemma faces the Pan-Africanist. On the one hand is the fact that Pan-Africanism demands an African consciousness and an African loyalty; on the other hand is the fact that each Pan-Africanist must also concern himself with the freedom and development of one of the nations of Africa. These things can conflict. Let us be honest and admit that they have already conflicted.

Later in the lecture Mwalimu said:

Those who would like to advocate complete concentration on national interests, and those who would demand the sacrifice of all national interests to the cause of African freedom and unity, both have an easy road to tread. The one can appeal to 'realism' and 'pragmatism', and can appear to be devoted to the practical interests of the people. The other can appeal to the hearts of men, and can appear courageous, self-sacrificing, and revolutionary. But both would lead Africa to disaster – the one to early stagnation and alien economic domination, and the other to chaos and disintegration of the units already existing. No; we must undertake a new and hard way forward and upward.

Bearing in mind these admonitions, which remain relevant more than 45 years after they were made, we must still answer the question 'what do we need to do to advance the Pan-Africanist project?' What is the "new and hard way forward and upward" of which Mwalimu spoke?

To attempt to answer these questions, the *Strategic Pan-Africanist Task* we face today is to work to advance towards the achievement of the interlinked objectives of the *Unity of our Continent* and its *Renaissance,* engaging in both bottom-up and top-down processes.

To achieve this *Strategic Pan-Africanist Task,* also bearing in mind our obligation continuously to engage the *African Diaspora* in our common project, the following are the *Pan-African Operational Objectives* (OOs) which must inform our united actions in the short and medium term.

- *Pan-African Operational Objective 1:* With regard to the bottom-up process, we must strengthen the regional political and economic processes led by our Regional Economic Communities;
- *Pan-African Operational Objective 2:* In terms of the top-down process we have to work to ensure that all our states implement the continental policies agreed through the OAU and the AU, including those spelt out in NEPAD and the APRM, the African Peer Review Mechanism;

- *Pan-African Operational Objective 3:* Given our continuing challenges in this regard, and relying on the agreed policies and programmes, we must act further to enhance the possibility for the AU to intervene throughout Africa to achieve the objective of peace, security and stability;
- *Pan-African Operational Objective 4:* We must empower the Pan-African Parliament to enable our continent's elected representatives, acting together, to participate in the implementation of the Pan-Africanist project, as well as provide effective oversight in this regard;
- *Pan-African Operational Objective 5:* We must take all action to ensure the engagement of the African Diaspora with the Pan-Africanist project, working to guarantee that it also addresses the challenges facing this diaspora; and
- *Pan-African Operational Objective 6:* We must ensure that the broad African masses take ownership of the Pan-Africanist project in all the elements we have mentioned, and therefore that the necessary steps are taken at least to keep the organised formations of these masses properly informed and engaged in all actions focused on the pursuit of this Pan-Africanist project, including through the AU ECOSOCC, the Economic, Social and Cultural Council.

With regard to both the *Strategic Pan-Africanist Task* and the Pan-African Operational Objectives, you should ask yourselves the honest and difficult question whether Africa today, in terms of the actual practice of African politics, to which we are exposed every day, has the organisations and the leadership that are genuinely committed to the accomplishment of this Strategic Pan-Africanist Task and the Pan-African Operational Objectives listed above!

Thus must we return to the serious warning which Mwalimu Julius Nyerere sounded in 1966 at the University of Zambia, about the potentially negative impact of the contradiction between our individual nationalisms and the pursuit of the Pan-Africanist project.

It would seem obvious to me that – for reasons we should understand very well, and which all of us can explain for each of our countries, in detail – many of us serving at different levels among the current leadership in Africa are pre-occupied with our disparate national challenges, paying insufficient attention to the advancement of the Pan-Africanist project.

This has arisen from serious objective challenges which have emerged in many of our nation states, to which our respective national leadership collectives, including those in civil society, have no choice but to respond.

At the same time, as an important element in terms of the content and make-up of these national challenges, is the reality that these challenges emanate in part from serious weaknesses in our democratic practice, including the corruption of our electoral processes.

This is combined with the abuse of power resulting in some of our countries being treated as personal fiefdoms that are used as a base for self-enrichment against the interests of the people, which eminently destructive phenomenon many African thinkers have spoken about.

All this raises vitally important questions about what together, as African citizens, we should do to hold our political and other leaders to account, and thus fulfil our obligation as the African masses to remain truly our own liberators.

In this regard the members of the esteemed University of Dar Es Salaam would have paid some attention to the article that was published in the *African Sociological Review*, titled 'Nyerere: Nationalism and Post-Colonial Developmentalism', written by Chachage and Chachage.[2]

In this article in which, as you know, they discuss multi-party politics in this country, Chachage and Chachage make assertions which are not easy to substantiate but nevertheless sound particular alarm bells about the broader African experience that we must consider and take into account.

Let us present to you fairly extensive quotations from this article. Such observations include the following:

Political parties, as state-like structures working to occupy the state, like the colonial state itself, have tended to put a wedge between politics and economics by insisting that the only place for conducting politics is in the government and the parliament. They have often been afraid of the emergence and consolidation of independent labour, peasant, women, youth and people's movements. The tendency for these parties has been to distance themselves from such organisations and activities, except when it is to their advantage...

For democracy to make sense, it has to be linked to those who are victims of the prevailing circumstances, by taking into account issues of social justice and social democracy. It has to be directed to the questions of redressing imbalances, inequalities and exploitation etc., rather than simply setting up democratic institutions... We need a conception of democracy and human rights and its organisational forms which stands for peace, justice, equity and equality...

It has to address such issues as: in which way is production organised? Who is producing, and who is appropriating the surplus? What forms of accumulating are taking place? What kinds of social relations exist among individuals, groups and organisations as far as the control of resources is concerned?

Only social movements (territorial and pan-territorial), and especially those grounded on the foundation of peace, equality, equity, democracy, stability and Pan-Africanism can articulate emancipatory politics. Nyerere's contribution on nationalism and Pan-Africanism is a lesson to be taken seriously.

> For such movements to exist there must be the emergence and consolidation of politics in civil society (grassroots-based movements and people's organisations), leading to real transformations of the state...
>
> Civil society implies self-organisation, which defends the interests of the majority of the people and promotes civil liberty and social transformation.

The Chachage and Chachage article, regardless of its domestic Tanzanian relevance, raises important matters relevant to the pursuit of the Pan-Africanist project, relating to the content of the vision of the African Renaissance, the empowerment and mobilisation of the African masses to act as their own liberators and the centrality of the Pan-Africanist perspective to the achievement of these objectives.

We should also refer to the important observations made recently by the eminent Ugandan and African intellectual, Mahmood Mamdani, in his book *Define and Rule: Native as Political Identity*.

Among others, in this 'little book', Professor Mamdani says:

> By 'equality and dignity', Mwalimu understood, above all, equality in the face of law, or, put differently, equality in spite of differences and privileges – those based on race and tribe – institutionalised and enforced by colonial law...
>
> We have seen that the indirect rule (colonial) state identified the population it governed as members of a group, either a race or a tribe...When it came to the political domain, punishments too were meted upon groups, and not just to individuals...
>
> In the face of growing political opposition (in post-colonial Africa), it became a convention to identify, brand and target the race or tribe of individual opponents. It created a regional (East African but also African) political environment marked by ethnic cleansing and extreme violence. To this general tendency, there was one exception: mainland Tanzania. The political credit for this, I believe, goes to Mwalimu Nyerere.

The Chachages advised that all of us should respect what they called "Nyerere's contribution on nationalism and Pan-Africanism".

Independently and in support, Mahmood Mamdani argued that what Mwalimu Nyerere stood for and did for this sister country of Tanzania gave an eminently practical example of what all of us as Africans should do to bridge the divide between nationalism and Pan-Africanism.

In his book, Professor Mamdani argued that Mwalimu Julius Nyerere taught all of us both to respect and manage our national and regional divides and also, at the same time, practically to live up to the objective to promote the Pan-African objective of the unity of all Africans, at all times avoiding the deadly and false trap, cultivated during the colonial years, that as Africans we are different tribes and races with mutually exclusive interests.

It was to defeat the pernicious practice of 'divide and rule' based on 'tribe and race', which unfortunately continues to inform much of our continental politics, that Mahmood Mamdani appropriately titled his 'little book', *Define and Rule: Native as Political Identity*.[3]

In the context outlined above, let me now say something about the six short and medium-term *Pan-African Operational Objectives* mentioned earlier, and especially the challenges we face in this regard.

The African Union held its 9th Ordinary Assembly in Accra, Ghana, at the beginning of July 2007 essentially to focus on what was described as the "Grand Debate on the Union Government". This 'Grand Debate' was about the steps our continent needed to take to achieve the unanimously agreed objective of the unity of Africa. In essence the 'Grand Debate' boiled down to a contest between two groups.

The one argued for a top-down process according to which, for instance, the AU would immediately establish an African Union Government, which would cover certain portfolios such as Foreign Affairs and Defence. Accordingly, the individual member states of the AU would immediately lose their sovereignty in these areas, ceding such sovereignty to the African Union Government.

The other and opposing group, which proved to be the majority, argued for a bottom-up process, according to which Africa would progress towards the formation of the African Union Government by using our regions, and the Regional Economic Communities, as the necessary building blocks towards the achievement of the African Union Government.

This divide in Accra in 2007 mirrored the debate that had taken place at the foundation of the OAU 45 years earlier in 1963, with the then top-down group led by Kwame Nkrumah, and the bottom-up group led by Mwalimu Julius Nyerere.

With regard to the matter of an African Union Government; majority opinion on our continent favours a bottom-up process, exactly for the reasons which Julius Nyerere explained in his lecture in Lusaka in 1966.

However, the concrete reality which must inform our actions is that our continent has in fact correctly decided that to advance its continuing commitment to the objective of African unity we must implement, simultaneously, both the top-down and the bottom-up processes.

To borrow from a slogan once used in China, this means that Africa has taken a correct decision – to walk on two legs!

Accordingly, those of us genuinely committed to the interlinked objectives of the African renaissance and African unity must ask ourselves the vitally important question – are we, in fact, today, walking on two legs?

Obviously we have to do a lot more to strengthen our capacity to build towards the unity of our continent both from below and from the top.

Obviously, this means that we have to pay very close attention to strengthening our Regional Economic Communities. In this regard, it may be that the East African Community can set a good example which others of our regions could emulate.

It also means that we have to pay similarly close attention to strengthening the African Union and all its institutions. Of equal importance, it is critical that we devise ways and means to ensure that policies decided at the continental level find expression in the national programmes implemented in our individual member states, and *vice versa*.

All this leaves unanswered a critically important question – who will drive the processes aimed at accelerating that advance towards African unity, acting both from the top and from below?

To answer this question we must return to where we started the formation of the ANC a century ago.

When it was formed, the ANC represented the most progressive movement in our part of Africa. That progressive character was defined by the fact that this was a movement for the liberation of all Africans from colonialism and imperialist domination.

This was clearly the most important and urgent progressive task all Africans faced until, with the exception of Western Sahara, colonialism and white minority rule on our continent were defeated.

Indeed we can say without fear of contradiction that the continent-wide movement for the liberation of Africa developed into the biggest progressive movement that Africa has seen.

It drew millions of Africans into struggle as conscious activists for progressive change, led by organisations such as the ANC and TANU (Tanzania African National Union), composed of patriots whose only objective was the liberation of the oppressed.

And indeed so powerful was the movement that, even after our countries gained their independence, they continued to count themselves as continuing activists in the struggle for the liberation of Africa – a sentiment expressed in Kwame Nkrumah's famous words, that "our independence is meaningless unless it is linked up with the total liberation of Africa".[4]

And so it is that we can indeed say that one of the outstanding achievements of the OAU was the mobilisation of our entire continent for that total liberation of Africa, within which context this sister country played the outstanding role earlier mentioned, as a Frontline State in that struggle.

Undoubtedly one of our greatest successes as Africans during the century of the existence of the ANC has been the total liberation of Africa, including the liberation of

South Africa itself. With this great victory achieved, the question must arise and has arisen – what are the new tasks of the African progressive movement?

My own answer to that question is that the central task of the African progressive movement must surely be the matters we have mentioned, namely the pursuit of the dialectically inter-connected objectives of African unity and the renaissance of Africa, directly linked to the objective to eradicate poverty and underdevelopment.

In this regard the progressive approach to the important issue of African unity should indeed be informed by what Mwalimu said in Lusaka, in 1966, that:

> It was as Africans that we dreamed of freedom; and we thought of it for Africa. Our real ambition was African freedom and African government. The fact that we fought area by area was merely a tactical necessity... simply because each local colonial government had to be dealt with separately.

This means that those of us who identify ourselves as progressives must do everything we can to overcome the inertia that comes from a narrow parochial nationalism, thus to find ways to give practical expression to the vision that 'when we dreamt of freedom, we thought of it for Africa', as well as defeat what Mahmood Mamdani warned against, the perpetuation of divisions among ourselves based on tribe, race and nationality.

And with regard to the progressive content of the unity and renaissance we seek, among others, we should pay attention to some of the things the Chachages said, for instance that:

> We need a conception of democracy and human rights and its organisational forms which stands for peace, justice, equity and equality... It has to address such issues as: in which way is production organised? Who is producing, and who is appropriating the surplus? What forms of accumulating are taking place? What kind of social relations exist among individuals, groups and organisations as far as the control of resources is concerned?

And with regard to some of the organisational challenges in the progressive movement, we could cite part of what the Chachages said, that:

> Political parties, as state-like structures working to occupy the state... have tended to put a wedge between politics and economics by insisting that the only place for conducting politics is in the government and the parliament. They have often been afraid of the emergence and consolidation of independent labour, peasant, women, youth and people's movements. The tendency for these parties has been

to distance themselves from such organisations and activities, except when it is to their advantage.

Thus, recalling the outstanding success of the earlier popular movement for the liberation of Africa, as progressives we must build and mobilise a genuinely popular movement for African unity and Africa's renaissance, which would therefore not allow for the perpetuation of the negative political processes and arrangements to which the Chachages referred.

During the recent past, two developments occurred on our continent which convey deeply worrying messages about the future of our continent.

Reference should be made to the manner in which the protracted crisis in Côte d'Ivoire was 'solved', and what happened in Libya which resulted in the violent overthrow of the Libyan government and the murder of Colonel Muammar Gaddafi.

The supposed 'solution' of the crisis in Côte d'Ivoire has left our continent with the challenge that this important African country could once again slide back into civil war, having moved further away from the strategic task to achieve the national reconciliation and unity which stands at the centre of the Mwalimu Nyerere heritage.

Libya remains in the grip of an internal violent conflict and, as we had predicted, the overthrow of the Gaddafi regime by the NATO-led forces has created a very dangerous situation throughout the African Sahel, currently dramatically represented by the rebellion in Mali which has split the country into two parts.

These two events are highlighted because the outcomes that were achieved did not emanate from strategic decisions we took as Africans but from decisions taken by others outside our continent. It is a matter of deep concern that we have entered into a new period during which the threat of our continued neo-colonial domination will increase.

The possibility of its success will be enhanced by division among ourselves because we have not moved far and fast enough towards achieving the objective of African unity, because we have not as yet united around the perspective of Africa's renaissance and because we have failed to constitute the all-Africa progressive movement for African unity and the renaissance of our continent.

It is important to insist that progressive Africa has a grave responsibility to act now, and as a matter of urgency, exactly to ensure that we guarantee the true meaning of what we celebrated when, in 1994, Africa and the rest of the world joined the ANC and the people of South Africa to celebrate both the end of white apartheid minority rule and the total liberation of Africa.

Conclusion

We started this chapter by quoting statements made by African patriots in 1897, 1906 and 1961. All of them foresaw a day when all Africa would be free, giving us as Africans the possibility to use that freedom to achieve both our unity and our renaissance. Surely, the best and only way for us properly to celebrate the centenary of the ANC, our continent's first modern organised movement for the liberation of Africa, would be to ensure that progressive Africa lives up to its current and historic responsibilities in the aftermath of our seminal achievement, the total liberation of Africa.

In the past, all of us, Tanzanians and South Africans together, asked ourselves the vital question about what we should do to achieve the total liberation especially of Southern Africa, including South Africa.

We answered that question by constituting a durable partnership for liberation, which led to the defeat of the most stubborn forces of colonialism on our continent, apart from the French in Algeria.

As we proudly celebrate the centenary of the ANC, all of us, Tanzanians, South Africans and all other Africans, including those in the African Diaspora, must answer the question, practically – what must we do to advance the progressive Pan-Africanist project, building on what progressive Africa achieved in the past, the total liberation of our continent, mindful of what Albert Luthuli said half-a-century ago, that "the call of the hour is to redeem the name and honour of Mother Africa."?

Endnotes

1   Adapted from the lecture in honour of the centenary of the ANC. 2012. 22 November. University of Dar-es-Salaam.

2   See Chachage, C.S., 2004. Nyerere: Nationalism and post-colonial developmentalism. *African Sociological Review* (Debates), 8(2).

3   For details on this subject, see Mamdani, M., 2012. *Define and rule: Native as political identity*. Cambridge: Harvard University Press.

4   Kwame Nkrumah made this call during his *Independence Speech* of 6 March 1957. Also, see an incisive critique by Tanzanian scholar Godfrey Mwakikagile in Mwakikagile, G., 2009. *Africa after independence: Realities of nationhood*. New Africa Press.

CHAPTER 14

Class dynamics and state transformation in South Africa

Joel Khathu Netshitenzhe

Introduction

The African National Congress turned one hundred years old in 2012, a moment that has, understandably, sparked robust discourse with many streams of thought contending the significance and content of the centenary.[1]

In various presentations, an attempt was made to dissect the state of the post-1994 South African state as well as class dynamics that attach to the challenge of the liberation movement's ascendancy into formal organs of political power. In this chapter these ideas are integrated, with issues selected to illustrate the strategic challenges that South Africa faces as it strives to speed up social transformation, complex issues that are playing themselves out at state and party political levels.

For purposes of this treatise it is not necessary to trace the evolution of the state as such – the Athenian and Spartan versions, the pre-colonial manifestations of social organisation as in the Mapungubwe and other African civilisations and the mfecane wars of nation-formation, or the rise of the colonial state in the geography today called South Africa. Nor need an attempt be made to interrogate the Weberian, micro-foundational and Marxist theories of the state and their utility.

Drawing from this tapestry, some generalisations are made on the state of the country today, its interplay with class dynamics and the actions required to ensure that the state plays an optimal role in leading the efforts to improve people's quality of life.

Concept of the state and class dynamics within the colonial state

Why is the state central to social organisation, at least during particular periods in the evolution of human society? It has been argued quite cogently that the very existence of the state arises out of the need to manage social conflict. Friedrich Engels in his seminal work, *The Origin of the Family, Private Property and the State* makes this assertion in the following manner:

> The state is… by no means a power forced on society from without; just as little is it 'the reality of the ethical idea', 'the image and reality of reason', as Hegel maintains. Rather, it is a product of society at a certain stage of development; it is the admission that this society has become entangled in an insoluble contradiction with itself, that it has split into irreconcilable antagonisms which it is powerless to dispel. But in order that these antagonisms, these classes with conflicting economic interests, might not consume themselves and society in fruitless struggle, it became necessary to have a power, seemingly standing above society, that would alleviate the conflict and keep it within the bounds of 'order'; and this power, arisen out of society but placing itself above it, and alienating itself more and more from it, is the state.[2]

But should we infer one-directional causality between the level of development of economic organisation and industry, on the one hand, and instruments of social organisation, on the other? As many would argue, forms of social organisation can evolve and assume autonomous identities. Indeed, Engels himself makes this qualification in his *Letter to Bloch*:

> According to the materialist conception of history, the ultimately determining element in history is the production and reproduction of real life. Other than this neither Marx nor I have ever asserted. Hence if somebody twists this into saying that the economic element is the *only* determining one, he transforms that proposition into a meaningless, abstract, senseless phrase. The economic situation is the basis, but the various elements of the superstructure – …political, juristic, philosophical theories, religious views and their further development into systems of dogmas – also exercise their influence upon the course of the historical struggles and in many cases preponderate in determining their form.[3]

The evolution of the state in a unified South Africa bore all the hallmarks of a colonial imposition, promoting and protecting the material interests of the colonial settlers.

The formation of the Union of South Africa in 1910 represented racial solidarity founded on dispossession, exclusion and repression of the black people.

However, within this racial solidarity, and indeed reflecting what Engels in the *Letter to Bloch* refers to as 'an infinite series of parallelograms of forces', various secondary contradictions played themselves out. While issues of language and culture were an important veneer, the essence of these tensions was about how to narrow the divide between numbers and real power, between the statuses of a ruling political elite and a ruling class. With the introduction of racially circumscribed 'democracy', the Afrikaners, as the majority within the white community, not only ensured through corrective or affirmative action that their political dominance translated into general socio-economic benefits but also sought to translate their position as the political ruling elite into becoming a full part of the ruling class across South Africa; that is, owners of the means of production beyond agriculture.

As this happened, and as is in the nature of the capitalist system, massive stratification also took place within the Afrikaner community, putting a strain on the nationalist project of mutual solidarity. Thus the supposed communal nationalist cause had to be re-invented and rationalised afresh. In 'Die Calvinistiese beskouing van die arbeid'[4] in the journal *Koers* of October 1946, the point is made by the ideologues of Afrikaner Nationalism about the white lower classes that:

> No one's task is too humble, because in the national economy we are all members of one body, in which there is indeed a head and a heart, but also the lesser members without which the body would be crippled. There is nothing wrong with the types of work we do... it is all needed to serve the church, the volk and the state.

One of the unique features that attach to this experience is that this political ruling elite had the possibility to use job reservation, land dispossession and other forms of racial discrimination and super-exploitation of black people, to accord the white lower classes privileged status. This somewhat ameliorated the intra-communal tensions and delayed their acute manifestations which later took the form of the intense *broedertwis* of the 1970s and beyond.

Where is all this quasi-historical meandering leading to?

Tragedy or farce or neither?

In his observation on Hegel's remark, 'somewhere that all great world-historic facts and personages appear, so to speak, twice', Karl Marx[5] says Hegel 'forgot to add: the first time as tragedy, the second time as farce'.

And so, to become more explicit, contained in this experience of the Afrikaner nationalist movement are three illuminating dynamics about:

- firstly, the conduct of a political elite that is not as such the ruling class, using political office to capture part of the commanding heights of the economy, and for a section of this elite to ascend to higher socio-economic status,
- secondly, how such progress can also be facilitated by the extant ruling class courting the political masters by ceding some of its economic power, and
- thirdly, how advancement of a supposedly communal nationalism, within a capitalist socio-economic formation, may benefit all its adherents somewhat, but this in fact also results in a small minority rising to the very top, and thus generating disquiet within the nationalist broad front.

In other words, if this truncated account of the experience of Afrikaner nationalism does invoke familiar images about the present it is because there are instructive parallels. At the centre of this is the question of the capture of political power by a coalition of forces in a 'nationalist movement', its attempt within an unchanged (capitalist) socio-economic formation to use political power to re-order the distribution of income and wealth, and the stratification and tensions that ensue, as the elite within this political elite climb faster and higher in the economic stakes than the rest.

It can be argued that in the past 19 years, within an unchanged socio-economic formation, the black political elite has been striving to use political power to re-order the distribution of income and wealth. The new elite, much as the Afrikaner elite did throughout the apartheid period, has been straining to use such power to ensure that the elite within the nationalist movement rises to become part of the ruling class, the owners of the means of production.

The established white ruling class has in turn been courting this elite in various ways, thanks to the post-apartheid transformation instruments such as black economic empowerment and affirmative action. As in the past, it is a begrudging compliance, but they are doing it nevertheless. Stratification and inequality have intensified within the black community; and the disquiet of the mass is manifesting on a grander scale than in the *broedertwis*, as reflected in the August 2012 Marikana tragedy and the ensuing mineworkers' and farm workers' revolts.

The challenge with these social dynamics is that the changing class structure within the black community, the bourgeoning of black middle and upper strata, is largely driven by the political project itself and consequently raises concerns of patronage and parasitic tendencies.

Another challenge is that this mainly first generation middle and upper strata quite legitimately aspire to and pursue the artificially high standard of living of the white community. This endeavour is legitimate because it forms part of the project of social change and non-racial equality. Yet, unlike their white counterparts, these emergent middle strata do not have historically accumulated assets, and they have large nuclear and extended families to support.

As a consequence, they have to rely on massive debt and the windfall of patronage. Having dipped their toes into that lifestyle but with no such historical assets as are available to the white middle and upper strata, some then try to acquire the resources by hook or by crook.

Ascendancy to these higher rungs of the social ladder happens through a variety of channels, including:

- management positions in the civil service and state-owned enterprises,
- 'streetwise' unemployed people who get into political leadership positions at local level and by the stroke of a pen become councillor or parliamentarian and migrate to the middle strata (of course, other streetwise peers then want to displace them in 'phuma singene' mobilisation),
- the university student leadership where, besides perks attached to SRC positions, some student leaders now demand a seat in university tender committees to get kick-backs, and
- trade union leadership which exercises authority over pension funds amounting to billions of rands, or even at shop-floor level where shop-stewards can influence catering and other service tenders.

While there is a new crop of young black professionals and entrepreneurs who are rising on the social ladder only due to their skills and acumen and do not require affirmative action, these are still the exception that proves the rule.

In the main, the position of the emergent middle and upper strata is tenuous and insecure. The consequence of this is that, unlike the middle strata in 'mature' class societies, the raison d'être of these emergent strata is not so much pride in the professions, or engagement in discourse on the nation's vision, or the shaping of positive value systems for society. Rather, it is survival and climbing up the steep social ladder.

The 'sins of incumbency' derive in large measure from this. Within parties, intra-party patronage and corruption take root. The political centre is unable to connect the local mediators to mass constituencies and the foot-soldiers on whom it relies to garner votes. In pursuit of numbers, a price is attached to a conference delegate's vote. And to paraphrase a lecturer at a Gauteng ANC political education workshop, a toxic leadership then begets toxic members, some of whom actually demand financial and other incentives to vote in particular ways.

Within society, there develops among rebel-rousers a nationalism of convenient victimhood, where radical slogans are used to hide incompetence and greed. The logic in this instance is: because you were oppressed or because you *delivered* at conference, you can mess up, steal and plunder; and shout 'racism' when challenged.

The entire apartheid project manifested similar narratives, *albeit* with particular undertones.

But it would be correct to pose the question: is such a characterisation not too simplistic? Even if we may be dealing with dynamics within one socio-economic formation, aren't there nuances? Is this an inevitable course of a nationalist cause within a capitalist socio-economic formation?

Without going into detail on the theorisation of the National Democratic Revolution (NDR), which aims to create a National Democratic Society (NDS), it is critical to highlight the nuances, some of which may reflect qualitative contrasts.

The African National Congress and indeed the liberation movement at large argue that the purpose of struggle was to resolve the basic contradictions spawned by apartheid colonialism: national oppression, class super-exploitation and gender discrimination. It is a nationalism of the oppressed that trumps narrow confines to embrace non-racial equality.

The NDR, it is argued, should result in the building of '...a society based on the best in human civilisation in terms of political and human freedoms, socio-economic rights, value systems and identity'.[6]

The economic system of a National Democratic Society would essentially be capitalist 'shorn of ... racial and gender exclusions... and freed from barriers to entry and competition' and it will have:

> [A] mixed economy, with state, co-operative and other forms of social ownership, and private capital. The balance between social and private ownership of investment resources will be determined on the balance of evidence in relation to national development needs and the concrete tasks of the NDR at any point in time.[7]

The NDR further emphasises that '[i]f there were to be any single measure of the civilising mission of the NDR, it would be how it treats the most vulnerable in our society'.

We would all agree that the results of Census 2011 and other data do underline the progress that has been made in improving the quality of life of the overwhelming majority of South Africans over the 19 years of democracy. One can quote instances such as the slight narrowing of the racial income gap, the extension of basic services to the majority of the population and a social wage unequalled in many parts of the world, the reduction of absolute poverty and the opening of access to opportunity undreamt of under apartheid colonialism (see chapter by Gumede for details on these trends).

Yet there is a need to drill deeper into the ebbs and flows of inequality trends within and among races, which the grand narrative of Census 2011 may not fully clarify. Among others, the aggregates on the racial income gap conceal the income inequality within the black community. Extension of access to basic services does not necessarily translate into quality of such services. Unemployment remains a terrible blot on the humanity of our society. While the state has played an important role as an instrument of redistribution, its effectiveness in this regard is hampered by poor capacity, patronage and corruption (see chapters by Hirsch and Ngcaweni for further reflections on state capacity and challenges facing the public service).

These truths all South Africans are aware of, and there is consensus that the political economy as currently configured is unsustainable. To use the metaphor of Colonialism of a Special Type: the pace at which the state (and the new political elite) can address all these issues, as compared to the historical period referred to above, is also constrained by the reality that the current political elite cannot resort to, but should in fact eliminate, the super-exploitation of the masses in the 'internal colony'. Such super-exploitation previously made it possible for the white political elite to buttress the living standards of the white lower classes in the 'internal me-tropolis'. Besides, the inherited impoverishment of the black majority, compared to the 'poor white problem' of yesteryear, is much more massive in terms of intensity and extensiveness.

Once again, while reflections of this kind oblige us to look at our weaknesses, we should not, in doing so, lose sight of the progress that our society has made since 1994. We should be proud that we have used the beachhead of the transition as a platform for political and socio-economic change, even if in many areas this may have been too slow and too tortuous.

Therefore we ask, is the evolution of class dynamics in post-apartheid South Africa a tragedy, a farce or neither?

In search of a new development trajectory

In the maelstrom of a political elite striving to rise to the status of a ruling class, in intimate embrace or shadow-boxing with the established white economic elite, and in the midst of mass disquiet and tragedies such as Marikana, we can be forgiven for the temptation to invoke, quite extensively, Karl Marx's observations after the 1871 defeat of the Paris Commune:[8]

> During the subsequent regimes [*after the 1789 French Revolution – author*], the government, placed under parliamentary control… became not only a hotbed of huge national debts and crushing taxes; with its irresistible allurements of place, pelf, and patronage, it became not only the bone of contention between the rival

factions and adventurers of the ruling classes; but its political character changed simultaneously with the economic changes of society...

After every revolution marking a progressive phase in the class struggle, the purely repressive character of the state power stands out in bolder and bolder relief... The bourgeois republicans, who, in the name of the February Revolution, took the state power, used it for the June [1848] massacres, in order to convince the working class that 'social' republic means the republic entrusting their social subjection, and in order to convince the royalist bulk of the bourgeois and landlord class that they might safely leave the cares and emoluments of government to the bourgeois 'republicans'...

Under its sway, bourgeois society, freed from political cares, attained a development unexpected even by itself. ...[F]inancial swindling celebrated cosmopolitan orgies; the misery of the masses was set off by a shameless display of gorgeous, meretricious and debased luxury. The state power, apparently soaring high above society and the very hotbed of all its corruptions.

These observations by Marx, perhaps not entirely applicable to the state of South Africa today, do send a chilling reminder of what should not be; for the arrival of the worst in our body politic may not announce itself by knocking on the front door. It is an injunction that the national democratic state should urgently organise itself into an effective instrument of rapid growth and development, or consign itself to monumental irrelevance as the revolution strays from its course. For, without this, the state will be rejected as a mere dispensary of elite patronage, mocked as an instrument of pork-barrel regional or ethnic 'delivery', and attacked as a defender of super-exploitation.

By avoiding this, we shall escape the fate that befell the pre-colonial Mapungubwe 'civilisation' which failed to negotiate the vicissitudes of environmental change, allowed social stratification to rend society apart, suffered marginalisation as new neighbouring 'civilisations' emerged and trade routes changed and failed to contain the excesses of a debased leadership.

South African leaders of transformation believe that there is a way out of pedestrian economic growth and development in which we are currently trapped. This is reflected, in part, in the expression of intent to build a developmental state, in the manner of the so-called Asian 'tigers' which have historically sustained high rates of growth and social inclusion over decades, and thus lifted hundreds of millions of people out of poverty. Such a state, it is argued, should have the strategic orientation for development, premised on the political will of the leadership to stake their all on a developmental project. It should have the legitimacy to mobilise society behind a vision and programmes to attain set objectives. Such a state should be optimally organised to meet its objectives, and it should have the technical capacity within the bureaucracy to bring its intentions to life. We should, however, acknowledge that the trend in most of these Asian developmental states was to rely on the trickle-down economics of high growth rates. Further, in the earlier phases of the evolution of most of these polities, authoritarianism held sway. In contradistinction to this, South Africans assert that ours should be a democratic developmental state, and that social policy should continue to feature prominently as part of speeding up the drive for social inclusion or 'developmental citizenship', values espoused in the country's Constitution which are inspired, among others, by the African Claims of 1943 and the Freedom Charter of 1955.

That the South African leadership is striving *a priori* to build a developmental state is itself a positive reflection on the commitment to deal with the social challenges we face. In the words of Professor Linda Weiss, for South Africa to have set itself:

> ... the unusual and challenging goal of becoming a developmental state... is a unique and noble enterprise: unique in so far as no state has ever self-consciously set out to become a Developmental State; and noble in so far as such a project draws inspiration from the experience of certain countries that achieved shared growth – growth with equity. Predatory states have appeared in abundance; developmental states are a much rarer breed.[9]

In terms of effort, two striking instances of progress deserve mention. Firstly, it is the adoption by Cabinet and endorsement by Parliament and the 'ruling party' of the National Development Plan (NDP), and the commitment that where there may be conflict between current policies and programmes and the NDP the latter will take precedence. This is reinforced by the apparent support of all political parties and most of society for Vision 2030 as elaborated in the NDP.

Secondly, the setting up of formal monitoring and evaluation capacity and the performance agreements within the executive that attach to this have the potential to increase accountability and thus the implementation of what has been decided upon.

If there was any urgent challenge to address in this regard, it would be ensuring that these latest initiatives are effectively operationalised and become truly embedded across all the spheres of government.

Political will and capacity of the state

The question has been raised quite legitimately whether, beyond declarations, there is the will and capacity to implement the NDP.

This question should be approached differently: so popular and so legitimate should the NDP be that, in the election hustings in 2014, the basic question posed to all parties should be how their manifestos accord with Vision 2030, and what concretely they are going to do in the five years of their mandate to ensure that it is implemented. The performance of government should be monitored against that yardstick. In other words, all of society should be the guardians of, and active participants in, ensuring that the NDP is implemented.

Besides this, let us reflect on a few critical actions that success in implementing a development plan requires, and how the South African state and society at large are faring. The first one is about a social compact. Professor Thandika Mkandawire, a leading development scholar, elaborates this notion thus:

> Social compacts refer to the institutionalisation of consultation and cooperation on economic policy involving representation from the state, capital, labour and other organisations of civil society. Social compacts have been used to address distributive and growth objectives of society at the micro-level; to improve labour management at the firm level and, as in the current usage of 'social pacts' in Europe, to manage the distributional issues of macroeconomics policies...
>
> The proactive initiatives emerge when societies aim at a future objective that requires high levels of cooperation and trust... and are evoked when nations seek to embark on ambitious projects that require coordination and co-operation in both the political and economic spheres. Nation-building and economic development are good examples of such efforts... Social compacts play an important role in such situations to assure citizens that their current sacrifices will be duly and fairly rewarded in the future.[10]

As such, in our situation, a social compact will have to be pro-active and all-embracing, covering such issues as investment, employment and wage policy, interest rates, inflation and cost of living, competition policy, spatial issues and so on. It will require commitment on the part of all sectors of society to facilitate high economic growth and social inclusion, encompassing the totality of things required progressively to attain a decent standard of living for all.

This demands activism across all sectors, and preparedness on the part of the broad leadership to weigh trade-offs and to make choices for the common good. It requires the will and the acumen to eschew narrow self-interest; and leadership capacity to accept and communicate decisions that may not entirely be popular with one's own constituency.

It is therefore critical to avoid the danger of devaluing the notion of a social compact by confining it merely to immediate responses to a wave of strikes or even short-term measures to minimise the impact of the current global economic crisis.

This, in the view of some, is one of the weaknesses of the outcome of the 2012 High Level Dialogue on the Economy, besides the fact that it did not at all refer to Vision 2030 and the NDP.

The second issue is about coherence in policy development and co-ordination. Researchers on developmental states do caution that we should not expect an artificial homogeneity within as large an organisation as the state. In the words of Linda Weiss:

> The state is not a unitary structure like an orange where all the segments fit neatly together. As a complex of political institutions, states are actually quite messy configurations... As power structures, we say that they are polymorphous. So the state may well be free-market in one sphere (like finance), yet developmental in another (e.g. industry and technology), a promoter of free trade in some sectors (financial services), yet mercantilist in others (agriculture or textiles).[11]

But all scholars of developmentalism do correctly argue that, precisely because states are 'messy configurations', one of the most critical and necessary attributes of a developmental state is a central institution, a pilot agency, with the strategic capacities, leverages and authority to drive economic policy and ensure its implementation. One of the weaknesses in the South African state currently is the multiplicity of centres from which economic policy is driven – Economic Development, Trade and Industry, National Treasury, Public Enterprises and so on – with each actually believing that it is the ultimate authority.

As such, we run the danger of re-living the words of Alexei Tolstoi in his epic work, *Ordeal*:

> The hurricane of events roared and the sea of humanity swayed. Everyone considered himself commander, and flourishing his pistol directed that the helm be turned now to port and now to starboard. All this was illusion... The illusions were born of brief glimpses of the mirage.[12]

The third issue is the balancing act by the state in providing societal leadership: what Peter Evans[13] refers to as 'embedded autonomy'. On the one hand, the state should be so networked across society as to be able to exercise ideational leadership or what Antonio Gramsci refers to as 'hegemony'.

On the other hand, the state should be buttressed by a professional bureaucracy that is insulated from undue political interference and patronage. The state as a whole should have the will to break logjams in the interactions among various sectors of society – to prevent narrow sectoral interests paralysing the capacity of society to move forward. In a society such as ours, with its wide social fissures, deadlocks among social partners should be expected. While the National Economic Development and Labour Council (NEDLAC) was set up primarily to resolve critical issues among these partners, it has become fossilised in its approach; each constituency pursues frozen mandates; representation has been juniorised and the interactions are technocratic.

For example, paralysis around interventions to deal with youth marginalisation, and the proposed youth wage subsidy in particular, reflects this malaise. And the state is too indecisive to act autonomously of the interest groups, even if it meant running extensive pilot projects on the youth wage subsidy, in two or three provinces – the better to address concerns that currently are discussed only in theoretical terms. At the same time, informal forums of interaction such as the Working Groups of government and a variety of other social partners have been jettisoned, worsening levels of mistrust across society.

The last issue is about the state's sources of legality and legitimacy. On the face of it, issues of legality and legitimacy should not arise in the context of our state, given the generations of rights that the Constitution proffers, the separation of powers and the institutions to protect and enforce these rights. But, in the context of tragedies like Marikana and the 2012 mine and farmworkers' revolts, we may need to drill deeper to assess whether, unsighted, there aren't worms eating into the very edifice of the state colossus.

And so, beyond the constitutional and formal legalities, we need to examine the sturdiness of the system of rule of law in relation to the most ordinary of citizens all the way to the highest echelons of society. When strikers and demonstrators carry weapons and murder others with impunity; and when an impression is created that court orders are not honoured, we need to ponder whether the 'threat of threat', combined with civilised and intelligent conduct, that should underpin state hegemony, is not in fact hollow – ready to unravel in insidious and profoundly destructive ways.

We need to examine how the intent and capacity to provide services by all spheres of government impacts on the legitimacy of the state. Needless to say, because of the levels of poverty and inequality in our society, an unavoidable feature of our nation for a long time to come will be the inflammable tinder ever ready to catch fire. In some cases it may not be actual 'delivery' that douses the fires of expectation; but the evidence of general progress and the hope that tomorrow will be better than today; as well as visible and effective measures to deal with corruption and patronage.

Where, as in the Marikana informal settlement, the social wage is virtually non-existent – with both the state and the mine-owners seemingly having washed their hands – the lack of hope is the spark that sets the tinder alight.

We need to examine whether our theoretical distinction between government and the state, as well as between the state and societal leaders, does matter in terms of the legitimacy of the state and the broader socio-economic formation. As such, unethical conduct by leaders in government, business, the trade union movement and the rest of civil society, impressions of lack of respect for public resources and the ostentation of the elite delegitimise not only the party political and societal leadership but also the state as such.

We need to do all this, appreciating that ours is essentially a capitalist system, with a state that seeks, through developmental programmes, to bridge deep and wide fissures inherited from the system of internal colonialism. As the ruling elite, quite naturally, seeks to raise itself and those in its courtyard to the position of the ruling class, failure more effectively to socialise the benefits of economic growth has the potential to unleash a conflagration much more destructive than the *broedertwis* of yesteryear.

The reconfiguration of this capitalist system should entail more than just the racial dimension at elite level, the so-called 'black economic empowerment' to which 'economic transformation' is usually reduced. The time has come, in addition to all the other programmes of economic transformation, for the political ruling elite and the ruling class together to contribute to forging stakeholder capitalism in which the working class is a real beneficiary.

The aim in raising this matter is not to delve into various aspects of economic transformation, ranging from the structure of the economy, efficiency and cost of infrastructure, skills training, the multifaceted role of the state and so on. It is merely to emphasise that, at the core of the ownership component of economic empowerment programmes going forward, in mining, manufacturing, services and other industries, should be meaningful employee share-ownership schemes (ESOPs) and community participation, which should be emphasised above all other ownership elements of broad-based black economic empowerment. This should be part of our contemplation on the place and role of labour: *'die beskouing van die arbeid'* of the current age.

Cleansing the sins of incumbency

Can the 'sins of incumbency' referred to above at all be eliminated?

The Organisational Renewal document considered by the ANC at its December 2012 conference made many proposals on how to deal with the challenges of political incumbency. Some of the proposals are new, and others are a consolidation of old ideas that were unfortunately rejected at that fateful ANC National General Council in 2005. Some of these proposals include:
• building a new corps of cadres with political and ethical as well as academic and technical acumen,

- strengthening ANC headquarters to be able to manage not only the exercise of political power and constitutional statecraft as well as the multitudes of members and supporters but also how to relate to civil society – including intellectuals, artists and media – not as victim and protestor; but as leader,
- the operationalisation of the decision on the Integrity Commission: a commission that will have the legitimacy and authority to call members who stray to order, and
- a radical shift in the management of leadership contestation so we can dispense with the current pretence that everyone waits for nominations to open, while people organise factional meetings about slates in the middle of the night.

On the latter, the ANC may need to go even further and state clearly that members who wish to stand for particular positions should declare, get vetted, be afforded a platform in the branches and regions to explain their proposed value addition and get disqualified if they break the rules. In this regard, there is much to learn from sister parties such as Chama Cha Mapindudzi in Tanzania and FRELIMO in Mozambique.

Conclusion

This then is the central message: the state of the South African state and its legitimacy cannot be divorced from the state and legitimacy of the socio-economic system that it manages, and the conduct of the elite beneficiaries of this system.

Is the extant and aspirant ruling class capable of behaving as more than just 'a class in itself'; that is, also as 'a class for itself'?

As Professor Thandika Mkandawire and other accomplished African scholars have suggested, this is perhaps one of the crucial questions of the political economy of our times that researchers on our continent need to interrogate. Combined with party political renewal and the construction of a capable developmental state, addressing these issues will be critical in defining South Africa's trajectory going forward.

Endnotes

1   Earlier versions of this article were presented by the author as Netshitenzhe, J.K., 2012. *The state of the State*. Harold Wolpe Memorial Lecture; as well as Netshitenzhe, J.K., 2012. *Competing identities of a national liberation movement versus electoral party politics: Challenges of incumbency*. The Young Communist League. May.

2   See Engels, F., 1884. *The origin of the family, private property and the State*. pp.157-158.

3   Engels, F., n.d. *Letter to J. Bloch* in Königsberg. Available at: http://www.marxists.org/... 1890/letters...

4   Quoted from O'Meara, D., 1983. *Volkskapitalisme: Class, capital and ideology in the development of Afrikaner Nationalism, 1934–1948*. Koers.

5   Marx, K., n.d. *The Eighteenth Brumaire of Louis Bonaparte*. Available at: http://www.marxists.org/archive/marx/works.

6   African National Congress, 2007. *Strategy and tactics document*, December.

7   Ibid.

8   Marx, K., 1871. *The Civil War in France, the third address*. The Paris Commune.

9   Weiss, L., 2010. *Transformative capacity and developmental States: Lessons for South Africa*. Sydney: University of Sydney.

10 Mkandawire, T., 2012. *Building the African State in the age of globalisation – The role of social compacts and lessons for South Africa*. Mapungubwe Institute Inaugural Annual Lecture. Johannesburg.

11 See Weiss, 2010, op.cit.

12 Quoted from Denga, A.C., p.105, see Tolstoi, A., 1986. *Ordeal*.

13 Evans, P., 1995. *Embedded autonomy: States and industrial transformation*. New York: Princeton University Press.

PART 4

The Future We Choose

CHAPTER 15

Organisational renewal: aspiration or necessity?

Kgalema Motlanthe

The future is not a result of choices among alternative paths offered by the present, but a place that is created – created first in the mind and will, created next in activity. The future is not some place we are going to, but one we are creating. The paths are not to be found, but made, and the activity of making them, changes both the maker and the destination. – John Schaar

Introduction

On January 08, 2012, the African National Congress (ANC) celebrated its centenary attesting to its enduring courage as a political formation whose ideals resonated with the masses of the oppressed on which the organisation was based. But what are the historical lessons to be drawn from this experience?

This stage in its history is only of use if it elevates the ANC to a higher level of conception, enabling it to expedite the process of realising its most cherished principles, including unity, democracy, non-racialism, non-sexism and justice, in the context of economic transformation, reconstruction and development.

Necessarily, the question that arises is whether the ANC still commands the moral authority both to lead society and meet its historical goals. Given the imperatives of the current epoch, this cannot only be based on the ANC's exalted history but should also reflect the organisation's acquired moral, ethical, ideological and behavioural consistency, as well as honesty and truthfulness to its principles as it wades into the second centenary of its existence with the burden of social transformation on its shoulders.

My view is that tension has emerged between ANC incumbency and objective conditions that define the post-liberation landscape during this process of correcting the socio-economic ills of the past.

Largely, this tension has been occasioned by our access to and employment of state power to effect social change within the framework of a capitalist economic system. We are carrying out the exacting task of socio-economic transformation under given conditions that are inevitably impacting on us as an organisation as well as our membership. It is therefore useful to reflect on this socio-historical configuration of the post-apartheid landscape with the hope of understanding how possession of state power in a post-colonial capitalist system may impact on the envisioned historical trajectory of the ANC and, in turn, what the ANC can do to reclaim its defining DNA.

However, such an understanding and the concomitant attempts it should suggest for us to stay on course does not inherently disavow the ineluctable fluidities peculiar to our historical period.

The burden of history

The ANC was formed in 1912 with the view to both uniting and representing the aspirations of the oppressed people of our country who had been subjected to colonial rule since the arrival of the Dutch settlers in 1652, a process which culminated in the exclusion of black people from the formation of the Union of South Africa in 1910. The impelling force behind the ANC's historical trajectory has been social emancipation and economic transformation through the destruction of the political and economic structures that served as the scaffolding for racial domination manifested in racial inequality. Characteristically, the ANC is a national liberation movement with the following as its objectives:

- Uniting the oppressed and spearheading the struggle for political, social and economic change;
- The ANC's key objective is the creation of a united, non-racial, non-sexist and democratic society;
- This means the liberation of Africans in particular and black people in general from political and economic bondage. It means uplifting the quality of life of all South Africans, especially the poor.[1]

From its formation, unity of the oppressed forces in society was the bedrock upon which the ANC stood. This element of unity was further enhanced by struggle for the moral values of human compassion and solidarity, and an element of humanism which was more than just opposition to the colonial and apartheid systems. For instance, throughout its history the ANC has invariably stressed love and respect for the collective and, in the context of the struggle, de-emphasised the individual, while conscious not to empty the notion of individuality of its innate content and legitimate existence and thus open up our movement to all sorts of insidious tendencies.

Emphasis on the collective over the individual was a way of cultivating selflessness as a virtue, this being key to the survival of the organisation and a future free society.

With time, and after incremental experience in the theatre of the struggle, the ANC came round to the view that concrete historical conditions had made national minorities an undeniable feature of the South African society. Firstly, when it was formed the ANC sought to unite all ethnicities in South Africa, prompted by the realisation that colonial conquest succeeded where unity among the African people had failed to take root. It followed then that with continued ethnic divisions Africans could not defeat colonial rule and reconstitute a new inclusive nation under conditions of modernity.

As the struggle gained impetus the concept of the oppressed was broadened to include all South Africans facing political oppression, social discrimination and economic exploitation. In consequence a nascent inter-racial solidarity with other progressive forces emerged as a current that eventually decanted into a non-racial stream within the ANC itself. In this way the struggle against colonialism and apartheid did not stop at ending this aberration but dared to posit ontological relations that were pitched at a higher socio-historical level.

In order for the revolutionary role of the ANC to have an upper hand, the movement itself had to reflect higher morality, thereby unleashing wider social forces, including minorities and, subsequently, other motif forces of the struggle such as workers, peasants, the youth, etc. So, from a non-racial, non-sexist, democratic, just and moral viewpoint, the struggle promised a new dawn inspired by the ideals of the ANC.

From this historical character and the conditions under which it was born flow two pivotal implications. The first is that the ANC was formed out of recognition of necessity at a particular stage of social development. In turn this necessity imposed a particular shape and form on the movement. Throughout its history the ANC had to take this objective reality into account in order to respond to the challenges it was going through as it worked towards attaining the stated goals of liberation struggle.

It is worth noting that chances of survival in the hundred years of its history would have been as good as zero had the ANC failed from time to time to studiously study these objective conditions and respond accordingly. As such, from the beginning its character, norms and values were the outcrop of a given situation.

Therefore, the ANC's character was not a pre-ordained act frozen in time; instead it has evolved over the years, adapting to the peculiarities of historical stages while retaining the essence of its vision. In hindsight, it is indeed plausible that this character, this unique shape into which the ANC has evolved in the furnace of the liberation struggle, has proven effective, as validated by the democratic breakthrough in 1994.

Yet, as social conditions change in the post-1994 era, a question that arises is whether this shape that defined the essence of the ANC during the course of the liberation struggle remains relevant. While there is seamlessness running through both the pre- and post-1994 eras in terms of the need to bring about economic justice and social equality as well as reconstruction and development, there are also indications that the post-1994 period has seen fundamental changes in social conditions.

Among others the current membership makeup of the ANC in terms of class, strata, gender, age group and demographics is likely to unleash particular idiosyncrasies on the movement itself. Care should therefore be taken not to lag behind these changing, fluid times that are apt to vitiate any stagnant social force, no matter how commendable its history.

The second implication stems from the challenges inherent in access to state power. Unlike the pre-liberation stage of our struggle when we aimed to dismantle and dismember the apartheid state and in its place construct a democratic one responsive to the needs of all South Africans, the present conditions see the ANC ensconced in power.

Some of the unintended consequences of state power entail the propensity to employ this state power for reasons other than serving the needs of society, particularly the section still trapped in historical disabilities. This sad scenario, which is peculiar to post-liberation landscapes elsewhere, is shown by incessant government and media reports pointing to corruption and abuse of state power.

A worldwide phenomenon, corruption has prompted some nations to take active steps to address it in varied forms. For example, the State of New South Wales in Australia defined corruption thus:

> As public officials we have specific powers, functions and knowledge because of the positions we hold. Corrupt conduct occurs when an official uses or attempts to use position for personal advantage. Corrupt conduct can also occur when a member of the public influences or attempts to influence a public official to use his or her position for purpose other than the benefit of the public.[2]

To illuminate the challenge of corruption in the post-colonial polity let us locate it in the broader historical context where distinction is drawn between the national liberation struggle and the class struggle. Such a distinction separates the goals of the class struggle from those of a national liberation struggle. In the former the overarching aim is to dismantle a social system, in this case capitalism.

With the victory of the working class through the vanguard party, the entire warp and woof of the capitalist state, including social, economic and political institutions, is smashed. In its place are engineered new institutions meant to lead to a new social order – these being norms, value system, ethos and culture. This post-revolutionary society assumes a new human personality with a totally new system of thought.

This scenario is contrasted with the national liberation struggle, whose core vision is to replace the colonial state or in our case the apartheid state with a democratic one. This objective is normally attained through the process of transforming state and society. It is worth noting that the process of social change takes place within the context of capitalism as a social system, and does not seek to dismember the latter. To be sure, the process of social change does take into account the history of relations between capital and racial oppression as the basis for formulating policies that will redirect the workings of capital so that it serves the needs of the democratic order.

Whether the political goals of social change are obtained or not, capitalist relations of society remain intact. As in almost all cases the world over where capitalism holds sway, social existence will therefore be moulded by the economic system in which it is rooted. In brief, it is my contention that, cast in a capitalist mould, post-apartheid society inevitably reflects this social reality. I submit that if we proceed from this theoretical understanding we will be better able to have a broader perspective of the nature and scope of the challenges we face.

This point is further thrown in bold relief when we take an even closer look at the conditions that germinate corruption in a capitalist society. It is widely accepted that capitalism is about individual success, especially in terms of wealth accumulation. In this connection, the struggle stalwart Toussaint is worth quoting at length:

> The characteristic corruption of capitalism, for example, is related understandably enough to money. The whole motivation of the capitalist system is the accumulation of private wealth by exploiting the labour of others. Status and privilege accrue to those who accumulate most. Personal enrichment with small regard to the interests of the rest of society is both acceptable and admired. Such society is thus a hothouse for breeding a financial corruption, which seeps through the stock exchanges, the multi-national corporations, the political parties and the administration, into every centre of power.[3]

To be sure, while the above citation raises the morally deformed nature of a capitalist society, it does not seek to paint all humanity living under the system with the same brush. Many decent human beings driven by probity do exist and are able to hold out despite the alluring power of such a questionable ethical system. Nevertheless, the contention remains that in a society where individual worth is largely judged on the grounds of material possession and not the content of one's character, it follows that the unimpeachable values that are the heritage of the ANC will naturally come under severe strain when juxtaposed with the dominant value system that shapes social life.

Most of the well-meaning ANC cadres, coming from humble social origins and suddenly wielding amazing political power that awards millions worth of contracts and tenders, find themselves caught up in these conditions. In the event that these tempting values should supplant one's sense of duty, as is likely to be the case, the result is a slippery slope where there is no stopping as the culture of venality sets in like an opportunistic disease.

These fluidities are reflected in the dichotomy between the epochs before and after democracy which Toussaint[4] usefully designates 'before power' (BA) and 'after power' (AP), respectively. Each of these epochs represents totally different philosophical orientations espoused by the individual members of the ANC. Even though not all members of the ANC embraced a socialist outlook during the era of the liberation struggle, socialism was the popular political outlook that shaped the post-apartheid thinking of many an ANC cadre. Following this observation, we can understand the prevailing political attitudes among ANC members 'before power' in these Toussaint terms:

> Socialism's moral and ethical codes are based on the concept that acceptable personal advance depends on the general advance of the whole society; that the individual rises with society as a whole, not from it. It is this code which provides the motivation for socialist leaders before they attain to power in the state. It explains why they willingly follow a life of personal hardship and privation; why they pass up a lifestyle of ease and comfort in order to devote themselves to winning the advance of the group, be it party or nation.[5]

As we have tried to show, this idealism is likely to recede into the background in proportion as the capitalist system sucks many of our cadres into its vortex. Of course, this does not suggest that the entire membership of the ANC has been compromised by these dominant values of acquisitiveness and greed. On the contrary, there are just as many men and women inspired by the ideals that saw political activists, the educated social segment, the clergy, traditional leaders and ordinary Africans from across Southern Africa gather in Bloemfontein to form this mighty movement a century ago. Perhaps this segment which refuses to give ground to these encroaching corrosive values represents the hope that all is not lost and that with a totally new approach that takes account of current historical realities the organisation can still impose its monogram on history.

ANC's renewal post-liberation

Our key challenge in this post-liberation era is to strive for organisational renewal with an eye to attuning to current historical imperatives. Organisations are sustained through long-term visions resulting from conscious actions taken today in the interest of present and future generations. Unwillingness to renew may result in ossification of time-worn approaches to doing things, with stultifying effects on internal organisational dynamism. Because each epoch is marked by unique conditions that throw up specific challenges, we are ineluctably enmeshed in circumstances that require a commensurate response.

In consequence, renewal helps us clear away the cobwebs of the present incumbency, opening our minds in a manner that affords our movement an opportunity to know what is no longer workable and the pitfalls we are encountering, thus preventing us from going off course due to the allurements of power.

These considerations therefore necessitate some honest introspection on our part and assume particular importance, given that the masses still trust the ANC to carry out its historical mission in a manner that upholds its founding principles while pushing back the frontiers of poverty, illiteracy, ignorance and hopelessness.

Renewal requires re-emphasising the traditions and core values of the movement and preventing the ANC's quintessence from being corroded by sins of incumbency. In essence, the ANC needs to work to ensure that it emerges from this current period fully consistent in outlook and orientation with the character of a modern progressive party. This is nothing new to the ANC as it has from its inception had the versatility to reorganise itself in the light of new experiences and to keep up with the historical process.

Practical experience over the last few years requires that we re-look the issues of organisational systems and processes with the object of strengthening existing internal democracy and leadership systems. History is only relevant to the extent that key lessons that have sustained us over many years are brought to the surface for modern generations to draw on as a reference point.

The culture of debate

One of the common refrains in the ANC's arsenal of principles is the issue of open, free and unfettered debate within its ranks. For many decades a spirit of open debate, constructive criticism and self-criticism has been the bedrock upon which the organisation has been able to stand firmly.

Allowing free voice from all and sundry, whether they are in leadership or not, enabled the movement to unite behind a single goal, because members are guaranteed say in the direction their organisation is taking.

In this way, the organisation serves as a people's assembly, giving branches, and by extension communities, the opportunity to voice their views, including those on election of public representatives. It also allows members to participate in the policy-making processes through a free contestation of ideas so that, once consensus emerges, a mandate is created for those in leadership.

As a result, the key lesson we may want to draw from this practice is to uphold and at all times defend the rich culture of debate that has sustained the organisation over the years. Our movement has not shied away from opening up the floor for a multiplicity of voices aimed at arriving at the best possible and most widely accept-able policy choices.

Emergence of slates

Historically, elections in the ANC serve as a mechanism for strengthening and renew-ing the organisation in the context of the challenges and tasks that would have been identified through this democratic decision-making process. Elective conferences provide an opportunity to elect a leadership best suited to the historical epoch. Thus when leadership is elected, it is based on the tasks that lie ahead. It is not the prede-termined result of slates, as has been the case in recent history.

Yet slates have become one of the harmful post-1994 viruses that have crept into the bloodstream of the ANC. Slates steal away the voice of members through buying of votes and treating the ordinary membership as voting fodder, serving no other purpose than to corrupt the organisation.

Slates represent a deformed character of the organisation in which factions and groups motivated by personal gain scramble with no holds barred for leadership positions.

Taken to its conclusion, we cannot but infer that slates serve to push away mem-bers from the ANC and to disorganise it, destroying the unity that has stood it in good stead for more than one hundred years. Conferences should not be preoccupied with elections of leadership as this is inconsequential to the struggle that the organisation must advance. When there is a healthy organisation, it does not matter who leads.

Members should remain loyal to the organisation, not to individuals, and should seek to enhance its prestige among the people. This prestige is a function – it depends on what we do and/or what we say as individual members. This is all the more reason we should always guard against the pernicious habit of – no matter how well-intended at first – allowing a cult of personality to develop in our midst, characterised by the practice of idolising leadership. Leadership is a reflection of an organisation and must not be personalised.

We must appreciate and understand the role of individuals in the organisation, but must always bear in mind that the organisation is more than the sum total of its individual members. As such slates are also antithetical to the principle of open and free debate and represent a degenerate version of the organisation in which factions and groups less motivated by what the ANC stands for use all manner of surreptitious means to gain leadership positions.

Slates are odious because the victorious factions spend time after conferences meting out a victor's justice; while those seen to have been on the opposite side during the conference are made to pay the price in many ways, including marginalisation. In the process, organisational work suffers. Leaders and membership are no longer united behind a common vision reaffirmed in the conference and expressed through appropriate organisational resolutions that require implementation.

Governance also suffers because the winning slates invariably overlook individuals perceived to be sympathetic to the losing ones. Part of punishing such individuals is removing them from work or depriving them of opportunities irrespective of their ability to excel in their duties; an act that ultimately undermines transformation and development.

In spite of voting in our conferences being by secret ballot there are those who pretend to know how delegates voted and on the basis of this single out certain individuals for marginalisation. In this case elections then lose meaning as an instrument for strengthening the organisation and become an apparatus for rewarding factions, irrespective of the decisions reached through consensus. On a broader scale, slates prevent the organisation being itself; that is, allowing multiplicity of views around the required leadership to take the ANC forward. As a consequence slates create conditions for factionalist imposition on the organisation; such leadership does not enjoy universal approval and may very well turn out to be a dead weight rather than a vital, dynamic leadership attuned to the imperatives of the time.

One of the irreparably harmful effects of slates is the hollowing out of the principle of non-racialism. After a hundred years of existence the composition of the ANC's membership seems to give the lie to its principle of non-racialism. Because they are virtually cloak and dagger affairs, and discriminatory by nature, slates do not allow for open, transparent and all-inclusive interactions. Currently many leadership structures of the ANC are not balanced in terms of demographics, which is uncharacteristic of the movement. If one casts one's eyes back to the 1950s and 1960s where progressive South Africans from all racial backgrounds made common cause in pursuit of freedom whether in formulating policy, open confrontation with the system, exile or even the battle tranches, it becomes a historical anomaly that today more than ever the practice of non-racialism seems to be on the retreat. Our poor showing in the 2011 local government elections in the predominantly white areas lends colour to this assessment.

Slates have eaten away at the heart of the organisation, leaving a trail of divisions, vengeance, internecine feuds and mutual mistrust, much to the mortal detriment of the ANC as an organic whole. Going into the next century, the ANC has to take stock in order to prevent the very real possibility that our movement's historicity of non-racial heritage is devitalised of meaning. We should not leave a distortion to posterity where they learn of the principle of non-racialism in the ANC as if it was an evanescent moment that has since passed into the obscurity of history.

Improving the debate within the organisation

At the national level, the ANC National Executive Committee (NEC) consists of one hundred and ten members and representatives meeting bi-monthly for two to three days. From observation the size of the NEC constrains debate because time prevents members from engaging each other. Each speaker can at most make one statement without the opportunity for debate to convince each other of the correctness of his or her views. Some of the NEC members who also have responsibilities in government find it difficult to carry out some of their organisational tasks.

This challenge also manifests itself at branch level where branches are modelled according to municipal wards that are too large to facilitate meaningful debate. To resolve these challenges the organisation will need to look into reducing the size of the NEC or meeting over many more days – perhaps for one week.

At a branch level, the organisation may want to create units or cells, as under the Mandela Plan (M Plan), in order to improve communication and co-ordination. This must take into consideration the modern means of communication and the open and democratic society in which we live. The notion of the M Plan can be re-modelled to suit current conditions in terms of the operation of the ANC. For instance, a cell or a unit comprises a few activists and so can enable all of them to have effective roles in carrying out the duties of the organisation and also meet where it is most convenient for them. The branch may also need to organise itself according to sectors in areas such as universities, mine villages, hospitals and industrial zones.

Political education

Part of the tasks that a post-liberation movement must pay attention to is the reality that after freedom it is more difficult to organise people because there is no visible, common struggle that unites them in their everyday experience.

After liberation, objective conditions embedded in the social system beget stratification according to class, which becomes more pronounced with time and which may dilute the historical cohesion that had sustained the struggle for decades. From the viewpoint of subjective conditions, we need to focus on political education with content geared to modern conditions in order to heighten political consciousness about the post-liberation struggle.

Most of the post-liberation challenges facing the ANC stem from the rapid growth of the organisation, with no corresponding effort to educate members and leaders about the minimum expectations that come with the responsibility.

With under-developed consciousness, members do not appreciate the high value and honour of serving the interests of the people before their own. They are also unable to grasp the malignant effect of corruption, factionalism, careerism and patronage on the character of society.

Based on correct curriculum, political education can sensitise people to the historical responsibility they have towards the future, showing them how accumulated acts of political irresponsibility such as stealing from the public purse may cripple the whole nation over time, thus undermining the gains of more than a hundred years of history. If ANC members are ideologically trained to fully grasp the post-apartheid vision of the organisation as well as their role in history as activists at an individual level, long before they serve in leadership capacity, we may begin to make headway.

Thus, the issue of political education is one of the key tasks that we must seek to take beyond discussions into concrete programmes and application throughout the organisation. Part of the question to be addressed through political education is whether members see themselves as observers or participants in pursuing the vision of a united, democratic, non-racial, non-sexist, just and prosperous society.

At the heart of this is whether the attainment of freedom has allowed the ANC to manifest non-racialism or not. It also impels us to examine whether the haves in society are conscious of the struggle to create an economically just and prosperous society over and above the achievement of democratic rights. Political consciousness in times of freedom is therefore acquired through a subjective process of continued political education.

Along with political education is the imperative to transform our internal mechanisms, processes and workings such that not only do we lead by example as elected leadership of the organisation but that we also subject ourselves to the policies and principles that govern our party. In practical terms this means equal measure of the internal application of rules to members that fall foul of the rules, including the laws of the country.

Once we are able to apply our own rules equally, fairly and consistently in an accountable and transparent fashion, it will be easier for our general membership to follow suit, not only inspired by the upholding of the law on the part of leadership but fully aware that law enforcement units will come down hard on anyone breaking the law. Examples elsewhere in the world of progressive political formations firming up their internal disciplinary mechanisms to forestall unlawful acts by cadres abound.

The *New York Times* of September 2006 reports a case of an arrest of a Mr Chen Liangyu, who was at the time the Shanghai Communist Party chief and a member of the Politburo. Mr Gan Yisheng, secretary general of the party's Central Discipline Inspection Commission, is reported to have said to the media that "any party member who violates party discipline, no matter how high or low his rank, will be thoroughly investigated and seriously dealt with."[6]

Indeed the Chinese Communist Party employs a system known as 'shuanggui' to investigate and prosecute cadres suspected of corruption. It is widely reported that this system has resulted in successful investigation and prosecution of many corrupt cadres, which included powerful and high-ranking party officials.

Even though the ANC does not have to replicate the internal party anti-corruption mechanism of the CCP, this model has resonant bearing for our case. Our movement needs an emphatic and decisive overhaul of internal contours with the view to enforcing a party value system and a culture of transparency, accountability and exemplary conduct to which society can look with admiration. In this regard, we trust that the establishment of 'the Integrity Committee' as per the 53rd ANC Conference in Mangaung represents renewed emphasis of this system of thought.

While political education is as critical in this task, it needs to be accompanied by these appropriate forms of sanctions against party members that show scant regard for the laws of our country. Before such malfeasance, corruption and other forms of violations of the law can take their course in terms of the laws of the country, the movement needs to have acted first, without either pre-empting or interfering with the national system of justice. Only then, when the ANC's clean governance record and commendable levels of discipline precede its name in society can our movement begin reclaiming the gravitas of its struggle days when, despite challenges of the time, it commanded unprecedented moral authority.

Conclusion

At this point in our history there is no time for dalliance and we must never ever as the ANC gloatingly claim that we have accomplished our mission. Yes, there has been progress since the dawn of democracy 19 years ago and we are still taking notable strides in many critical areas of our socio-economic life as a country. However, we must also remember that freedom is the recognition of necessity!

When someone is homeless or lives in a lean-to shack or a mud house which is a death trap, and then is given a brick and mortar RDP house, it does not mean that all the needs of his or her family have been met.

On the contrary, we have only met one aspect of their needs since there are many more basic necessities such as electricity and potable water that guarantee a decent lifestyle. That is the reason it is said that *freedom means recognition of necessity*. For this reason we have no grounds as members of the ANC to ask our members or non-members, or indeed poor and hopelessly indigent people to 'wait and be patient'. They have a right to be impatient; they have a right to demand that all their needs should be met today and not in the next five years or ten years.

Once again we need to recognise that we are confronted with different conditions, on two levels. The first are objective conditions, which are not of our making and to which we can only respond effectively by re-engineering our organisation to be equal to the challenges imposed by such conditions, the same way the ANC did when it was formed.

The second set of conditions, subjective ones, are within the realm of possibility for us as an organisation to change as we see fit. For instance, moral uprightness is a goal we can achieve by ensuring that no comrade is above the code of conduct of the ANC and the laws of our land. Acts of corruption should be punished accordingly, in a manner that is fair and consistent. Such consistency on our part would not only lend credence to our principles but would also raise the prestige of our movement among our people and peoples of the world.

The period leading up to the next century will be an acid test for the ANC as to whether or not it is equal to the task of bringing about social change in South Africa. As the above argument shows, the ANC needs internal renewal in accordance with the needs of the times to be able to execute its historical mandate. For this internal renewal to happen we first need honesty and openness in the light of recent organi-sational experience, especially since we ascended to power in 1994. If we continue to do things the same old way we are likely to keep producing the same results. In the past the ANC managed to stay afloat because from the 1960s to the 1980s it kept up with developments.

Let us remember Lenin's teaching that 'the fighting party of the advanced class need not fear mistakes. What it should fear is persistence in a mistake, refusal to admit and correct a mistake out of a false sense of shame'.[7]

Necessarily, organisational renewal is an aspiration and a necessity, not an op-tional luxury. We owe it to history, the present and the future.

Endnotes

1 Sisulu, W., 1957. *South Africa's struggle for democracy by W.M. Sisulu*. Available at: http://www.anc.org.za/show.php?id=4598.
2 This was a resolution adopted by the Independent Commission Against Crime of New South Wales.
3 Toussaint, 1991. Corridors to corruption. *African Communist*, 1st Quarter, p.31.
4 Ibid.
5 Ibid.
6 Khan, J., 2006. *The New York Times*, 27 September.
7 See Lenin's *Selected Works*, Volume 9.

CHAPTER 16

State, democracy and statistics in the making of the new South Africa

Pali Lehohla

Introduction

From Madiba to Zizi, to Bakone to Msholozi, the narrative of a country in transition has been written in statistics. In particular, the South Africa I know and the home I understand cannot be better narrated than by its statistics, more generally and more specifically by the censuses of 1996, 2001 and 2011.

Upon receiving the figures about South Africa from Census 1996, the first to be conducted under democratic rule, President Mandela said something very much unlike him. So clear, so granular, so penetrating, so elucidating and so painful were these figures that the naked truth about apartheid and its profound consequences on the country were laid bare. Madiba the peacemaker, the nation builder, the reconciler, the forgiver and indeed the father of the rainbow nation must have been pushed by these figures from his written speech. A stirred and emotion-filled Mandela, moving away from his written speech, dared and surprised everyone when he launched Census '96 and said 'whites will never rule this country again, never again...be part of the majority like Alec Erwin'.[1] Madiba's response to Census 1996 captured the power of statistics and the profound need and challenge of delivering on the burning platform of a better life for all.

Origins of statistics

Statistics is derived from a Latin word *status* and the Italian *statista*, both meaning 'political state'. Kings and rulers of the time concerned themselves with the statistics of size of land, population and commerce. Statistics, in the parlance of matters of state, are known as the science of statecraft. The notion of science in state affairs alludes to the prospect of a technocratic state and statistics underpinning this eventuality. In modern statehood a branch of this science known as 'official statistics' has taken root. Germany is generally recognised as the earliest of adapters and the most aggressive in taking on official statistics. This it did towards the end of the eighteenth century. In France, Napoleon Bonaparte was known to have depended on statistics for statecraft, and renowned for thinking probabilistically. When assessing generals for appointment he also paid premium attention to whether the track record of the would-be general attested to such a general being lucky.

Official statistics as part of modern statecraft have since grown in importance in many jurisdictions and are a common feature of the statutes of many countries. As a body of organised and systematic enquiry beyond information about the state, and particularly its mathematical and academic foundation and the study of probability, statistics as a discipline was formalised in the seventeenth century by Blaise Pascal (1623–1662) and Pierre de Fermat (1607–1665). Their applications have been widespread in medical applications of antibiotics, spearheaded by Florence Nightingale, and in social science.

Today, with the explosion of information technology, statistical applications have become so pervasive that they affirm the view by H.G. Wells[2] (1866–1946) that one day numeracy would be as necessary for humankind as the ability to read and write. The unfortunate side, especially for South Africa, was Verwoerd's address to the minority parliament in 1953, in which he questioned the use of teaching a Bantu child mathematics when it could not use it in practice.[3] By that declaration, when he was responsible for education as a minister, Verwoerd ushered in a legacy reflected in the Census 96 results – a society divided. President Mandela confronted these results and all presidents after him have taken to heart their meaning. They reflect on what the results mean substantively: how democratic South Africa continues to transform itself from its apartheid past.

Statistics: A burning platform for action

Statistics present a knowledge base on which a profound understanding of human endeavour in its political, social and economic manifestations is possible. Statistics therefore create an evidence-based platform for action. The pain of apartheid presented in statistical facts enables profound depth of knowledge and understanding about South Africa. However, before overplaying the role of statistics above all else, let us acknowledge that arguably 'not all things that get counted count, and not all things that count get counted'. There is a profound question as to what gets measured. Does the community of practice measure what they treasure? This question has as yet not been answered in full and worrying signs have emerged. In particular, these questions were addressed by the Stiglitz Commission.[4]

Taking recommendations from this commission are the resolutions of Rio+20 on GDP and beyond. The philosophical concern in this regard is practically 'what gets measured gets done' and the question philosophers ask is 'whether that which gets done is what is treasured'. Does the world treasure happiness, morality, riches, longevity, health, culture, education, values and traditions? The world as it seesaws and as we know it today has been influenced by Marxist and free-market philosophies. These outlooks to life yielded outcomes with major technological breakthroughs and advancements, as well as economic booms, on the one hand, and on the other hand economic busts, market failures and subsequent economic crisis and the spectre of conflict, war, disease and hunger. The basic philosophy that drives official statistics is that if it is a matter of social concern it needs to be managed, but for it to be managed it has to be measured.

When he received the results of Census 2001, President Mbeki[5] asked for facts and only facts. Such facts would constitute the basis for political will and policy action. When he was inaugurated as president of the republic, President Zuma created two institutions, the Planning Commission and the Department of Monitoring and Evaluation. He thus concluded the cycle for application of evidence for decision making. Statistics define and underpin all stages of the value chain and the discipline of evidence-based decision making, the science of statecraft. In the main, they do so by establishing, describing and explaining the nature and chain of relationships and causations from issues of identification, beneficiaries, policy choices, planning and programme design, implementation, monitoring and evaluation.

Statistics are the pillars of a modern state. As he launched the enumeration phase of Census 2011, Zuma[6] said he sought to know where South Africans lived, worked and played. When finally Census 2011 results were presented on 30 October 2011, the South African society was able to reflect on what had happened over the previous 17 years. Zuma now knew where South Africans lived, worked and played. The narrative of a country in transition was scribbled down.

This chapter is a tale of statistics and statistical practice in the making of a modern human-rights-based statehood in post-apartheid South Africa. The key issue being addressed is whether establishing it could have been enabled by the use of statistics or whether this occurred in spite of statistics.

To ground the South African case there is need to examine the global context within which statistical development evolved. For elaborating on this I explore the interplay between political statistics and statistical politics, South Africa and statistical development in Africa, and finally statistical development in South Africa since 1980 and policy responses to it.

Political statistics and statistical politics in the global agenda

Political statistics consist of a sequenced narrative of political events, with consequences for the evolution and emergence of the statistical agenda across space and time. The prime mover in the development of statistics consistently appears to be the nature of institutional responses to economic crises at different epochs of history. These to a large extent have remained the triggers to statistical progress and development. This history of development in statistics significantly begins with the crash of the stock market in 1929[7] and is currently a developing narrative as the stop-and-start responses to the 2008[8] financial crisis play out their drama into the second decade of this, the second century. The stock market crash of 1929, followed by the recession of 1930 and the Great Depression of 1933, opened new areas of statistical development.

Maynard Keynes[9] (1883–1946), British economist, was amongst the first to put forward the idea of deficit financing. Roosevelt, President of the United States, adopted it with great zeal and initiated the New Deal which saw America drag itself out of the depression. This medicine was further administered in war-battered post-Second World War Europe through Marshall Aid. Keynes's major contribution to statistics was the national accounts. The United Nations[10] was born on 26 June 1945, replacing the League of Nations. One of the first commissions the UN established was the United Nations Statistics Commission (UNSC) in 1947, the first task of which was to create a framework for national accounting. The aim of this framework was to provide a national accounting system that would provide tools for macro-economic stability and predictability and mitigate against financial and economic bubbles. Today, the statistics fraternity following the 2008 economic meltdown has adopted natural capital accounting.

The United Nations System of National Accounts was thus born out of Keynes's work and the intellectual work of the Soviet-American Leontief,[11] and Leontief's algebraic input-output matrices expanded the horizons of the national accounting framework by adding what is now known as a social accounting matrix. This invention underpinned models for national planning approaches. Keynes and Leontief were Nobel Peace Prize winners, as were three of the students of Leontief. These developments were followed in 1953 by the Europeans establishing a statistics body, Eurostat,[12] which guided the establishment of various bodies working for European political cooperation. The Lisbon Treaty[13] of 2009 created the European Union and a single currency for the Eurozone. Statistical compliance remains a key condition for accession to and remaining in the Eurozone.

The first edition of *A Handbook of Statistical Organisation*[14] guided the implementation of official statistics. Following the end of the Cold War in 1991, the

United Nations Fundamental Principles of Official Statistics,[15] which became the cornerstone for guiding emerging democracies in statistical principles and practice, in particular for Eastern Europe, was adopted. In 1990, the United Nations Human Development Index (HDI)[16] was introduced as a measure of quality of life. Although criticised throughout its 22 years by the UNSC, led by the chief statisticians of Australia (2001), South Africa (2005 and 2010), and Morocco and Brazil (2010), the HDI has remained one of the important indicators that the global system of measurement holds dear.

In 1998, the Argentinean and Russian economic crises prompted the International Monetary Fund[17] (IMF) to establish a statistical compliance standard that would assist in improving the science of statecraft. The framework consisted of two standards, the Special Data Dissemination Standard[18] (SDDS), which had more stringent conditions, and the General Data Dissemination Standard[19] (GDDS), which was less demanding. These had the objective of improving on the level and degree of transparency amongst countries' statistical systems and thereby also strengthening statistical practice. However, despite these measures, the world was revisited by yet another economic crisis, this time prompted by financial and mortgage sector indiscretions in the United States and Europe. The Pittsburgh meeting of G20[20] in May 2009 sought to find solutions to this world crisis. The questions that were asked, beyond blaming banks and global financial systems for greed and bad practices, related to the robustness of systems of accountability and in the main the statistical systems.

Side by side with these global developments, the Stiglitz Commission on GDP and beyond, an initiative of then French President Sarkozy,[21] gained traction and indeed drew more attention than it would have had the crisis not provided the context. The recent Rio Plus Twenty Conference had amongst other resolutions firmly put the GDP and Beyond as a treasured agenda for measurement. The OECD, on the other hand, moved on, piloting what is called *How's Life* reports. This measured what the OECD perceived to be treasured by society.

The agenda on the African continent

On the African continent the agenda for statistics, particularly the undertaking of population and housing censuses, accompanied the wave of independence from colonialism in the 1960s. However, from the mid-sixties this development was rudely disrupted by dictatorships that plagued the continent for at least three to four decades. Despite the bleak picture, the ministers responsible for economy and finance adopted the Lagos Plan of Action for statistics and the Minimum Integration Programme (MIP) for Africa in 1980.[22] Twenty years later, in 2000, the heads of states globally committed to Millennium Development Goals[23] (MDGs) as the development language that gave capital to Partnership in Statistical Development in the 21st Century (PARIS21).[24]

Under this rubric, the Marrakesh Plan of Action for Statistics[25] (MAPS) was born in 2005, followed by the Busan Plan of Action for Statistics[26] (BAPS) in 2011. The African Regional Reference Strategic Framework[27] (RRSF) for statistics and Poverty Reduction Strategy Papers (PRSP)[28] gave momentum for a statistical agenda for the continent, since the dividend of poverty burden remained largely in Africa.

More recently, on the continent the countries and the pan-African institutions, namely the African Development Bank[29] (AfDB), the Economic Commission for Africa[30] (ECA) and the African Union Commission[31] (AUC), together with the African Symposia for Statistical Development, the Chairperson of whom is Pali Lehohla, South Africa's Statistician-General, focused on the development of statistics on the continent. In this regard the African Charter[32] on Statistics was adopted by the heads of state, and the Strategy for the Harmonisation of Statistics in Africa[33] (SHaSA) was approved by the heads of African Statistics offices. The SHaSA has 14 programmes that draw from the African Union integration agenda focusing on three primary areas, namely political, economic, and social and cultural integration. The integration agenda is underpinned by, amongst others, joint projects and programmes on population census undertaken in the 2010 Round of Census, the International Comparisons Programme[34] (ICP) Africa and the Infrastructure Statistics programme.

Political statistics and statistical politics in South Africa

South Africa, the last bastion of settler colonialism and despotism of a special kind known as apartheid, had a particularly unique development path in statistics. A number of statistical collections were undertaken in the country, including the censuses of the colonies. These statistical operations of the late 1800s, as contained in the Blue Book of the census, had hallmarks of discrimination against the native populations. In 1910 a Union government was established in present-day South Africa. Subsequent to its formation, a Census Act[35] was one of the only 11 acts of parliament legislated then. This, the Census Act, was followed by the first Statistics Act[36], enacted in 1914, shortly after the 1913 Land Act. These pieces of legislation, together with a battery of other acts of parliament, were applied to direct the path the Union, and then the post-1961 Republic would follow – a grand apartheid scheme.

Of significance is that one of the 11 founding legal instruments of the 1910 Union was an act that dealt with the science of statecraft, the Census Act. A significant change in the statistics terrain in the late 1970s was the move from decennial to five-yearly censuses, with the change starting from 1980 onwards, and in terms of statute this practice continues to date. Of importance was that the grand apartheid schema was nearing completion with nominally independent homeland administrations in place. Statistics offices were established in all the independent homelands and self-governing territories.

Another important feature of the science of statecraft in South Africa was the fragmentation of statistical service. The Central Statistical Service (CSS)[37] was the preserve of white South Africa who would conduct all economic, population and social statistics. Such surveys as the income and expenditure surveys, crucial for measuring price movements (consumer price index – CPI), were the terrain of the Bureau of Market Research (BMR)[38] at the University of South Africa (UNISA), and they had a niche market across all black communities, including independent homelands and self-governing territories. The Development Bank of South Africa[39] (DBSA) also entered this fray of statistical collection, as did the Human Sciences Research Council[40] (HSRC) and many private individuals who became household names in official statistics.

Five-yearly censuses instead of a decennial one would become an important instrument for monitoring the changes, but the liberation of Southern Africa, in particular of Namibia, was to destabilise this rhythm just ten years later. Five-yearly censuses were undertaken on the years ending with zero and five, 1980, 1985, with the next census for the 'Southern Africa region' including South West Africa, the Independent Homelands of TBVC and self-governing territories scheduled for 1990. However, the independence of Namibia was imminent and changes in South Africa were written on the wall. This made a 1990 census not feasible politically. The Census of South Africa and the homelands was subsequently held in 1991, but failed to mobilise public participation. There were even wide protests against it from the liberation movements.

Statistics: a burning platform for post-apartheid South Africa

In May 1994, following the April elections, Nelson Mandela was inaugurated as the president of the Republic of South Africa, thence to preside over the making of a constitution that entrenched human rights and created conditions for eliminating all forms of discrimination and prejudices, a constitution that held promise for a better life for all. The Reconstruction and Development Programme[41] (RDP) became the policy instrument through which restoration of dignity, creation of a better future and ultimately a better life for all were to be attained. Yet the RDP document, however brilliant, was devoid of statistical information. Where a semblance of statistics existed it was rather fragmented. Where offers of statistics were made they were presented by very clumsy, incompetent and competing factions, consisting of homeland offices, CSS, BMR, HSRC and DBSA to mention the most prominent of this ugly contestation. None of them had the mandate of a full picture yet they were not prepared to cooperate. Instead they paraded their shameless wares in front of would-be new political masters of change. It was a seriously sorry state of affairs, a gigantic implosion of statistical affairs.

The RDP therefore became a very difficult and challenging shell to direct and implement. The only nationally representative data was the World Bank/SALDRU study of 1993, but having been involved in the discussion of the design and implementation of the survey I would be painfully aware of how far short this 'jewel' was from informing the RDP. It needed structural statistics more than the cyclical statistics it provided. Far more important were sub-provincial statistics which were critical, while the survey could only be nationally representative. It is not surprising that a scatter-gun approach to housing, education and medical services characterised the developmental path of South Africa at this early stage.

Another study that was hurriedly implemented by the Central Statistical Service was that of the October Household Surveys (OHS) of 1993 and of 1994. In conducting this study in 1994, Dr Du Toit[42] could not agree to the imperative of integrating the statistics offices provincially and managing the surveys in the context of that infrastructure, as this would be administratively efficient and politically it would be legitimate. For instance, managing surveys as though Bophuthatswana still existed did not make any sense from a sampling design and field operation perspective.

The reporting domains were provinces and geographical structures below them. Designing a sample and running a survey in desperate non-contiguous domains of Bophuthatswana remnants in the Free State, in Gauteng, in the Northern Cape, in Limpopo and in the North West, as though Bophuthatswana were still alive and kicking, represented a field operations circus and a political insult to the new geographical framework of the post-apartheid era. Du Toit could not heed the plea for organising differently; consequently a planned protest was mounted to have CSS see the point. However, this also fell on deaf ears. It was clear then that the consequence of non-participation would fall on the new government, so a compromise had to be reached. Unfortunately, the leadership of the Transkei statistics office was in such disarray that the command structures could not fall in line under the compromise deal to conduct the survey. Thus there remains a deep hole for Transkei in the South African 1994 OHS data.

Census 96: The evidence

Mandela had been thrust into an environment that had very few social or population statistics to inform his newly formed government on how to target poverty and social disparities that had so divided the country for centuries. Census 96 provided the quantitative evidential base and illustrated the challenges and what was to be done. It quenched the thirst for data and directed in a targeted fashion what needed to be done. It comes possibly as little surprise that Madiba, while welcoming the results, made the statement that white people would never rule South Africa.

Statistical product expansion and quality improvements

As Census 96 came to pass, new products of an improved October Household Survey and the Income and Expenditure Survey were introduced. The first mapping of poverty in South Africa was derived from the Income and Expenditure Survey and Census 96. The 2001 Index of Multiple Deprivation was a successor to the innovative groundbreaking study on poverty information provided at lower levels of geography. On the economic statistics front, Stats SA signed up to the stringent IMF Special Data Dissemination Standard in 1998 and Ms Annette Myburgh,[43] then Chief Director Economic Statistics, was instrumental in setting Stats SA on this uncomfortable but necessary path. This farsighted decision ensured that we would keep the discipline of statistical production on the narrow route of quality.

Under the SDDS, changes in the production of economics statistics included shortened lead periods to release data and an increase in the slate of products. Among other important innovations that would be easy to facilitate from the SDDS perspective was the smoothness with which the South African Reserve Bank would adopt inflation targeting based on the robustness of the consumer price index (CPI). The Gross Domestic Product (GDP) figures laid the basis for macro-economic management and creating a predictable economic environment. In 1999 the Statistics Act, Act 6 of 1999 replaced a moribund statistics act as well as repealing all homeland-based ones. The Act also allowed for the appointment of a Statistician-General. At the same time plans were made for Census 2001.

By June 2000, after serving a five-year term, Mark Orkin's term at Stats SA came to an end and the position was advertised. This marked another major transition. Ros Hirschowitz[44] acted for a period of five months before I would be appointed as the Statistician-General in November 2000. The period over which Ros presided was quite stormy and the preference by labour was that none of the then chief directors should run or be considered for the position of Statistician-General. I applied and was appointed. While I appreciated the promotion to Statistician-General, the timing of the transition that saw Mark leave with a census of the population only 15 months away, in hindsight could perhaps have been dealt with differently.

Strategic interventions upon appointment

Five strategic interventions in the period 2001 to 2004 were the basis for change. The first was the establishment of an Organisational Development Task Team (ODETT),[45] chaired by Mr Risenga Maluleke.[46] Risenga and I had worked together to have statistics offices in provinces and through my intensive interactions with him he became an ideal binary as I prepared my application for the position of Statistician-General and heading Stats SA. ODETT consisted of labour and management. The second was implementing a study programme in official statistics, which in the main was a foreign study programme as there were and are still not enough universities equipped for teaching official statistics in South Africa. The third was focusing on the quality of economics statistics, the fourth on implementing an international statistical development agenda, and the fifth and immediate on preparing for and conducting Census 2001.

Is this change or a wrong set of statistics: the rollercoaster rocks?

The South African politicians, industry practitioners and academia continue to indulge in official statistics and keep the integrity of the information in constant check through the use and critiquing of statistics. This no doubt is done because official statistics are recognised as a *sine qua non* for development planning and addressing social concerns. In this regard I can open the 2001 to 2004 window and reveal how some of the developments took root. These years were a rollercoaster as we attempted to implement changes in statistical collections. In the main, Jairo Arrow,[47] an internal methodologist, was instrumental in critiquing the quality of the statistical series. In what was to be known the 'Acid Test Report', seminars and rejoinders were prepared to debate and improve on the quality of the series. The discourse was largely useful, albeit very acrimonious, and left many scars that are not easy to heal in the organisation. From this initiative more robust sampling frames were used for businesses statistics, yielding results with better accuracy. However, during this time we also committed major errors in our statistical compilations.

The tax law had been amended in 2000 to provide access to tax records for statistical purposes, but these improvements were disrupted by fault-lines in the statistical production systems. The first major crisis was the CPI debacle of 2003, whereby for 15 months as the Statistician-General, I overstated the CPI and this came with serious financial losses to the state.

Accompanying this painful mistake of the CPI, in 2005 voices of academics, such as Professor Makgoba of the University of KZN, lampooned Stats SA and decried it as affirmative action gone wrong. In his Sunday newspaper article he heaped praise on *Transnet*, *South African Airways* and *Eskom* as model institutions which cannot and should not be left in the hands of incompetent bureaucrats like me. Earlier on, at the beginning of 2000, we had run-ins with Professor Makgoba on his claims over increased AIDS deaths. Stats SA's retort to his assertion was that the statistics were only the consequence of amalgamating data from homelands with those of white South Africa. The *Sunday Times* had a front page splash on the mortality rate of HIV and AIDS, while the numbers reflected little more than a cumulative effect of deaths over years that were now being reported in a national picture for the first time. The photogenic display of mortality in the newspaper was a bag of ecological fallacy and asked the wrong questions. Unfortunately it drove the discourse into debates that became less useful.

The 2001 Census had the highest undercount with almost one in six missed. This was the most difficult of times. The most intriguing was the public response that reflected our inability to communicate and differentiate change from mistakes. In the end the results of change that were managed and deliberate were confused with the litany of statistical errors that accompanied the process.

Funding the fact finder of the nation

Despite these very trying times, the fiscus for statistics improved considerably from 2002 to 2008. While there were difficulties emanating from improvements in the production of statistics and downright errors, the political environment, particularly in the person of Minister Manuel, though harsh at all times, remained supportive to the institution and its staff. With President Mbeki he appreciated statistics and understood the depth of the challenge of change.

Sailing in calmer waters

By 2005 Stats SA had begun to sail in calmer waters. Improvements in statistical production came thick and fast. Governance had improved and since then the organi-sation has received unqualified audits, except in 2011, the year of Census 2011. The results of Census 2001 compared to those of 1996 pointed out what remained to be done. Mbeki, ironically echoing Charles Dickens's pedantic schoolmaster, called for 'facts and only facts'. In so saying he outlined what a modern state requires, scientific facts that inform action. At a later stage, in 2007, when the Community Survey was released it provided further evidence on progress made in the 13 years since liberation from apartheid. Karin Maughn,[48] a journalist at the *Star* newspaper, led with a headline that the 2007 Community Survey results were a waste of the fiscus. She went further, arguing that the results were rushed in order to increase the chances of Mbeki being elected as the ANC President in Polokwane, a claim that was echoed by the South African Communist Party. Stats SA and Council took this matter to the ombudsman, who after months of waiting instructed the newspaper to withdraw its story and publicly apologise.

One of the statements that has remained a classic for the official statistics fraternity was from Minister Manuel when he articulated the importance of statistics and the need for them to be independent. Addressing the launch of the national statistics system (NSS) in 2002, he said 'politics is my life, I like good news, I like to tell stories that GDP is growing at double digit, inflation is low and employment is rising, but please do not give me what I like, give me what I need to touch the lives of those who waited for a long time for democracy to touch their lives'.[49] This undergirded the philosophy of and practice in official statistics in South Africa.

Stats SA and the global statistics system

The global statistics system uses the United Nations Fundamental Principles of Official Statistics as the framework for practice. Though *A Handbook on Official Statistics* predated the adoption of the principles, subsequent releases of the handbook have more explicitly embraced the ten principles.

The priority areas of South Africa are ten and amongst them is priority ten. This priority is for a better South Africa, in a better Africa and a better world. This priority is in keeping with three of the fundamental principles of official statistics, namely principles eight, nine and ten, which address matters of international cooperation and international standards, and their contribution to statistical development globally. Priority ten also gives effect and meaning to Section 7(1)h and i of the Statistics Act, Act 6 of 1999, which empowers the Statistician-General to endeavour to fulfil the Republic's international statistical reporting obligations and liaise with other countries and their statistical agencies. As a consequence of these enabling instruments, the system of statistics in South Africa has reaped tremendous mutual benefits from the global system. Its stature and resilience has grown out of these global engagements.

As early as 1998, Stats SA immersed itself in the SADC agenda and played a leading role in the undertaking of censuses. It was subsequently selected as a focal point for censuses. By taking up this role it partnered with the African Census Analysis Project (ACAP) at Pennsylvania University in driving the agenda. One of the important outputs of this collaboration was the implementation of common SADC questions in the 2000 and 2010 Round Censuses of Housing and Population, the SADC monographs on population and the publishing of *After Robin Island: The Demography of South Africa* in the Demography of Africa Series.[50] In 2002, Statistics South Africa chaired PARIS21,[51] which remains the major driver of statistical development. Through the PARIS21 dimension the agenda for African Statistical Development was firmly placed on the global agenda.

Conscious of the lacklustre manner in which Africa was approaching statistics, Stats SA and South Africa took specific steps to remedy the situation. As of today we can proudly say for the first time that African countries have universally had their populations counted in the 2010 Round of Censuses. This gives Africa prospects for implementing public policies on the basis of evidence. The Africa Symposium for Statistical Development (ASSD) has been the prime mover of this development and Stats SA is host to the Secretariat of ASSD.

Threats to official statistics

No doubt statistics play a critical role in development and increasingly occupy space that is often dangerously close to the political life of society. This space is uncomfortable to statisticians themselves as they are trained to manage data and not so much to manage a development agenda and/or communication. As statistics become more visibly important, as in the Greek crisis and requirements for accession to the Eurozone, it is clear that many a chief statistician will be in trouble with political systems. As in the past three years, chief statisticians and staff in statistics offices have had or have been forced to step down. It has happened in Canada over a matter of the Census of 2011 with Munir Sheikh,[52] who succeeded Ivan Fellegi,[53] having had to resign after just less than three years in office. Expressing disappointment at political interference, Fellegi wrote that statistics are like water and for consumption must be clean. Public policy cannot be based on dirty evidence he regretted. So, this institution of accountability which represents statistics for transparency, accountability, results and transformation indeed requires leadership and deliberate empowerment in leadership, including constitutional and legislative checks and balances in order to remain true to its cause and course in the twenty-first century.

Threats to official statistics in South Africa

South Africa has been well positioned regarding official statistics in that it has a modern legislative prescript that accords the Statistician-General independence, and reinforces such independence with the establishment of a Statistics Council. The test of this independence has been demonstrated during the release of Census 2011 results, where the national statistics system has been defended by an independent Statistics Council when some experts decided to cast doubt on the integrity of the numbers. The results of Census 2011 have been released and they are being shared, explained and critiqued by a variety of stakeholders. Generally, the results have been well received as they shed light on policy decisions and action. They form the evidence for hard choices that have to be made at the political, business and individual levels. They are the template of evidence from which all and sundry have to draw.

What are the lessons for the relationship between the state and statistics?

In South Africa there are very important signs that signify that official statistics occupy a place of importance and benefit in society. This position has to be strengthened and protected as a treasured intellectual heritage that will provide an invaluable time series for evidence-based decision making and as a veritable facilitator of rational social discourse.

We have illustrated how at a political level statistics as facts about the nation are delivered, received and deliberated in South Africa. We have also illustrated how statistics as an institution are protected by legislation and practice. The democracy of South Africa remains to be better served by the prospect of indulging in evidence for hard political choices. Statistics will always be part of this discourse and those who run the office and collect data cannot remain behind computers and stay in rarefied environments and throw data over the fence for policy to catch it and hope that they will survive for long. The value of statistics is in disseminating them, and explaining and deliberating them with users. In short, engaging with society about what the statistics mean and how best they can be applied is the responsibility of a modern statistics office. In South Africa we have in time learnt how this space is navigated and how statistics can be a useful tool for policy.

Conclusion

As I have served in the statistics office over a period of 30 years, thirteen of which as the Statistician-General, it is possible to make some informed assessment of how statistics have influenced the South African state. In the main, the RDP document became the catalyst for statistical information. The policies it espoused required evidence as the basis for issue identification, policy design, planning and intervening, progress monitoring and impact evaluation. The parlous state of development information and the fragmented statistical system made it a more urgent duty for the state to build an institution that would provide this critical information. In doing so, and as a creature of history, the institution's gestation window towards competency was fraught with problems of improving statistics and immense errors of omission. However, in time the institution was able to hold its own and be counted amongst institutions that have a lot to offer not only in South Africa but also globally. Importantly, it was anticipating the introduction of the Planning Commission as well as the Monitoring and Evaluation Ministry, for which the Statistics Act in espousing the NSS was farsighted. The full implementation of the NSS remains the major task of the decade.

The chapter is not about government administration generally and it seeks not to address the specific reference of the relationship between ministers and directors-general, nor does it seek to address the tenure of the latter. It is about the use of evidence as the basis for decision making. I would, however, be remiss as the longest-serving director general in the public service of South Africa if I did not share an observation regarding the often vexed relationship between ministers and directors-general. I have served as Statistician-General for thirteen years, too long probably given the average tenure of directors-general in the civil service, and under the same minister too. Too long again given that (i) a mandating government has a five-year term, (ii) there are periodic cabinet reshuffles and(iii) there is perennial redeployment of directors-general. The fact that I have served for thirteen years as Statistician-General under the same minister is a statistical observation of momentous improbability. Manuel informing me that he is still responsible for statistics as minister after being appointed Minister in the Presidency responsible for Planning quipped that our forebears must have done something terrible in their lives. The period has been long and indeed, and importantly, long enough for achieving the hard slog of institution building. It might be necessary, time permitting, to unpack what ingredients made it possible for such partnership to prevail. Manuel has often said, and publicly so, there is no legislative formula for a minister-and-director-general working relationship. The formula is about committing to the work at hand and simply working on the relationship. It is my experience too, and there it is important to know that there is nothing rosy or romantic about it least I provide false expectations and explanations.

I thus can conclude without fear of contradiction that what made Statistics South Africa work was and remains the quality of political leadership that makes for good institutions. It is the patient impatience they exercise in allowing for errors to be made and corrected in the process, as the basic requirement for developmental learning. It is the stability they provide and provided for the institution and the respect they have for its independence. It is the ability to engage internationally and be transparent about weaknesses, but above all it has been the robust engagement that the political system pushed into the field that made the office stronger. The professional conduct of the staff and their intellectual engagement, investment in their training and eagerness to learn earned the institution credibility and stature. Above all it is the humility, service and care with which the institution delivers the South Africa I know and the home I understand to the public that makes for an enduring institution of service to the state. To a large extent, South Africa's transition and change over time have been evidence-based. The use of statistics has been the prime informer of change, although more in the use of evidence as the basis for decision making could be done for better outcomes.

Endnotes

1   President Nelson Mandela's address launching South Africa 1996 Census results. 1998. 20 October. Pretoria.

2   H.G. Wells (1866–1946) is considered as the father of science fiction.

3   Minister of Education Dr Hendrick Verwoed introducing the Bantu Education Act 1953.

4   President Sarkozy of France established the Stiglitz Commission.

5   President Mbeki launching the results of Census 2001, 08 July 2003.

6   President Zuma calling on residents of South Africa to participate in Census 2011.

7   Stock Market Crash of 1929.

8   President Obama, G20 Pittsburgh meeting of 2009.

9   Maynard Keynes is credited to have introduced deficit financing. Currently there is a re-emergence of Keynesian thinking post the 2008 economic crisis.

10 The United Nations was born to foster peace, and encourage multilateralism and détente.

11 Leontief is the father of the input-output matrix which also includes modern day social-accounting matrix.

12 Eurostat is an organ of the Eurozone that regulates statistical production and their quality framework.

13 The Lisbon Treaty created the Eurozone and the implementation of a single currency, the Euro and created statistical oversight powers for Eurostat.

14 The *Handbook of Statistical Organisation* is an important manual for guiding how these institutions are governed taking into account the political and production systems of countries.

15 The UN Fundamental Principles for Official Statistics will be twenty years in 2014 and in 2010 the UNSC held a seminar to consider challenges and prospects.

16 The Human Development Index is one of the premiere indicators of the UN Reports received a scathing critique from in particular Ian Castles, a former head of the Australian Bureau of Statistics.

17 The IMF introduces statistical standards by which the world could verify the quality of country statistics.

18 SDDS was a standard that was adopted by Stats SA in 1998 and by 2012 seventy countries acceded.

19 GDDS is a less demanding standard and there are now 105 countries on this standard including Timor Leste which acceded to the standard in October 2012.

20 The G20 meeting of Pittsburgh created an opportunity for the notion of the Global Impact and Vulnerability Alert System (GIVAS) which was adopted by the UN Secretary General.

21 President Sarkozy is the former president of France.

22 The MIP outlined what at the minimum Africa needed for regional integration. It was an integral part of the Lagos Plan of Action adopted in 1980.

23 The MDGs will have run their course by 2015, in their trail they raised the profile of evidence as the basis for decision making.

24 PARIS21 was very instrumental in bringing partnerships for technical support and funding the planning for statistics particularly in the developing world.

25 MAPS, adopted in Marrakesh in 2005, became the tool of advocacy for driving investments in statistics and policy dialogue on matters statistics.

26 BAPS followed on MAPS six years later and assessed the progress thus achieved over the period.

27 RRSF is the instrument by which Africa interpreted the MAPS and started implementing National Strategies for the Development of Statistics.

28 PRSPs were papers and blueprints that aimed at reducing poverty, and for the first time measurement and indicators became deliberate and central pillars of these papers.

29 AfDB has been at the forefront of funding statistics on the continent and notably International Comparisons Programme Africa (ICP-Africa) and many other statistics activities on the continent.

30 UNECA is the technical arm of the UN in Africa and its role has been the provision of stewardship in statistics on the continent.

31 The AUC was established by a constitutive Act in 2002 and was inaugurated in Durban, South Africa.

32 The African Charter on Statistics will become AUC law once 15 or more countries ratify it.

33 SHaSA is a Khoisan word meaning precious water and was researched by the Young African Statisticians. It was adopted as an acronym in a process of discussing the strategy in Pretoria in December 2009. The strategy discussions first started in Ribavu in Rwanda, Abidjan in Ivory Coast, Addis Ababa Ethiopia and finally in East London and Pretoria in South Africa.

34 To date, under the 2010 Round of Censuses, Africa has enlisted in excess of 38 countries that have conducted a census and in as far as the ICP is concerned, Africa has adopted a strategy for continuous ICP with five-yearly reporting in order to compare with other regions.

35 The Census Act of 1910 was a forerunner to the Statistics Act of 1914. Statistics are necessary and form the cornerstone for political management.

36 In 2014 South Africa will have experienced a century of statistical practice – a prospect for commemorative centenary reflections would be in order as statistics mirrors the history of the country.

37 Except for messengers, the CSS was a white minority preserve that was uninterested in understanding the human endeavour of other race groups.

38 BMR at UNISA was responsible for running Income and Expenditure Surveys in all areas in South Africa that were not white, thus participating in a disparate statistics system.

39 The DBSA was created as a funding arm for homeland development and invariably entered the fray of production of statistics.

40 The HSRC conducted social research and training in research methods and undertook several demographic surveys in homelands.

41 The RDP is a programme of transforming the South African society. The CSS reported to the minister responsible for RDP.

42 Dr Du Toit was the then head of the Central Statistical Service (CSS). The CSS presided over the statistics of what was nominally South Africa excluding self-governing territories and Transkei, Bophuthatswana, Venda and Ciskei (TBVC-countries); he was the last head of the service to preside over an officially disjointed statistics system.

43 Ms Annette Myburgh is currently head of Programme, Project and Management Information System Office in the Office of Statistician-General.

44 Dr Ros Hirschowitz was Deputy Director General retired in 2006 after nine years of service to Stats SA.

45 ODETT became a platform through which management and staff shared the most difficult conversation of transition.

46 Risenga Maluleke was known to me since 1994 and was part of the leadership team that expressed transformational views against the CSS as early as in 1994. He was drafted into the CSS in 2007 as the head of provinces and he is Deputy Director General.

47 Dr Arrow was the Deputy Director-General for Methodology and Standards.

48 Karin Maughn was a journalist at *The Star* newspaper.

49 Minister Manuel at the launch of the National Statistics System (NSS) in 2002 in Somerset West. He later became a critique of the NSS as a concept that was too much ahead of its time and advocated a more measured approach to statistical development which in the main focused on strengthening the capability of Stats SA to do statistics. Such was then the focus of the organisation for at least nine years.

50 Under the ACAP flag, the African continent has the possibility of raising its intellectual prospects and publishing its own demography for use at institutions of higher learning. The Robin Island series of books, with the first being *The Demography of South Africa* edited by African scholars, holds prospect for African scholarship and scientific enquiry.

51 Partners in Statistical Development in the 21st Century (PARIS21) has grown from strength to strength and has been recognised as a professional entity that brings policy and statistics together. Its catalytic role in the use of evidence for decision making has been most felt in Africa.

52 Dr Munir Sheikh succeeded Dr Ivan Fellegi as Canada's Chief Statistician.

53 Dr Ivan Fellegi was Chief Statistician for Canada for more than two decades and he transformed the StatCan into a formidable professional organisation, yet when confronted with political interference on the fundamental principles of official statistics, it became clear that good practice is good, but it is not good when not supported by clear and unambiguous legislation. Canada is looking at reviewing its statistical legislation to protect statistics. Dr Fellegi is Chief Statistician Emeritus.

CHAPTER 17

Socio-economic transformation in post-apartheid South Africa: progress and challenges

Vusi Gumede

Introduction

Judging from various policy pronouncements and documents of the African National Congress (ANC), it can be argued that the organisation has always been clear about the nature of its envisaged post-apartheid South Africa. The social and economic transformation that has been pursued since 1994 is informed by, among others, the 'Ready to Govern' (R2G) discussion document of 1992. At minimum, arguably, it provides a robust analysis of the social and economic challenges that the post-apartheid South Africa was to confront, in pursuit of a new political-economic order.

The question that this chapter addresses relates to whether, almost two decades since the dawn of democracy, South Africa is on course to be the country that was conceptualised and pursued for decades by the broader liberation movement. In other words, to what extent has the 'legacy of inequality and injustice created by colonialism and apartheid' been overcome? Put differently – looking at the ANC's 'vision for the future' just before the dawn of democracy – have the 'sustainable economy and state infrastructure that will progressively improve the quality of life of all South Africans' been developed, 20 years later?[1]

Since 1994, the ANC-led government has undertaken extensive policy reforms in an effort to transform society. The broad objectives that it has continuously pursued are the creation of a united, non-racial, non-sexist, democratic and prosperous society. The strategic path towards this better life has translated into a programme in the 1994 Reconstruction and Development Programme[2] (RDP), followed by an economic policy framework in 1996, Growth, Employment and Redistribution (GEAR) – A Macroeconomic Framework. GEAR was intended to stabilise and rescue an economy that was already falling apart, effectively in recession when the ANC came into office in 1994. It is again in recession 20 years later.

GEAR was replaced in 2005 by the Accelerated and Shared Growth Initiative for South Africa (AsgiSA), intended to accelerate the growth of the economy and wealth redistribution. However, it was short-lived and soon replaced by the NGP in 2010, with an emphasis on job creation, the need to create decent work and a new policy orientation towards labour-intensive approaches. It aspired to increase employment opportunities by five million by 2020 and reduce unemployment by ten per cent, largely through a public infrastructure programme.

In 2012 emerged the National Development Plan (NDP) or Vision 2030 of the National Planning Commission (NPC).[3] More than being a policy document, it is a consensus-building mechanism towards some envisaged end state in which poverty, inequality and unemployment would have been drastically reduced. Given that it takes time to implement any policy, it is hard to assess the effectiveness or lack thereof of AsgiSA and the NGP. However, this chapter attempts to highlight the direction the NGP in particular is taking. It would seem the NGP, although comprehensive in its analysis of the economic challenges, falls short on appropriate policy prescriptions.

A macro-level evaluation of all the broad policy reforms since 1994 points to the conclusion that the government has made concerted efforts to deal with the historical socio-economic challenges; however, much still needs to be done to establish the envisaged post-apartheid society. Significant achievements have been registered, for instance, in the expansion of access to education, healthcare, housing and basic services, yet there are fundamental policy constraints on economic performance and the general wellbeing of society.

A review of post-apartheid South Africa

The R2G document, released in 1992, was the ANC's most robust attempt at spelling out the kind of society that democratic South Africa would be like. It can be argued that other important discussion documents of the ANC and those of government during the 1990s were significantly influenced and informed by it.

The R2G discussion document, in particular, indicates what the role of a 'democratic developmental state' would be in a post-apartheid SA.[4] In addition, it presents thinking and proposals on all aspects of development, including social policies. Informed by the Constitution and Bill of Rights, it is a summary of the thinking of the liberation movement, and more so of the various leaders of the ANC over the decades.

The RDP and its associated projects played an important role in laying the foundation, by providing a framework towards service delivery. Much has thus been achieved with specific regard to the implementation of the government's priority on addressing the lack of access to basic social services. However, there is still a long way to go in ensuring that the 'Better Life for All' that the RDP promised will become reality.

Overall, either from Statistics South Africa (Stats SA) data or government records, there is evidence of impressive progress in access to basic services, though there are still many people without access to piped drinkable water.[5] The challenges of service delivery remain unabated and progress is mixed, as Table 1 shows.

Table 1: Access to services and type of dwelling South Africa (1996–2011)

Type of main dwelling	1996	2001	2011
Formal	65.1	68.5	77.6
Informal	16.2	16.4	13.6
Traditional	18.3	14.8	7.9
Other	0.4	0.3	0.9
Household basic services			
Piped water (tap)	80.3	84.5	91.2
Electricity (lighting)	58.2	51.4	84.6
Toilet facilities			
Access to a flush toilet	82.9	82.3	90.6
Bucket toilet	4.7	4.1	2.1
No toilet	12.4	13.6	7.3

Source: Census (2011)

As the table demonstrates, there are ample causes for public protest.

Another area of concern is the social assistance programme. As Table 2 indicates, South Africa has an extensive social assistance programme which has raised the income levels of the poor considerably. As of 2010/11, about 15 million people have been receiving social grants, constituting more than 3.2 per cent of GDP. This figure rose to 15.6 million in 2011/12 and is expected to rise to 16.8 by 2015. The majority of grant recipients are the 10.4 million who receive a child support grant, provided to children in need up to the age of 15 (and it is expected that children below age 18, over time, will also receive it through a means test). There has also been a reduction of men's age requirement for the social old age pension to 60 years.

Table 2: Social Assistance (2000–2011)

Grant type	2000/01	2002/03	2004/05	2006/07	2008/09	2009/10	2010/11
Old Age Grant	1 900 406	1 943 348	2 124 984	2 195 018	2 390 543	2 546 657	2 678 554
War Veterans Grant	5 617	4 638	2 963	2 340	1 500	1 216	958
Disability Grant	655 822	840 424	1 293 280	1 422 808	1 286 883	1 264 477	1 200 898
Foster Child Grant	66 967	83 574	195 454	400 503	474 759	510 760	512 874
Child Dependency Grant	33 574	42 355	86 917	98 631	107 065	110 731	112 185
Child Support Grant	1 111 612	1 998 936	4 165 545	7 863 841	8 765 354	9 570 287	10 371 950
Total	**3 773 998**	**4 913 275**	**7 869 143**	**11 983 141**	**13 026 104**	**14 004 128**	**14 877 419**
Growth Rate	40.4%	23.4%	21.5%	9.5%	5.2%	7.5%	6%
Grant-in-aid	10 107	12 625	25 667	31 918	46 069	53 237	58 413

Source: Development Indicators (2011)

The challenge with the social assistance programme is its financial sustainability and possible unintended consequences. Although it is stabilising as a share of GDP, it is still very high (over three per cent). As for unintended consequences, the fundamental issue has to do with the kind of society South Africans aspire to. Ideally, there should be more people in gainful employment than in social assistance, as in Brazil and India. The grants, however, especially in the context of a small informal sector, play an important role in mitigating severe hardship. As some of the findings on poverty show, the grants could have played an important role in cushioning against the global economic recession.

The economy grew relatively quickly after 1994, but is now beginning to stagnate as a consequence of the global economic recession and poor economic management.

Gross Domestic Product (GDP) per capita has been increasing at an impressive rate, particularly since 1996, and this is an important indicator – with all its shortcomings – of improving standards of living in a society. Since 2004, growth has exceeded four per cent per year, reaching about five per cent in 2005. Whereas the steady growth of the economy could be interpreted as positive, however, the pace has not been matched with the requisite elements to support such an economy. In other words, although the improvement of GDP (per capita) cannot be entirely attributed to macroeconomic stabilisation it does coincide with key macro-economic interventions, in particular GEAR. For an economy to perform well, macroeconomic stabilisation is a prerequisite.

As Table 3 shows, GDP itself, not per capita income per se, has been performing relatively well. Looking at the recent period, after the macroeconomic stabilisation programme of the 1990s, GDP has averaged – barring the recent global economic recession – about 3.5 per cent. However, the expected jobs have not been forthcoming. An exception was the relatively high number of jobs created when it grew relatively well during 2005–2008.

Although the GDP performance could be celebrated, South Africa has not performed well enough for the size of its economy or comparative context. Looking at Botswana, India, Brazil and Malaysia in Table 3, the economic performance has been low. The low GDP growth rate supports the argument that it is not only the global economic recession that has lowered SA's economic performance.

Table 3: Gross Domestic Product, SA and other countries (2000–2010)

	2000	2001	2002	2003	2004	2005	2006	2007	2008	2009	2010
SA	4.2	2.7	3.7	2.9	4.6	5.3	5.6	5.5	3.6	-1.5	2.9
Botswana	5.9	3.5	9.0	6.3	6.1	1.6	4.5	4.8	2.9	-4.9	7.2
Brazil	4.3	1.3	2.7	1.1	5.7	3.2	4.0	6.1	5.2	-0.6	7.5
India	4.0	5.2	3.8	8.4	8.3	9.3	9.3	9.8	4.9	9.1	9.7
Malaysia	8.9	0.5	5.4	5.8	6.8	5.3	5.8	6.5	4.7	-1.7	7.2

Source: Development Indicators (2011)

It could be argued that South Africa was going to be in recession anyway from about 2009 because of its own poor economic management, especially the management of public finances from about 2008. Compared to similar economies, the relatively low rate of GDP growth has meant that fewer jobs are created, and more lost.

GDP projections substantiate the view that this poor economic performance has little, if anything, to do with the global economic recession. The annual percentage changes in GDP will continue being lower than those of its counterparts, for instance that of Sub-Saharan Africa.[6]

One of the most critical challenges facing the government and society broadly is employment creation and poverty. The goal is to cut unemployment by at least half between 2004 and 2014, and to a maximum of 14 per cent in 2014. However, the employment performance of the economy has not adequately met the needs of society. The number of jobs created has lagged behind the demand for jobs. A number of the newly created jobs have been precarious and of poor quality and many of those jobs are under pressure or have disappeared as a result of the recession and poor economic management.

An unemployment rate of 25.2% in the first quarter of 2012 compared to 23.9% in the fourth quarter of 2011 was recorded, which is considerably higher than the global average. The 2011 Census found an unemployment rate of 28.9%. Using the expanded definition of unemployment, it stands at about 40%, reflecting the high volumes of discouraged work seekers. Since the low point in 2010, there has been a gain of a total of 447 000 jobs. From 2000 until 2008, the unemployment rate averaged 26.3%, reaching an historical high of 31.2% in March of 2003 and a relative low of 23% in September of 2007. The majority of the unemployed are low-skilled or poorly educated workers, mostly women and youth in rural areas, for whom demand has been shrinking due to changes in the domestic structure of production.[7]

South Africa is further faced with the complexities relating to an uneven labour market environment, the changing nature of work, lack of labour market measurement instruments, and that of serving a multi-class of service beneficiaries: vulnerable workers and unemployed job-seekers. The fragmented nature of the labour market and its increasing informality, casualisation and externalisation have worsened the job crisis and the economic status of the working class. Millions of workers are trapped in informal, temporary, involuntary part-time or casual work that offers few benefits and limited prospects for advancement. This is the case particularly for youth, women and immigrants, who constitute the largest sector of the workforce.

Bloch[8], among others, is of the view that although many challenges remain, there were significant achievements in turning around apartheid education in the first decade of democracy. This has, according to Kraak,[9] been evident in increased access, headcount enrolment, investment by government and the private sector in education, and institutional rationalisation processes and regulation respectively.

The changes pursued in the education sector in South Africa have resulted in great strides forward. Government has made some progress in the expansion of education access, particularly improving access for disadvantaged groups. Progress is also visible in the different sectors, as presented in the 2008 review of national policies for education in South Africa by the Organisation for Economic Co-operation and Development (OECD). For instance, the OECD[10] noted that what government had been able to achieve in the space of 14 years was commendable and that it was understandable that some of the policy goals had not yet been realised.

In this instance, data from the 'Towards a Fifteen Year Review'[11] indicated that education participation had increased since 1994, especially in the case of primary schooling. This is attributed to those interventions geared towards increased access. In terms of the growth in enrolments for the age cohort 7 to 15 between 2002 and 2007, enrolments of 5-year-olds improved from 40% to 60%, of 6-year-olds from 70% to 88%, and of 15-year-olds from 96% to 98%.

Data for 2010 from the Department of Basic Education's Education Statistics in South Africa report,[12] as Table 4 shows, have relatively high gross enrolment rates: 94% for primary phase (grades 1 to 7), 86% for secondary phase (grades 8 to 12) and 91% for grades 1 to 12. In essence, the country has been successful in facilitating access to primary and tertiary education, particularly for girls. This is a target that the country has reached before its deadline of 2015, from the perspective of the Millennium Development Goals (MDGs).

Corroborating this point, according to the OECD report referred to above, South Africa can be said to be close to achieving universal basic education, with 96.6% enrolment of 7- to 15-year-olds, almost all children of school-going age entering school and the majority reaching the end of Grade 9.

Table 4: Gross Enrolment Ratios by gender and level of education

Gender	Primary phase (Gr.1–7)	Secondary phase (Gr.8–12)	Total (Gr.1–12)
Female	92 %	89 %	91 %
Male	96 %	83 %	91 %
Total	**94 %**	**86 %**	**91 %**

Source: Department of Basic Education (2012)

Table 5 shows improved access to education – in support of reports such as the OECD's one referred to above – between 2001 and 2011. Although there are still large numbers of those without school attendance, the percentage of those with school attendance increased from 71.5% in 2001 to 73.4% in 2011, while the percentage of those without school attendance decreased to 26.6% in 2011 from 28.5% in 2001. There are also increases in percentage shares, in terms of attendance, for all types of educational institutions except pre-school. In the ten-year period (2001–2011) there has been an increase of about 100 000 for universities, which confirms that numbers of those seeking higher education increase over time, in any society, and as such more universities are needed.

Table 5: Access to education in South Africa (2001–2011)

Education	2001		2011	
	Number	Percentage	Number	Percentage
School attendance				
Yes	13 727 893	71.5	13 837 961	73.4
No	5 463 823	28.5	5 023 110	26.6
Type of educational institution				
Pre-school	575 936	4.2	128 719	0.9
School	12 584 818	91.7	12 862 961	92.9
FET college/College	191 234	1.4	359 228	2.6
University/Technikon	315 592	2.3	410 063	3.0
ABET	26 505	0.2	22 730	0.2
Other	33 809	0.2	57 883	0.4
Public or Private				
Public	13 028 486	94.9	11 924 285	92.7
Private	699 407	5.1	934 480	7.3

Source: Statistics South Africa (2012)

In terms of enrolments it is noted that the extent to which the higher education system can actually produce highly skilled graduates is predicated on three important factors: the number of school leavers who qualify for entry to higher education institutions, the number who choose to enter higher education institutions, and the number who complete their qualifications.[13] However, the quality of Grade 12 school-leaving passes is said to be questionable. Bloch elaborates on the issues bedevilling the education system in South Africa in detail.

Other important areas are literacy and numeracy. Various datasets and publications show a steady increase in the literacy rate in South Africa. The 2011 Development Indicators[14] show that, according to the General Household Surveys, the literacy rate has increased from 70.7 per cent in 2002 to about 80 per cent in 2009. Therefore, although there are improvements there is still a long way to go in ensuring that the 20 per cent classified as illiterate can be literate. Bloch shows that despite high levels of educational spending South Africa is amongst the worst performing countries internationally on literacy and numeracy.

Despite improved literacy rates and access to education it remains evident that key historical factors have continued to constrain and limit the successful transformation of the education sector. Over the past year and a half, it has become increasingly evident that South Africa's education institutions remain untransformed. There is emerging consensus that the quality is poor, the curriculum is poorly structured and the legacy of the Bantu education system remains.

Recent data from the latest census highlighted the reality that access to education, not to mention the quality of the education system, remains a challenge. For instance, the number (at above five million) and the share of those not attending school remains very high. Also of importance is that there is slow progress in rolling out early learning. Although the enrolment of Africans in higher education institutions has increased, detailed analysis of data reveals historical disparity in participation rates among population groups. The total gross participation rate remained similar in early to mid 2000, at about 15.7, and increased marginally to 16.18 in 2007. While the numbers of those enrolled in higher education have been increasing, participation rates for the black student population do not seem to be increasing at any significant rate.[15]

Of concern is that even qualified graduates are struggling to find employment. For instance, Moleke[16] found that the majority of the unemployed fall under the categories of Africans, females, those who studied humanities and the arts, and those who studied at historically black universities. The unification of the education system and standards also remains an issue. The two-tier education system is accentuated by an increasing share of those receiving private education. Also, it remains to be seen whether the approach adopted in restructuring the higher education landscape was appropriate. The Higher Education Monitor of the Council on Higher Education (CHE)[17] reflects on a number of pertinent issues pertaining to the challenges confronting the South African higher education landscape. Overall, the picture is not good, but there is some progress, especially in the context of proposals contained in the 2012 Green Paper for Post-School Education and Training.[18]

Two important development issues that continue to haunt post-apartheid South Africa are poverty and inequality, linked to the structure of the South African economy. On the one hand, the economy or the labour market are not creating jobs or addressing structural poverty. On the other hand, the structure of the economy reproduces inequality through benefiting those with certain skills or political connections while keeping the rest of society, within the black African community in particular, at lower levels of economic or financial wellbeing.

Since 2000, because of the challenges relating to healthcare, education and the labour market, South Africa's human development – that is, the general wellbeing of society or the quality of life – has been slow. The Human Development Index (HDI) measures human development as a composite indicator made up of life expectancy, literacy and per capita income, while the Human Poverty Index (HPI), introduced in 1997, is an attempt to bring together in a composite index the different features of deprivation in the quality of life to arrive at an aggregate judgment on the extent of poverty in a community. A more applicable HPI for developing countries is notated as HPI-1, which combines measures of life expectancy, child nutrition status, access to improved water sources and income. For developed countries, HPI-2 takes into account social exclusion and jobs, over and above measures relating to life expectancy and standard of living.

Human development, as quantified by the HDI, is actually doing relatively well compared to similar countries, although South Africa's has remained unchanged, at about 0.61, since 2009. Table 6 presents HDIs of selected countries, including South Africa. Norway has the highest HDI globally and the USA is third. Some other countries can be said to be comparable to South Africa (i.e., India, Brazil, Malaysia, Mauritius, China and Botswana).

Table 6: Human Development in South Africa and Selected Countries

	1980	1990	2000	2005	2009	2010	2011
South Africa	0.564	0.615	0.616	0.599	0.610	0.615	0.619
India	0.344	0.410	0.461	0.504	0.535	0.542	0.547
Brazil	0.549	0.600	0.665	0.692	0.708	0.715	0.718
Botswana	0.446	0.594	0.585	0.601	0.626	0.631	0.633
Mauritius	0.546	0.618	0.672	0.703	0.722	0.726	0.728
Malaysia	0.559	0.631	0.705	0.738	0.752	0.758	0.761
China	0.404	0.490	0.588	0.633	0.674	0.682	0.687
United States	0.837	0.870	0.897	0.902	0.906	0.908	0.910
Norway	0.796	0.844	0.913	0.938	0.941	0.941	0.943

Source: UN Human Development Report (2011)[19]

South Africa's HDI is higher than that of India but below other comparable countries. Even for India, it would seem that the HDI has been catching up. Interestingly, Botswana's HDI overtook in 2005, while that of Brazil was comparable in 1990, albeit now far higher than that of South Africa. Mauritius – one of the so-called developmental states in Africa, alongside Botswana – had an HDI comparable to that of South Africa in 1990 but it is now far higher, although the latter has marginally increased in the past few years.

Looking at specific indicators of human development, such as literacy and enrolments, the recent progress is somewhat mixed. Table 7 gives some of the indicators calculated from the National Income Dynamics Study (NIDS) datasets for 2008 and 2010[20] – a longitudinal survey and panel study using data collected at two-year intervals. 2008 was the inception year and 2010 the second data collection phase.

Table 7: Human Development Indicators

	% below poverty line		Adult literacy		Lack of access to water		Gross enrolment	
	2008	2010	2008	2010	2008	2010	2008	2010
Total	46%	45%	90.40	90.56	6.91	5.52	76.72	68.05
Gender								
Male	43%	41%	91.78	92.28	6.51	5.29	76.04	68.75
Female	49%	48%	89.18	89.07	7.27	5.72	77.42	67.33
Race								
African	55%	53%	88.58	89.11	8.67	6.72	79.32	69.33
Coloured	26%	23%	93.30	92.71	0.52	0.50	63.45	57.04
Asian/Indian	9%	8%	92.90	94.45	0.00	0.00	61.59	64.20
White	1%	2%	100.00	99.50	0.00	0.55	63.59	66.02
Province								
Western Cape	23%	25%	95.54	95.25	0.17	0.19	58.51	56.95
Eastern Cape	63%	62%	86.87	88.18	24.89	23.18	83.73	72.52
Northern Cape	33%	38%	88.07	89.46	0.37	0.89	69.91	65.37
Free State	45%	44%	93.47	94.06	0.52	0.04	78.39	69.90
KwaZulu-Natal	62%	56%	85.48	85.84	13.86	9.80	78.29	65.04
North West	42%	42%	87.44	89.91	1.18	0.48	72.99	68.44
Gauteng	28%	27%	96.44	96.79	0.00	0.00	70.06	69.09
Mpumalanga	42%	41%	90.50	90.43	0.37	0.21	80.12	66.18
Limpopo	63%	62%	85.06	85.00	4.43	2.31	87.23	74.74

Source: Own calculations based on the National Income Dynamics Study 2008 & 2010 Datasets

The calculations on poverty and literacy substantiate other analyses which suggest that South Africa is meeting targets related to poverty and literacy. Regarding poverty, the share of those below a poverty line of R515 per person per month in real 2008 rands has declined, though marginally, from 46 per cent in 2008 to 45 per cent in 2010.

In terms of geographical locations, poverty has remained similar for the North West but increased, relatively significantly, for the Northern Cape during 2008 and 2010. One hypothesis is that such an increase in the share of those below the poverty line can be attributed to the effects of the global economic recession.

Another important indicator of human development, or human poverty, is access to a clean water source. The percentage of those who lack access to clean water declined from seven per cent (in 2008) to five per cent (in 2010). Water is important for other indicators, especially those that relate to health and mortality. The improvement of access to water, therefore, should be commended.

Literacy rates improved effectively for all provinces, and also for Africans, though marginally. Interestingly, there has been a marginal decline in literacy rates for the white population group (and an increase in the share of the white population group below the poverty line). Literacy is measured for those 15 years of age and above.

Of major concern, among other issues, is education, which remains a major challenge. Gross enrolments have deteriorated, significantly, in a short time. Between 2008 and 2010, for example, there was a decline from 77 to 67 females and for Africans from 79 to 69. The same trend can be discerned in the provinces. The challenge relating to education is also demonstrated in Table 8, in the education index, though general improvements in wellbeing may be noted.

The deprivation index declined from 7.91 to 6.14, at an aggregate level, showing an improvement because it is a measure of the level of deprivation, particularly access to a clean water source and children's nutrition status. Therefore, except for the education index, all other indices show an improvement. For instance, the life expectancy index, one of the main variables for human development, improved during 2008–2010. In the aggregate, it was 0.41 in 2008 and 0.46 in 2010. However, the index did not change for females (at 0.44). The province with a notable improvement was KwaZulu-Natal (0.34 to 0.43).

Table 8: Indices of Human Development

	Life expectancy index		Education index		GDP index		Deprivation index	
	2008	2010	2008	2010	2008	2010	2008	2010
Total	**0.41**	**0.46**	**0.86**	**0.83**	**0.47**	**0.47**	**7.91**	**6.14**
Gender								
Male	0.38	0.46	0.87	0.84	0.48	0.49	7.33	6.39
Female	0.44	0.44	0.85	0.82	0.46	0.46	8.56	5.90
Race								
African	0.34	0.43	0.85	0.83	0.37	0.38	8.94	6.81
Coloured	0.62	0.43	0.83	0.81	0.47	0.50	4.10	4.27
Asian/Indian	0.86	0.73	0.82	0.84	0.65	0.65	0.00	0.00
White	0.82	0.68	0.88	0.88	0.72	0.71	4.12	0.28
Province								
Western Cape	0.57	0.54	0.83	0.82	0.52	0.52	1.40	2.38
Eastern Cape	0.42	0.38	0.86	0.83	0.35	0.40	15.96	12.65
Northern Cape	0.47	0.57	0.82	0.81	0.45	0.47	9.67	8.80
Free State	0.23	0.37	0.88	0.86	0.45	0.48	5.04	1.83
KwaZulu-Natal	0.20	0.39	0.83	0.79	0.43	0.45	9.86	8.54
North West	0.44	0.43	0.83	0.83	0.45	0.45	7.73	6.21
Gauteng	0.63	0.50	0.88	0.88	0.55	0.53	5.45	3.27
Mpumalanga	0.34	0.35	0.87	0.82	0.50	0.48	5.80	2.34
Limpopo	0.47	0.48	0.86	0.82	0.37	0.38	8.95	6.65

Source: Own calculations from the National Income Dynamics Study 2008 and 2010 data

The human and poverty indices themselves show improvements, as Table 9 shows.

Table 9: Human Development & Human Poverty

	HDI		HPI-1		HPI-2	
	2008	2010	2008	2010	2008	2010
Total	0.58	0.59	27.11	21.42	46.95	42.35
Gender						
Male	0.58	0.60	25.88	20.80	47.25	42.11
Female	0.58	0.57	28.14	22.12	47.70	44.43
Race						
African	0.52	0.54	31.25	24.20	53.26	47.72
Coloured	0.64	0.58	10.51	16.58	31.42	34.64
Asian/Indian	0.78	0.74	4.92	3.85	19.12	9.66
White	0.80	0.73	10.13	8.12	12.43	12.61
Province						
Western Cape	0.64	0.63	14.40	10.52	28.84	34.54
Eastern Cape	0.54	0.54	23.35	29.36	54.51	52.52
Northern Cape	0.58	0.62	27.23	12.96	41.69	31.79
Free State	0.52	0.57	37.27	26.90	52.43	48.95
KwaZulu-Natal	0.49	0.54	48.11	28.68	62.67	49.33
North West	0.57	0.57	25.59	16.03	44.24	48.90
Gauteng	0.68	0.64	10.28	28.89	34.39	32.19
Mpumalanga	0.57	0.55	40.43	29.00	45.54	53.56
Limpopo	0.57	0.56	19.44	23.18	48.25	46.71

Source: Own calculations from the National Income Dynamics Study 2008 and 2010 data

Both HPI-1 and HPI-2 show improvements across the country. The HDI has marginally improved, from calculations of 0.58 in 2008 to 0.59 in 2010. KwaZulu-Natal had the most notable improvement of the HDI (0.49 in 2008 and 0.54 in 2010) while Gauteng showed a marginal decline from 0.68 in 2008 to 0.64 in 2010.

Another important issue that the human development calculations show is inequality in outcomes as a result of inequality of opportunity. South Africa has one of the highest economic inequalities in the world, reported to have a Gini Coefficient of 0.69.[21] From the perspective of human development and human poverty, there are significant differences in indices for the white and black population groups. For instance, for the latest estimates, Africans have an HDI of 0.54 while whites have one of 0.73. The interracial differences are also evident in other measures that make up the HDI. For instance, the GDP index of Africans is 0.38 while that of whites is 0.71 – and whites have an almost zero deprivation index while that of Africans is 6.81, as Table 8 illustrates.

Possible policy options

South Africa requires a new mix of policy instruments that would ensure that the economy grows substantially and, most importantly, jobs. In other words, over and above robust social policy, it needs an economy that works better for society – not a society that adjusts to the so-called needs of an economy. To achieve this, South Africa needs to be an agile and capable developmental state.

South Africa's greatest threat would be government and policy failures to transform the structure of its economy. This view is supported by Edigheji and Moyo, who contend, for example, that South Africa is unlikely to achieve its developmental state agenda because of its Minerals-Energy Complex (MEC), deindustrialisation, as well as slack agrarian and land reforms. The question of structural transformation of the economy therefore remains central to the debate on its developmental trajectory.[22]

The economy has, in the recent past, been the main obstacle to social and economic transformation on two levels. First, its structure has remained relatively unchanged from the predominantly MEC bias as well as in terms of ownership patterns. Second, the economy, after stabilising in the 1990s, has not been able to emulate those of its peers (such as India, Brazil, Malaysia and Mauritius). The National Planning Commission (NPC) acknowledges these issues; therefore it is simply a matter of reshaping economic policy to address the conundrum. Policies for the economy – including a robust industrial one –should make up the vision, as an explicit economic model that would be agreed upon by all relevant role players. It is not enough, anymore, to have a mixed and capitalist economy, but rather South Africa should have used the opportunity presented by the global economic recession to craft its own socio-economic development model.

The second most important issue for social and economic transformation is jobs. South Africa needs to resolve the challenge of unemployment broadly, and youth unemployment, which has since reached crisis proportions, in particular. This is another broader economic policy issue, and more narrowly a labour market one. The restructuring of the economy should alleviate the unemployment challenge. To fully address the unemployment challenge, however, the labour market should function differently. The demand side of the labour market, firm behaviour in particular, requires more attention. The requirements on experience, especially for graduates, should be revised. Graduates, in particular, should receive in-service training and there should be a set of active labour market type interventions to increase the probability that graduates in particular are absorbed by the labour market.

At a broader level, the informal economy should not be discouraged. South Africa's peers (India, for instance) have an informal economy that is effectively above the formal economy. As a temporary cushion, the informal sector plays an important role in alleviating unemployment and poverty. To address unemployment, consensus is needed on the vision for the economy, not similar to the wide-ranging NPC's 2030 National Development Plan but more focused on restructuring the economy and creating jobs for the people rather than those needed by the economy.

The gains on social development and social welfare in the post-apartheid South Africa are commendable, although clearly not enough to date. Besides challenges of wider reach, as the data discussed indicate, the country is confronted with the challenge of the quality of social services – various government reports also highlight this challenge. Therefore, implementation of programmes for social upliftment should be improved. Education and skills development should be improved. Healthcare services should be improved. These are challenges that all countries face, in one way or the other.

To successfully transform society, as Mkandawire[23] contends, collective interventions directly affecting transformation in social welfare, social institutions and social relations are critical. In other words, social policy should transform social welfare, social institutions and social relations. It can be argued that social policy – if it exists – has not been successful in transforming social institutions and social relations. The labour market is one of critical social institutions that remain significantly untransformed. Broadly, there is merit in the argument that social relations remain largely untransformed too.

It is in this context that SA needs to rethink its social policy. Social policy should work in tandem with economic policy towards advancing wellbeing, both subjective and objective wellbeing. Therefore, rethinking social policy should be undertaken jointly with improving economic policy. These policies can only work with a clear vision for the economy and society.

Conclusion

This chapter has reviewed social and economic transformation since 1994. The overwhelming conclusion is – as others have concluded – that South Africa has achieved significant social and economic development in about two decades of democracy. The economy was stabilised in the mid-2000s, and social development has improved.

However, from a policy perspective, the country has fallen short significantly. The necessary reforms in the economy, in particular, have been weak because of poor policy development and lack of vision for the economy. In social development, it is argued that lack of social policy has constrained the advancement of wellbeing. Broadly, from the mid-2000s, South Africa has effectively been standing still compared with the robust reforms of the 1990s. We are taking for granted that implementation is a challenge, but implementation is more of a challenge – we argue – particularly when policies are inappropriate or weak.

The answer to South Africa's woes, from a policy perspective, is reform, of the economy in particular. The strategies and programmes that have been introduced since the mid-2000s have not addressed the policy constraints that needed reform, but rather programmes and strategies not informed by policy have been followed. Therefore, more policy thinking should be exercised for both social and economic transformations. Most important, policy should be pursuing the vision for the economy agreed upon through national consensus. Failing this, the envisaged South Africa – as per R2G and Strategy and Tactics documents – remains a pipedream.

In short, as the ANC enters its second centenary, the key question is: will it introduce policy reforms and enhance state capacity in a manner that will meaningfully transform the political economy of South Africa and thus deliver the masses into a national democratic society characterised by a better life for all?

References

Ministry of Higher Education and Training, 2010, *Transformation, Social Cohesion and the Elimination of Discrimination in Public Higher Education Institutions*. Pretoria

Statistics South Africa, 2009, *Quarterly Labour Force Survey*. Stats South Africa, Pretoria.

United Nations Development Programme, 2007, *Human Development Report*. New York: Palgrave Macmillan.

Endnotes

1   The 'Ready to Govern' discussion document of 1992 spelt out – upfront – very specific goals for a democratic South Africa. The points quoted in the paragraph come from what was said, in the 'Ready to Govern' discussion document, to be the ANC's Vision for the Future.

2   African National Congress, 1994. *RDP White Paper*. Available at: http://www.anc.org. za/232. Also see African National Congress, 1994. *Reconstruction and Development Programme: A policy framework*. Johannesburg: Umanyano Publications.

3   National Planning Commission, 2012. *The National Development Plan 2030*. Pretoria: Ministry of Planning. The Presidency.

4   In simple terms, what role would the state play in economic development post-1994? Gumede explains the notion of a developmental state in detail – see Gumede, V., 2011. Policy making in South Africa. In Landsberg, C. & Venter, A. (eds), 2011. *South African government and politics*. 4th edition. Pretoria: Van Schaik; and Gumede, V., 2013. Public sector reforms and policy-making: A case of education in an emerging developmental South Africa. In Kanjee, A., Nkomo, M. & Sayed, Y. (eds), 2013. *The search for quality education in post-apartheid South Africa*. Pretoria: HSRC Press.

5   According to the 2011 Census there were about 1 265 907 people in 2011 without access to piped water, of which 1 234 087 were black Africans – this supports the point that most of the socio-economic challenges confronting South African society remain predominantly problems of black Africans.

6   All estimates, whether from the World Bank or IMF or the South African Treasury or the South African Reserve Bank, imply that SA would lag behind its counterparts and would be below the Sub-Saharan Africa GDP average in the next two years.

7   Statistics South Africa, 2012. *Census 2011*. Pretoria: Statistics South Africa.

8   Bloch, G., 2006. *Building education beyond crisis*. Johannesburg: Development Bank of Southern Africa.

9   Kraak, A., 2008. The education–economy relationship in South Africa, 2001–2005. In Kraak, A. & Press, K. (eds), 2008. *Human Resource Development review 2008: Education, employment and skills in South Africa*. Cape Town: HSRC Press.

10   Organisation for Economic Co-operation and Development (OECD), 2008. *Reviews of national policies for education: South Africa*. Available at: http://www.oecd.org/ southafrica/reviewsofnationalpoliciesforeducation-southafrica.htm.

11   The Presidency, 2008a. *Towards a fifteen year review, synthesis report on implementation of government programmes*. Pretoria: Government Communications and Information Systems. Available at: http://www.thepresidency.gov.za/main.asp?include=docs/15year/main.htm.

12 Department of Basic Education, 2012. *Education statistics in South Africa 2010*. Pretoria: Department of Basic Education.

13 Breier, M & Mabizela, M., 2008. Higher education. In Kraak, A. & Press, K. (eds), 2008. *Human Resource Development review 2008: Education, employment and skills in South Africa*. Cape Town: HSRC Press.

14 Ministry of Monitoring and Evaluation, 2012. *Development indicators 2011*. Pretoria: The Presidency.

15 Refer to Kraak & Press, 2008, op. cit. and Steyn, 2009.

16 Moleke, P., 2006. *Finding work: Employment experiences for South African graduates*. Cape Town: HSRC Press. Also see Moleke, P., 2005. *Inequalities in higher education, and the structure of the labour market*. Human Sciences Research Council Paper Series. Employment and Economic Research Programme, South Africa.

17 Council on Higher Education (CHE), 2007. *Higher education monitor: A case for improving teaching and learning in South African higher education*. Pretoria: Council on Higher Education.

18 Department of Higher Education and Training (DHET), 2012. *Green Paper for the post-school system*. Pretoria: DHET.

19 United Nations Development Programme, 2011. *Human Development report*. New York: Palgrave Macmillan.

20 Wave I had 28 247 respondents and Wave II had 28 641. For more details, available at: http://www.nids.uct.ac.za/home.

21 Bhorat, H. & Van der Westhuizen, C., 2010. Poverty, inequality and the nature of economic growth in South Africa. In Misra-Dexter, N. & February, J., 2010. *Testing democracy: Which way is South Africa going?* Cape Town: IDASA.

22 Cited in Edigheji, O., 2010. *Constructing a democratic developmental state in South Africa: Potentials and challenges*. Cape Town: HSRC Press.

23 Mkandawire, T., 2001. *Social policy in a development context*. Social Policy and Development Programme Paper 7, United Nations Research Institute for Social Development, Geneva.

CHAPTER 18

Aspirations to an elusive developmental state: the obstacles to deep reform

Alan Hirsch

Introduction: the developmental challenge

Many, especially in the ANC, believe that South Africa has or should be a developmental state.[1] This chapter explores what a developmental state is, and how difficult it might be to establish one that is fully functioning. In very broad terms it is a society in which a strong and empowered state administration drives capitalist economic development effectively.

The transition to democracy in 1994 was not simply about setting up a new governance structure of a society that was otherwise functioning quite well. Beyond the political system, the education and health systems were fragmented disasters, the social infrastructure for Africans was in an appalling condition and the economy was not only deeply unequal but also seriously in trouble.

In the decade before 1994, the economy actually shrank, with per capita incomes 15 per cent lower than in 1984. Unemployment was rising, and the overall government deficit was close to 10 per cent, and rising sharply. It was not a matter of taking over a going concern. Apart from simply installing democracy, the challenge was to fix systems, institutions and programmes that were poorly designed and badly damaged. The challenge for reformers was great.

The ANC's Reconstruction and Development Programme (RDP) set out the economic challenge simply: 'The South African economy is in a deep-seated structural crisis and as such requires fundamental reconstruction'.[2] The RDP was designed as a programme to transform the whole of society: education, healthcare, housing and the economy.

It was the kind of challenge that had been faced by many states before, typically newly liberated colonies that had been sucked dry by a colonial power. African countries had not done well after decolonisation, as after a relatively short honeymoon period fuelled by strong commodity prices in the 1960s and early 1970s, many had slipped into economic weakness and political inertia.

The ANC was conscious of the challenge, and rebuilding would not be easy. It recognised that the challenge of reconstruction meant that deep reforms and institutional transformation were needed, and yet it also knew that as a newly free African country South Africa faced deep scepticism amongst the economic elite at home and abroad, as well as expectations of failure which instilled in the new government a fear of making mistakes.

This was not a trivial issue. The ANC came to power representing the powerless, plus the organised working class. The economic elite within South Africa were not part of the ANC in any way. As the Ten Year Review pointed out,[3] one of the great challenges faced by South Africa was that unlike most societies there was almost no overlap between the economic elite and the political elite, especially within the ruling party. In addition, as an open economy dependent on foreign sources of investment funds, a great deal of economic power was held outside South Africa, and this formed a major constraint.

Contemporary developmental states

The notion of using political power for reconstruction and development implied a government which would play a considerable role in reshaping the society and the economy. The ANC approached this challenge, not as a traditional socialist party which believed in the centrality of the state, but rather as a social democratic party which accepted the role of the market. It had begun to learn how in some market-based societies economic reform was driven by the state.

The economic rise of East Asia had a considerable influence on thinking within the ANC. Japan, Korea, Taiwan and, later, mainland China were non-Western societies that played the capitalist game to their own advantage through an effective state apparatus and goal-driven relationships between political and economic society.

Influential academic work on East Asian economic development by writers such as Chalmers Johnson, Alice Amsden and Robert Wade, on Japan, Korea and Taiwan respectively, had an impact on thinking within the ANC's intelligentsia.[4]

One of the main lessons of contemporary development economics is that the institutional path that supports economic growth always reflects the distinctive historical experience of the country concerned.[5] There is not one path, although there is a common view that economic success is unlikely in the absence of a basically functioning state with a sufficient degree of macroeconomic stability. Nevertheless, ANC economic thinkers tried to learn the reasons for economic success in East Asia.

Though it is unwise to generalise about paths to economic growth, the East Asian developmental state does have some characteristic features, across Japan, South Korea and Taiwan, and to a large extent China. A useful attempt to sum up these common features was made by Meredith Woo-Cummings.[6]

One characteristic is a collective cultural commitment to development that derives from an anti-colonial or anti-imperialistic struggle. Wartime mobilisation and nationalistic unity around a goal of economic independence is a feature of all four of the East Asian tigers: Japan resisting the US and Europe's domination; China throwing off Japan; and Taiwan and South Korea involved in their own struggles deriving from two unresolved civil wars.

Entailed in this description is the implicit argument that citizens imbued with strong nationalistic values are prepared to give up more sovereignty than perhaps is typical in liberal democratic states. However, it is not conventional authoritarianism. As Johnson has put it, 'In the true developmental state the bureaucratic rulers possess a particular kind of legitimacy that allows them to be much more experimental and undoctrinaire than in the typical authoritarian regime. This is the legitimacy that comes from devotion to a widely believed-in revolutionary project.'[7]

Another important common feature of East Asian developmental states is in the management of finance by the state. All four countries had financial systems without a great deal of depth, complexity or openness. Unlike conditions in small open economies such as South Africa in the current era, the state had significant financial leverage. It was able to channel limited resources, sometimes derived from foreign assistance, into sectors and companies that were favoured at the time. It was able to segment financial markets between industrial finance and consumer finance, so that industrial borrowing rates were low in favoured sectors and consumer interest rates discouraged spending scarce savings on consumption. Such market segmentation and rationing is very difficult in modern open financial systems where arbitrage would tend to eliminate the divisions between these market segments.[8]

At least as important, probably more so, is the nature of the bureaucracy in East Asian developmental states. East Asian bureaucracies are highly meritocratic and relatively immune to politics, and are therefore able to deploy their greater autonomy with some significant degree of skill. A notable characteristic described in depth by Peter Evans is their embedded nature. The developmental bureaucracy had to be embedded in society through 'a concrete set of connections that link the state intimately and aggressively to particular social groups with whom the state shares a joint project of transformation'.[9] This embeddedness could nevertheless not compromise the developmental project; the state was neither captured nor captor: 'the archetypal developmental state is', for Evans, 'that rare beast with its tentacles reaching deep into the society, while managing to keep its corporate integrity intact'.[10]

The key partner of the East Asian developmental state is business. In Japan and South Korea there has been an intimate relationship between the state and the big business conglomerates, the zaibatsu in Japan and the chaebols in South Korea. In Taiwan, the state managed to create an environment supporting medium-sized businesses.

East Asian developmental states were by no means the first developmental states in history. Some would argue that virtually all successful growing countries arise from developmental states.[11] The East Asian model was by no means the only one, and valuable examples of effective state developmentalism exist in Northern Europe and Scandinavia, North America and, one could argue, contemporary Latin America.

The experience of Ireland since the late 1980s is an important example of a different kind of developmental state, relevant in many respects to South Africa. Ireland represents a more flexible form of a developmental state operating as a small open economy in an era of fully fledged globalisation. In a democratic context, neo-corporatism allowed Ireland not only to drive a macroeconomic stabilisation programme but also to actively develop a competitive advantage in the information technology sector.[12] The Irish experience shows that a kind of developmental state is possible even for an open economy in an era of deep global integration.

There may even be incipient forms of developmental state in Africa, and the leaders of Ethiopia and Rwanda certainly believe that they are driving such developmental projects. However, the East Asian experience had the greatest impact on the ANC in the early stages because of its timing and its global intellectual impact. As the East Asian economic development experience has been well studied, it provides a valuable set of criteria against which to measure the developmental capacity of other states.

Views of development in the ANC during the transition

The context of the transition was that the Washington Consensus was still close to full strength in global thinking. In 1990, the Reagan era still dominated the US, Margaret Thatcher was still Prime Minister of the United Kingdom and the Soviet Union was about to become a thing of the past. Thinking within the ANC about the relationship between state and the market was contested.

There were no longer two clearly opposed camps, and thinking about the state was in flux. One powerful argument derived from the recent and contemporary history of Latin America; the risk of fiscal populism was one of the shadows cast over the ANC. The fear of a Latin America-style bail-out, with debt-asset swops and risks to policy-making sovereignty, was palpable to the extent that ANC economic leadership considered expansive fiscal proposals in a World Bank Report to be irresponsible and risky.[13] The fear of populism was sometimes accompanied by a low estimation of the capabilities of the South African state before and after the political transition and the notion that, therefore, the economy was best left largely to the market.

At the opposite end of the spectrum, the formulation of the left included elements of developmental interventionism by the state, including fiscal and monetary policy and trade and industrial policy. Some trade union formulations included elements of worker control, not directly of the state but of a degree of executive power in firms. In addition, there was a fear of imperial powers and global corporations which led many on the left to endorse fiscal conservatism as a defence against foreign interests.

Among ANC intellectuals there were a wide variety of views, in various combinations. Some were freemarketeers on trade policy but interventionist on industrial policy and the capital account. Some combined macroeconomic conservatism with microeconomic interventionism, others the reverse.

The tensions were symbolised in the ANC in the Macro-Economic Research Group (MERG) which, in addition to many valuable policy projects, tried to produce a synthesis position of ANC economic thinkers in a book called *Making Democracy Work*.[14] Rather than producing a workable synthesis the book included a number of contradictory positions. The overall tone set by the editors was interventionist. Concerns about explicit interventionism and the fractious public history of the MERG led the ANC to distance itself from the report. This event is sometimes cited as one of the key moments when the ANC moved to the right, but elsewhere I argue that this view does not comprehend the intellectual history of the ANC very well.[15]

Despite many meetings and conferences, economic thinkers in the ANC were unable to craft a broadly understood and accepted coherent approach to economic development. The RDP had conventional macroeconomics, more preoccupied with stabilisation than growth, but it had no clear, coherent or modern approach to economic development.

Perhaps the best attempts to develop a coherent approach to economic growth were the Industrial Strategy Project reports and its synthesis book: *Improving manufacturing performance in South Africa*.[16] This was a bold attempt to combine modern theories of competitiveness in production with light borrowings from East Asian developmentalism, grounded in a coherent South African approach to the roles of the state and the market in economic growth. For one reason or another, the Industrial Strategy Project did not become a significant part of the discourse of the ANC or of the trade union movement that had commissioned it.

Constraints of transition

Did South Africa have a 'collective cultural commitment' to a common vision of development in 1994? Sadly, the elementary truth is that it had few cultural collective commitments in 1994, and certainly not to a common view of development. The response of the *Financial Mail*, a voice of established business, was to write an editorial about a draft of the RDP headed 'The Road to Hell'. The response of other representatives of the economic elite was similar.[17] This was in spite of the ANC having engaged intensively with business in various public and private arenas since and even before 1990, and the fact that the RDP was not a radical revolutionary programme. It was a very carefully prepared social democratic manifesto.

One problem was that the cultural gap between government and business was unusually large. The entire domestic economic ruling class was white, with the few black business people having no real power and tending to have a dependency relationship with white-owned businesses. The black political leaders and white business leaders had not gone to the same schools or universities, they spoke different languages at home and they did not play or watch the same sports or listen to the same music.

The focus of Mandela's presidency was on reconciliation, on building trust in a very general kind of way. There was no real effort to build a common developmental vision, even though one of the first acts of the new government was to establish the National Economic Development and Labour Council (Nedlac).

The new government commissioned a macro-economic policy report, and received a weak and anachronistic document from the Central Economic Advisory Service, which was disbanded shortly afterwards. Then the RDP office, which was a ministry in the Presidency, produced a draft National Growth and Development Strategy. A significant weakness of the document was that it became an omnibus for a disparate range of economic policy issues, and consequently it lacked a simple, clear and accessible message. Moreover, when an ANC Minister of Finance was appointed in March 1996, the Treasury began to assert its core role in economic policy and the RDP office was disbanded.

Nedlac focused on rewriting the labour laws of the country and devoted its key resources to intensive negotiation around four new labour laws. The Minister of Labour had also set up a Presidential Labour Market Commission, which commission proposed a National Accord on Employment and Growth, based on a broad-ranging social compact.[18] Unfortunately, the proposal was overshadowed by the launch of the Growth Employment and Redistribution Strategy (GEAR) by the Minister of Finance.

On reflection, the simultaneous preparation of three key reports on growth and employment by the RDP Ministry, the Labour Department and the Treasury shows an unhealthy degree of discordance and rivalry in the Mandela cabinet and a lack of common purpose in the ruling party. Without a strong consensus in the ruling party, any notion of a developmental state was unlikely.

In this environment, uncertainty reigned and deep relationships were not built between the economic and the political elites. While the Trade and Industry Chamber in Nedlac tried to cement agreement between government, business and labour around a range of economic development strategies and programmes, the opportunity for a grand agreement was lost. The failure of the Jobs Summit in 1998 made this even clearer. Sadly, the main objective of the government in the jobs summit, in the context of a build-up to an important ruling party elective conference, was not to lose face in public.

Ideological tensions

Sometimes rivalries are disguised as ideological differences; in the ANC these differences were real. The gulfs were not so wide that strong leadership focused on building bridges then could not have closed them, but they remained unresolved. GEAR became symbolic of these differences, but if it had been implemented differently GEAR might have been less divisive. Also, the Minister of Finance's indication that its parameters were 'not negotiable at this stage' made it more vulnerable to partisan attacks.[19]

Apart from its orthodox commitment to a tight fiscal regime, tariff reductions, privatisation and gradually liberalising foreign exchange rules, the GEAR document had significant developmental elements. It had tax incentives for investment, a commitment to expanding infrastructure investment to address deficiencies and backlogs, a commitment to support for small businesses and a clear commitment to 'maintain the current competitive advantage created by the depreciation of the rand... [though keeping] the real effective rate of the rand at a competitive level' (Department of Finance, 1996:10).

While the evident intention of GEAR was to tighten fiscal policy to allow a looser monetary policy to encourage higher investment and consumption, the South African Reserve Bank continued raising the interest rate until it killed off any possibility of a GEAR-driven boom. The Reserve Bank was concerned that the growing money supply was contributing to higher inflation and that a weaker rand would make it more expensive to repay the foreign currency obligations of the Reserve Bank. The financial crises in Asia, Russia and Brazil in the late 1990s encouraged further monetary tightening. South Africa was solvent but growing very slowly. There was little money outside of the state-owned enterprises to invest in infrastructure, and an *Eskom*-driven electrification programme had a short-lived impact.

Another commitment of GEAR that was not followed through was the commitment to co-ordination amongst government departments and agencies in the implementation of economic policy. The Treasury failed to follow through on this commitment, and maintained a tight hold on economic policy.

The tax incentive programme was rushed through parliament to ensure its rapid implementation. Some of the authors of GEAR, including myself, felt that the programme's credibility depended on putting through pro-investment/pro-growth reforms as quickly as possible. The tax incentive legislation was passed quickly because concessions on its design were made freely to interested parties – there should be a spatial element and a labour intensity element, and we should not disadvantage existing businesses. The result was too clumsy to implement effectively.

The elements of GEAR that were effectively implemented, apart from a successful reform of the budgeting system, tended to be the classic Washington consensus structural adjustment elements. Eventually, improved fiscal management bore fruit. In the early 2000s the social welfare system was greatly enhanced and investment in public infrastructure was reinvigorated. By the mid-2000s growth was stronger and employment grew relatively quickly. When the financial crisis came in 2008, reserves were available to counteract some of its impact, but GEAR did not receive much of the credit.

GEAR was seen by many on the left in the ANC alliance as symptomatic of a conservative triumph within government. Communist Party members later called it 'the class project of 1996', implying that it was through GEAR that the bourgeoisie, or more specifically the financial oligarchy, took control of government economic policy. This notion gave ammunition to supporters of Jacob Zuma in his campaign to topple Thabo Mbeki as ANC president in 2007, as he drew some support from a disaffected left in the ANC and its alliance partners.

The diffusion of power

The alternative to an orthodox liberal approach to development has not always been clearly stated. Perhaps this is because in the absence of a capable state – one that is efficient and meritocratic and is strongly endorsed by the political elite – liberal economics seems to make the most sense. Liberal economics says get the basic environment for investment right. Leave the rest to business.

In many countries in Africa, especially democratic ones, political power is spread wide. It can be parcelled out along ethnic lines. There could be economic class divisions with significant power in trade unions and/or business. The ruling party might comprise a group of factions that need to be appeased, or the ruling coalition might be fractured. There might be regional leaders with effective veto power. Though the state may have the capacity to undertake its minimal functions competently and some intermediate functions, it struggles to achieve all its ambitions for many intermediate and most activist functions (using the terminology of the World Bank, 1997).

In South Africa, the ANC itself is characterised with fissures which have the capability of weakening the decisiveness of the ruling party and the government. There are tensions along ethnic, urban–rural and class lines. None of these tensions have the capacity to fundamentally undermine the integrity of the ANC, but they do have the ability to make the ruling alliance and the government far less effective than it could be. Many have the ability to throw sand into the machinery.

Although the ANC has more than 60 per cent electoral support, the veto on effective decision-making is widely distributed within the ruling alliance. When there is no deep national consensus about who we are and where we are going, and specially about how to get there, how do we make effective policies in order to escape an equilibrium of slow growth and high inequality?

Nevertheless, the ambitions of the ruling party are not modest or simple. Take for instance the 2007 Polokwane conference resolution on the Democratic Developmental State. The centre-piece of the economic transformation resolution was the commitment 'to build the strategic, organisational and technical capacities of government with a view to [establishing] a democratic developmental state'. Subordinate commitments included:

- establishing a capacity for 'government-wide economic planning',
- the integration of planning across different tiers and organs of government,
- improving the quality of the civil service,
- strengthening the ability of the state 'to engage with, understand and lead the development of globally integrated economic sectors',
- to play a direct role in strategic sectors of the economy such as energy and transport, and
- a few additional elements that assume that a more effective state can help solve problems of growth and jobs.[20]

While the resolution was valuable because it made clear a commitment to ensure that the state supported economic development, it erred in as much as it frequently conflated or confused developmental interventionism with state control and ownership.

Is a DDS possible in South Africa? When an international team of development economists was asked to advise South Africa on developmental and growth strategies, one of the recommendations was a subsidy to encourage the employment of never-yet-employed youths (Levinsohn, 2007). There were several legitimate concerns about the proposal, mainly that it would favour young workers, who could displace employed workers, and that it could lead to wage undercutting. For every one of these concerns there is a potential solution in the design of the programme. However, the outcome, six years on, is interminable debate, sand in the machine.

Another contemporary example is the Gauteng toll-road saga. It seems to be far easier to block the implementation of decisions than to arrive at agreement on developmental programmes. Second guessing is a national pastime and there is no single simple truth.

The Irish experience shows that a DDS that neutralises the class divisions and fractionalisation of society is possible. Neocorporatism, a politically mediated pact between the major classes and their fractions, gave Ireland the space to experiment with and implement developmental strategies in a systematic way. The South African state lacks that space.

The weak authority of the bureaucracy

Meritocratic bureaucracies in developmental states have much greater authority than civil servants and the experts on whom they draw in South Africa. There are several possible circumstantial reasons for this. The first is that many political leaders and senior civil servants came through the struggle against apartheid together. The result is that their roles in government are sometimes blurred or confused. The second is that the senior leadership of the civil service are political appointees. Directors general and their deputies are appointed by Cabinet, and although this is by rule-bound recruitment procedures they remain political appointees.

This can weaken their credibility and authority in relation to their political principals. Some argue that empowerment considerations in appointments can also contribute to the lack of authority of senior officials.[21] Empowerment considerations can also lead to posts being left vacant for excessive periods of time.[22] A third reason is that, as a result of the historical legacy of apartheid, a large proportion of experts are white and they are not drawn from the same cultural background as most political leaders. This can easily lead to a trust deficit. Von Holdt also notes that, while the apartheid state operated within a firm hierarchy of power, there is much more contestation within the post-apartheid state.

Gathering courage

Addressing these cleavages requires an approach to policy formation and implementation that specifically attempts to overcome the divisions in society and deliberately build a common national vision. This requires a new kind of nationalism that is able to give real support to the kind of 'widely believed-in revolutionary project' symbolised in the Asian developmental states:

> The question confronting us as society, and confronting too the ANC, is what sort of state we want, and how we might go about constructing it. At its root this is a question of how we want to define post-apartheid nationalism and modernity.[23]

There have been several recent attempts in this direction. Under the second Mbeki government, the Deputy President, Phumzile Mlambo-Ngcuka, led the accelerated and shared growth initiative: AsgiSA. The programme was carefully crafted in government, with a time-consuming process of to-ing and fro-ing between technocrats and political leaders. Eventually a draft was ready, with a platform of six initiatives: infrastructure investment, prioritised skills development, small business support, sector development initiatives, macroeconomic adjustments and strengthening the capacity of the state.

Mlambo-Ngcuka and her team took the proposals, provisionally endorsed by Cabinet, into the field, testing them out with all significant political parties, with business and with labour. I remember presenting a draft of AsgiSA to a COSATU shop-stewards gathering in Johannesburg. In spite of tensions within the ANC and the surge of discontent that targeted the President and the Deputy-President's husband, AsgiSA was widely accepted and endorsed. Important parts of it were effectively implemented. A tripartite leadership group representing business, government and labour that drove the Joint Initiative on Priority Skills Acquisition (JIPSA) demonstrated the considerable achievements of AsgiSA. The early end of the Mbeki regime included the resignation of Mlambo-Ngcuka, however, and this meant that the AsgiSA brand was damaged beyond repair.

Another effort to build a new nationalism is embodied in the New Growth Path or NGP. The NGP is driven by the Minister of Economic Development, Ebrahim Patel, a very experienced trade unionist and an intellectual widely respected on the left in South Africa and abroad. The New Growth Path is the Zuma Government's variation on AsgiSA, through it takes it further in a number of important respects. It is too soon to say whether the NGP will be successful in establishing a 'widely believed-in revolutionary project' and how much it can contribute to building a new form of post-apartheid nationalism.

Recent initiatives on infrastructure investment deriving from the NGP have garnered wide support. Patel's tripartite agreements on a range of issues including skills development and green growth are less widely known and not yet deeply understood, but they have the potential to support a new, widely supported national development project.

Alongside the NGP is the National Development Plan of the National Planning Commission (NPC). The NPC is meant to address longer-term planning issues, to develop a vision for South Africa a decade or two ahead. The NPC presented its draft NPD to the public in November 2011 and published a final version in August 2012. It engaged in wide-ranging public consultations, more oriented to general public involvement than to engaging political formations in the style of AsgiSA and the NGP. The NDP could contribute to modernising our nationalism, but its relationship to the NGP is a confusing one.

Are the NGP and the NDP complementary or in competition? They could be seen as complementary as the NGP is a medium-term (to 2014) and the NDP a long-term framework (to 2030). However, can the government present them both to the people in such a way that it builds a common national project, or will their coexistence lead to the kind of confusion that emerged in 1996 between the Treasury, the RDP Office and the Presidential Labour Commission?

Conclusion

It is too early to say that a Democratic Developmental State is impossible in South Africa. Our political society is so young and immature that it would be unfair to form a final judgement at this time. It took China 30 years after the revolution to reach maturity on its developmental strategy. It took India even longer.

It may be useful to summarise here some of the most important preconditions, were we to get there.

Firstly, we need a clear common purpose as a nation. This means in the first place a clear common purpose in the ruling party. It would not be too hard to sketch out such a common purpose, as the recent histories of AsgiSA and the NGP show. The challenge is unity in the ruling party and the neutralisation of destructive competitive rivalries.

Secondly, we need a bureaucracy which is essentially meritocratic, and is respected by society and by political leaders.

Thirdly, we need to negate the diffusion of power through a broad, effective social compact. As Peter Evans said, we need 'a concrete set of connections that link the state intimately and aggressively to particular social groups with whom the state shares a joint project of transformation'. Unlike the East Asian states, this cannot simply mean the state and business. It has, at least, to mean an effective pact between business and organised labour, mediated by the democratic state. Ireland shows that a democratic developmental state in an era of global integration is possible with a deeply effective social partnership.

References

Amsden, A. 1989. *Asia's Next Giant: South Korea and late industrialisation*. New York and Oxford: Oxford University Press.

Johnson, C. 1982. MITI and the Japanese Economic Miracle: The Growth of Industrial Policy 1925–1975. Stanford: Stanford University Press.

Johnson, C. 1999. 'The developmental state: Odyssey of a concept', in Meridith Woo-Cumings (ed), *The Developmental State*. Ithaca: Cornell University Press, p. 52.

Levinsohn, J. 2007. 'Two policies to alleviate unemployment in South Africa', Michigan: University of Michigan.

Wade, R. 1990. Governing the Market: Economic Theory and the role of government in East Asian industrialisation. New York: Princeton University Press.

World Bank. 1994. Fallon, Peter; Pereira de Silva, Luiza. 1994. *South Africa: Stimulating Economic Growth*. © World Bank, Washington, DC. Available at: https://openknowledge.worldbank.org/handle/10986/10014

World Bank. 1997. *World Development Report: The State in a Changing World*. Available at: ttp://wdronline.worldbank.org/worldbank/a/c.htmlworld_development_report _1997

Endnotes

1 Insightful comments from Anver Saloojee, Anne McClintock and an anonymous reviewer helped to improve this essay.

2 African National Congress, 1994. *The Reconstruction and Development Programme*, Johannesburg: ANC.

3 See The Presidency, 2003. *Towards a ten year review*.

4 See Johnson, 1982, op. cit.; Amsden, 1989, op. cit. and Wade, 1990, op. cit.

5 Rodrik, D. (ed.), 2003. *In search of prosperity: Analytical growth narratives*. New York: Princeton University Press.

6 See Woo-Cumings, 1999, op. cit.

7 See Johnson, C., 1999. The Developmental State: Odyssey of a concept. In Woo-Cumings, M. (ed.), 1999. *The Developmental State*. Ithaca: Cornell University Press.

8 However, as the performance of BNDES in Brazil has shown, for example, segmentation in financial markets for the purposes of industrial policy is not impossible in open and deep financial systems.

9 See Evans, P., 1995. *Embedded autonomy: States and industrial transformation*. New York: Princeton University Press.

10 Woo-Cumings, 1999, op cit., p.15.

11 Chang, H-J., 2007. *Bad Samaritans: Rich nations, poor policies and the threat to the developing world*. London: Random House.

12 See Ó Riain, S., 2000. States and markets in an era of globalization. *Annual Review of Sociology*, 26, pp.187-213.

13 Fallon, P. & Pereira de Silva, L., 1994. *South Africa: Stimulating economic growth*. Available at: https://openknowledge.worldbank.org/handle/10986/10014.

14 Macro Economic Research Group, 1993. *Making democracy work: A framework for macroeconomic policy in South Africa*. A report to members of the Democratic Movement of South Africa from the Macroeconomic Research Group, Centre for Development Studies, Belleville, South Africa.

15 See Hirsch, A., 2005. *Season of hope: Economic reform under Mandela and Mbeki*. Scottsville and Ottawa: University of KwaZulu-Natal Press and IDRC.

16 Joffe, A., Kaplan, D., Kaplinsky, R & Lewis, D. (eds), 1995. *Improving manufacturing performance in South Africa: The report of the Industrial Strategy Project*. Cape Town: UCT Press.

17 See Hirsch, 2005, op. cit.

18 See Labour Market Commission (LMC), 1996. *Restructuring the South African labour market: Report of the Presidential Commission to investigate Labour Market Policy*. Available at: http://www.polity.org.za/polity/govdocs/commissions/fintoc.html.

19 See Hirsch, 2005, op. cit.

20 See ANC, 2007. *Economic transformation resolution*. Available at: http://www.anc.org.za/show.php?id=2536#economic.

21 Von Holdt, K., 2010. Nationalism, bureaucracy and the developmental state: The South African case. *The South African Review of Sociology*, 41(1), pp.4-27.

22 Chipkin, I., 2008. Set-up for failure: Racial redress in the Department of Public Service and Administration. In Bentley, K. & Habib, A. (eds), 2008. *Racial redress and citizenship in South Africa*. Cape Town: HSRC Press.

23 See Von Holdt, 2010, op. cit.

CHAPTER 19

The next frontier: building a capable public service

Busani Ngcaweni

Background

This book began by discussing events, personalities, organisations and decisions that characterised the early years of the ANC. Suggestions were made about what kept the organisation cohesive in its early years, with one main conclusion: the all-embracing vision to free the oppressed from colonialism and apartheid. Moving from that premise, subsequent chapters of the book discussed how the ANC – throughout the history of anti-colonial and anti-apartheid struggles – organised itself philosophically, tactically and organisationally as it experienced changing local dynamics and global balance of forces. Recognising that none of this evolution was monolithic, we moved to present some of the major debates that shaped the ANC over the years; doing so under the rubric: *the battle of ideas*.

The last part of the book, a prospective look at the present and the future, identified a few strategic challenges that the ANC as a political party and the ANC as a governing party needs to prioritise. As this last chapter suggests, one of those challenges is the building of a capable public service or, alternatively, what are simultaneously called the Public Service Mandarins.

This chapter does not purport to be a conclusion for the entire edition. However, given all the successes and challenges problematised in previous chapters, it proposes that, apart from internal party contradictions and the changing balance of forces, the ability of the public service to deliver services to the people will determine how the electorate and the international community judges the ANC in its second centenary. While it is true that possibilities abound for introducing ambitious social and macro-economic reforms (that can lead to the progressive realisation of socio-economic rights guaranteed in the Constitution), it is equally true that it is even more difficult to rapidly transform the public service which, in any developmental state, occupies the engine room of the state delivery machinery. It is against this backdrop that we title this chapter *the next frontier*, emboldened by the ANC's own admission that a weak bureaucracy stands between it and the realisation of its vision recently elaborated upon in the National Development Plan.

Introduction

In 1954, the famed French feminist author and existentialist philosopher Simone de Beauvoir produced a landmark novel titled *The Mandarins*. The storyline of this novel develops around a cohesive group of French intellectuals operating in the aftermath of the Second World War. De Beauvoir drew the title from imperial China, in which what became known as 'scholar-bureaucrats' had evolved over centuries and mastered the art of administering state affairs.

Among the essential preoccupations of the novel was questioning their capacity, roles and effectiveness and the extent to which they could play a leading part in the theatre of transforming Europe after the Second World War.

Key to their contemplation was self-recognition as reformers, intellectuals and scholar-bureaucrats, and not just typical public sector employees. Their posture was that of public servants ready to lead a renaissance. In short, they were fully conscious of the role of senior bureaucrats in transformation.

In recent times, all manner of uncertainties have been occasioned by the global economic crisis, the rise of China, the Arab Spring and country-specific political dynamics that have affected nations in both the developed and developing world. In Europe, once again, we have seen the *Mandarins* stepping up their game to save countries like Greece and Italy from the apocalypse of a continuing global economic crisis.

Here, in South Africa, it has become a common refrain to question the capacity and complicity of bureaucrats when discussing service delivery shortcomings, weak economic performance and policy failures.

It is disconcerting that bureaucrats themselves are absent from this debate. Indeed, they might be seized with the matter, yet the public is not aware – and hence their diminishing confidence. The situation is not helped by countless reports of public funds being either stolen or mismanaged by the bureaucrats.

Theoretical underpinnings of a capable state

As a public servant, I write this chapter to contribute to the state capacity and developmental state debate, convinced that the deficit of confidence in state institutions is unsustainable, for it threatens to undermine our democracy and the pursuit of social justice. The dearth of trust is bad, breeding cynicism and delegitimising the state.

The latter is antithetical to the South African developmental state initiative, a phenomenon explored in the previous chapter by Alan Hirsch.

Chalmers Johnson[1] says this about the legitimacy of the bureaucracy:

> In the true developmental state the bureaucratic rulers [the mandarins] possess a particular kind of legitimacy that allows them to be much more experimental and undoctrinaire than in the typical authoritarian regime. This is the legitimacy that comes from devotion to a widely believed-in revolutionary project.

As if foretelling what post-apartheid South Africa would need to consider for reforming its civil service and to settle the political–administrative interface quagmire, Chalmers Johnson concluded in his seminal 1982 work, *MITI and the Japanese Miracle*,[2] that developmental states are nations where politicians reign and bureaucrats rule!

In this connection, we might even accede to the observation that bureaucratic authority is partly dependent on political authority. After all, it is the ruling politicians who ought to delegate authority to the reigning bureaucrats. This is the symbiosis that might untie the knot of political-administrative interface.

In *Thinking about Developmental States in Africa*, Thandika Mkandawire[3] argued that the developmental state has two components – ideological and structural. The former pertains to a government whose ideological underpinnings are developmentalist. The structural aspect concerns the institutional (that is, technical and administrative) capacity of the state to implement.

It must be stated from the onset that, as elaborated on by Francis Fukuyama in *The Patterns of History*,[4] there is centuries-old evidence of bureaucrats playing a central role in advancing the civilisation of societies. Citing examples such as China, Japan and Korea, Fukuyama argues that the presence of high-quality public administrators sustained the development of societies in East Asia, with China bestowing upon its neighbours 'traditions of coherent centralised states and meritocratic bureaucracy'.

A note on the political context

Moving forward to the South African ruling party's fifty-third elective conference in Mangaung, many observers and interest groups (bureaucrats included) were keenly watching, speculating about the meaning and implications of policy outcomes for various sectors and the country as a whole.

'Mangaung', as the conference has come to be known, was however not just about the ruling party's leadership contest, although the subject of elections satiated the palates of commentators and journalists hungry for nerve-wracking headlines.

More important, Mangaung ratified, modified and adopted key policy positions that had already been discussed by the branches of the ANC and processed at the June 2012 Policy Conference, where the imperative of creating a National Democratic Society gained impetus.

Before the conference, the private sector was contemplating what could be on the horizon as the party made known its intention to play an active role in the economy through state-owned enterprises and direct ownership and control of strategic assets in the economy. What will direct state involvement in the mining (through the state mining company), cement and steel production value chains mean in an environment grappling with low demand?

Organised labour and the young lions on the other hand were asking themselves: are we winning the debate on nationalisation, labour broking and the proposed youth wage subsidy?

Those in the agriculture sector watched the space for any new proposals to speed up land reform. These came and so the debate continues on how to speed up land reform. It is important to note that decisions on the land question could not escape the November–December 2012 Western Cape farm workers strike which, once again, illuminated the tragic conditions under which farm workers toil almost 18 years after the introduction of the democratic dispensation. The conference of the one hundred year old organisation could not escape the looming one hundredth anniversary of the 1913 Land Act, which actually institutionalised the dispossession of the African majority.

As the conference progressed, social activists were asking: based on the entire post-94 experience, is the organisation finally adopting a radical stance towards decisive transformation of the economy, thus altering patterns of apartheid production and wealth accumulation and distribution?

The media – normally positioned as observers – were somewhat relieved because the idea of a Media Tribunal was, for all intents and purposes, buried; meanwhile, it remains enthralled by real and imagined internal party contestation beyond the conference and what majority percentage the party will reach in the 2014 national elections.

Veterans are contemplating: is the organisation reclaiming its hegemony to the extent that it can influence, lead and drive the revolutionary agenda towards the attainment of a national democratic society? We can extend this and mention general concerns about the relationship between party and state and their respective roles in driving the transformation agenda.

A more ponderous question is: what new ideas will emerge that will intensify the transformation of the South African economy to the point of negating Michael Moore's conclusion that 'capitalism means that a few people will do very well, and the rest will serve the few',[5] thus achieving a 'further restructuring of the economy in order that it benefits all'?[6]

One thing is fairly certain: given ongoing debates about organisational renewal, the ANC seems set to reassert the values and principles that inspired its formation, growth and programmes over the last century.

But then again this is not a paper about the thousand flowers blooming within the governing party or about the pre- and post-Mangaung political discourse dominating our headlines.

This chapter calls for the rise of the South African mandarins and then explores their role in the management of the aforementioned complexities, whatever the policy outcomes are, and taking into account persisting market and geopolitical contradictions.

The principal presupposition here is that it is senior bureaucrats who carry the responsibility of accelerating transformation and of managing policy changes to the extent that such changes do not interrupt but accelerate service delivery.

Once again, the reality of diminishing public confidence in our ability to ethically and efficiently lead public institutions and to deliver services necessitates introspection. The mandating party's intention of building a responsive and capable developmental state and the initiative to professionalise the public service offer space for such reflection.

Addressing contradictions arising from the political-administrative interface is not unique to South Africa and nor is it a twenty-first century phenomenon. It requires thorough research and analysis, especially as South Africa continues to face challenges of public service transformation nearly two decades after the 1994 democratic elections.

And so we proceed with these unmandated reflections, inspired by the optimism that a renaissance in the public service is possible. In their book *Manufacturing Consent*, Edward Herman and Noam Chomsky[7] say the following about optimism:

> Optimism is a strategy for making a better future. Because unless you believe that the future can be better, you are unlikely to step up and take responsibility for making it so.

Where are the Mandarins?

There is a generally accepted assertion that many of government's best-performing programmes and institutions (for example see Acemoglu and Robinson,[8] Diamond,[9] Rodrik,[10] Stiglitz[11] and Francis Fukuyama[12]) are characterised by their clarity of vision, the stability of their leadership and their policy approach.

However, it is also well documented that the level of political influence over the day-to-day operations of the public service often undermines this stability, especially when accountability mechanisms are weak.[13]

Let us immediately disclaim that, as demonstrated by scholars like Sachs[14] and Fukuyama,[15] the strength of political institutions is not a silver bullet that propels the growth of nations. Other variables, such as inherited political economy, geopolitics, natural resources and innovation, contribute significantly to the advancement of nations and, dialectically, impact on political institutions.

In this connection, Alan Hirsch, a long-serving public servant, has this to say about blind spots in our developmental state aspirations in comparison to our counterparts in East Asia:

> Meritocratic East Asian bureaucracies have much greater authority than senior civil servants in South Africa. There are several possible reasons for this. The first is that many political leaders and senior civil servants came through the struggle against apartheid together. The result is that their roles in government are sometimes blurred or confused. Secondly, there is the fact that the senior leadership of the civil service are political appointees. Though they are appointed after rule-bound recruitment procedures, they are nevertheless political appointees, which can weaken their credibility and authority in relation to their political principals.[16]

Hirsch hastens to point out, however, that this situation is not the sum total of the root causes of problems undermining the performance of public sector reforms and institutions.

Over the years, the state has tried and succeeded in innovation, as exemplified by the reformation of the South African Revenue Services and Statistics South Africa, the turnaround at the Department of Home Affairs and the successful hosting of the 2010 FIFA World Cup.

Maphunye says the challenge is stability in public sector leadership, and argues that political leaders have defined tenures before moving on to their next portfolios. These changes are less likely to be disruptive if the public service is able to retain a degree of stability and continuity, much as fast-developing countries have been able to do.

Hirsch goes on to say that for this developmental state aspiration to be realised, South Africa needs a:

> ... Clear common purpose as a nation. This means in the first place a clear common purpose in the ruling party. Secondly, we need a bureaucracy which is essentially meritocratic, and is respected by society and by political leaders. Thirdly, we need to negate the diffusion of power through a broad, effective social compact... A

democratic developmental state requires in South Africa a deeply effective social partnership.

President Jacob Zuma has been repeatedly quoted as saying South Africa needs public servants that always uphold the interests of the people they are employed to serve by building an administration that knows where people live and what they think, and acts fast, efficiently and effectively on the issues raise raised by the public.

In an endeavour to bolster the thesis that the task of creating excellence in the bureaucracy is feasible, let us characterise key features of the mandarins while simultaneously problematising ideological questions inherent to this exercise.

At a basic level, the mandarins must be inspired by a conviction that public service is a revolutionary practice; not only a vocation of interpreting problems facing society and finding palliatives for such but also a practice that expresses itself in the search for and cure of the root causes of problems facing society. In South Africa's new National Development Plan, this characterisation is treated as part of the developmental state.

The mandarins ought to be a cadre that envisions their mandate beyond mundane implementation of strategic plans and annual programmes.

Society expects the mandarins to 'push the envelope' in a manner that permanently alters the socio-political economy and propels the nation onto a greater development trajectory. In pedestrian terms, this means they ought to see their work without the lenses of, and outside the domain of the daily routine and the meeting of targets.

Public service mandarins should constantly work hard to find solutions to persistent poverty and inequality, asking why our rates of growth and social cohesion are performing unspectacularly when, at a political level, the mandate and resources are provided to aid efforts to alter these menacing challenges.

They should constantly ask 'what can we do to achieve even better outcomes?' instead of being satisfied with the clichéd comeback that 'there is improvement'. The mandarins should do so believing that it is a feature of advanced detachments to do and achieve more instead of being content with routine.

As an act of national duty, the public service by its very nature negates the notion that a government and even society can ever meet targets, since social advancement is a moving target. The day such absolutes as 'we have met the targets' is reached will mark the end of history and a reversal of the inalienable human endeavour of learning.

Perhaps as a reminder of the mammoth task before us, we should recall the words of Founding President Nelson Mandela, who had this to say when addressing the outgoing commissioners of the Public Service Commission in 1996:

For the majority of South Africans, the Public Service was seen as a hostile instrument of an oppressive minority. We have an immense challenge to build a state that is truly oriented towards the service of all South Africans; that is equitably representative of our society; that is guided by the broad vision of a better life for all; and that is dedicated to making efficient use of public resources. No less demanding are the tasks of rooting out corruption ... Achieving all these goals at the same time as we find the right size for our Public Service, will no doubt produce some testing times...

Public servants are employees of the state and accountable to elected leaders. The nature of this accountability should be managed in such a way that it does not blur the distinction between political party mandates and the need for professional, non-partisan obligations of the bureaucracy. It is critical for public servants to forge a cohesive professional identity and loyalty to the values of the Constitution and concomitant national priorities that are usually informed by ruling party manifestos.

At the very least, a professional public service equal to the challenge posed by the first democratic president should evince the following virtues (in no particular order):

Political competence/attitude

This means full appreciation of the mandate of government and selflessly executing this mandate, conforming to the highest ethics and values, and in accordance with the prescripts of the Constitution of the Republic. Serving should be inspiring when one comprehends the genesis, object and expected outcomes of such policy priorities as improved education and health standards, creation of decent work and accelerating rural development, as well as fighting crime and corruption, among others. The desire to build a developmental state must be embraced by the public service as a call to action and not just a grand intellectual project with no substantive impact in the creation of a new civilisation.

This is not blind loyalty, as some who doubt the mandating party's intentions have observed. It is about deploying 'Catholics as altar boys' – a people who believe and share philosophical underpinnings and the greater good intended.

Along the same lines, President Barack Obama had this to say in the 2011 post-State of the Union Address:

Every administration bequeathed unto itself the manifest responsibility of delivering on a promised electoral mandate. It has no one to blame if it fails, but itself. Therefore deploying the most competent with the most profound understanding of how to deliver that mandate, is putting in place a system of extreme excellence balanced with dependencies where meritocracy thrives on the altar of obsessive competence and performance.

Again, in all these cases, the qualifying criteria ought to be proven competence and a commitment to the ideals of reconstruction and development; that is, to building a caring, non-racial, non-sexist, united, democratic and prosperous South Africa.

Technical skills and competence

This relates to the ideal of employing one's technical skills to the extent that the service we provide is according to specification and is delivered effectively and efficiently. There are many technically competent people in the public service. We must aspire to efficiently use their skills in the right positions and under enabling conditions.

Skills in the public sector require management, since many competent people wander about and under-serve because of poor management. Worse still, poor management creates a perverse incentive and a loophole through which underprepared public servants slip through into higher positions. For their part, the mandarins should take very seriously the meritocratic appointment of senior and middle managers and talent retention.

By international standards our public service pays competitive salaries. Moreover, there is now the Occupational-Specific Dispensation – a remuneration structure that incentivises scarce-skills professionals such as engineers to stay in the public service. Therefore, remuneration can no longer be cited as the cause of poor performance, as much as poor performance management is. The number of senior managers with tertiary qualifications has increased substantially over the years. Advanced tools of trade are being made available, as are professional development opportunities.

What about those with poor occupational competencies? The leadership has said they should be retrained and/or redeployed to positions that are fit-for-purpose.

There are many such people in government; however, failure to accurately plan and cost a construction project is different from manipulating this project for nefarious ends. This distinction is critical in order for the public service and society in general to separate (and up-skill) under-qualified public servants from the corrupt ones who must be purged – just as we should clinically treat data on corruption, wasteful expenditure and unauthorised expenditure. These are not synonyms.

In my limited time in government, I have observed that we do have some of the best brains in the land. The challenge is often application; that is, people fail to apply themselves optimally to the fullness of their capacities. This immediately cheats the public of a timely and quality service. In the long term these colleagues rob themselves of learning and professional development opportunities. Hence, we have doctors who overdose patients, quantity surveyors who overspend and accountants who cannot keep proper records of expenditure.

Political commentator Adam Habib was once quoted as saying the democratic state brought people into government *with technical competencies* [some without] but not *management skills*, and has done very little to provide mentorship, management or leadership training. The result is a level of senior managers who are indubitably qualified in their fields but inadequate at working with, motivating and transferring skills to their subordinates. In contrast, management and leadership training is a norm in the private sector.

Social conscience, technical competence and professional excellence are among the most vital virtues for which all public servants should strive. The bulk of government's training budget should go to enhancing technical skills, enabling innovation and deepening creativity at the same time as we build vital normative attributes such as discipline, commitment, customer care, integrity and respect. To paraphrase a recent *Newsweek*[17] caption: potent pressure has grown, the pressure to stay aloft, to stay prolific and flawless. The National Development Plan takes this forward by calling for a balance between a core standard of training for all public servants and specialist training that is tailored to the needs of individuals.

Discipline, commitment and excellence

These are qualities that the mandarins must aspire to and personify. This requires us to exercise diligence in the application of public resources (e.g. money, time and infrastructure) and strive for superior outcomes in the work we do. Such basics as teachers being at school on time and teaching will go a long way in improving the quality of life of all South Africans. For our part, we must be inspired by these words of former President Nelson Mandela addressing Parliament in 1994:

> Our single most important challenge is therefore to help establish a social order in which the freedom of the individual will truly mean the freedom of the individual. We must construct that people-centred society of freedom in such a manner that it guarantees the political liberties and the human rights of all our citizens.

There seems to be an emerging culture of entitlement among us, which is often divorced from the requisite work ethic imbued with a sense of discipline and excellence. We often accommodate mediocrity without necessarily counting its social and material costs to the nation. Senior bureaucrats should avoid the 'democratic indifference trap' – a phenomenon I describe as public servants with a high sense of entitlement and a low sense of commitment to their duty. Consequently, these civil servants celebrate and enjoy the spoils of freedom while denying the accrual of the same to the majority.

In this connection, Martin Luther King wisely observed:

A true revolution of values will soon cause us to question the fairness and justice of many of our past and present policies. On the one hand, we are called to play the Good Samaritan on life's roadside, but that will be only an initial act. One day we must come to see that the whole Jericho Road must be transformed so that men and women will not be constantly beaten and robbed as they make their journey on life's highway. True compassion is more than flinging a coin to a beggar. It comes to see that an edifice which produces beggars needs restructuring.[18]

Trust, honesty and integrity

These are other important virtues to be embraced by public service mandarins. We must be truthful to our work, taking into account the mission, vision and mandate of the employer – the state, and therefore the people. Trustworthy people act honestly and with integrity. They are honest with themselves (they know what they can and cannot do and therefore seek necessary remedies) and in their dealings with others. A grievance with one's employer should not translate into a grievance with the public whose trust we betray by providing sub-standard services.

For those among us fast becoming common denominators in government corridors, we should serve with humility and be self-critical. We hold no monopoly over the answer to the question: 'How to do things in government?' If we did, society would be far ahead!

Our vantage point is that the state has invested in us and so we should humbly pay our dues through excellence, efficiency and pride. We must avoid what Lance Buhl,[19] a scholar at the Terry Sanford School of Public Policy calls 'delusions of grandeur' and 'delusions of adequacy', for 'delusions of adequacy corrode the generative premises about effective leadership in the public'. One of those premises is that effective leaders are those who are servant-leaders. Instead, he argues, the mandarins should seek to use their 'power, position and talent to serve those they are entrusted with leading'.

Delusions of grandeur can be pervasive to some among us who declare: 'I have been here for too long so I know what I am doing.' This contradicts a natural phenomenon of the continuity of change and of learning as a ceaseless process.

It is well and good for the mandarins to inspire public trust and confidence. Politicians must also trust us.

Accountability

Here the point is simple, and requires no peroration. We must be accountable for our decisions and deeds. And we should hold those we are responsible for accountable. This would require a complete revamp of the performance management system and overcoming of perverse incentives that dominate the current performance management regime. Quality and impact need to feature prominently in the gauging of performance of the mandarins.

Creativity and innovation

These are the qualities that were demonstrated during the implementation of the 2010 FIFA World Cup. In executing that project, senior managers across three spheres (working with highly driven elected representatives) found creative ways of breaking inter-governmental huddles which are often blamed for sluggish delivery.[20] This negated the 'colonial unconscious'[21] practice of doing things the same old way, the way we inherited the public service, the way we think things ought to always be.

Possibilities abound for further innovation in our delivery approaches. For example, we need to implement process-cycle and total quality management systems that map out every step in decision making and the delivery of public goods and services. This will increase efficiency and promote transparency and accountability. Already, the Presidential Infrastructure Coordinating Commission (PICC) is institutionalising the use of technology and modern project management approaches in the management of the multibillion rand infrastructure programme.

The realm of possibilities

Even as we grapple with the nauseating news of corruption, conflict of interest, 'democratic indifference', missing of targets and over- and unauthorised expenditure, we should equally take comfort in the emergence of a new public service cadre; a cadre that evinces the qualities discussed earlier, which include discipline, commitment, productivity, humility and, most of all, appreciation of the constitutional imperative of transforming the public service.

Conscientious observers of the evolution of the South African public service will affirm this. The growing impatience from the executing authorities (elected officials) as well as the public will fuel the renaissance flame.

Added to this mix is a rapid increase in the number of young energetic graduates who are joining the public sector.[22] Class formation and inequalities also play a critical role here, since even for black engineering and commerce graduates the only way to get ahead is to go into the public sector as discrimination persists in the private sector.

They do so believing that 'there's something civil servants have that the private sector doesn't. And that is the duty of loyalty to the greater good – the duty of loyalty to the collective best interest of all rather than the interest of a few. Companies have duties of loyalty to their shareholders, not to the country' – as asserted by the comptroller general of the United States, David Walker, in a *New York Times* interview in 2007.

Recruiting young, energetic graduates will raise the bar and redefine the performance discourse, from the meeting of targets to achieving excellence.

In this connection, speaking at the 2009 public excellence awards, Nancy Lee, best-selling author and co-author with Philip Kotler of 'Marketing in the Public Sector', said:

> The Public Sector Excellence initiative is an inspirational model for recognising and showcasing excellent agencies and programmes, as well as high-performing public servants, which will lead others in moving 'from good to great'.[23]

Also noteworthy is the renewed 'activism' of the Public Service Commission which, seen in the context of the work of the Auditor General and the Performance Monitoring and Evaluation Department, will inculcate a new culture of professionalism, productivity and accountability. Importantly, their focus is shifting from compliance to performance.

There is therefore a firm foundation in South Africa from which generations of public service mandarins can flourish. Under this political ecology and a commitment to build a democratic developmental state, a platform has been created for the mandarins to raise their hands higher.

But first, like *The Mandarins* in Simone de Beauvoir's tome, the senior management service in South Africa must shift its mindset and develop a political attitude towards its work. By political attitude we do not mean overt party-political allegiance but rather an uncompromising commitment to transformation. It must be rigorous, prolific and valiant in the tackling of the country's niggling challenges.

The political attitude of the mandarins should be grounded in Franz Fanon's injunction that: 'Each generation must, out of relative obscurity, discover its mission, fulfil it, or betray it.'[24]

Saloojee and Pahad[25] remind us that developmental states are different from other forms of governance and political institutions:

> Developmental states create specific institutional structures, consciously articulate political purposes and harness nationalism and a sense of national cohesion towards economic growth and development and towards overcoming late and uneven development. The critical difference between developmental states and liberal and neo-liberal states is the extent to which they concentrate power in a bureaucracy... Developmental states are strong states characterised by a very high degree of 'embedded bureaucratic autonomy' and insularity, a capable small bureaucratic elite

in a pilot Ministry given the political space to set national development objectives, public-private cooperation and the ability to secure compliance...

In the hope of legitimating these unmandated reflections, let us end with a citation from a Cuban revolutionary, Manuel 'Barbarroja' Pineiro, who long challenged public officials to act differently:

> Let us increase our vigilance against complacency and arrogance – which may appear like weeds in our work and, if we don't uproot them in time, wind up by invading everything. Let us oppose them with revolutionary unpretentiousness... Let us oppose this with the careful administration of resources, systemisation, planning, and the most intelligent use of all human and technical resources we have.[26]

Conclusion

There is hope for the realisation of this aspiration, because, as Chomsky postulates: 'If you assume that there is no hope, you guarantee that there will be no hope. If you assume that there is an instinct for freedom, that there are opportunities to change things, then there is a possibility that you can contribute to making a better world.'

The apartheid state had a vicious bureaucracy with a common purpose: to advance race-based capital accumulation and to oppress black people. The post-apartheid state – especially with the benefit of governing for eighteen years – requires a disciplined, committed, competent, prolific, caring, selfless bureaucracy: the mandarins, steeped in liberatory philosophy, to advance national reconciliation, reconstruction and development, and to champion the attainment of a better life for all South Africans.

After land reform and the meaningful inclusion of the black majority in the mainstream of the economy, building a capable, caring and responsive bureaucracy is arguably the next frontier that the ANC must confront – not in a stop-and-start process but as an integral part of the mandate the party carries into the future.

Behavioural science tells us that we become what we think and expect of ourselves. If we think of ourselves as *The Mandarins*, facilitating the great leap forward towards the attainment of a National Democratic Society, that is what we will become.

After all, history will judge us against Fanon's injunction: did we discover and fulfil our mission to advance the principal objectives of the National Democratic Revolution? Or, will we quickly evaporate into the footnotes of the past as a generation who failed to seize their moment in history, who when asked to step up in the best traditions of *The Mandarins* elected instead to write themselves into the script as extras in the British production – in *The Thick of It* and *Yes Minister*?[27]

Endnotes

1   Chalmers Johnson is highly regarded for his early conceptualisation of a developmental state characterised by a society where politicians reign and bureaucrats rule

2   Johnson, C., 1982. *MITI and the Japanese miracle*. Stanford: Stanford University Press.

3   Mkandawire, T., 1997. *Thinking about developmental states in Africa*. Tokoyo: United Nations University.

4   See Fukuyama, F., n.d. China and East Asian democracy: The patterns of history. *Journal of Democracy*, 23(1).

5   See *Quotable Quote: Michale Moore*. N.d. Available at: www.goodreads.com/quotes/231578-capitalism.

6   Gumede, V., 2012. The South African Developmental State in the making. *The Thinker*, 25.

7   Chomsky, N. & Herman, E.S., 2010, *Manufacturing consent: The political economy of the mass media*. New York: Random House.

8   Acemoglu, D. & Robinson, J.A., 2012. W*hy nations fail: The origins of power, prosperity and poverty*. New York: Crown Publishing Group.

9   Diamond, J., 2012. *What makes countries rich or poor*. New York: The New York Review of Books.

10 Rodrik, D., 2000. *Institutions for high-quality growth: What they are and how to acquire them*. NBER Working Paper no.7540.

11 See Stiglitz, J., 1998. The private uses of public interests: Incentives and institutions. *Journal of Economic Perspectives*, 12(2).

12 Ibid.

13 Maphunye, K.J., 2009. *Public administration for a democratic developmental State in Africa: Prospects and possibilities*. Centre for Policy Studies Research Report, p.114.

14 Sacks, J.D., 2012. *Government, geography and growth: The true drivers of economic development in Foreign Affairs*. Council on Foreign Relations, October.

15 Fukuyama, n.d., op. cit.

16 Hirsch, A., 2013. Elusive aspirations to a Developmental State: The obstacles to deep reform. In Ngcaweni, B. (ed.). *The Future we chose: Emerging perspectives on the ANC centenary*.

17 Zakaria, F., 2012. Plagiarism and the lynch mob. *Newsweek*, August.

18 See King, M.L., 1967. *Why I am ppposed to the war in Vietnam*. A Sermon. April 30. Ebenezer Baptist Church.

19 Buhl, L.C., 2004. *Delusions of adequacy: Thoughts on leadership, democracy and its institutions*. Durham: US-SA Centre for Leadership and Public Values, Duke University.

20 Ngcaweni, B., 2011. A new public service cadre can do things differently. *Public Sector Manager Magazine*, August.

21 Hudson, P., 2012. The state and the colonial unconscious. *PARI Public Lecture Series*, June.

22 Programmes like graduate recruitment present an opportunity for public sector transformation. But for it to work, the working environment they go into should be changed to ensure that graduates develop necessary skills; lest we face the danger of them quickly become jaded and cynical. This is where the NDP story of getting career paths for new public servants right is gain more currency.

23 See Lee, N.R. & Kotler, P., 2009. *Marketing in the public sector*. Public Sector Excellence.

24 Fanon, F., 1961. *The wretched of the Earth*. New York: Grove Press.

25 Pahad, E. & Saloojee, A., 2012. *The bureaucratic, flexible and democratic developmental State(s): Lessons for South Africa*. Unpublished manuscript.

26 Pineiro, M., 2006. *Che Guevara and the Latin American Revolution*. Minneapolis: Ocean Press.

27 *Yes Minister* and *The Thick of It* (a more recent spoof on the Blair era) provide two different accounts of how the public service can go wrong. In *Yes Minister*, the public service is a deeply conservative body that blocks everything in order to protect its own interests – a very real risk of a public service that is too autonomous and less accountable. In *The Thick of It* we see a bureaucracy obsessed with spin over substance. None of these is desirable in South Africa.

Lightning Source UK Ltd.
Milton Keynes UK
UKOW05f0217210815